15/5/12

WOMEN AND HUMOR IN CLASSICAL GREECE

Women and Humor in Classical Greece examines the role of women as produc-ers of joking speech, especially within cults of Demeter. This speech, some-times known as *aischrologia*, had considerable weight and vitality within its cultic context. It also shaped literary traditions, notably iambic and Attic old comedy, which have traditionally been regarded as entirely male. The misog-yny for which ancient iambic is infamous derives in part from an oral world in which women's derisive joking voices reverberated. O'Higgins considers this speech from its mythical origins in the Homeric *Hymn to Demeter*, through the reactive iambic tradition and into old comedy. She also examines the po-ems of Sappho and Corinna as literary jokers, responding in part to their own experience of joking women. The book concludes with a fresh appraisal of the three great "women's" plays of Aristophanes: *Lysistrata*, *Thesmophoriazousae*, and *Ecclesiazousae*.

Laurie O'Higgins is Associate Professor of Classics at Bates College, where she has served as Chair of the program in Classical and Medieval Studies. She has written extensively on Greek and Latin poetry and on women in antiquity.

Women and Humor in Classical Greece

LAURIE O'HIGGINS

Bates College

PUBLISHED BY THE PRESS SYNDICATE OF THE UNIVERSITY OF CAMBRIDGE
The Pitt Building, Trumpington Street, Cambridge, United Kingdom

CAMBRIDGE UNIVERSITY PRESS
The Edinburgh Building, Cambridge CB2 2RU, UK
40 West 20th Street, New York, NY 10011-4211, USA
477 Williamstown Road, Port Melbourne, VIC 3207, Australia
Ruiz de Alarcón 13, 28014 Madrid, Spain
Dock House, The Waterfront, Cape Town 8001, South Africa

http://www.cambridge.org

First published 2003

Printed in the United Kingdom at the University Press, Cambridge

Typefaces Utopia 9.5/13 pt. and Rusticana   *System* LATEX 2$_\varepsilon$ [TB]

A catalog record for this book is available from the British Library.

Library of Congress Cataloging in Publication Data
O'Higgins, Laurie, 1958–
    Women and humor in classical Greece / Laurie O'Higgins.
        p.   cm.
    Includes bibliographical references.
    ISBN 0-521-82253-X (hardback)
        1. Greek wit and humor – History and criticism.   2. Greek wit and humor – Women
authors – History and criticism.   3. Women and literature – Greece.   4. Women in
literature.   5. Women – Greece.   I. Title.
PA3249.037   2003
887′.0109 – dc21   2003043805

ISBN 0 521 82253 X hardback

In memory of my father, Frank O'Higgins, 1932–1990.
For my husband, Jim Richter
And in loving tribute to our eloquent little daughter, Ellen Richter,

Do mhúchas léan le gáire
You have quenched grief with laughter

CONTENTS

ACKNOWLEDGEMENTS

Many people have helped me write this book. My greatest intellectual debt is to Jeffrey Henderson, who has read and commented on more than one draft, and has shared his ideas with me most freely. I owe much to Kevin Clinton who helped me with many questions relating to the Thesmophoria and Greek religion generally. Gayle Holst-Warhaft, Laura McClure, Ralph Rosen, Louise Pratt, Madeleine Henry, and Allaire Chandor Brumfield shared their work and ideas in progress. Nick Lowe wrote kindly and promptly when I asked for permission to use his work. Thank you. The readers for Cambridge University Press were tremendously helpful to me in thinking through the book's ideas. Blame the remaining follies and infelicities on the intransigent author. Speaking of infelicities, I hope that readers will forgive a somewhat eclectic system of transliteration from Greek.

I am also grateful to Jane Snyder, Nancy Rabinowitz, Sarah Johnston, Bruce Heiden, and Froma Zeitlin for sharing ideas and friendship over the years. Here at Bates College, in the Classical and Medieval Studies Program, I am blessed with good colleagues, including most recently Margaret Imber and Lisa Maurizio. Dennis Grafflin in the History Department gave invaluable, trenchant criticism of a draft of the introduction and Chapter 1. Pam Chenea also read and commented wisely. Thanks to Tom Hayward, Reference Librarian and classicist, and to the hardworking staff of the Bates Inter-Library Loan Department.

The former Bates Dean of Faculty, Martha Crunkleton, encouraged me to focus on this project, saying that life is too short to do anything other than what you love. The current Dean of Faculty, Jill Reich, has supported me and my colleagues gracefully through tough times and good.

Thanks to Julia Zhukova for your diligence, tact, and courtesy in helping me find some of the visual evidence.

Thank you to the heroes of Pooh's Country Pre-School in Greene, Maine, who have cared for my daughter so well, while I worked on my book and on teaching. Bonnie Goudreau, Christine St. Germaine, Vickie McBride, Sherrie Higgins, Gayle Eaton, Kim Spence, you have done a wonderful job.

God bless you all. Thank you Linda Dufour. I don't know what I'd do without you.

Sylvia Hawks and Lorelei Purrington, thank you for your professionalism and generous help with technical matters as I produced and edited the manuscript here at Bates. Thank you to Beatrice Rehl, Senior Editor, Arts and Classics, at Cambridge, and Eleanor Umali, Senior Project Manager at TechBooks. You have been superbly helpful and efficient.

Thanks most of all to my husband Jim Richter, whose careful readings of numerous drafts and whose loving support generally have sustained me throughout.

1. Naked old woman, holding a phallos and seated on an altar. Published with permission from the State Hermitage Museum, St. Petersburg. BB 176.

2. Grotesque, clothed old woman drawing a veil before her face. Published with permission from the State Hermitage Museum, St. Petersburg. BB 165.

3. Grotesque, clothed old woman with swollen belly (Demeter?). Published with permission from the State Hermitage Museum, St. Petersburg. BB 164.

4. Statuette of an old woman carrying an infant. From an Athenian grave. The Metropolitan Museum of Art, Rogers Fund, 1913 (13.225.26). Published with permission from the Metropolitan Museum of Art.

5. Statuette of an old woman, holding her chiton and himation in front of her. The Metropolitan Museum of Art, Rogers Fund, 1913 (13.225.17). Published with permission from the Metropolitan Museum of Art.

WOMEN AND HUMOR IN CLASSICAL GREECE

INTRODUCTION

I HAVE LONG THOUGHT ABOUT silence and oblivion, their power, and the strategies that writers, ancient and modern, employed to impose or to shatter them. I began my scholarly life working on the figure of Ajax within Greek tradition, and later I turned to women in Greek literature. This drew me to consider real women in archaic and classical Greece, their speech and silence, and their one-sided relationship with the literary tradition.

A striking asymmetry marked women's joking traditions, it seemed; they participated actively in cultic joking, but in the satiric and comic literatures of ancient Greece they appeared chiefly as targets. If, as in old comedy, they functioned as agents, it was in fantastic situations, perhaps intended to shock and amuse by their implausibility or incongruity. In short, the literary tradition gave little direct evidence of women as makers of humor in their own right. In recent scholarship on ancient comedy, attention has been given to women, but scholars have viewed them generally as emblems of larger comic issues, or as the means – as in tragedy – for ancient playwrights to explore male identity. It is time to focus (again) on the – admittedly vexed – question of women's agency, women's voice, in order to understand both men and women more fully.[1]

The very possibility of women's "own" voice has been much debated. In its most radical form, theorists have posed the full question, is there such a thing as a women's authentic voice? French feminists have tended to take a skeptical view; in a patriarchal culture man "owns" language. He is consistently the subject and positive reference point of his own discourse. This leaves women to occupy the position of negative pole, or object. As speakers, as literary creators ("writers"), they cannot but work within a language and conceptual system that is essentially masculine.[2] Women cannot resist their secondary status without some kind of linguistic transgression.[3]

Irigaray, who has been especially influential in classical scholarship, has traced this alienation of the female from language back to the classical period, and to Plato in particular.[4] As Skinner has pointed out, however, Plato is not representative of classical Greece in general. The highly segregated nature of ancient societies made possible a women's culture that offered a degree of independence from the male-run world. This in turn raises the possibility that within their semiautonomous culture women could deploy language in distinctive ways. I believe that women's cults facilitated the evolution of a tradition of "women's speech," a speech that could in some cases nourish a women's literary tradition but that mostly existed simply to sustain, connect, and amuse its practitioners. In this position I follow Skinner, Showalter, and others,[5] but I also take it a step further. Women's voices, and women's deployment of "their" Greek language, whatever that may have sounded like, reverberated throughout the society as a whole, leaving a mark on what has survived into our world.[6]

In the course of this brief introduction, I show the importance of the Homeric *Hymn to Demeter* for our understanding of women's cultic joking. I also posit a relationship between the joking that took place in (mostly women's) cults of Demeter, the women's and men's cults of Dionysus, and the hypermasculine ancient genres of iambic and old comedy. On the face of it, this seems unlikely. Cultic joking served to strengthen social bonds by focusing members of the worshipping group on each other, mocking and teasing so as to level differences, but not so as to wound or humiliate. Yet the iambic genre perfected the kind of joking that tightens a group through rejection and contemptuous assaults on some designated outsider(s). Nonetheless, I believe that women's cultic joking affected and indeed inspired the ancient genre that we know as iambic.

This leads to comments on the importance of the spoken word in antiquity generally and on how any student of ancient literature (oral or written) must bear in mind that what we read (usually in silence) was produced in a world filled with and shaped by the human voice. Then I turn to the issues facing anyone attempting to read the various sources on women's cults and on women's role in ancient life generally. A section on the terminology used by ancient authors to describe women's cultic speech precedes a chapter-by-chapter outline of the book.

The Hymn to Demeter

Years ago an incident in the Homeric *Hymn to Demeter* caught my attention. This early-sixth-century B.C.E. epic tells how Hades kidnapped Persephone from Demeter. The bereaved goddess, disguised as an old woman, entered the palace at Eleusis but refused a seat or refreshment

πρίν γ᾽ ὅτε δὴ χλεύης μιν Ἰάμβη κέδν᾽ εἰδυῖα
πολλὰ παρὰ σκώπτονσ᾽ ἐτρέψατο πότνιαν ἁγνὴν
μειδῆσαι γελάσαι τε καὶ ἵλαον σχεῖν θυμόν·
ἦ δή οἱ καὶ ἔπειτα μεθύστερον εὔαδεν ὀργαῖς.

until decorous Iambe, with jokes
and many a mocking jest moved the holy lady
to smile and laugh and have a gracious heart.
Even afterwards she used to cheer her moods. (202–5)

The *Hymn* presents this jesting as the *aition* or foundation story for the joking practiced by women within certain cults of Demeter. Iambe's intervention occurs without a request, without a preamble or permission. Iambe's speech, as far as we can tell, included no specific message or instruction. In and of itself, however, it seems to have functioned as a transformative, healing act and a gesture of welcome to the community.[7] Furthermore, it began a sustained, joyful relationship, breaking the tension that had marked Demeter's entry into the circle of women.

The descriptions of both Iambe's speech and Demeter's reaction are important.[8] Iambe "intervenes with jokes and mockery." The goddess smiles, laughs, and has a joyful heart – and is cheered again on subsequent occasions. There is a continuum in each case: from jesting to tempered aggression, from mild acknowledgment to hearty laughter, and to sustained graciousness and repeated joy. When we go on to consider its "afterlife" (in women's cults of Demeter), we must bear in mind this breadth of implication. This cultic speech covered a range of tone and attitude. It inspired a range of reaction in its immediate addressee (Demeter), and within the microcommunities of her cult the speech has an enduring, bonding, and stabilizing effect.

The author(s) of the *Hymn* spotlighted Iambe's jokes as a symbolic prototype for cultic abuse, mockery, and obscenity, practiced especially in the worship of Demeter and Dionysus. Men and women could engage in such speech, although in the rites of Demeter it tended to be a female preserve. I am concerned with women's use of such speech here. The *Hymn*'s Iambe episode, which took place within an all-female group, probably referred to the Thesmophoria, a vital Demetrian rite, exclusive to women.[9] The poet(s) of the *Hymn* invented the eponymous heroine Iambe to "explain" a preexisting cultic phenomenon: women's cultic joking. At the same time, the Iambe myth, as told within the *Hymn*, can be understood as an aspect of the women's cult to which it refers.[10]

Cult and Literature

Joking generally was – and is – shared. A person jokes, and at least one other listens and reacts. Joking builds or strengthens a group, sometimes deliberately and self-consciously. In archaic and classical Greece this group-building could occur in two ways, which were not mutually exclusive but which tended to work asymmetrically, with one mode predominating on a given occasion. One was exclusion, that is, marking boundaries or a power differential. A group defined its boundaries by joking contemptuously at individuals perceived as outsiders. This type of joking established a hierarchy or "pecking order." The other type of joking emphasized connection within a community – even within a cultic community subdivided into mock rival groups. This joking focused group members on each other, not on those outside the pale. It tended to break down hierarchies within the community.[11]

Cultic joking tended to belong to the latter type of group building, I believe. Although it could be abusive, it was not intended to rupture the worshipping group but to foster a collective identity. One might imagine that such introverted joking – often occurring in secret cults – would be less likely to migrate to new environments. Alternatively, the more "extroverted" joking could flourish in literary, semisecular contexts, such as poetic competitions. The literary genre of joking, iambic or satire, was indeed weighted toward the extroverted end of the joking spectrum – an expression of contempt for persons perceived as alien. Yet many poems in the iambic genre, and the men credited with creating those poems, were affiliated with Demeter's cult, as I show in Chapter 3. Moreover, the "speaking name" of the *Hymn*'s mocking servant, Iambe, suggests that literary *iambos* drew some of its breath and life from cultic antecedents.[12]

Iambic poems, usually coarse in tone and often in iambic meter, were recognized as belonging to the iambic genre through the type of occasion at which they were performed – originally festivals of Demeter and Dionysus in all likelihood. Iambic poetry, like the ritual mockery with which it was linked, also already existed at the time of the *Hymn*'s composition; its heyday was the seventh and sixth centuries.[13] By the classical period, cultic jokes and practices and literary jokes existed side by side, and people undoubtedly recognized their kinship. The *Hymn*'s "Iambe incident" thus inevitably evoked both versions of *iambos*, cultic and literary.

From the point of view of the *Hymn to Demeter*, Iambe bore a "double" progeny: a long-lived practice of cultic abuse and joking, often uttered by women in all-female contexts, and literary iambic, which was predominantly male. Iambic poetry brutally targeted women and debased them with venom that seemed propelled from the genre's very core. Iambe's twin offspring provoked questions for me: how to unravel the complex relationship of women with speech, cultic and literary, and how to recover, or at least find the echoes of, a type of women's speech that did not attain literary status.

Iambic's as yet unborn fifth-century sibling, Attic comedy, also would evolve from a range of cults, especially those of Demeter and Dionysus. In comedy's case, the sixth-century B.C.E. Athenian boom in Dionysus worship meant that Dionysian cult became the city's preeminently visible and renowned context for cultic joking. The hypermasculine civic cult of the City Dionysia has tended to obscure the role of women in Athenian cultic joking and mockery, but women played a crucial part in the cults that also would nurture Attic comedy. Furthermore, despite the momentum of Dionysian cult and despite the legal restrictions on women's participation in certain "licentious" cults, women continued to joke and mock in vital cults throughout the fifth century and for long afterward. Thus, the genres of iambic and comedy not only had roots in cults in which women joked (in some cases, these cults being exclusive to women), but they flourished in a world in which such cultic speech was a living reality. Ancient comedy and iambic evince substantial interest in women, their actions, worship, thoughts, fantasies, and flaws – and speech.

A deeper understanding of the connections between Greek cultic joking (in which women's voices carried considerable power) and literary joking makes clear that the context in which the ancient literary genres flourished was partly shaped by women.[14] The literary evidence may better be understood not only as part of a literary tradition, but as an element of a polemical, joking dialogue between men and women. Almost by definition, surviving poetry, whether comic or iambic (satiric), is the product of male élites with some degree of power and autonomy within their respective political systems. The survival of literary texts and the total loss of the oral culture in which these texts grew has distorted our view of the culture as a whole and blinkered our vision of its surviving fragments.

Joking and laughter constituted a mode of engagement, in which power was negotiated. It was precisely because women's cultic joking was so formidable a force that it generated such a strong response among male satirists and comic poets. I am not suggesting that women's cultic joking was enacted unequivocally against men en masse. The fact that women could and did joke among themselves was, however, threatening to men – even as it was essential within certain major cults. This was a locus off limits to men and with its own legitimacy and power. Thus, when Aristophanes and others portrayed women as jokers or as jokes, they were appropriating women's voices and using them for their own ends. Part of the objective of this book is to revive the context of ancient satire and comedy. We need to understand these genres not as unilateral expressions of individual men or simply as voices within self-reflective traditions, although they were, in part. Rather, they were elements within a negotiation of power, deriving from complex and integrated societies.

The Power of the Spoken Word

Because our sources have not recorded women's cultic speech, there is a natural inclination to throw up our hands and consider only those data we have.[15] This, however, is as irresponsible as it is seemingly safe. There are reasons for pressing forward, albeit cautiously. In the essentially preliterate world of classical Greece, the spoken word weighed more than it does for us.[16] We often regard the spoken word as evanescent; for fifth-century Greeks it constituted a permanent reality. We may shrug when a politician admits to having sworn falsely; the Athenians were aghast when Euripides' Hippolytus said just that. It toppled a bastion of reality: the oath. The spoken word's power, both normative and transgressive, was particularly felt in religious contexts, in which it constituted a crucial and fragile link between gods and mortals; a single misspoken utterance could invalidate an entire ritual.

All speech was weighty, potentially destabilizing, and destructive and so was controlled in many contexts. These controls could be legally pre-scribed or function as part of an uncodified system of social constraint. Contraints on women were tighter, given the widespread belief that women could not control their own conduct. Thus, the transgressive speech of women, including, paradoxically, the iambic speech required by certain cults, potentially was more subversive and thus more powerful than that of men.[17]

Iambic literature explicitly depicted itself or was seen as having emerged from a polarized context in which a disagreement had occurred. One need not postulate an actual dispute, but it is vital, when reading ancient iambic, to keep in mind the ancient belief in its disputatious beginning – the in-volvement of two parties. The modern world has inherited a fragment of one party to the dispute, or one pole of the antithesis. We do not hear and we neglect to consider the perspective of the "other." Although women are not often directly addressed in iambic, they routinely appear as key figures in the dispute.

One way to view their involvement is to say that they functioned (merely) as the means by which the iambicist could attack his male enemies. Certainly there is truth to this proposition in a world where a man's honor depended on the chastity and decorum of his female relatives, it being his responsibility to maintain order in the household. Yet there is more to iambic's hostile interest in women, I believe. Women played a role in their own right. When, as was often the case, women functioned as the targets of iambic, they were routinely mocked and rebuked for crass sexuality. I present the following as hypothesis, to be tested over the next four chapters: iambic censured women's licentious cultic speech in a "secular" world where the license of cult no longer protected it. The abusive and obscene speech of women within their cults seemed to have "invited" a quarrel, of which iambic was the voice of the surviving combatant: the angry "response." The genre must be recontextualized by modern readers if it is to be understood.

Aischrologia

Of all the types of speech associated with women, none exceeded cultic joking in power and impact. As I noted in discussing the "foundation" story of the *Hymn to Demeter*, Iambe's address to Demeter explictly covered a range of tone and attitude, from jest to mockery. I suggest that some of the terms describing this speech are inclusive of the whole range (terms such as *aischrologia*), whereas others single out some aspect of it (such as *blasphemein*).

Cultic mocking speech was variously described in ancient sources on the rites of Demeter: speech "such as one would find in a brothel"; *aischrologia* (shameful speech), *arrheta*, *aporrheta* (unspeakable things); verbs connoting abuse (*loidorein*), mockery (*diaskoptein*) and blasphemy (*blasphemein*). In Demeter's worship it occurred in exchanges between women in segregated contexts.

"Speech such as one would find in a brothel" alerts us to the sexual content of this speech. As Henderson has noted, *aischrologia* and terms like it imply shame, the feeling that accompanies the exposure of what ought to remain private. It is not the same as our modern notion of obscenity, which implies dirt and pollution, something inherently nasty. For the Greeks sexual congress was natural, enjoyable – but private.[18] Those parts of the body associated with sex similarly were not in themselves dirty but were private. To render them public was to transgress. The speech that exposes sexual parts or sexual behavior was expected to have a shaming effect – on the speaker, the addressee, a larger audience, or a party being described or implicated within the speech. Thus, such shame-inducing speech routinely implied aggression and could be perceived as insulting to the person at whom it was directed. The question is, how do we weigh and understand that shame, that aggression, especially within the marked context of cult? Is it felt equally by women and men, by participants, and by observers?

The terms *arrheta* and *aporrheta* refer to what should not or cannot be spoken. This taboo may be interpreted in different ways. Either the subject was not supposed to be divulged, or the words were so shameful as to make it virtually impossible to utter them under normal conditions.[19] Both readings of *arrheta* imply challenges for the modern scholar. Obviously taboos regarding disclosure impede the transmission of information and render suspect the accounts that do survive. If we consider the implications of shameful speech – *aischrologia* – we face questions of perspective and attitude.

Most of the terms imply or connote sanction or disapproval. Outsiders, invariably men, deployed these terms and descriptions. The standards and norms implicit in them are those of a public, authoritarian, male-run world. Some, such as the Church Fathers, disdain the practices they describe. From their perspective, the speech appears defiant. We may conclude that even if the women engaged in such speech would have recognized the terms, they might have contested their use or meaning. The practitioners might not have endorsed fully or shared the notions of shame and transgression implicit in some of the terms.

The Greek αἰσχρόν (the first element in the word *aischrologia*) also has an aesthetic dimension, which is crucial to our understanding of *aischrologia*. τὸ αἰσχρόν suggests something opposed to the proportion, grace, containment, and harmony of σωφροσύνη, for example. This speech (and again, of course, we face the problem of whose perspective is being considered) is identified as ugly, intemperate, even repellent. I argue in my discussions of the women's cults that a celebratory and self-conscious *grotesquerie* marked both their speech and their behavior.

Archaic and classical Greece was a culture obsessed with male honor. Modern scholars have explored the implications of this worldview, using comparative evidence from modern anthropological studies of Mediterranean and other cultures.[20] The maintenance of a man's personal honor was a heavy responsibility and constant concern to him in an environment where watchful eyes monitored every move. It entailed control of his female relatives, whose chastity and sexual decorum (at least as known to the rest of the world) reflected on his manly capacity to police the boundaries of his household. Women, too, had a stake in the system, but they were not understood to be capable of self-regulation, as was a virtuous and competent man. Their relationship with "honor" and its antithesis "shame" was a function of their role in a man's world. Within the world of women's cults, however, a woman might not have felt her conduct and speech as equally constitutive of her family's honor.[21] Instead, detached from father, husband, brothers, and sons, she looked at other women, like herself, and created, with ribald and mocking speech, a new community.

Perhaps practitioners or observers perceived in the speech a challenge to "real-world" norms and values. Without women's own testimony, we cannot know their spectrum of opinion. As I show, however, the partial evidence that survives indicates that men perceived this cultic speech as significantly unsettling and contestatory, in addition to its presumable value within "fertility" cults.[22]

Reading between the Lines

In assessing ancient evidence, one must remember that sources often spoke prescriptively about the role of women in society; they reflected an official view of a world segregated along gender lines, with women relegated to the private sphere of the home and family.[23] Such "packaging" of the world means that women's (often secret or separate) activities affecting the public world of state or community as a whole did not usually receive explicit acknowledgment, even though such activities were indeed felt to be important.[24] In the case of iambic abuse – of women's errant sexual behavior – we are seeing a form of social control whose very virulence suggests fear: that women did not, or might not, conform to societal codes. The vehemence suggests contestation, not unanimity.

Most scholars know better than to take literally what a comic or iambic poet says about women (or anything else), but the problems of contextualizing and assessing evidence apply across all genres. The fact that a theme received particular attention among historians, philosophers, or orators may mean that it was the subject of controversy and not that our author is stating his society's consensus for the benefit of future generations.[25]

We may learn more from what is assumed or taken for granted than from what is pointed out deliberately. In addition to the trickiness of assessing authors' complex agenda and purposes in writing, there may be questions regarding their insight and understanding. Almost by definition, for example, our sources on secret cults did not share the reverence felt by many in the communities in which they were practiced. The *Hymn to Demeter*, for example, emphatically prohibits speaking of the Mysteries of Demeter.[26]

Ideally we would have women's views on their own activities to complement what men said about them. We don't.[27] Winkler's work has shown how great the potential difference between what women may have thought themselves to be doing in cults and what men thought – or said – about them. I modify his argument, however.[28] There did exist a woman's perspective and knowledge that differed from men's, but I do not think that this perspective and collective wisdom was entirely a closed book to their male contemporaries.[29] Male sources, even hostile male sources, although obviously not ideal, nonetheless yield real insights into the "alien" world(s) of women.

Whether in the field of religion or of literature, men's and women's voices invariably were part of a single system. It is crucial to consider the total entity – especially when one is dealing with a seemingly all-male phenomenon such as old comedy or iambic. Brumfield has suggested that ancient feminine consciousness was "expressed in ironic coda to the masculine point of view" and may be imagined as "like a double star whose invisible member's orbit can only be plotted from the movement of its visible twin."[30] To take her thesis further, I believe that we can hope to comprehend the male perspective only by tracking that feminine star that so often moved in its shadow.

Summary of Chapters

In Chapter 1 I discuss women's joking and its function(s) within the cults of Demeter and Dionysus. I focus particularly on the Thesmophoria. My approach to women's ritual here and throughout the book is synthetic, broadly feminist, and influenced by recent anthropological theory, especially practice theory.[31] Women's minds and bodies were shaped by their experience of culture. At the same time, they were makers of ritual, agents in reproducing and defining their festivals in an ever-changing political and social context. I take another look at *aischrologia* at the end of Chapter 1, considering how one might imagine women's perspective(s) as counterpoint to the male readings of "shameful" speech necessarily imposed on us by our sources.

Chapter 2 analyzes the Iambe incident within the *Hymn* and against the background of joking scenes from epic. Iambe's mockery, with its magical aftermath, differed profoundly from mockery scenes in the *Iliad* and *Odyssey*. Typically, mockery in epic was a bloody affair, often pointing the way to the exclusion, humiliation – and even death – of one individual or many; in the *Hymn*, Iambe's mockery led to the inclusion of a former "outsider" and her retreat from death toward joyful affirmation of life. Iambe's joking led to the formation of a community of women and an interlude during which the goddess magically nurtured the infant prince of Eleusis in their midst, secretly dipping him in the fire to purge his mortal flesh and render him divine.

The "Iambe incident" shone briefly in a generally somber story that sent complex signals about relations between women, men, and the divine world. A subsequent interruption by the infant's mother as Demeter was attempting to immortalize the child reawakened the goddess' lethal rage and grief and shattered the community of women. The *Hymn* closed with the well-known "shared custody" arrangement between Demeter and Hades and with the transmission of Demeter's famous cult of the Mysteries – to the priests and kings of Eleusis. The local women, so critical to her initial welcome and her relenting, seem to have moved from center stage to the periphery and to have lost the initiative in relation to the goddess, yielding their place to men. What does this suggest?

Demeter's cult of the Mysteries at Eleusis – which was open to Greek speakers, men and women – did not in fact displace the Thesmophoria or any other women's cult, but the *Hymn*'s suggestion of a transition contains an important truth nonetheless. With the development of the *polis* of Athens, public, largely masculine institutions grew, which appropriated or tended to appropriate the introvert, secret powers of women. As Brumfield put it, "the Eleusinian Mysteries can be seen as a public and rationalized version of the local mysteries traditionally celebrated by women."[32] Similarly, literary iambic did not displace women's cultic joking, which continued throughout antiquity, but women's voices generally failed to make the transition from cult to iambic literature.

The *Hymn* is not just telling a history, of course. It has its own perspective on that history. I suggest that the *Hymn* as a whole reflects the patriarchal standpoint of the poem's creators. Yet there are also hints within it of a perspective and a history quite at odds with that enshrined in this, its final version. Chapter 1's discussion of the pomegranate seed and *cyceon*, for example, shows the stratigraphy of these opposed perspectives, where a "vein" of women's cultic lore lies beneath the poem's "masculinist" surface.

Chapter 3 tracks the connections between the iambic genre and the Iambe stories that developed after the *Hymn*. It follows the fortunes of the character Iambe, after her earliest appearance in the *Hymn to Demeter*. She came to function as a – significantly but paradoxically – feminine symbol of literary iambic in a series of stories. She became for ancient scholars a "double" symbol, representing the practice of iambic mockery, especially within the cult of Demeter and becoming its archetypal victim, a person driven to suicide by the cruelties of an iambic poet. This harsh fate was more likely in situations in which the connection to Demeter's cult seemed relatively attenuated.

Chapter 3 also examines the female characters – generally targets – of iambic. Iambic's voice, which was deeply personal, seems quintessentially male, and often hostile to women. Yet reading between the lines of these misogynistic texts, one also can perceive the profound importance women's (now largely silent) voices had in the development of the genre. One may also see traces of women's Demeter cults in extant iambic, which otherwise shows no sympathy toward women. Chapter 3 concludes with consideration of women's agency, as evinced within male iambic.

Chapter 4 considers whether women actually created literary iambic and what this iambic might have looked like. Sappho's poems of mockery (both harsh and lighthearted) complicate the notion of iambic as a male monopoly. Thinking about Sappho's iambic "face" also creates a more complex vision of this ancient poet than has been traditional in British and American scholarship.[33] I also briefly consider some fragments of the poet Corinna.

In Chapter 5 I analyze women's joking in a specifically Athenian context, showing how the developing Athenian *polis* in the sixth and fifth centuries moved toward restricting women's roles in the public sphere. These restrictions, attributed to Solon, targeted both lamentation and "disorderly and licentious" behavior at religious festivals. Subsequently, the great City Dionysia, where comedies were first performed, became a focal point – the city's most ambitious and extravagant expression of cultic joking. The City Dionysia did not replace women's cultic mockery, but it drew energy and resources and contributed to the shift of the city's cultic balance as a whole toward men. No women took part in the plays, either composing or performing in them.

Loraux and Holst-Warhaft have argued that the city of Athens partially appropriated the traditional women's function of lament.[34] Tragedy and the funeral oration embodied these functions at the state level. I suggest that comedy played an analogous role with regard to women's cultic laughter. It did not replace women's joking, but it represented the centralizing tendency in the way Athenians mediated relations between the community and the gods, with a concomitant lessening of women's importance as credited public agents in the religious sphere.

I show how comedy shared iambic's origins in cultic joke exchanges, iambic's coarseness, and (to an extent) its subject matter but differed from iambic in form (i.e., having extended plots) and so in its potential to develop complex roles for women.[35] To understand "women," as depicted by Aristophanes and others, I examine the fragmentary evidence of old comedy, showing how the roles of women became increasingly differentiated over time and how they reflected certain social realities, if not the lives of actual women. By looking at the whole range of fragments, we can evaluate Aristophanes' treatment of women. His use of women as a theme, if not idiosyncratic, characterized a variant of old comedy and was not universal. For Aristophanes women constituted a "shadow polis," a parallel world that he could use to discuss the city as a whole. He also viewed women as an interest group, however, with important collective concerns in their own right. He did not concern himself with women as individuals and lampooned dramatists – comic and tragic – who did.

I end Chapter 5 by discussing the crucial question of whether women attended the plays. I argue that they did; the fact that they were not explicitly acknowledged as part of the audience by the playwrights made their presence something of a paradox, duly reflected by contradictory and debated evidence. I argue for the presence of women in the audience before turning to individual plays, so as to introduce this feminine "gaze" through which the plays might have been viewed.

Chapter 6 discusses the two "women's plays" of 411, the *Lysistrata* and *Women at the Thesmophoria* (*Thesmophoriazousae*), and scenes from the *Acharnians*, the *Women at the Assembly* (*Ecclesiazousae*), and *Plutus*. Aristophanes' women's plays of 411 drew on the preexisting comic tradition regarding women, but their scope and concentrated focus on women reflected unique and new concerns of the poet and also owed much to the turbulent year in which they were written. The Spartans had occupied Deceleia in 413, and year-round farming had halted in Attica for the first time since the beginning of the Peloponnesian war, twenty years earlier.

Aristophanes' parody of the Thesmophoria presented itself as an offering to Demeter as well as to Dionysus: mockery for a goddess whose worship included mockery. The play's mimesis of the Thesmophoria attempted to coopt the voice and authority of its target. His parody of this vital women's cult appropriated, for the City Dionysia, voices and powers he felt to be missing from the Athenian stage. The evident, outrageous inauthenticity of Aristophanes' version of the Thesmophoria made it an apt, iambic offering to Demeter, and the ludicrously ineffectual efforts of the character Mnesilochus to disguise himself as a woman and infiltrate the festival reenacted genuine Themsophorian mythic and ritual motifs. When addressed together with Demeter, Dionysus transcended his role as patron of drama. Together with the city's patron, Athena, he represented the (endangered) fertility of Attic soil: grain, olives, and vines – and humankind.

More important than the fact of the borrowing, however, is the larger dynamic context in which we should view it. As with iambic, so with comedy, what we have inherited was not, I believe, a unilateral, self-reflective voice, but rather a performance that formed part of a larger debate, or series of debates. In brief, I suggest that we should view the *Lysistrata* and *Thesmophoriazousae* not as the exclusive products of a man writing for men, from within a male-centered traditition, but rather as the surviving piece of a dialogue between Aristophanes and women, whose voices, cultic and domestic, he undoubtedly heard and cared about.

Chapter 6 concludes by reversing our thinking about gender and audience in fifth-century Athens: considering women as spectators, not just spectacle, men as spectacle, not just spectators. If, as was the case in my view, women watched old comedies, how might they have responded to its depictions of "women?" Women's shared cultic experience shaped their response to the sexual jokes, the laughter at female ugliness and old age, the portrayal of women's cults on the Dionysiac stage.

Much of old comedy's humor paralleled that of women's cults, exposing, mocking, and enjoying publicly, what was normally kept hidden. The explosive power of old comedy's humor lay in outspoken revelation and imagined social upheaval. Its program seemingly challenged the city's pattern of silencing and restraining so many of its inhabitants – women, slaves, and metics. Yet old comedy was an all-male affair, its thunder borrowed from cultic jesting, uttered – often exclusively – by women. This work listens, beyond the uproar of the Dionysian theater, for those laughing women's voices, both those imagined by the comic playwrights and their real counterparts, heard and unheard by men.

◇ 1 ◇

CULTIC OBSCENITY IN GREECE, ESPECIALLY ATTICA

B ELIEF IN THE RESTORATIVE POWER of women, produced through mingled solemnity and raucous joking, was powerful, in Greece and
elsewhere.[1] Ancient Egypt, Scandinavia, and Japan had traditional
stories in which a woman or goddess cheers a mourner by making obscene jokes or by exposing herself.[2] In Greece most evidence for women
as active participants in obscene insult exchanges occurs in relation to the
cults of Demeter. In this chapter I analyze certain rituals of Demeter that
featured such obscene joking and insult. Only through careful analysis of
the context can one begin to understand the force and impact of the speech
associated with it. Then I discuss the joking, and women's relationship to
it, in more detail.

My approach to ritual is eclectic, drawing on structuralist theory while
attending to the question of ritual's ever-shifting relationship with social
identity. Like other classical scholars in recent years, I have found useful the
insights of cultural anthropologists in thinking about ancient rituals.[3] In
analysis of the Demetrian Thesmophoria, which is where one may glean
the most detail, I see the ritual as a site of interaction between cultural
ideas and women's social experience. The Thesmophoria enacted and
celebrated continuity, but it also was a place where social structures and
cultural ideals might undergo critique – even transformation. In times of
stress and social change, such as marked Athens in the final third of the fifth
century B.C.E., rituals such as the Thesmophoria or Adonia could become
lightning rods for tensions, especially intergender tensions.

Groups of men and women mocked each other with obscene banter in
connection with the cult of Demeter and other deities, but our knowledge
of this practice derives from locations other than Athens.[4] This probably is no coincidence. Archaic and classical Athens seems to have segregated men and women more than other cities.[5] At the Hybristica at Argos,
men and women exchanged clothes and fought; according to myth, the
fight commemorates a victory by the women of Argos, led by the poetess

Telesilla, against the Spartans.[6] The leadership of a poet suggests that there were verbal exchanges involved in addition to ritual fighting. At Pellene, in the Peloponnese, Pausanias records a festival of Demeter Musia in which choruses of men and women hurled insults at each other.[7] At a sacrifice for Apollo Aigletes on Anaphe, there was a traditional intergender exchange of insults, because maidens given by the Phaeacian queen Areta to Medea had once "mocked the nobles" (presumably those accompanying Jason).[8]

Herodotus describes the Aeginetans stealing statues of Damia and Auxesia from Epidaurus and instituting in their honor "certain ceremonies."[9] These statues had been set up on the advice of the Delphic oracle following a crop failure at Epidaurus. They were made (on Delphic advice) from the wood of the cultivated olive. The ceremonies instituted by the Aeginetans in honor of the purloined "fertility" statues consisted of sacrifices and of "women dancers and singers in the satirical and abusive mode." Each chorus was trained by its own (male) chorus leaders, of whom there were ten. Herodotus notes that the women's attacks were directed at no man but at the local women. His emphasis suggests that his readers might otherwise assume the women directed their mockery across the gender line, at men. The Aeginetan ceremonies resembled similar rites that had been taking place at Epidauros, according to Herodotus.

Attica

Worship of various deities, in their different aspects, took place throughout the Athenian year. The liturgies varied from formal and spectacular state festivals like the Panathenaia (every four years) or the annual City Dionysia; to international cults such as the Eleusinian Mysteries (administered by a body of priests and existing outside the city and its political structures); to small local affairs, taking place at deme level or within individual neighborhoods. The latter were sometimes arranged quite spontaneously, without "official" support. In some cases deme festivities corresponded roughly with what was taking place at a grander level elsewhere.

At Attic festivals of Dionysus, wagons passed through the streets bearing masked revelers who shouted obscene insults at bystanders; hence came the expression ἐξ ἁμάξης, or "from the wagon," to mean something rude or obscene.[10] It is not clear whether women participated in this rude banter; Greek masculine adjectives and participles may refer either to an all-male group or to a mixed one.[11] A scene in the *Acharnians* of Aristophanes depicts a married Athenian woman told by her husband (Dicaeopolis) to watch his celebration of the Rural Dionysia from the roof (*Ach.* 262) – an interesting compromise.

Demeter

Demeter's cults had been dominated by women since time immemorial. Festivals such as the Thesmophoria possibly dated to the Stone Age, at a time when women were responsible for crop production and animal husbandry.[12] Scholars have challenged interpretations of rituals that seek meaning in "origins," however, and certainly even if one could establish the primacy of one context over another for "reading" a ritual, this would not necessarily remain true for all time. Changing political and social structures surely produced new, or more layered, interpretations of the rituals among the participants.[13]

Crude and aggressive joking featured in many of the major Demeter festivals: the Stenia and Thesmophoria, the Haloa, and the Eleusinian Mysteries. At the Stenia, which preceded the Thesmophoria, Photius tells us that the women abused each other (he uses the verb *loidorein*).[14] Hesychius mentions that the women at the Stenia "blaspheme and mock" *blasphemein, diaskoptein*).[15] Women's cultic speech also was characterized as *aischrologia* (shameful speech), *arrheta*, or *aporrheta* ("unspeakable" words). As I mentioned in the Introduction, "unspeakable" words bespeak problems for the modern scholar intent on assessing them. Whether the implied prohibition refers to a taboo on divulging the secrets or speech so shameful as to problematize utterance, the door seems firmly shut in our face. Furthermore, the "shame" implicit in *aischrologia* unleashes problems of perspective and attitude. Who is ashamed? Or who imputes shame to others? As if these problems were not sufficient, the sources on the women's festivals track through an impenetrable forest of antecedents.

The Source(s)

The principal ancient sources for the Demeter festivals are especially problematic, and require a brief commentary. Two long scholia, or ancient commentaries, on the text of Lucian's *Dialogs of the Courtesans* purport to describe the Thesmophoria and Haloa festivals.[16] There is also a passage from the Church Father Clement of Alexandria's *Protrepticus* or *Exhortation* to the Greeks to abandon the Pagan religions.[17] These accounts all derive from a single ancient source, whose identity and date is still very much in doubt, and who combined in his narrative both description of the activities and interpretation as to what they might mean (detailed subsequently). As Lowe has observed, this ancient venture into explanation is unique in the history of Greek religion and therefore of enormous interest. As to how this unknown scholar knew what he did about these secret festivals and which elements subsequent writers (including the highly polemical Church Fathers) may have rewritten and reinterpreted for their own purposes, these difficult questions remain to be answered. Obviously we are at the mercy of many unknowns. Nonetheless, as I observed in the Introduction, I believe that, as in the case of all of our (male, élite) sources to view the evidence, even here, as pertinent only to the state of mind, the preoccupations, of its author is to throw the baby out with the bathwater. For obvious reasons these data are particularly problematic, but as with contemporary sources such as Aristophanes, I suggest that they emerge from a world shaped and conditioned by women's presence, by women's voices. Whoever these sequential writers may have been and whichever audiences they may have addressed, they wrote in a context in which the Demetrian cults, and the women who practiced them, still spoke with an authoritative voice.

The Demeter Festivals

I borrow Lowe's translation of the scholion to the *Dialogs of the Courtesans*, vii.4:

Ἀλῶα· ἑορτὴ Ἀθήνησι μυστήρια περιέχουσα Δήμητρος καὶ Κόρης καὶ Διονύσου ἐπὶ τῇ τομῇ τῆς ἀμπέλου καὶ τῇ γεύσει τοῦ ἀποκειμένου ἤδη οἴνου γινόμενα παρὰ Ἀθηναίοις, ἐν οἷς προτίθεται αἰσχύναις ἀνδρείοις ἐοικότα, περὶ ὧν διηγοῦνται ὡς πρὸς σύνθημα τῆς τῶν ἀνθρώπων σπορᾶς γινομένων, ὅτι ὁ Διόνυσος δοὺς τὸν οἶνον παροξυντικὸν φάρμακον τοῦτο πρὸς τὴν μῖξιν παρέσχεν. δέδωκε δὲ αὐτὸ Ἰκαρίῳ, ὃν καὶ ἀποκτείναντες ποιμένες τῷ ἀγνοῆσαι, ὅπως διατίθησι ποθεὶς οἶνος, εἶτα μανέντες διὰ τὸ καὶ πρὸς τὸν Διόνυσον ὑβριστικῶς κινηθῆναι καὶ ἐπʼ αὐτοῦ τοῦ τῆς αἰσχύνης σχήματος καταμεμενηκότες χρησμὸς παύσασθαι τῆς μανίας αὐτοὺς διηγόρεσυε πήλινα ποιήσαντας αἰδοῖα καὶ ἀναθέντας· οὗ δὴ γενομένου αὐτοὶ μὲν ἔστησαν τοῦ κακοῦ, ὑπόμνημα δὲ τοῦ πάθους ἡ τοιαύτη ἑορτή. ἐν ταύτῃ καὶ τελετή τις εἰσάγεται γυναικῶν ἐν Ἐλευσῖνι καὶ παιδιαὶ λέγονται πολλαὶ καὶ σκώμματα. μόναι δὲ γυναῖκες εἰσπορευόμεναι ἐπʼ ἀδείας ἔχουσιν ἃ βούλονται λέγειν· καὶ δὴ τὰ αἴσχιστα ἀλλήλαις λέγουσι τότε, αἱ δὲ ἱέρειαι λάθρα προσιοῦσαι ταῖς γυναιξὶ κλεψιγαμίας πρὸς τὸ οὖς ὡς ἀπόρρητόν τι συμβουλεύουσιν. ἀναφωνοῦσι δὲ πρὸς ἀλλήλας πᾶσαι αἱ γυναῖκες αἰσχρὰ

καὶ ἄσεμνα βαστάζουσι εἴδη σωμάτων ἀπρεπῆ ἀνδρεῖά τε καὶ γυναικεῖα.
ἐνταῦθα οἶνός τε πολὺς πρόκειται καὶ τράπεζαι πάντων τῶν τῆς γῆς καὶ
θαλάσσης γέμουσαι βρωμάτων πλὴν τῶν ἀπειρημένων ἐν τῷ μυστικῷ, ῥοιᾶς
φημι καὶ μήλου καὶ ὀρνίθων κατοικιδίων καὶ ᾠῶν καὶ θαλαττίων τρίγλης,
ἐρυθίνου, μελανούρου, καράβου, γαλεοῦ. παρατιθέασι δὲ τὰς τραπέζας
οἱ ἄρχοντες καὶ ἔνδον καταλιπόντες ταῖς γυναιξὶν αὐτοὶ χωρίζονται ἔξω
διαμένοντες ἐπιδεικνύμενοι τοῖς ἐπιδημοῦσι πᾶσι τὰς ἡμέρους τροφὰς
παρὰ αὐτοῖς εὑρεθῆναι καὶ πᾶσι κοινωνηθῆναι τοῖς ἀνθρώποις παρ'αὐτῶν.
πρόσκειται δὲ ταῖς τραπέζαις καὶ ἐκ πλακοῦντος κατεσκευασμένα ἀμφοτέρων
γενῶν αἰδοῖα. Ἁλῶα δὲ ἐκλήθη διὰ τὸν καρπὸν τοῦ Διονύσου· ἁλωαὶ γὰρ αἱ τῶν
ἀμπέλων φυτεῖαι.

Haloa: A festival at Athens of Demeter and Kore and of Dionysus, encompassing mysteries, held among the Athenians at the cutting of the vine
and the tasting of the wine previously laid in storage. In these [subject
missing] in the form of male privates are set out, which they explain as
symbolic of the seed of men's generation, because Dionysus in making
the gift of wine provided that stimulating drug as an incitement to sex. He
gave it to Icarius, whom the shepherds having also [?] slain through their
ignorance of the effects of wine-drinking, and subsequently being driven
mad on account first of their blasphemous impulse towards Dionysus,
and secondly having remained under the very aspect of shame [?] – an
oracle commanded them to desist from their madness by fashioning clay
genitals and dedicating them.[18] This done, they were released from the
curse, and the present festival commemorates the events. In it, there is
also presented a woman's *telete* at Eleusis, and many jokes and frivolities
are uttered. The women go in alone, and may say what they wish; and
indeed they do then say the most disgusting things to one another, and
the priestesses approach the women secretly and into their ear urge them
to commit adultery, as though it were some holy secret.[19] All the women
shout disgusting, blasphemous things at one another, handling the while
indecent images of the body, male and female alike. Here there is a great
deal of wine laid ready, and tables laden with all the victuals of earth and
sea save those forbidden in the mysteries; I mean pomegranate, apple,
domestic fowl, eggs, and among fish the red mullet, erythinus, black-tail,
crayfish and dogfish. The Archons prepare the tables and leave them inside for the women, while they themselves depart and wait outside to
show all visiting foreigners that civilized foods originated with them and
were communicated to all mankind by them. Also laid on the table are
private parts of both sexes fashioned of cake. It is called Haloa after the
fruit of Dionysus, for *aloai* are where vines are grown.[20]

At the Eleusinian Mysteries both men and women were initiated to im-
prove their lot in the afterlife.[21] The festival began with a procession from

Athens to Eleusis, bearing the statue of Iakkhos and other sacred objects.
At a bridge over the Cephisus the initiates engaged in an exchange of insults (known as *gephurismos* or "bridge-ism") with a person or persons
stationed there.[22] Accounts of the assailants vary – unidentified masked
figures in some; according to Hesychius it was a prostitute, or a man "deeply
veiled" and so possibly disguised as a woman. One scholar has described
this stage in the ritual as follows:

> We have found a similar pattern underlying many of the most character-
> istic Dionysiac rituals: when the masks go into the city, they utter insults
> that can hardly be understood as personal statements by the individuals
> behind the mask, or by whomever, indeed. Neither can the "insults of
> the bridge" in the way to Eleusis possibly be personal statements of any-
> body, and not even real insults aimed at a particular person. They again
> seem more like a sort of welcome: in both cases, the procession marks the
> entrance into something different (indeed, into something that may be
> called an experience of otherness), and the insults are the threshold.[23]

The Scira, a midsummer Demeter festival, was celebrated with a procession out of the city of the priestess of Athena and the priests of Poseidon
and Helios.[24] It appears to have been primarily a dissolution festival, marking the end of the Attic calendar year. The Sciron itself was a hero precinct
but lay next to a shrine of Demeter and Persephone on the road to Eleusis. Thus, as Burkert put it, "Athena and Poseidon are received there as
guests by the Eleusinian goddesses." The women of the city participated
as a group "according to ancestral custom." They feasted together, as a
group, and it it was a high honor to be selected to preside.[25] They ate garlic, an anaphrodisiac, as part of a general abstinence from sex during the
festival.[26] There is no direct evidence for *aischrologia* at the Scira, but it is
likely to have occurred in such a festival of license and mock-autonomy for
women, involving a procession similar to that which began the Eleusinian
Mysteries. The Scira is the festival at which the Assemblywomen hatched
their plot in Aristophanes' play – indeed the abusive "Ionian song" between the old woman and the girl (877–937) probably reflected the iambic
banter characteristic of the festival.[27] The Calamaia also, probably a festival associated with threshing the grain, was celebrated at Eleusis and at
the Thesmophorion at Piraeus.[28] Like the Scira, the Calamaia probably
resembled the Thesmophoria in some respects.[29]

Of the Demeter festivals, the Thesmophoria – a November festival that
directly preceded cereal sowing, pruning, and trenching fruit trees and

the olive harvest and pressing – was the best-known and most widespread of Demeter's festivals, being attested in at least thirty cities in mainland Greece, the islands (including Crete), Asia Minor, North Africa, and Sicily.[30] It followed closely upon the Stenia, and together the series of rituals were believed to correspond with the mythical events surrounding Demeter's loss of her daughter. Only women took part, although it required the support – financial and otherwise – of the men in the community.

Again, I quote Lowe's translation of the relevant scholion (to Lucian, *Dialogs of the Courtesans* ii.1):

Θεσμοφόρια· Θεσμοφόρια ἑορτὴ Ἑλλήνων μυστήρια περιέχουσα, τὰ δὲ αὐτὰ καὶ Σκιρροφόρια καλεῖται. ἤγετο δὲ κατὰ τὸν μυθωδέστερον λόγον, ὅτι, [ὅτε] ἀνθολογοῦσα ἡρπάζετο ἡ Κόρη ὑπὸ τοῦ Πλούτωνος, τότε κατ᾽ ἐκεῖνον τὸν τόπον Εὐβουλεὺς τις συβώτης ἔνεμεν ὗς καὶ συγκατεπόθησαν τῷ χάσματι τῆς Κόρης· εἰς οὖν τιμὴν τοῦ Εὐβουλέως ῥιπτεῖσθαι τοὺς χοίρους εἰς τὰ χάσματα τῆς Δήμητρος καὶ τῆς Κόρης. τὰ δὲ σαπέντα τῶν ἐμβληθέντων εἰς τὰ μέγαρα κάτω ἀναφέρουσιν ἀντλήτριαι καλούμεναι γυναῖκες καθαρεύσασαι τριῶν ἡμερῶν καὶ καταβαίνουσιν εἰς τὰ ἄδυτα καὶ ἀνενέγκασαι ἐπιτιθέασιν ἐπὶ τῶν βωμῶν· ὧν νομίζουσι τὸν λαμβάνοντα καὶ τῷ σπόρῳ συγκαταβάλλοντα εὐφορίαν ἕξειν. λέγουσι δὲ καὶ δράκοντας κάτω εἶναι περὶ τὰ χάσματα, οὓς τὰ πολλὰ τῶν βληθέντων κατεσθίειν· διὸ καὶ κρότον γίνεσθαι, ὁπόταν ἀντλῶσιν αἱ γυναῖκες καὶ ὅταν ἀποτιθῶνται πάλιν τὰ πλάσματα ἐκεῖνα, ἵνα ἀναχωρήσωσιν οἱ δράκοντες, οὓς νομίζουσι φρουροὺς τῶν ἀδύτων. τὰ δὲ αὐτὰ καὶ Ἀρρητοφόρια καλεῖται καὶ ἄγεται τὸν αὐτὸν λόγον ἔχοντα περὶ τῶν καρπῶν γενέσεως καὶ τῆς τῶν ἀνθρώπων σπορᾶς. ἀναφέρονται δὲ κἀνταῦθα ἄρρητα ἱερὰ ἐκ στέατος τοῦ σίτου κατεσκευασμένα, μιμήματα δρακόντων καὶ ἀνδρείων σχημάτων. λαμβάνουσι δὲ κώνου θαλλοὺς διὰ τὸ πολύγονον τοῦ φυτοῦ. ἐμβάλλονται δὲ καὶ εἰς τὰ μέγαρα οὕτω καλούμενα ἄδυτα ἐκεῖνά τε καὶ χοῖροι, ὡς ἤδη ἔφαμεν, καὶ αὐτοὶ διὰ τὸ πολύτοκον εἰς σύνθημα τῆς γενέσεως τῶν καρπῶν καὶ τῶν ἀνθρώπων οἷον χαριστήρια τῇ Δήμητρι, ἐπειδὴ τοὺς Δημητρίους καρποὺς παρέχουσα ἐποίησεν ἥμερον τὸ τῶν ἀνθρώπων γένος. ὁ μὲν οὖν ἄνω τῆς ἑορτῆς λόγος ὁ μυθικός, ὁ δὲ προκείμενος φυσικός. Θεσμοφόρια δὲ καλεῖται, καθότι θεσμοφόρος ἡ Δημήτηρ κατονομάζεται τιθεῖσα νόμους ἤτοι θεσμούς, καθ᾽ οὓς τὴν τροφὴν πορίζεσθαί τε καὶ κατεργάζεσθαι ἀνθρώπους δέον.

Thesmophoria: a festival of the Greeks encompassing mysteries, also known as Skirophoria.[31] It was [*or* they were] held, according to the more mythological explanation, because [when] Kore, picking flowers, was being carried off by Pluto, one Eubouleus, a swineherd, was at the time grazing his pigs on that spot, and they were swallowed up together in Kore's pit; wherefore, in honour of Eubouleus, piglets are thrown into the pits of Demeter and Kore.[32] The rotten remains of what was thrown into the megara below are recovered by women called "dredgers," who have spent three days in ritual purity and descend into the shrines and when they have recovered the remains deposit them on the altars. They believe that anyone who takes some and sows it with the seed will have a good crop. They say that there are also serpents below about the pits, which eat up the great part of the material thrown in; for which reason they also make a clatter whenever the women dredge and whenever they set those models down again, so that the serpents they believe to be guarding the shrines will withdraw. The same thing is also known as the Arretophoria, and is held with the same explanation to do with vegetable fertility and human procreation. On that occasion too they bring unnameable holy things fashioned out of wheat dough, images of snakes and male members.[33] And they take pine branches because of that plant's fertility. There are also thrown into the megara (so the shrines are called) those things, and piglets, as mentioned above – the latter because of their fecundity as a symbol of vegetable and human generation, for a thanksgiving offering to Demeter; because in providing the fruits of Demeter she civilized the race of humans. Thus the former reason for the festival is the mythological one, but the present one is physical. It is called Thesmophoria because Demeter is given the epithet "Lawgiver" for having set down customs, which is to say laws, under which men have to acquire and work for their food.[34]

As Lowe has warned, although the scholiast takes the anomalous step of giving explanations for what took place at the Thesmophoria, he does not say what many modern scholars have thought him to say: that the festival was intended to promote human and agrarian fertility. His two explanations are, respectively, etiological and and symbolic. The pigs are thrown in to commemorate an earlier fall of some piglets. The pinecones and piglets symbolize the generation of crops and humans, who benefited from Demeter's gift by becoming civilized. The actions could be seen as thanksgiving and as celebratory of Demeter's former gift, not necessarily intending to invoke her powers in the future. Recent scholars have very much sharpened our sense of the festival's potentials – and of the pitfalls inherent in "reading" it.

The word χοίριον/χοῖρος (piglet) was also a term for the vulva, and so the magical core of next year's crop was a symbolic and potent mixture of extremes: the unripe youth of the piglet and its decomposition; an emblem of female immaturity and of female overripeness or decay. The snakes thought to inhabit the underground pits and feed on the offerings similarly expressed paradoxical meanings. From the Bronze Age they were linked with death and the dead – but also with the miraculous ability to shed old age and regain lost youth; the word γῆρας means both old age and the skin that a snake sloughs off every spring.[35] The old age of the snake was a husk, beneath which youth waited to reemerge. The very underground chasms or chambers, simultaneously evoked both the formlessness of decay, absorption, and death on one hand, and the female genitalia and fertility on the other.[36]

During the Thesmophoria the women withdrew to a place of their own and imitated an "ancient" way of life.[37] In some cases they built huts of leaves and pine branches; in Athens, buildings, or Thesmophoria, were designated for the festival. It appears that there was no state celebration at Athens; rather, women gathered within their various demes.[38] Scholars have tended to argue the contrary, however – that there *was* a single, Athenian festival and that its building was located on the Pnyx.[39] Clinton has shown the extreme flimsiness of the grounds for regarding the Thesmophoria at Athens as a citywide celebration and taking the Pnyx as the site of the festival.[40] There is no archaeological or epigraphic evidence for a statewide feast, whereas there is substantial evidence, literary and epigraphic, for deme-level Thesmophoria. Evidence elsewhere suggests that the festival originally may have been celebrated on a small scale, rather than by a very large group of women, which would have required elaborate accommodations.[41] As a source (in favor of a poliswide festival at the heart of the city) Aristophanes is obviously not entirely trustworthy. He may be rendering the notion of a "shadow polis" run by women as deliberately preposterous. At the same time, he may be appropriating for his own comic purposes an institution with preexisting parodic elements.

None of this is to imply that the festival was not tremendously important to the Athenians and that it did not generate hope, anxiety, and excitement throughout the city. The festival made an impact on civic activity, because on the second day prisoners were released and law courts and council meetings were suspended. The women formed temporary, self-sufficient societies, with their own magistrates and governing bodies, mimicking (conceivably mocking) the male institutions that ruled the city as a whole.[42] Augustine suggests that this "parliament of women" may itself have been felt to hark to a "prior" time in which women participated in running the city, before a catastrophe barred them from politics forever.[43] There is no reason to assume that the women of any era believed this, however. The "parliament" was a parallel city (or cities), perhaps re-formed every year, but not a sign of lost privilege for women.

The Thesmophoria proper was usually divided into three days at Athens (sometimes longer elsewhere): the Ascent, the Fasting or Middle Day, and the Feast of Fair Offspring.[44] It was the Middle Day, during which the women lamented and fasted and placed a curse on anyone revealing the "things that may not be spoken" which forms the backdrop to Aristophanes' play, the *Thesmophoriazousae*.[45] They also joked and abused each other, in memory of the joking that cheered Demeter. The jesting and laughter among the women – who probably came from all walks of life, perhaps including slavery – drew them together and focused their generative powers.[46] It is likely that the women broke their fast by drinking the *cyceon*, the suspension of partially ground barley and pennyroyal in water.[47]

Cleomedes compares the speech of the women at the Thesmophoria with that used in a brothel.[48] Both Diodorus Siculus (in his description of the Sicilian Thesmophoria) and Apollodorus explain that festival's coarse abuse in terms of the joking that cheered Demeter when she was grieving for Kore (Persephone). In addition to the abusive speech, we are told that the women beat each other with pieces of bark (the μόροττον), a ritual associated with fertility magic.[49] One important feature of this festival was the prescribed chastity of the women participants, an element of the Skira festival of Demeter also. In some versions of the Thesmophoria the women slept on the anaphrodisiac λύγος – the *vitex agnus* (*castus*) or withy.[50] This abstemiousness magically enhanced the fertility rites by marking out the special nature of the festival.

As many ancient writers observed, and as some modern studies suggest, the *vitex castus* has gynecological functions, including regulation of menstruation; encouragement of conception, labor, and lactation; treatment of uterine and ovarian problems; and abortion.[51] Likewise the pennyroyal in the *cyceon* was known for its various reproductive functions, including opening the uterus for cleansing, hysteria, stimulating the onset of menses, abortion, stimulation of childbirth, and the expulsion of the afterbirth. Pine, which featured both in the sacrificial pits and in the temporary structures, also had a regulatory role in gynecological processes. Pine was known in antiquity as a contraceptive and an aid in lactation. Pomegranate seeds, whose chief function seems to have been as a contraceptive and abortifacient, apparently also were consumed by the women at the Thesmophoria. Clement of Alexandria notes that the women were forbidden to eat those seeds that had fallen on the ground; presumably, therefore, they were eating others.[52] I suggest that those that fell on the ground were understood as being sacred to Persephone, the famously infertile bride of

Hades, who consumed pomegranate seeds in the *Hymn*. Nixon concludes as follows: "The references to pennyroyal and pomegranate in the *HHD* [the *Hymn*] (and to pine and vitex in allusions to the Thesmophoria) imply that any woman with knowledge of these plants could regulate her own reproductive life as she chose."[53]

Nixon makes the crucial point that, in the eyes of the women participants, the object of the festival need not have been "fertility" pure and simple, but rather a fertility that women controlled and managed. The "fair offspring" that were the festival's most explicitly named desideratum might have been so precisely because of management and choice by women. Thus the Thesmophoria's objective was not simply the production of male heirs within a strongly patriarchal system, but also the handing down of critical and empowering gynecological knowledge from older to younger women.[54] The sexual jesting and mockery may have functioned, in part, to transmit a variety of information.

In addition to the (mock-)hostility directed by the Thesmophorian women at each other in the form of abusive speech, there are hints of more serious hostility against men.[55] Herodotus mentions that the Danaids brought the Thesmophoria from Egypt to Greece.[56] These were the fifty daughters of Danaus, who had quarreled with his brother Aegyptus over their joint rulership of Egypt. Danaus fled with his daughters to Argos and foiled his brother's efforts at *rapprochement* by requiring his daughters to murder their husbands (Aegyptus' fifty sons) on their wedding night. All of the girls except Hypermnestra complied by decapitating the sons of Aegyptus.

It seems odd that the ill-omened Danaids should have been regarded as responsible for introducing the Thesmophoria to Greece. Like the goddess they celebrated, they were death-dealing as well as life-bringing. They found themselves in a curious fix, required to repudiate one form of patriarchal management of women's lives and bodies (marriage and childbearing) in favor of another (service to Danaus's vengeance). The Thesmophoria would continue to transmit complex and mixed messages: cooperation and collision of men and women; acceptance and rejection of sexual relations and of the consequences; destructive openings of the body (decapitation, rape, abortion, castration, as described later) versus benign – if still ungentle – openings (laughter, childbirth, the obscene display of genitals by Baubo, a crone attempting to cheer Demeter).

The tale of Battus illustrates a recurring motif in relation to the festival: that of the intruder. At Cyrene King Battus is said to have been castrated by the Thesmophorian σφάκτριαι or "Sacrificers" because he attempted to spy on them.[57] The "Chalcidian Pursuit" was the name given to a mysterious element of the Thesmophoria that celebrated the pursuit of the enemy, following prayers of the women.[58] Yet at the same time, Aristophanes' parody of the festival, the *Thesmophoriazousae*, with its tale of a male spy's escape from harm, was also true to the festival. Pausanias tells of how Aristomenes of Messenia was overpowered and captured by the women celebrating the Thesmophoria, but that he was saved by the priestess of Demeter, who fell in love with him, a tale that corresponds to the famous story of Hypermnestra's clemency.[59] Thus, Detienne's theory, that the stories of women's violence expressed male fear of gynocracy and of women wielding sacrificial knives, does not fully account for the complex meanings of the cult.[60] The Thesmophorian myths seemingly expressed the belief that an all-female group was essential to the functioning of the cult and that a disruption of the group could have catastrophic consequences. At the same time, the varied outcomes and implications of the infiltration stories suggest that the categories of male and female were not as antithetical as first impression suggests. Interaction between men and women might have been hostile or bloody, but counterforces of trust, cooperation, affection, and sexuality were also present. And interaction occured, albeit in defiance of prescribed rules and norms. This was the paradox that lay beneath the official protocol of "women alone."

Indeed, the unmanned infiltrator Battus may not simply represent failed interaction between male and female. Rather, like the imposter of Aristophanes *Thesmophoriazousae* who unconvincingly masquerades as a woman, he occupies an ambiguous and vital category: neither male nor female – or perhaps *both* male and female. I shall return to this theme in my discussion of the *Thesmophoriazousae*.

I suggest that we should modify our notions of the Thesmophoria and similar festivals, beyond what seemed broadly to serve the common weal: good harvests and new generations of citizens. The Thesmophoria had the effect (and among women, undoubtedly, the purpose) of reforming and strengthening bonds among women, bonds that marriage might otherwise attenuate. Mothers, daughters, sisters, friends, and cousins would find each other at this and other festivals, even if geography and other constraints of married life had made it difficult for them to see each other on a daily basis. Male anxiety about what the women were "plotting" suggests that the Thesmophoria provided more than simply a service to a patriarchal system.[61] Furthermore, as Nixon has demonstrated, one must

distinguish between "fertility," broadly defined as "lots of children" or agricultural plenty, and managed fertility.

The Figurines

Material evidence enhances our understanding of the Thesmophoria. For
example, Kron has described votive objects (numbering more than twenty
thousand!) deposited in the Thesmophorion at Bitalemi, beginning in the
mid–seventh century B.C.E.[62] They include pottery from different parts
of the Greek world, terracotta protomes or masks, figurines of women
carrying sacrificial piglets, throned goddesses, sacrificial knives, axes and
other utensils, stamped bronze ("pre-money"?), and jewelry. Similar votive
deposits have shown up in Knossos, Cyrene, and elsewhere.[63]

A woman's early-fourth-century grave collection from the Taman peninsula on the Black Sea (Phanagoria) included terracotta figurines, like others
found elsewhere in the Bosphorus and North Black Sea area.[64] The grave
(listed as number 4) is one of a series found in a two large grave mounds.
The graves also produced objects unambiguously associated with the goddess Demeter. Grave number 2, for example, contained a big painting with
a head of Demeter, and so it became known as the grave of a Demeter
priestess. Grave number 1 (not plundered in antiquity) contained many
gold plates with representations of the heads of Demeter, Kore, and Heracles. There were also headdresses typical of Demeter priestesses, a golden
kalathos, and headbands. Grave number 4 also included the Demeter head
decorations, and so this, too, has been described as a Demeter priestess
grave.

The terracottas included old women holding infants; a naked old woman
holding a phallos and sitting on an altar (Plate 1); solitary old women
(clothed) (Plates 2 and 3); solitary old men; models of a rooster, sheaf of
corn and a pig; young women wearing crowns or bearing vessels or baskets
of loaves or fruit. Peredolskaya, who published these terracottas, judged
them to be associated with the Eleusinian Mysteries. Clinton has argued
that the Taman figurines in fact are connected with the Thesmophoria
rather than the Eleusinian mysteries.[65]

Figurines like these have shown up in sites all over the Greek world
(Plates 4 and 5). Pfisterer-Haas's comprehensive study of visual representation of old women in antiquity includes a section on those she regards
as unequivocally cultic: clothed figurines bearing baskets and/or piglets,
or squatting naked old women, from the classical through the Hellenistic

period.[66] Some of the squatting naked old women are also pulling their mouths open with their hands and sticking their tongues out.[67] She suggests that such figurines may have had an apotropaic function.

In addition to the Taman grave collection, there are examples of grotesque terracottas from Attica, Argos, Olynthus, Tarentum, the sanctuary of Demeter and Kore on Acrocorinth, the sanctuary of Demeter at Knossos, the necropolis at Meligunìs Lipára in Sicily, Pantikapaion (Kerch), and other graves of the Bosphorus and Black Sea region.[68] Interpretation of the clothed or less obviously obscene old women figurines has tended to take place from the perspective of the Greek theater.[69] Scholars such as Webster, Pickard-Cambridge, and Bieber have used these figurines in filling out the scanty evidence for old and middle comedy's development. "They demonstrate to us the characters popular with the audiences who bought them as souvenirs."[70] Yet as Pickard-Cambridge noted, the figurines' connection with the theater is not always incontrovertible. After noting the arguments in favor of a theatrical link – the similarity of their faces to the comic masks attested on other monuments, and the dearth of imaginable explanations for the figurines, especially the phallic ones – he says, "But even when the case for taking some as representations of the comic stage is accepted, individual cases are always problematic, and such rule of thumb tests as that an open mouth ought to point to a comic mask do not always work."[71]

He goes on to note that the problem is exacerbated by the fact that the terracottas were so widely spread over the Greek world and that a "type" might have an afterlife quite separate from whatever impulse first brought it into existence. I do not wish to argue that such figurines never be linked with the comic stage. Rather it is clear, certainly in the case of the Taman grave collection and in the case of the figurines found in the Sanctuary of Demeter and Kore on Acrocorinth, for example, that another interpretative frame would be helpful. By insisting that such figurines only represent old or middle comic actors and by failing to consider a cultic dimension, we risk misreading them, or reading them too narrowly. This is not to engage in the question of their value in reconstructing the early history of old and middle comedy.

One further point, even in a hypothetical case in which one might be confident that the figurines are "just" theatrical, their marked physical similarity with unambiguously cultic figurines (i.e., those coming out of clearly cultic contexts or with obviously cultic attributes, such as the *calathos* or offering basket) invites a more nuanced interpretation. Cultic connotations surely tempered and enriched reception, at least some of the time. Given that they often show up in women's graves, it seems reasonable to conclude that they touched on important issues for the women with whom they were found. When we consider how women might have "read" Greek comedy, the parallels between the appearance of the actors playing women and the figurines linked with Demeter's worship may have shaped women's reception of the genre.

The old women figurines in particular seem to draw on a strain of women's cultic values at odds with the aesthetic and ideology of classical Greek "high" culture. Peredolskaya describes the grotesque face of one old woman in particular as resembling a caricatured mask of old comedy.[72] The bodies, male and female, also resemble the lumpish silhouettes of comic actors. One of the characteristic features of the old women figurines is a protruding belly. Some scholars argue that this is merely comic rotundity, such as would characterize a comic actor's padding. Bakhtin, on the other hand, sees their large bellies as a supernatural pregnancy, the grotesque fecundity of a woman who seems destined only for the grave[73]:

> In the famous Kerch terracotta collection we find figurines of senile pregnant hags. Moreover, the old hags are laughing. This is a typical and very strongly expressed grotesque. It is ambivalent. It is pregnant death, a death that gives birth. There is nothing completed, nothing calm and stable in the bodies of these old hags. They combine a senile, decaying and deformed flesh with the flesh of new life, conceived but as yet unformed. Life is shown in its twofold contradictory process; it is the epitome of incompleteness. And such is precisely the grotesque concept of the body.

Given the Thesmophoria's paradoxical mixing of decay with premature life, I believe with Bakhtin that these figurines express, in the most striking way, women's uncanny reproductive powers, agrarian and human. They are pregnant crones. These and other figurines represented characters in recurring cultic "dramas," lost to us now. The joke that the pregnant crones represent is the discrepancy between women's own aging and often unlovely bodies and the ever-renewing life cycles over which they keep watch. At the same time their bodies emphasize an exuberant connectedness with the natural world. As has been noted:

> The classical statue has no openings or orificies whereas grotesque costume and masks emphasize the gaping mouth, the protuberant belly and buttocks, the feet and the genitals. . . . The grotesque body is emphasized

as a mobile, split, multiple self, a subject of pleasure in process of exchange: and it is never closed off from either its social or ecosystemic context. The classical body on the other hand keeps its distance. In a sense it is disembodied, for it appears indifferent to a body which is "beautiful," but which is taken for granted.[74]

The pregnant crones combine grotesquerie, death, and new life. When held up against the prevailing model of the female in Greek literature, they form the antipode. Pandora, Helen, Deianeira, Eriphyle, Clytaemestra, and many others represented the ruin that inevitably underlay a beguiling exterior, whether the woman herself was conscious of it or not. They seemed to promise to men gratification, children, a safe and prosperous hearth. Yet their stories formed a persistent and oppressive pattern that undermined the credibility even of those women who succeed in living out men's ideal, such as the *Odyssey*'s Penelope. The ghost of Agamemnon in the *Odyssey* pointedly observed (twice!) that his unfaithful wife, Clytaemestra, had darkened the fame of all women forever. As one scholar has it: "Clytemnestra is said at xi 433 to have made **aiskhos** not only for herself but also for all womankind in the future by way of betraying Agamemnon. At xxiv 200, this same betrayal turns the very concept of Clytemnestra into a **stugere . . . aoide** 'hateful song' that will survive into the future (xxiv 201) and will bring a bad name to all womankind. We have here one of the clearest instances of blame as blame *poetry*."[75]

    Grace, persuasiveness, fidelity, and self-control – no sum of these virtues could cancel the expectation that womanly charm brought only trouble and death to men. Yet in the Kerch figurines we can identify a different system of reckoning. Out of a seemingly charmless, undignified, aged, and intemperate vessel spills an incongruous hope – and a rebuttal to death. The ugliness of the Thesmophorian figurines and the coarseness of the women's speech, stood in apparent antithesis to the "fair offspring" toward which the Thesmophoria seemingly moved. I suggest that the indecorousness, abusive speech, and flouting of other societal norms by women was an end in itself. Such speech and action celebrated *grotesquerie* within a frame of norms and values independent of the male world.[76]

Male Attitudes toward Women's Cultic Speech

Much ancient theory on joking and laughter dates from the fourth century B.C.E. or later – a period that had seen a sharp change in attitude toward crude humor.[77] In the *Nichomachean Ethics* Aristotle praised the modern preference for subtlety or innuendo (*hyponoia*) in contrast to the old comedy's coarse abuse and the "phallic songs" from which old comedy derived.[78]

In general ancient philosophers focused on curbing coarse humor.[79] In a competitive society the dangers of public mockery and humiliation were very great – for men as well as for women – and the ancient theorists spoke repeatedly to the question of what was fitting and decorous and what exceeded norms of responsible behavior. Joking and laughter were permissible only in certain contexts – festivals and banquets, for example. Ideally they formed a kind of "play" or παιδιά that allowed the individual a respite from the rigors of normal life – and ensured his return to normal life's restraints. The word παιδιά made its own point; it was essentially for children, and for adults who were willing to be childlike for a while. This suspension of adult responsibilities and restraints was strictly temporary; as Anacharsis, the friend of Solon said, according to Aristotle: "Be merry, that you may be serious."[80]

What was true of "respectable" men was even more so for "respectable" women, although in this case, the evidence is inferential rather than in the form of direct admonitions, which would be seen as being the prerogative of male relatives, and a private matter. Pliny tells us that the fourth-century sculptor Praxiteles made two statues: a mourning matron and a laughing harlot – a telling opposition.[81] The *Odyssey* made a symbolic contrast between Penelope's persistent tears and her maidservants' laughter, suggesting that suspicion of women's laughter and its connection with ungoverned sexuality had existed from an early date.

This dichotome between tears and laughter constituted part of a larger pattern of distinction and antithesis, which shaped Greek logic, and structured most speech except that of certain cults. In the world of literary genres, tragedy abstracted certain themes from cult's mélange, comedy and satire accruing motifs from the other end of the spectrum.[82] Yet the women of the Thesmophoria, in remembering Demeter and reenacting Iambe's words, mingled grief and raucous laughter. Their reaction formed a shifting chiaroscuro of outrage and hilarity, despair and hope, rage and tenderness. Similarly the women's cult of the Adonia, spotlighted by Aristophanes in the *Lysistrata*, featured a combination of mourning and raucous laughter. This noisy brew of hilarity and lamentation is condemned by the Magistrate who shows up in that play's opening scene. He berates the women who have assembled and suggests that their earlier celebration of the Adonia disrupted the Assembly – and jinxed the Sicilian expedition! Yet within a world organized and articulated by antithesis (expressed by Greek's ubiquitous particles *men* and *de*) cultic women seem to have derived energy from this doubleness.[83]

Given our lack of direct evidence for cultic speech of any kind, it is impossible to say without doubt whether this doubleness, or mingling of mourning and hilarity, was a preponderantly female form of expression or whether it characterized cultic speech in general. Undoubtedly it was perceived as a characteristically feminine discourse, a breaching of boundaries.[84] Because we know that women were traditionally charged with the emotional work of lamenting the dead, it seems likely that they had unique opportunities for mixing mourning with hilarity and bawdy humor, whether in cultic or in noncultic situations.[85]

In the Introduction I referred to the "problematizing" of women's speech (of any kind) by recent theorists such as Irigaray. In her vision of history the Greeks instituted a patriarchal discourse that has molded Western culture to this day. In classical Greece (and thereafter) men owned normative discourse, logic, and narrative. Women cannot own that language or logic but simply, as ciphers, occupy a place in the system, as the "other" or the object. For Irigaray and for other French feminists, linguistic transgression (variously defined) is the only way for women to communicate as women. I suggest that this cultic speech and joking among women was indeed an authentic women's speech. It was generated by women not using the preexisting rules and the dichotomous systems of Greek logic and language as known to men – and women. It was not a simple reaction against hegemonic speech either, but the production of a subculture with its own agenda. It had a diffuse, multiple, and emotionally shifting quality, was highly charged (hence the frequent accusations of drunkenness), and it reached out informally to divinities and the dead as well as the living.[86]

Whose Party Was It?

There are questions to be asked regarding cultic *aporrheta* or *aischrologia*, cultic unspeakable or shameful speech. Did it seem shameful to everyone? Did men and women perceive it differently? Would *aischrologia* have taken different form in the mouths of women than when uttered by men? Certainly abuse and obscenity had a different value and impact when expressed by women rather than by men, given the decorum and silence that society officially enjoined upon respectable women.[87] The taboo being broken was stringent, and the impact of transgression proportionately greater. At the same time, it was a commonplace that women lacked self-control – in speech as well as action. Their sexual and transgressive natures gave an authenticity and power to their sexual and transgressive cultic speech, a power absent from comparable men's speech. Women also held within them potentially explosive secrets, knowing – as no one else could – the paternity of the children they brought to birth. "Speaking the unspeakable" (*aporreta* or *arrheta*), the repressed or concealed thing, mirrored their ability to unlock the womb and its secrets.

It is impossible to say for certain whether the actual jokes, the actual obscene terms used by the women, would have differed from those employed by men in cults of Dionysus and elsewhere.[88] When one looks at obscenity in the comic poets, one sees mostly double entendres, drawn from everyday life.[89] The category of what we call "four-letter words" is relatively small. It is possible that women developed an exclusive vocabulary of such words, now inevitably lost, but I suspect that such a vocabulary, if it existed, was not large. Rather, women's obscenity drew on their everyday vocabulary, words connected with spinning, weaving, and food production.[90] Their jokes and slang terms would have drawn on their domestic world and so would have been somewhat – but not profoundly – different from men's. We know from a fragment of Eupolis that women's word for the chamber pot was *skaphion*; no doubt there were a few such terms circulating among women.[91] The vessel used by men, the *amis*, may have had a narrow opening at the top and thus been unsuitable for women. In fact Mnesilochus, disguised as a woman in Aristophanes' *Thesmophoriazousae*, speaks as if an *amis* were preferable, thus betraying himself as an imposter, through his use of the man's term.[92]

What did women think themselves to be doing, and how did they conceive of their speech at the Thesmophoria? Our direct testimony from antiquity derives almost exclusively from privileged (male) élites. Furthermore, these élites recorded what they wished to be said or known about their world, and often not those things that disrupted this vision. Third, as Lowe has well observed, our sources on women's cults comprise such a concatenation of sources, countersources, scholarly interpreters, and judgmental Church Fathers that there is little hope of discovering "meaning" as presumably felt by the cultic practitioners themselves. So where does this leave us when we wish to assess what women themselves may have thought about their own use of cultic joking? I make a few modest suggestions as to a course of inquiry.

I suspect that women, who certainly knew and understood what was expected of them by those who established their society's public norms, may additionally have recognized the existence of a world not run by men. In other words, they knew that their speech was "shameful" in the eyes of men, but they might not have regarded it as such themselves.

Women's View of "Shameful" Speech

I begin with an anecdote from antiquity, cited by Athenaeus in a section of the *Witty Diners* in which men exchange stories about famous and clever courtesans.[93] Lais may have been the kind of "educated woman" that Plato had in mind in the *Laws*, as being fond of tragedy.

Λαίδα λέγουσι τὴν Κορινθίαν ποτὲ
Εὐριπίδην ἰδοῦσαν ἐν κήπῳ τινὶ
πινακίδα καὶ γραφεῖον ἐξηρτημένον
ἔχοντ᾿· "ἀπόκριναι, φησίν, ὦ ποιητά μοι,
τί βουλόμενος ἔγραψας ἐν τραγῳδίᾳ
'ἔρρ', αἰσχροποιέ';" καταπλαγεὶς δ᾿ Εὐριπίδης
τὴν τόλμαν αὐτῆς, "σὺ γάρ, ἔφη, τίς εἶ, γύναι;
οὐκ αἰσχροποιός;" ἡ δὲ γελάσασ᾿ ἀπεκρίθη·
"τί δ᾿ αἰσχρόν, εἰ μὴ τοῖσι χρωμένοις δοκεῖ;"

They say that Lais, the Corinthian woman, once saw Euripides in a garden, having his writing tablet and stilus hanging by his side. "Tell me, Mr. Poet," she said, "What did you have in mind when you wrote in a tragedy: "'get out you evildoer'?" Euripides was stunned by her gall and said: "As for you, what are you, madam? Are you not an evildoer yourself?" She laughed and replied: "But what is evil, if it does not seem so to those who engage in it?"

Lais asks Euripides to explain to her what he intended when he had Jason call Medea an αἰσχροποιός. Lais's reply to the poet's angry rebuke also quotes Euripides, a line from the *Aeolus*, mocked by Aristophanes also.[94] The famous hetaira, a foreigner in Athens, considers a dramatic insult delivered to another infamously assertive foreign woman. The trap for Euripides – for such it proves – echoes the kind of abuse visited by Aristophanes upon Euripides, when he quotes notorious lines [My tongue swore, but my heart remained uncommitted!] out of context. Although her object in raising the question seems to be showing Euripides' his (unintentional) sexual pun, the dispute has broader implications.

The insult (αἰσχροποιός "evildoer") directed by Jason at Medea occurs at the end of the tragedy, after she has revealed the children's bodies to him. His meaning seems unmistakable at first glance. But Lais is leading Euripides into a snare. αἰσχροποιός can also mean fellator or fellatrix, a meaning that Euripides is quick to acknowledge as he retorts, "And that's what you are yourself!"[95] Lais does not deny the charge – but disputes the meaning of αἰσχρός – "foul," "evil," or "shameful." One's evaluation of behavior (of a real person or a character in a play) depends on one's perspective. She repudiates Euripides' definition of shameful behavior and reveals – at least as ancient audiences might see it – inconsistencies in his thinking. How could he, the (in)famous moral relativist, insist on a transcendent value to αἰσχρός?[96]

Lais's glib argument suggests that she identifies herself as one of Athens' fashionable intellectuals, a sophist. Euripides himself was regarded as a sophist, making her trap for him ironically apt. Yet Lais was also a woman living in Athens, someone with whom Athenian women would have felt affinity – just as the women in Euripides' play immediately expressed sympathy with Medea when they discovered how Jason has treated her. Lais would have participated in some religious festivals, together with Athenian citizen women of all ranks and slaves.[97] Lais's questioning of Euripides' use of αἰσχρός as a term of opprobrium directed by a male character at a female character in response to her revenge for his manipulation of the sexual rules, and Lais's subsequent mockery of Euripides' second use of the insult, this time in his own voice, at a real woman, this time for her own sexual rule breaking, suggests a gendered pattern, a gendered – rather than a purely individualistic – definition of what was shameful.

A wealthy courtesan would not always speak for all women, but it would be unwise to assume that she could not ever speak for other women. The story indeed suggests that women's notion of what constituted "shameful" behavior or speech differed from men's.[98] This difference would alter their interpretation of a play – comic or tragic. Men characterized women's cultic speech as "shameful," for example, recalling that used in a brothel. As I have suggested, women might have simultaneously recognized public (i.e., male) norms of "shameful" speech for women while acknowledging a semiindependent world, where different norms applied.

Language in the public sphere belonged to men, but it might be read differently by women. Sophocles' representation of the famous debate between Creon and Antigone illustrates how a woman, focused on her obligations to family, contested the king's rebuke for breaking the law: "Are you not ashamed? (οὐκ ἐπαιδεῖ;)". "No," she answers, "It is no shame (οὐκ αἰσχρόν) to revere one's blood kin."[99] Their lethal conflict is reflected in their opposing applications of virtually the same term.

"Shame," I suggest, in women's case largely associated with sexual morality, was a function of identity within a male-centered world, a world of distinction and contested rank. Within cults such as the Thesmophoria and Scira, rank (that is, a woman's husband's rank) may still have affected a woman's visibility and role to an extent, but the playful aggression of *aischrologia* made it difficult to sustain clear distinctions clearly. Indeed *hybris* is precisely about broaching boundaries, and the "shameful speech" in all of its manifestations – insult, obscenity, and mocking jest – broke through all that might separate women in the noncultic world. The women joked in memory of jokes made by Iambe to cheer Demeter. Thus the *aischrologia* enacted memory and re-created a moment in the infinite past. It evoked a dead and absent girl and in so doing called into the women's presence all dead and absent kin, sisters, daughters, and mothers. The *aischrologia* made of women's fertility – and women's sexuality – something to be sustained by an inviolable community of women, not merely a matter between a man and his wife. It brought into the light of the women's community a vivid sense of the illogicality, fragility, and indignity of flesh, and its power to re-create itself within the shadow of death. Similarly the women's community remade itself every year and faced death with grief and laughter.

◈ 2 ◈

IAMBE AND THE *HYMN TO DEMETER*

T HE HOMERIC *HYMN TO DEMETER* refers to a tradition of joking that differs sharply from joking practices in contemporary iambic or epic. Epic concerned itself with the establishment of a hierarchy and with efforts to challenge that hierarchy. The *Iliad* famously posed the question as to who was the best of the Achaeans. The *Odyssey* described the struggle of Odysseus to regain the kingship he had lost while absent. The mockery, joking, and laughter that accompanied these stories typically represents contestation, often bloody, of the hierarchy, followed by resolution. Whether the characters within the poem understood the implications of these conflictual moments, we, the audience, can appreciate their significance as "sites" of contestation and often as key turning points in the narrative.

Yet the *Hymn*'s joking scene had many of the elements that we see in the other epic joking episodes: a potentially dangerous individual of (unrecognized or unacknowledged) high status being "challenged" by someone much lower in status, an unaware internal audience, a sense of crisis. Yet in the Homeric *Hymn to Demeter*, the mockery and joking was marked by ambivalence – a juxtaposition of contradictory views, but without conflict. Furthermore, it made possible a remarkable mingling of different social classes, even of different orders of being: goddess and mortals, living and dead.

In this chapter I argue that the *Hymn* was formed by male hands, evincing a "masculinist" perspective in many ways but also retaining traces of women's cultic perspectives, embedded in the text, concentrated around the "Iambe incident" at Eleusis. Following description of this example of joking and its repercussions, I provide several contrasting incidents from other places in the hexameter epic tradition to make clear the *Hymn*'s anomalous nature. The chapter continues with discussion of Baubo – Iambe's Doppelgänger, found only in cultic contexts. I conclude with analysis of the "pomegranate seed" incident and the *cyceon*, the special beverage that Demeter drinks. These elements of the story constitute traces of the women's cults that the *Hymn* in effect displaces with the male-run Eleusinian Mysteries. The pomegranate seed incident in particular shows signs of a less than complete integration into the new narrative.

The Date and Circumstances of the Hymn's Composition[1]

The Homeric *Hymn to Demeter* probably achieved its current form between the late seventh and early sixth centuries B.C.E. in Attica.[2] Like the other Homeric *Hymns*, this one probably was meant to be sung at a festival, on its own or as a prelude to a longer poem. Although it belongs to an oral tradition, stylistic features suggest a conscious reworking of material, perhaps with the aid of writing.[3] Nonetheless, when we are thinking about its relationship to other mythic material (such as the Orphic Baubo stories, described later), one might imagine the alternative narratives as being in a process of continuous recomposition, with many opportunities for mutual influence or self-conscious distinction.[4]

The end of the seventh and the beginning of the sixth centuries B.C.E. saw rapid cultural development, in which several major cultic centers evolved – and competed – for eminence in the Greek world. The *Hymn* ends with Demeter's founding of the famous Eleusinian Mysteries and her transmission of them to the priests and kings at Eleusis. It makes ambitious claims for the Eleusinian Mysteries – they can benefit anyone on earth – and for the goddess: not some local deity, but an Olympian, with the power to confer blessings locally and abroad. The poem addresses Demeter as the mistress of Eleusis, Paros, and Antron (in Thessaly).[5] By so doing, it establishes itself as authoritative beyond Athens or Eleusis. This is an ambitious literary voice, whose international claims parallel and sustain those of the cult it celebrates.

The *Hymn* tells of the rape of Persephone by Hades and of Demeter's search for her daughter, visit to Eleusis, and encounter with Iambe, whose mocking jokes inspire her – against all seeming logic – to laugh. The Iambe episode stands as an etiology or mythical "beginning" for women's laughter within the cult of Demeter. At the same time the *Hymn* was also an epic poem in a highly evolved tradition. We can best appreciate the anomalous nature of the "Iambe incident" by seeing it in this context.[6] But first to the *Hymn's* own story.

Demeter's rage darkens the *Hymn* that bears her name. After she discovered from Helios that Hades had seized Persephone, and after Helios

advised her not to "cling to an insatiable anger – in vain" (82–3), Demeter
assumed the disguise of an old woman:

γρηῒ παλαιγενέϊ ἐναλίγκιος, ἥ τε τόκοιο
εἴργηται δώρων τε φιλοστεφάνου Ἀφροδίτης
οἷαί τε τροφοί εἰσι θεμιστοπόλων βασιλήων
παίδων καὶ ταμίαι κατὰ δώματα ἠχήεντα

Like a woman born long before, bereft of childbearing
And the gifts of Aphrodite, friend of wreaths.
Such as serve as the nurses of rule bearing kings
And are housekeepers in the echoing halls. (101–4)[7]

Following Helios's departure "a more terrible and more bestial (κύντερον)
anger settled in her heart" (90). In other words, both within and without she
seemed formidably changed. Her alienation was absolute; human form
signified her angry distance from the gods; her age, itinerant poverty, and
her grim bearing separated her even from human society. This was an
internal, uncommunicative grief and anger. Nonetheless Demeter turned
toward human society; the daughters of Celeus met her as they drew water
from the "Maiden's Well," near Eleusis.

Its narrative sequence marks the *Hymn*'s version of events as unique.
"Orphic" accounts of the story, probably already circulating when the
Hymn was composed, described Demeter as chancing upon Eleusis during her search for Persephone. In the *Hymn* there is no obvious reason for
Demeter to be wandering in Eleusis (or anywhere else), because she already
knew where Persephone was.[8] In the Orphic stories Demeter rewarded the
inhabitants of Eleusis for telling her about her daughter's whereabouts,
which they were in a position to do, having witnessed the seizure of Persephone by Hades. In the *Hymn*'s account, the Eleusis episode sticks out –
precisely because it seems to disrupt, rather than develop, the narrative.
Thus it has invited speculation as to its "meaning" outside of the narrative
context. Many scholars have commented insightfully on the cultic implications of the Eleusis section. Nonetheless, the placement of the Eleusis
events within the poem as a whole does indeed shed light on Iambe's joking
and its implications.

The disguised Demeter returned to the palace with the daughters of
Celeus and Metaneira, the local rulers, having suggested that she might
care for an infant or perform other domestic tasks in return for her keep
(139–44). Despite her disguise as an old woman, Demeter was suffused with

an unnatural radiance:

...ἡ δ' ἄρ' ἐπ' οὐδὸν ἔβη ποσὶ καί ῥα μελάθρου
κῦρε κάρη, πλῆσεν δὲ θύρας σέλαος θείοιο.
τὴν δ' αἰδώς τε σέβας τε ἰδὲ χλωρὸν δέος εἷλεν·
εἶξε δέ οἱ κλισμοῖο καὶ ἑδριάασθαι ἄνωγεν.
ἀλλ' οὐ Δημήτηρ ὡρηφόρος ἀγλαόδωρος
ἤθελεν ἑδριάασθαι ἐπὶ κλισμοῖο φαεινοῦ.
ἀλλ' ἀκέουσα ἔμιμνε κατ' ὄμματα καλὰ βαλοῦσα,
πρίν γ' ὅτε δή οἱ ἔθηκεν Ἰάμβη κέδν' εἰδυῖα
πηκτὸν ἕδος, καθύπερθε δ' ἐπ' ἀργύφεον βάλε κῶας.
ἔνθα καθεζομένη προκατέσχετο χερσὶ καλύπτρην·
δηρὸν δ' ἄφθογγος τετιημένη ἧστ' ἐπὶ δίφρου,
οὐδέ τιν' οὔτ' ἔπεϊ προσπτύσσετο οὔτε τι ἔργῳ,
ἀλλ' ἀγέλαστος ἄπατος ἐδητύος ἠδὲ ποτῆτος
ἧστο πόθῳ μινύθουσα βαθυζώνοιο θυγατρός,
πρίν γ' ὅτε δὴ χλεύης μιν Ἰάμβη κέδν' εἰδυῖα
πολλὰ παρὰ σκώπτουσ' ἐτρέψατο πότνιαν ἁγνὴν
μειδῆσαι γελάσαι τε καὶ ἵλαον σχεῖν θυμόν·
ἧ δή οἱ καὶ ἔπειτα μεθύστερον εὔαδεν ὀργαῖς.
τῇ δὲ δέπας Μετάνειρα δίδου μελιηδέος οἴνου
πλήσασ' · ἡ δ' ἀνένευσ· οὐ γὰρ θεμιτόν οἱ ἔφασκε
πίνειν οἶνον ἐρυθρόν· ἄνωγε δ' ἄρ' ἄλφι καὶ ὕδωρ
δοῦναι μίξασαν πιέμεν γληχῶνι τερείνῃ.
ἡ δὲ κυκεῶ τεύξασα θεᾷ πόρεν, ὡς ἐκέλευε·
δεξαμένη δ' ὁσίης ἕνεκεν πολυπότνια Δηώ.

But she stood on the threshold, and her head
grazed the ceiling, and she filled the doorway with divine light. Metaneira
was seized by reverence and awe and pale fear.
She yielded her chair and bade the other to sit.
But Demeter, Seasongiver, She of Glorious Gifts,
did not wish to sit on the shining couch
but remained silent, with her lovely eyes cast down
until decorous Iambe placed a jointed seat,
and above she threw a silvery fleece.
Then sitting down [Demeter] held her veil before her, in her hands.
Long she sat on the stool, sorrowing and silent,
nor did she welcome anyone by word or sign,
but unlaughing and without touching food or drink
she sat, pining in longing for her deep girt daughter
until decorous Iambe, with jokes
and many a mocking jest moved the holy lady
to smile and laugh and have a gracious heart.
Even afterwards she used to cheer her moods.

To her Metaneira offered a full cup of sweet wine,
but she refused. It was not right for her, she said,
to drink red wine. But she bade her mix barley and water
with tender pennyroyal, and to offer this to her, to drink.
Metaneira prepared the drink and gave it to the goddess, as bidden,
and mistress Deo accepted it, for the sake of the ritual. (188–211)

Despite its brevity, the *Hymn*'s description of Iambe's intervention and
Demeter's reaction covers a range. Iambe jests and mocks; Demeter smiles,
laughs, and then maintains a gracious disposition.[9] This sequence of jest
and reaction apparently repeated itself on subsequent occasions. The result of her mood change was Demeter's voluntary nursing of Metaneira's
last-born – and late-born – child, the boy Demophoon. The goddess
promised that her knowledge and experience would protect the baby from
evil spells and childhood ailments; she could wield an "anticutting" against
the "undercutter" (teething perhaps?) and a defense against spells. This
boast by Demeter evokes a theme that resounds throughout the *Hymn*
and the women's rituals connected with it, described in Chapter 1: plant
lore, and women's pharmacological expertise.[10]

Secret nightly baptisms in the fire together with daily infusions of am-
brosia caused the baby to grow at an amazing pace; Metaneira's suspicions
about her strange nurse drove her to interrupt the process, however, and,
as Demeter wrathfully explained, Metaneira's ill-timed intervention cost
Demophoon a chance to become immortal. As a consolation for the loss,
it seems, she promised that the boy would have ritual honor.[11] Demeter
goes on to identify herself and request the building of a temple, promising
instructions in her worship:

ἀλλ᾽ ἄγε μοι νηόν τε μέγαν καὶ βωμὸν ὑπ᾽ αὐτῷ
τευχόντων πᾶς δῆμος ὑπαὶ πόλιν αἰπύ τε τεῖχος
Καλλιχόρου καθύπερθεν ἐπὶ προὔχοντι κολωνῷ·
ὄργια δ᾽ αὐτὴ ἐγὼν ὑποθήσομαι ὡς ἂν ἔπειτα
εὐαγέως ἔρδοντες ἐμὸν νόον ἱλάσκοιθε

But come, let the entire people build me a great temple
and an altar below it, under the steep wall of the city
on the eminent hill, above Kallichoron.
I myself will establish rites so that then
you may appease my spirit with holy fulfillment of them. (270–4)

Ironically the building of the temple allowed Demeter to withdraw
from gods and mortals. The very focus of communication promised by
the goddess became a hermitage and allowed her to engage in a lethal

"showdown" with Zeus; universal famine resulted. Forseeing the end of humankind's worship, Zeus capitulated and negotiated Persephone's return. It was not a complete restoration, however, because Persephone had eaten a pomegranate seed while in the Underworld. Henceforth she would divide her time (unequally) between Olympus and Hades.

The significance of the "Iambe incident" in the *Hymn* begins to emerge in the light of its outcome – both the immediate consequences of the jest and subsequently the breaking of the spell by Metaneira and the final struggle between Zeus and Hades and Demeter and Persephone. First, Iambe's joking instituted a "carnival of women," embracing the serving woman, Iambe, and queen Metaneira, goddess and mortals. The joking acknowledged a community that extends even to the dead, because Demeter's laughter in the face of Persephone's disappearance from the upper world defied the gulf between life and death.

Psychologically speaking, it is easy to appreciate why Demeter withdrew in anger and grief, and it is possible to see how Hades and Demeter – and Persephone herself – eventually achieved a tense compromise, with Persephone spinning endlessly between husband and mother.[12] What seems incomprehensible from the narrative or psychological perspective was Demeter's initial mollification *before* the restoration of Persephone.[13] What did Iambe achieve with her jests? The answer lies in the world and in the logic of cult. It is necessary also to consider the goddess whom she addressed and whose state of mind she affected so profoundly.

Demeter was rarely conceptualized without her daughter. Indeed in parts of the Greek world Persephone and Demeter were twin aspects of a single divinity: mother and maiden.[14] Both goddesses were implicated in rape stories.[15] The false tale that the disguised Demeter tells the daughters of Celeus to account for her state of solitary wandering also bears an odd resemblance to the fate that has befallen her daughter:

Δωσὼ ἐμοί γ᾿ ὄνομ᾿ ἐστί· τὸ γὰρ θέτο πότνια μήτηρ·
νῦν αὖτε Κρήτηθεν ἐπ᾿ εὐρέα νῶτα θαλάσσης
ἤλυθον οὐκ ἐθέλουσα, βίῃ δ᾿ ἀέκουσαν ἀνάγκῃ.
ἄνδρες ληϊστῆρες ἀπήγαγον, οἱ μὲν ἔπειτα
νηῖ θοῇ Θορικὸν δὲ κατέσχεθον, ἔνθα γυναῖκες
ἠπείρου ἐπέβησαν ἀολλέες ἠδὲ καὶ αὐτοὶ
δεῖπνον ἐπηρτύνοντο παρὰ πρυμνήσια νηός·
ἀλλ᾿ ἐμοὶ οὐ δόρποιο μελίφρονος ἤρατο θυμός,
λάθρῃ δ᾿ ὁρμηθεῖσα δι᾿ ἠπείροιο μελαίνης
φεῦγον ὑπερφιάλους σημάντορας, ὄφρα κε μή με
ἀπριάτην περάσαντες ἐμῆς ἀποναίατο τιμῆς.

Doso is my name; my lady mother gave it to me.
But now I have come from Crete over the sea's broad back.
Unwillingly, since against my wish, by force and compulsion
pirate men stole me away. Then they
put in at Thoricus with their swift ship, where the women
disembarked in numbers – and the men also –
and they were preparing dinner by the stern cables.
But my heart did not desire pleasant food
but in secret I sped through the dark country,
fleeing my arrogant masters, lest they
reap the benefit of my price, having removed me unbought. (122–32)

"Doso's" bond with her mother, who has given her name and identity; her tale of kidnapping by male agents; the implication that escape from captivity was dependent on the eating of, or abstinence from, food prepared by a male person or persons – these are themes of Persephone's story also, as told by the *Hymn*. At the end of the poem (441–69) Rhea, Demeter's mother, travels to encourage her to restore fertility to the earth. Their reunion is marked by a mutual affection that recalls the encounter between Demeter and Persephone only a few lines earlier. In short, the *Hymn* presents Persephone's story as her mother's also.[16] Thus Iambe's magical joking may be seen as having a double, and reverberating, impact. Mother and daughter are simultaneously restored to themselves and to each other. This symbolic union and restoration defies the multiple ruptures brought about by Hades and Zeus, their effort to create distinctions of time, place, and identity. Iambe, by contrast, united living and dead, goddess and mortal, past and present, within a mystical community of women.

Her daughter's disappearance seemingly all but shattered the identity of the mother goddess; without her child Demeter could no longer represent motherhood. When the bereft goddess turned into an old woman "past the age of childbearing and of garland-loving Aphrodite," it was not a disguise as much as a symbolic representation of her impoverished state; Demeter seemed to have lost that part of herself belonging to the morning of a woman's life.

In response, Iambe did not add to Demeter's essential nature. Her jokes compelled the goddess to recognize and respond to a contradictory reality. Demeter belonged to grief and loss – but simultaneously to hope, strength, and bawdy life. This complex reality, indeed, is hinted at by the poem throughout the narrative. Demeter had disguised herself – almost as her own opposite. Yet in describing this old woman the poem signals not a complete crone, antithesis of the earth goddess, but a double presence.

She was old and young, feeble and strong, beautiful and a stranger to garland-loving Aphrodite; she was a giver of life and an omen of death. Most important – as Iambe reveals – Demeter was a childless mother, simultaneously fertile and infertile, an elderly woman who could breast-feed an infant.[17] Iambe made manifest Demeter's persistent and essential strength in causing her to laugh and relent.[18]

What did Iambe communicate to the goddess to restore her – as indeed she did, if only for a while? Ironically, while the *Hymn* gave such weight to the "Iambe incident," it was reticent about the details of her trans-forming jests. The cultic evidence, together with the details of the Orphic narratives, described later, suggest that these jests were sexual in nature and almost certainly were connected with Demeter's function as the pro-tector of fertility, both agrarian and human. The Greek words describing the joking (χλεύης...παρὰ σκώπτουσ') actually suggest mockery, a joke di-rected at Demeter; indeed the phenomenon of ritual joking (*aischrologia*) associated with the cult of Demeter seems to have consisted of insults and mocking banter exchanged between participants in her worship. Clay makes an interesting suggestion: "But mourners usually sit on the ground, whereas Demeter sits on a stool. I suggest, then, that Demeter's attitude resembles nothing so much as a woman in labor on a birthing stool, about to give birth. Iambe notes the resemblance – and its absurdity."[19] If this is right, Iambe is pointing to the grotesque paradox that lay at the heart of women's cultic jesting, in my view, the pregnant crone.

The *Hymn* says nothing directly of Iambe's status or appearance; in-stead twice it describes her as κέδν' εἰδυῖα ("knowledgeable about worthy things") – an expression that I translated as "decorous" and that generally applied to older, experienced women. Parallels from the *Odyssey* and the other *Hymns* (there are none in the *Iliad*) suggest that the formula affirms Iambe's good character – especially her sexual restraint.[20] This assurance, together with the silence regarding the details of Iambe's "many jests" and the somber introspection of the grieving goddess, give the scene a strange elusiveness; we can watch from a distance, as it were, but we witness only a graceful mime. It seems as if the epic tradition is struggling to assimilate an episode that strains epic decorum to the limit.

The palace described by the *Hymn* was essentially a woman's world, contained within the male political sphere, but authoritative and powerful on its own turf. Metaneira made the decision to hire Demeter, offering impressive rewards, without recourse to her husband (218–23). It was the women of Eleusis that Demeter had to thank for her shelter, and it was one of these women, Iambe, who broke through her morbid trance and caused her to join them.

This sense of a bond among women pervades the entire episode. Just as Demeter's bereavement brought her close to the mortal world, so her laughter had a human dimension; it was not the unquenchable laughter of the Olympians, remote from all suffering.[21] Rather, it was the laughter of Sarah, the eighty-year-old wife of Abraham, when she discovered that she was with child.[22] When Demeter laughed, together with mortal women she celebrated life and its capacity for renewal in the face of human limitation, old age, and death.[23] She might have been thinking already of her planned immortalization of the child Demophoon: a retaliatory seizure of a mortal from Hades, who had presumed to imprison a god among the dead. More than this, however, Demeter was sharing a joke with women – like herself – whose sexual and reproductive powers cannot easily be understood or dismissed. Like Metaneira who had produced a son – late born, beyond all hope – like decorous Iambe, surprising in her bawdy humor, so the seemingly ancient Demeter belied expectation.

Mockery and Blame in Epic

When we look elsewhere in the epic hexameter tradition, we can see how unusual Iambe's joking – and Demeter's reaction – is. Not surprisingly, the harsh and competitive environment of the *Iliad* bears witness overwhelmingly to the laughter of exclusion. In the *Iliad* gods and men laughed at the unexpected and "shameful" exposure of infirmity, folly, ugliness, age, failure, or death.[24] Women did not typically engage in mockery; the sneers privately uttered by Helen at Paris in book 3, 428–36, were a rare exception – and not intended to raise a laugh in anyone else.

In the *Odyssey* women's laughter bears strong – and negative – sexual connotations. The mockery and laughter of the unfaithful maids seemed to express a link between their unchastity and their arrogance and political treachery.[25] Penelope's famous weeping marked the antithesis. Even among goddesses, sexual laughter was taboo; *Odyssey* 8's story of Ares and Aphrodite is a case in point.[26] Only the male gods chose to witness the trap in which Hephaestus had snared his faithless wife with her lover, Ares. The goddesses stayed "each at her home . . . for modesty." The unquenchable laughter – a mixture of prurient pleasure and mockery of Ares – and mockery of the cuckolded husband who had published his own dishonor arose from an all male group of gods, just as the group seemed to be all male at the human level, listening to the song of Demodocus.[27] At the conclusion of the story, when Aphrodite was finally released, to flee to Paphos, Homer calls her "laughter-loving," an epithet that has been called inept in the circumstances. It may signify Aphrodite's unique status, however; she was the one goddess for whom sexual propriety could be a laughing matter.[28]

The mockery of the Achaeans at Thersites in *Iliad* 2 typifies the epic laughing tradition. Book 1 had witnessed the quarrel between Agamemnon and Achilles, Achilles's withdrawal from battle, and his prayer that the Achaeans would learn to regret his absence. The tide of war now indeed turned against them. Encouraged by a (false) dream from Zeus, Agamemnon tested the mettle of the troops with a disingenuous speech advocating immediate return to Greece. Unfortunately his manipulative address backfired, and the soldiers moved in earnest toward the ships. The officers started to halt the process, and in the midst of the fracas Thersites ("the ugliest man who came to Troy") spoke up:[29]

" Ἀτρεΐδη, τέο δὴ αὖτ᾽ ἐπιμέμφεαι ἠδὲ χατίζεις;
πλεῖαί τοι χαλκοῦ κλισίαι, πολλαὶ δὲ γυναῖκες
εἰσὶν ἐνὶ κλισίης ἐξαίρετοι, ἅς τοι Ἀχαιοὶ
πρωτίστῳ δίδομεν, εὖτ᾽ ἂν πτολίεθρον ἕλωμεν.
ἦ ἔτι καὶ χρυσοῦ ἐπιδεύεαι, ὅν κέ τις οἴσει
Τρώων ἱπποδάμων ἐξ Ἰλίου υἷος ἄποινα
ὅν κεν ἐγὼ δήσας ἀγάγω ἢ ἄλλος Ἀχαιῶν,
ἠὲ γυναῖκα νέην, ἵνα μίσγεαι ἐν ἐν φιλότητι
ἥν τ᾽ αὐτὸς ἀπονόσφι κατίσχεαι; οὐ μὲν ἔοικεν
ἀρχὸν ἐόντα κακῶν ἐπιβασκέμεν υἷας Ἀχαιῶν.
ὦ πέπονες, κάκ᾽ ἐλέγχε᾽, Ἀχαιΐδες, οὐκέτ᾽ Ἀχαιοί,
οἴκαδέ περ σὺν νηυσὶ νεώμεθα, τόνδε δ᾽ ἐῶμεν
αὐτοῦ ἐνὶ Τροίῃ γέρα πεσσέμεν, ὄφρα ἴδηται
ἦ ῥά τί οἱ χἠμεῖς προσαμύνομεν ἦε καὶ οὐκί·
ὃς καὶ νῦν Ἀχιλῆα, ἕο μέγ᾽ ἀμείνονα φῶτα,
ἠτίμησεν· ἑλὼν γὰρ ἔχει γέρας, αὐτὸς ἀπούρας.
ἀλλὰ μάλ᾽ οὐκ Ἀχιλῆι χόλος φρεσίν, ἀλλὰ μεθήμων·
ἦ γὰρ ἄν, Ἀτρεΐδη, νῦν ὕστατα λωβήσαιο."

Son of Atreus, what thing further do you want, or find fault with
now? Your shelters are filled with bronze, there are plenty of the
choicest women for you within your shelter, whom we Achaians
give to you first of all whenever we capture some stronghold.
Or is it more gold you will be wanting, that some son
of the Trojans, breaker of horses, brings as ransom out of Ilion,

one that I, or some other Achaian, capture and bring in?
Is it some young woman to lie with in love and keep her
all to yourself apart from the others? It is not right for
you, their leader, to lead in sorrow the sons of the Achaians.
My good fools, poor abuses, you women, not men of Achaia,
let us go back home in our ships, and leave this man here
by himself in Troy to mull his prizes of honour
that he may find out whether or not we others are helping him.
And now he has dishonoured Achilleus, a man much better
than he is. He has taken his prize by force and keeps her.
But there is no gall in Achilleus' heart, and he is forgiving.
Otherwise, son of Atreus, this were your last outrage. (225–42)

Odysseus rapidly intervened with a harsh rebuke, beating Thersites with Agamnemnon's sceptre – and prevented the Achaean retreat from becoming a rout.[30] In responding aggressively to an outburst by someone else, Odysseus has been likened to an iambic "blame" poet.[31] In general, as we shall see, the blame poet was not imagined as beginning a hostile exchange; his verbal aggression had the justification of being self-defense. Alternatively, one may see Odysseus's speech and action in a broader context, reflecting a norm of behavior familiar from Hesiod on: it was wrong to pick a fight, but legitimate to retaliate to insult.[32]

Despite his ultimate humiliation, we cannot dismiss Thersites as a buffoon.[33] His complaint echoed that of Achilles, voiced earlier, and it was only Thersites's lowly status and coarse manner that allowed Odysseus to dismiss him.[34] Agamemnon's assessment of the situation was in fact mistaken, as we know. Unlike us, Thersites was not privy to Zeus's chicanery or Agamemnon's rhetorical ploy, but his cynical suspicions ("This whole system is designed to the advantage of those at the top!") came close to the truth. When the Greeks (apparently) chose to be amused at Odysseus's rebuke and Thersites's humiliation, they also chose – for a while longer – to accept the status quo at Troy. Thersites may be said to function as a scapegoat, because his "expulsion" caused the Greek community at Troy to reconstitute itself and the hierarchy and ideology sustaining the war effort to fall back into place.[35] The Greek laughter at his expense bonded the all-male group, as they closed ranks against the outsider. Yet as the Greeks laughed, many of them unwittingly made an "Achillean" choice of short lives in Troy over longevity in Greece. The object of their derision was for them an omen of death rather than a "true" scapegoat, who purges destructive forces.[36] Thersites has been described as a "comic" Achilles, and indeed his alienation from the Greek host, following closely upon that of Achilles, set the stage for the massive destruction to be imposed by his tragic "double."

The suitors' laughter at Iros, an opprobrious beggar, played a similar role within the *Odyssey*.[37] Iros rudely challenged Odysseus, whom he took to be a fellow beggar, to a boxing match that Odysseus easily won. In laughing at Iros, the suitors believed themselves to be closing ranks against an outsider, a man whose weakness defined and accentuated their own superior status. Yet as with Thersites so with Iros, his bloodshed warned of their own imminent death; it was not a cathartic displacement or deferral of it.[38] At 18, 100 the suitors "died laughing" at Iros's mock death, a macabre phrase that later blossoms into the vision of the seer Theoclymenus.[39] To him their hysterical laughter "sounded like lamentation," and their rich banquet became a gory monstrosity. As in the Thersites episode, this laughter stood at the junction of life and death – and pointed the way to death.[40]

Both the Thersites and the Iros scenes represent "mocking" moments within epic. Iros's massive wound in the jaw, rendering him incapable of further gluttony or "mordant" abuse, reminds us of the carnivorous "fangs" of blame, a pervasive metaphor in the archaic and classical tradition.[41] In winning the boxing match, Odysseus proved himself not merely a superior warrior, but prefigured his future role as a more potent "blamer," the man who would have the last (cruel) laugh, at the suitors' expense (*Odyssey* 22, 5–8). One of the poem's ironies is Odysseus's adoption of the "blamer" role: the predatory "outsider," paradoxically savaging dwellers in his own house.

My final Iliadic example comes from the end of book 1, where Hephaestus quelled a row between Zeus and Hera by reminding her of Zeus's strength, to which his own limp bore witness. Hephaestus handed Hera a drink, and as he moved among the gods they erupted in "unquenchable laughter" at the clumsy cup bearer. Their laughter here had an element of exclusion – Hephaestus was the lone grotesque amid Olympian beauty. But Hephaestus had deliberately invited this laughter by his incongruous usurpation of Ganymede's role – a comic distraction *and* an implicit reminder of the Olympian status quo; no one could safely challenge Zeus.[42]

At the same time all the gods dwelt far from mortal suffering, and their deathless laughter, here and elsewhere, was nourished by this security, in which Hephaestus was included. Even at its cruelest, laughter among the gods lacked the bloody potential of human laughter. Indeed the carefree laughter of the gods heralded the displacement of truly dangerous power struggles from Olympus to the fields of Troy below, where the real stakes were being lost and won.

These characteristic epic examples of humor drew lines between insiders and outsiders, between those who were higher and lower in the social hierarchy. A human community might be strengthened by the laughing episode, but someone always paid a price, and the affirmation of social or metaphysical structure*s* foreboded bloodier future payment.

When we view Iambe's mockery against the backdrop of the Homeric "mockery and laughter" scenes described earlier, we observe how different it is. In the Iros and Thersites scenes, indeed even in the Hephaestus episode, jesting or mockery ended in the isolation of an individual. These incidents turned a society against a designated outcast (uniting it and affirming a ranking order in the process) and marked the exclusion with laughter. Iambe's jest and Demeter's laughter, on the other hand, marked the assimilation of a perceived "outsider" into the circle of the safe and privileged. Rather than humiliation, Iambe began the gradual restoration of Demeter from servile self-abasement to her true status as queen, mother, and goddess.[43] At the same time, Iambe's jokes formed a most remarkable – and unequal – community, in which a goddess mingled quietly with mortal women, virtually becoming one of them. This is remarkable in itself. I know of no other incident in Greek myth in which a mortal deliberately makes a divinity laugh and thereby creates a psychological bond between two orders of being. In general, when a Greek god laughed at a human "joke," it expressed contempt at mortal aspirations. One thinks of Athena's enjoyment of Ajax's ruin in Sophocles, Dionysus's uncanny smile in the *Bacchae*, or even (to revert briefly to epic) the address by Hesiod's Muses to their humble mouthpiece: "Shepherds of the field, wretched abuses, mere bellies!"

As I noted in the Introduction, the *Hymn* seemed to constitute Iambe's joking as an archetypal moment for the joking practiced by women in their worship of Demeter. The cultic joking that supposedly drew breath from this moment was especially characteristic of women's worship, and positive in tone and impact. If it mocked it did not do so ruinously. It emanated from a world quite alien from that of hexameter epic, in which it was preserved, like an insect in amber. As we shall see, however, this cultic joking in its turn formed the soil in which another literary tradition was rooted: the iambic genre. And the iambic genre, as we shall see, in many ways shared epic's grim, bloody, and competitive worldview.

The question of the Iambe episode's relationship with the literary genre of iambos will be addressed more fully in the next chapter. At first glance the ethic of this incident seems utterly antithetical to that of literary iambic. Iambic poetry was largely a male preserve.[44] It joked about women as though there were two categories, separated by an unbridgeable gulf: before and after; the young, nubile, and virginal versus the old, hideous, and sexually voracious. In the *Hymn* age and youth were not mutually exclusive opposites, and sexuality and reproductive powers were not confined to the young. The jest and the laughter took place within a circle of women; Demeter acknowledged the simultaneity of death and life, unlike the iambic poetic tradition, the power of which was measured by its murderous finality.

But there is another side to the goddess. Indeed if one looks again, one can see that the *Hymn's* Demeter is an apt patron for the deadly genre that evolved from her worship. Although the goddess relents when Iambe jokes, in much of the story Demeter shows a cruel and remorseless side; her grief is described as αἰνότερον καὶ κύντερον ("more terrible and bestial") at 90, when she first learns what has happened. When Metaneira interrupts her midnight therapy, she flings Demophoon to the ground, θυμῷ κοτέσασα μάλ' αἰνῶς, raging very terribly in her heart, and possibly killing him.[45] She is willing to destroy the entire race of mortals with famine. Thus Demeter's nature in the *Hymn* is persistently double; she is terrifyingly cruel and surpassingly kind; she acts in a tragedy – avenging a lost daughter – and a comedy of rescue and rejoicing. This doubleness, this refusal to demarcate, and this simultaneity distinguish her and her women's cultic tradition from the male world – divine and human – with which she negotiates. In the male world there is a "before" and "after," an irrevocable fall between the joy of possession and the grief of loss. The cultic carnival created by Iambe and presided over by Demeter belongs instead to a cyclical, or timeless, time. Thus the narrative as a whole emblematizes a larger dialogue, between two profoundly different voices.

The poem moves on, however, presenting a second narrative of restoration: Iambe's joking and its magical consequences are followed by the deal cut between Demeter and Zeus. The episodes appear sequentially, with the second arrangement displacing the first, which has broken down. The sense that one voice has the "last word" suggests the poem's ideological substructure. Demeter abandons the "carnival of women" and turns instead to the power tactics of that most polemical of epics: the *Iliad*. She withdraws from her own supporters, forcing through murderous isolationism an acknowledgment of her status within the world's hierarchy.

Demeter's intervention in the affairs of Metaneira's household begins with women's chatter and laughter but ends in anguished silence, broken only by the "pitiful voice" of an inconsolable child. As we shall see, this silence augurs the future for women. Within the narrative, Demeter's exclusive relationship with the women at Eleusis yields to a more public and general accessibility; she charges Metaneira to see that "the entire people" (270) build her a temple in which they may approach her with the appropriate rites. Following the return of Persephone Demeter instructs the Eleusinian princes, Triptolemus, Diocles, Eumolpus, and Celeus, in her rites: the Eleusinian Mysteries. Any mortal introduced to these rites will encounter a different fate after death.

Within the mythical narrative, the jesting began a brief period of magical intimacy with the goddess, abruptly ended with Metaneira's unfortunate interruption. Both the long-term benefits and the final, irretrievable loss of communion seem symbolically prophetic. The tale explains and sanctions an ending of privilege for women, and a beginning of blessings for all mortals, to be administered by

> θεμιστοπόλοις βασιλεῦσι
> δ[εῖξε,] Τριπτολέμῳ τε Διοκλεῖ τε πληξίππῳ,
> Εὐμόλπου τε βίη Κελεῷ θ᾽ ἡγήτορι λαῶν,

> law-giving kings,
> Triptolemus, Diocles the driver of horses,
> Mighty Eumolpus and Celeus, leader of the people. (473–5)

Baubo and the Cult of Demeter

When the *Hymn* describes Iambe – twice – as κέδν᾽ εἰδυῖα ("decorous," "knowledgeable about worthy things"), it stresses her (sexual) respectability. This formulaic character testimonial and the *Hymn*'s silence regarding the (sexual) subject of her joking distances her from her disreputable counterpart, Baubo, a woman associated with Demeter cults. I suggest that this careful distinction was part of the *Hymn*'s overall strategy: to appropriate the women's cultic material for a male-run social order. Baubo's unacceptable vulgarity was linked to a power and authority that the *Hymn*'s poets wished to retain, but in a sanitized alternative version.

There are two sources of evidence for Baubo: the "Orphic" fragments and archaeological material in the form of inscriptions and figurines.[46] The archaeological evidence dates to the fourth century B.C.E. or later and derives from several places in the Greek world, but not Attica itself. Like the *Hymn* itself, the Orphic poems cannot be dated precisely, but they probably existed alongside the *Hymn*, as it was being composed and recomposed.[47] The Orphic material has survived mostly in (hostile) accounts by the Church Fathers of Demeter's cult; while they clearly wish to emphasize the ludicrous and obscene nature of the pagan rites, the described events conform to fertility myths elsewhere.[48]

In the longest fragment (Kern 49) Baubo seems to be the mother of the infant Demophoon, and queen of Eleusis. In others, she is merely a local rustic, one of a cast of characters including her husband, Dysaules; the cowherd Triptolemus; the shepherd Eumolpus; and the pig keeper Eubouleus.[49] In Clement's version of the story (Kern 50, 52), Eubouleus and Triptolemus saw their animals being swallowed in the earth with Hades's chariot, and so they were able to tell Demeter – who had wandered to Eleusis still in search of Persephone – what had happened. Demeter's reward to the people of Eleusis is twofold: instruction in agriculture and in the Mysteries.[50] In Hesychius Baubo is defined as the wet nurse of Demeter, the opposite of the extant sources, in which Baubo is the mother, Demeter the wet nurse.[51]

During her visit to Eleusis, Demeter was cheered by an obscene gesture made by Baubo. Details of this gesture are found in Clement and Arnobius.[52] After failing to cheer Demeter with words, Baubo lifted her skirts to reveal her genitals.[53] Hesychius under "Baubo" suggests that, according to Empedocles, the name means "abdomen" or the body's cavity (κοιλία). Devereux and others have argued for an identification with the vulva, which fits this story.[54]

In addition to the fact that she performed an obscene gesture – as opposed to the words uttered by Iambe – Baubo differs from her counterpart in being a woman of childbearing years, whereas, as we shall see in the next chapter, whenever Iambe's age is specified in the post-*Hymn* literary tradition, she seems to occupy one of two extremes: girl or crone. Why is this? My explanation is that Baubo emblematized female sexuality and fertility, the power of the female displayed in a bold – even aggressive – epiphany. She revealed to the world what is normally inside, hidden. Iambe on the other hand, a girl or crone, represented the magic of cultic speech, invoking, but not embodying, the precarious and evanescent powers of the female and those of the dormant fields.

Two types of terracotta figurines dating from the fourth to the first centuries B.C.E. are linked with Baubo.[55] The Priene type features a nude woman, whose face – which is also her belly and vulva – is supported directly by two stumpy legs.[56] The other type – "of Egyptian origin" – also shows a nude woman, this time with an anatomically correct body. Her belly is swollen, her legs splayed. She appears to be about to give birth, although in one example she is riding a pig, the animal sacred to Demeter.[57]

Inscriptions on Naxos, Paros, and in Dion (Macedonia) testify to Baubo's cult status in these places. The fourth-century inscription from Naxos associates Baubo with the principal deities of Eleusis, Demeter, Kore, and Zeus Eubouleus.[58] A similar inscription appears on Paros.[59] At Dion the (Hellenistic) inscription, on top of a marble table, reads as follows:

Μενεκρίτη Θεωδώρου ἱερητεύσασα Βαβοῖ.

Menekrite, daughter of Theodorus, having served as priestess to Babo [sic].[60]

Nonnus preserves the story that Demeter herself performed just such an obscene gesture.[61] Like Iambe, Baubo reveals to Demeter something relevant to Demeter's own sphere and function, something present in Demeter herself. Baubo may be said to be a version or aspect of the goddess she confronts.[62]

Baubo clearly existed both as a cultic figure and a literary one. Iambe, on the other hand, has never shown up in inscriptions or any archaeological context.[63] Iambe was "cultic" only in the sense that she epitomized a cultic activity: the exchange of insults or *aischrologia*. In fact the evidence suggests that Iambe was the invention of the composer(s) of the *Hymn*: the necessary catalyst in the Eleusinian drama but one who avoided the crude pantomime of the traditional cultic tale. Within the *Hymn* she was the solitary servant in a conspicuous royal cast, of whom one member at least was worshipped in local cult.[64]

Nothing Like a Dame

Let me reprise here an important theme introduced in Chapter 1. If one casts a glance over Greek literature as a whole, it becomes easier to appreciate the significance – and anomaly – of Baubo (and Iambe) as feminine prototype. The famous originary woman of Hesiod, Pandora, embodies the characteristics of women in Greek literature. Pandora was a beautiful trap: in appearance a lovely young maid, but with a heart full of deceit. She was destined, and indeed designed by the gods, to put man in his place, as a creature bound to toil and to suffer. Like so many of the women in the Greek epic and tragic traditions, Pandora's lovely face and seductive voice belied the ruin that she carried within. Baubo, in contrast, held no seductive appeal for men but addressed herself to a female audience. In many accounts she is old, and in most accounts she lacks dignity and restraint. Visually she is grotesque, in the form of the Priene and Egyptian figurines. These Baubo models in turn recall the old women figurines – Thesmophorian grotesques, I believe – found all over the Greek world from the Black Sea to Sicily. The pregnant crone, like the sexualized crone, seems to hold no promise of life, yet out of this clumsy and unprepossessing vessel and out of a dark and death-filled situation, come joy, life, and hope.

The Pomegranate Seed

Like other elements of the *Hymn*'s story, the theme of the "pomegranate seed" reminds us of the existence of other narratives, other ways of considering the relationship between the *Hymn*'s protagonists. I suggest that here, as elsewhere, we can detect an "archaeology" of viewpoints, with women's cultic interpretations now subsumed beneath a very different, patriarchal and hierarchical perspective.

The *Hymn* refers to the seeds twice, once when we hear that Hades tricked Persephone into eating it, following the arrival in the underworld of Hermes, Zeus's messenger, with instructions to restore Persephone to her mother:

> αὐτὰρ ὅ γ᾽ αὐτὸς
> ῥοιῆς κόκκον ἔδωκε φαγεῖν μελιηδέα λάθρη
> ἀμφὶ ἓ νωμήσας, ἵνα μὴ μένοι ἤματα πάντα
> αὖθι παρ᾽ αἰδοίῃ Δημήτερι κυανοπέπλῳ.

> ... But he gave her to eat
> a honey-sweet pomegranate seed, stealthily passing it
> round her, lest she once more stay forever
> by the side of revered Demeter of the dark robe. (371–4)[65]

Later, however, when Persephone describes the incident to her mother (411–12), she indicates (a) that she knew what had happened; Hades' stealth and trickery – to which Persephone alludes – apparently sufficed only to perpetrate the deception, not to keep Persephone unaware of it afterward; (b) that Hades used force in addition to trickery – an oddly overdetermined account. This symbolic consumption of food means, as the poem twice explains, that Persephone must spend one-third of each year below the earth.

Pomegranate seeds were not just food.[66] According to ancient medical treatises they functioned as an astringent cleanser for the uterus and female genitalia. They were used as contraceptives, to expel the afterbirth, and as abortifacients. Recent studies reveal that pomegranate seeds contain female sex hormones, so that it seems likely that they did have a real effect. Pomegranate seeds featured in Demeter's cult of the Thesmophoria, as we have seen. Unlike other plants associated with the Thesmophoria, however, pomegranate seeds were not aids to fertility, but the contrary.

Thus the choice of this particular substance by Hades to give his "blossoming wife" (*thaleren . . . akoitin*, 79) seems pointless, even counterproductive, from his perspective.[67] He desired union with Persephone, and union with a god (even brief) normally produced children, an outcome the gods saw as inevitable.[68] Thus, for example, Zeus avoided the match with lovely Thetis to prevent begetting a son destined to be greater than his father, as an oracle had ordained.[69] From a marital point of view, children embodied and strengthened the contract.[70] The *Hymn* presents Hades as an effective negotiator, a wily – and forceful – manipulator of a deteriorating situation, eliciting from Persephone and her mother a part-time marriage in lieu of complete divorce. Was the pomegranate seed a miscalculation? I suggest that the *Hymn* deploys a version of the myth that attributes to Hades what was in fact Persephone's own doing in other accounts. Ovid depicted Persephone as helping herself to the seeds (albeit "unwittingly"), and accounts by Ovid, Nicander, and Apollodorus tell of the punishment of Ascalabus for spying on Persephone and informing on her, a motif that makes more sense if one imagines Persephone herself eating the seeds surreptitiously (i.e., with conscious intent).[71] If Hades fed her the seeds, what need of further witnesses? Ovid drew on a rich range of material, lost to us now, some of which may have derived from alternate narratives coexisting with the *Hymn*. In these alternative accounts Persephone herself may have attempted to undo the marriage by aborting her child. I suggest that such an interpretation of the events in the underworld belonged particularly to women's rites such as the Thesmophoria. The authors of the *Hymn*, working within a more patriarchal framework, and designing an account to celebrate the Eleusinian Mysteries, run by kings and priestly clans, attributed the crucial initiative to Hades.

The *Cyceon*

Iambe's jest brought about a meal that would be celebrated ever afterward at Eleusis – a tradition of communion with Demeter, who accepted the *cyceon* "for the sake of the rite" (ὁσίης ἕνεκεν, 211).[72] Like other elements of ritual, the *cyceon* was rich in meaning and implication. It was a drink, a suspension of partially ground (but uncooked) barley and pennyroyal, *Mentha pulegium* L. (often mistranslated as mint) in water.[73] The pennyroyal could function as a contraceptive and abortifacient and an aid in childbirth and nursing.[74] The raw but ground barley expressed the ambivalence of Demeter's nature, which celebrated the cultivated earth while shunning other features of "civilized" society, such as cookery.[75] At the same time, the *cyceon* could express other things. Plutarch tells of how the people of Ephesus asked Heraclitus about political concord. His answer was to drink the *cyceon* – without comment.[76] This cryptic response suggests how, just as Demeter's worshippers might mingle as one without losing their identity, so also Ephesus's citizens might become a unity, constituted by disparate elements.[77] This drink of women's cult represented (literally and figuratively) suspension: the capacity of essentially incompatible or alien elements to coexist amicably without coercion or restraint.

The *cyceon* contained no wine, a fact emphasized by Demeter's marked refusal to drink wine at 206–7. Thus Demeter's drink distinguished itself from that of Dionysus in an emphatic opposition. This opposition, this marked refusal, may have had particular weight in an Attic sixth-century context, in which Dionysian cult was rapidly expanding its sphere of influence. Whereas Dionysus's drink could transform individuals into something other than their rational selves, Demeter's drink restored the self, brought it back from a period of alienation.[78] In ritual, such a period might be marked by fasting or sexual abstinence, which was then ended by the drinking of the *cyceon*. Hipponax later was to call the *cyceon* "a remedy for suffering."[79] In contrast, Dionysus embodied a wilder, potentially dangerous and transformative drink, the components of which had been utterly and irrevocably transformed, often associated with violence and confusion. Like the *cyceon*, wine was a cultic drink, but whereas wine exacerbated the dangers of interaction between disparate classes of being (one thinks of the disastrous wedding banquet attended by Lapiths and Centaurs), the *cyceon* made for a magical harmony.

Demeter's choice marks a cultic distinction. The drink embodies certain values: sobriety, peace, and social harmony – values associated with women's cultic joking. As we shall see, however, both Demeter's and Dionysus's cults had links with the iambic genre through their use of *aischrologia*. When we encounter the mockery and joking of iambic literature, in contrast, we will find different values, blended in.

Scholars long interpreted the details of Demeter's interaction with the women at Eleusis as related to the famous Mysteries celebrated there in antiquity. Clinton has argued otherwise, however, making a persuasive case.[80] The mockery that is so central in the *Hymn*'s narrative was peripheral in the Mysteries (the *gephurismos* en route to Eleusis). The *Hymn* makes no mention of Eubouleus, who was a key figure in the Mysteries. It says nothing about the famed "Mirthless Rock," a key icon of the Eleusinian Mysteries. The goddess Hecate plays a significant role in the *Hymn*, yet she does not feature at Eleusis.[81] The *Hymn* features an all-female setting for its etiology, although men and women took place in the Mysteries. The nursing of Demophoon made no sense within the context of the Mysteries. Moreover, the *Hymn* presents the Mysteries as founded by Demeter and granted to humankind *after* describing the etiological sequence of ritual activities featuring Iambe. Why would it portray the goddess as inventing something already in existence? "Rather, the jesting, drinking of the *cyceon* and nursing of an infant fit the women's festival of the Thesmophoria.[82] I believe that this is so. Thus the poem structures a narrative shift from a private, female world to a public, male world. The Greater Mysteries appear to supersede the Thesmophoria; a state-wide worship with Panhellenic prestige replaces the more modest women's practices."[83]

With the poem's shift from the private world of women to the public world of "state"-run cult, I end this chapter. The Thesmophoria did not actually yield to the cult of the Mysteries, but the polis, with its prestigious and high-profile institutions, indeed tended to encroach upon some of the ancient prerogatives of the women's cults.[84] The *Hymn* reflected Athenian "international" aspirations at the end of the sixth century B.C.E.; its author(s) wished to assert themselves with a voice that carried far beyond the environs of Athens and Eleusis. Whereas the Thesmophoria was celebrated all over the Greek world, from the Black Sea to Sicily, the Mysteries belonged exclusively to Eleusis and drew people from many places.[85] The *Hymn*'s segue from the Thesmophoria to the Mysteries served the Panhellenic ambitions and reflected the patriarchal values of its author(s). In the next chapter I trace the "fate" of Iambe, because her stories express the threatened (and, I infer, the threatening) position of joking women in archaic and classical Greece.

IAMBIC'S RELATIONSHIP WITH THE FEMALE

I N CHAPTER 2 I EXAMINED the episode in the Homeric *Hymn to Demeter* in which Iambe cheered the goddess with her joking. I suggested that Iambe was a prototype both for the cultic laughter practiced by women in certain religious cults, and for the genre that bore her name. This second aspect of the etiology I examine here, because it is not universally accepted.

The *Hymn's* version largely reflects a male, patriarchal tradition, which is understandable, given that the *Hymn* belonged to a conservative epic genre that also included the *Iliad* and poems of the Trojan cycle. Yet the *Hymn to Demeter* also drew on women's cult. Overall, the *Hymn's* telling of the Iambe story – with its sequence of grieving goddess, Iambe's jests, and their inspiration of a short-lived "carnival of women," followed by the formal establishment of the male-run Eleusinian Mysteries – hints at a larger debate or struggle. The poem seemingly drew lines around women's joking, limiting it to a particular sphere and moment in time. Yet it also communicated the authority and reverberating impact of that joking. The carnival of women challenged the measure, limits, and hierarchy that structured and drove epic narrative. This implicit dialogue between male hierarchical orderliness – literary and societal – and the threatening disorder of women's cultic laughter was to shape the iambic genre, as I show here.

Defining *Iambos*

A passage in the *Poetics* of Aristotle has been the starting point for modern scholars' efforts to define literary *iambos*, a difficult matter given the paucity and scattered variety of the remains.[1]

διεσπάσθη δὲ κατὰ τὰ οἰκεῖα ἤθη ἡ ποίησις· οἱ μὲν γὰρ σεμνότεροι τὰς καλὰς ἐμιμοῦντο πράξεις καὶ τὰς τῶν τοιούτων, οἱ δὲ εὐτελέστεροι τὰς τῶν φαύλων, πρῶτον ψόγους ποιοῦντες, ὥσπερ ἕτεροι ὕμνους καὶ ἐγκώμια. τῶν μὲν οὖν πρὸ Ὁμήρου οὐδενὸς ἔχομεν εἰπεῖν τοιοῦτον ποίημα, εἰκὸς δὲ εἶναι πολλούς, ἀπὸ δὲ Ὁμήρου ἀρξαμένοις ἔστιν, οἷον ἐκείνου ὁ Μαργίτης καὶ τὰ τοιαῦτα. ἐν οἷς κατὰ τὸ ἁρμόττον καὶ τὸ ἰαμβεῖον ἦλθε μέτρον διὸ καὶ ἰαμβεῖον καλεῖται

νῦν, ὅτι ἐν τῷ μέτρῳ τούτῳ ἰάμβιζον ἀλλήλους. καὶ ἐγένοντο τῶν παλαιῶν οἱ
μὲν ἡρωικῶν οἱ δὲ ἰάμβων ποιηταί. ὥσπερ δὲ καὶ τὰ σπουδαῖα μάλιστα ποιητὴς
῝Ομηρος ἦν (μόνος γὰρ οὐχ ὅτι εὖ ἀλλὰ καὶ μιμήσεις δραματικὰς ἐποίησεν),
οὕτως καὶ τὸ τῆς κωμῳδίας σχῆμα πρῶτος ὑπέδειξεν, οὐ ψόγον ἀλλὰ τὸ γελοῖον
δραματοποιήσας· ὁ γὰρ Μαργίτης ἀνάλογον ἔχει, ὥσπερ Ἰλιὰς καὶ ἡ Ὀδύσσεια
πρὸς τὰς τραγῳδίας, οὕτω καὶ οὗτος πρὸς τὰς κωμῳδίας. παραφανείσης δὲ
τῆς τραγῳδίας καὶ κωμῳδίας οἱ ἐφ᾽ ἑκατέραν τὴν ποίησιν ὁρμῶντες κατὰ τὴν
οἰκείαν φύσιν οἱ μὲν ἀντὶ τῶν ἰάμβων κωμῳδοποιοὶ ἐγένοντο, οἱ δὲ ἀντὶ τῶν
ἐπῶν τραγῳδοδιδάσκαλοι,

Poetry then divided in two, according to the disposition (of the poets). For
the loftier souls imitated noble deeds, and the actions of people of this
sort, while the lower types imitated the deeds of unworthy men, at first
composing blame poems, just as the others had composed hymns and
praise poems. We are not able to name the work of any poet before Homer
when it comes to poems of this (i.e. unworthy) sort, but it is likely that
there were many. But from Homer on we can, like his *Margites* and works
of this sort. In these poems, according to a principle of apppropriateness,
the *iambeion* (iambic trimeter) appeared, which is why it is now called
the *iambeion*, because they used to *iambize* (mock) each other in this
meter. Of the ancient poets, some became authors of heroic works, others
authors of *iamboi*. Just as Homer excelled in serious compositions (for he
alone not only composed well but also composed dramatic imitations), so
he was also the first to illustrate the form of comedy, composing dramas
not as blame but in order to be funny. As the *Iliad* and *Odyssey* stand in
relation to tragedies, so stands the *Margites* in relation to comedies. When
tragedy and comedy came into existence, the poets rushed to each type of
poetry according to individual disposition; those who before would have
written *iamboi* became comic poets, and epic poets became tragedians.

The passage introduces key issues: the meaning of the verb ἰαμβίζω ("address in an iambic manner"); the subject matter of iambic; the relationship between the genre of *Iambos* and the iambic trimeter, the *iambeion*.
Regarding the first, Aristotle apparently takes ἰαμβίζω to mean "mock,"
"address mockingly." Certainly by the fifth century ἰαμβίζω meant to satir-
ize, without implying any particular meter.[2] As to the last of these issues,
Aristotle seems to suggest that the meter was named because it was especially appropriate for the genre of *iambos*. It was not exclusive to *iambos*,
of course, nor were all poems included within the genre of *iambos* in the
iambic trimeter. As West observes: "Iambic metre got its name from being particularly characteristic of ἴαμβοι not vice versa."[3] The Alexandrian
editors of archaic poetry also included poems in choliambics, trochaic
tetrameters, and epodic poems in their books of *iamboi*.[4]

West defines the iambic genre thus: "I suggest that we may recognize iambus most confidently in those types of subject matter for which elegiacs are never used: that is, in explicitly sexual poems, in invective which goes beyond the witty banter we found in elegy, and in certain other sorts of vulgarity."[5]

The question as to what properly constitutes iambic subject matter is tricky, given the variety of what survives, and Bowie has recently argued for a slight revision of West's position.[6] Rather than seeing archaic *iambos* as a genre built around the notion of blame or abuse, from which the metrical term was named, Bowie proposes a less distinctive thematic "core." "Iambos" was originally a hodgepodge genre, a "loosely linked network of poetic types." Blame poems were sufficently prominent within that group to inspire the term ἰαμβίζω, meaning "blame." If this is correct, then some of the nonvituperative or less vituperative poems of Archilochus and others might have been considered legitimate *iamboi* by ancient editors. At the least one may imagine a range of tones, including irony, mild amusement, lighthearted drollery – not just savage rage.

Early iambic flourished in the islands of the eastern Aegean: Paros and Amorgos – Lesbos too, if one may count Sappho and Alcaeus as iambic poets (at least part of the time) – and in Ionia. Hipponax traditionally was linked with Ephesus, on the Ionian coast.

Cult and Genre

In his discussion of the Iambe story, Bowie says the following:

> This story clearly related to the σκώμματα (jibes) later attested as part of Eleusinian ritual,[7] and shows that there was a conceptual link between *iamboi* and σκώμματα, but of course it does not demonstrate that the genre *iambos* had ritual origins. It is compatible both with the hypothesis that *iambos* began in a ritual context and then became secular, as it clearly has become by the generation of Archilochus and Semonides, and with the hypothesis that *iamboi* were a form of secular poetry that regularly or often involved σκώμματα, and that it was for this reason that the creator of the story of the woman who consoled Demeter gave her the name Iambe.[8]

I suggest, however, that Iambe's functional "double," Baubo, makes it difficult to sustain the second of these two positions. There is no doubt that Baubo embodies a nonliterary activity. She is a purely cultic phenomenon, a symbol of an interaction between a woman and a goddess. How could it be, then, that the *Hymn*'s creators, looking to supplant Baubo with a less outrageous figure, would find a name symbolizing abusive (noncultic) poetry? Rather, it makes sense to see in Iambe also a symbol of cultic interaction.[9] A question remains, of course as to the extent to which the genre's cultic origins still may have resonated within the genre. I do not think that iambic altogether forgot its cultic roots, as Bowie states.[10]

From the earliest period there are connections between the cult of Demeter and the iambic genre. Archilochus, among the first poets to use the term *iamboi*, is linked to the worship of Demeter. The worship of Demeter was introduced to Thasos by Cleoboea, fellow traveller in Charon's ferry with Tellis, Archilochus's grandfather, according to Pausanias.[11] Archilochus's father, Telesicles, also evokes a priestly role, and West has suggested that the priesthood was hereditary.[12] Paros, Archilochus's home, was called the island of Demeter by Stephanus of Byzantium.[13] An inscription there (noted in my discussion of Baubo in the last chapter) addresses Demeter Thesmophoros and Kore and Zeus Eubouleus and Babo.[14] The patronymic "Dot-ades" belonging to Lycambes, Archilochus' well-known "enemy" and target, is linked by West to the name "Doso" assumed by Demeter in the *Hymn*.[15] A fragment of Hipponax (Gerber 39) promises that the poet will strengthen himself for his iambic attacks by drinking the *cyceon*, the magical beverage offered by Iambe to Demeter in the *Hymn*. Hipponax thus suggests that his poetry takes place in a context of Demeter's cult and occurs alongside cultic *aischrologia* or insult exchange characteristic of her worship.[16] In short, from the outset, I suggest that Demeter's ritual joking nourished and validated the mockery of the genre that derived from it.[17]

While I believe that Demeter's cult was the most significant religious influence on the iambic genre, it must also be remembered that cults of Dionysus, which also featured *aischrologia*, had also an imporant impact.[18] Dionysus's cult welcomed both sexes – indeed it was unique in its long standing practice in this regard.[19] The cults of Dionysus and Demeter were nearly always linked.[20] Archilochus's famous lines about his spear, remind us that the island communities of the eastern Aegean, in which Demeter's crops and cults flourished, were also home to the ancient wine industry, and the god who protected it:

ἐν δορὶ μέν μοι μᾶζα μεμαγμένη, ἐν δορὶ δ᾽ οἶνος
Ἰσμαρικός, πίνω δ᾽ ἐν δορὶ κεκλιμένος.

In my spear is my kneaded bread, in my spear
Is my Ismarian wine. I drink leaning on my spear.[21]

The couplet simultaneously evokes the realm of Demeter, that of Dionysus, and glories in the life-sustaining violence that permeates Archilochus's poetic persona.[22]

Frag. 120 of Archilochus seems to derive from a festival of Dionysus, in which the poet is leading a song:

ὡς Διωνύσοι᾽ ἄνακτος καλὸν ἐξάρξαι μέλος
οἶδα διθύραμβον οἴνῳ συγκεραυνωθεὶς φρένας.

I know how to lead in the dithyramb,
The lovely song of Lord Dionysus, my wits thunderbolted with wine.[23]

Frag. 251, a verse passage deriving from a very fragmentary section of the Mnesiepes Inscription (discussed later) mentions the god Dionysus, together with unripe grapes, figs – and an epithet for Dionysus, Oipholios, which refers to sexual intercourse. The inscription continues, seemingly condemning something (probably these verses) for being "too iambic." Yet the criticism of the lines brought down a series of troubles on the heads of the Parians, until the Delphic oracle instructed them to honor Archilochus. The Archilocheion, or shrine of the poet, was probably the original site of the inscription, and may have been understood by the Parians as their response to this advice by Delphi.[24]

Also interesting in regard to the relationship between iambic and Dionysus is a passage by Semus of Delos, cited by Athenaeus.[25] He describes a number of different performers singing songs, apparently in honor of the god Dionysus. The first of these, the so-called αὐτοκάβδαλοι, who recited their poems wreathed in Dionysian ivy, were later called *iamboi*, as were their poems. Semus places these *iamboi* alongside costumed performers of *phallika* in a theater. The phallus-pole bearers sing a song explicitly in honor of Dionysus, and then some of them rush toward audience members, mocking them (the verb used is τωθάζω).

Cultic abuse and joking detached (partly) from cult to form the basis of literary iambic. Early poetry contests speeded the transition. Cultic jesting was acted and reenacted by participants who understood themselves to be part of a recurring process. With the evolution of competitions honoring a divinity – the individual sought in part to transcend the process, to make memorable or conspicuous his part in it. Archilochus, we are told, won such a poetry contest, seemingly with a *Hymn* in honor of the goddess Demeter, on Paros.[26]

Iambos, as a literary and social phenomenon, developed in the seventh and sixth centuries B.C.E. This was a time of rapid political and social change throughout Greece, as the traditional kingdoms and oligarchic fiefdoms reflected in the Homeric poems were riven by strife. A growing population put unprecedented pressure on land, resulting in the development of overseas colonies in some cases, wars and land seizures in others. In many places tyrants seized control of what were becoming city-states, sometimes with the avowed intention of aiding the common people against predatory élites. Ian Morris has argued that during the period extending from the eighth century to the fifth a profound ideological shift took place throughout Greece as a whole, making "rule by the demos" first a credible possibility, and then, often preferable to rule by the élite.[27] Such a belief was contested by conservative élites, who typically saw their authority as deriving from sources outside of the "state," such as the gods, aristocrats from other states, and the East, with its ancient traditions of luxury and elegance.

Iambic poetry was fueled by these class tensions and changes. As the *Hymn* describes it, iambic was radically egalitarian in origin. Iambe was a servant woman, yet she, and not Queen Metaneira, was able to persuade the disguised goddess to accept hospitality.[28] She spoke mockingly – to a goddess and a guest – and yet encountered a gracious response. She created a community of women that bound high and low born, mortal and divinity, living and dead. Iambic speech in cult had an exhilarating power. In its literary manifestation, however, its power emerged as more hostile and repressive. Iambic poetry became a significant voice within the political and class struggles taking place throughout the Greek world. Not surprisingly it emerged as the characteristic weapon of the antiaristocratic element, the little or middling man who mistrusts aristocrats and their pretensions. Archilochus's famous quatrain about his ideal comrade-at-arms sums up the perspective as follows:

οὐ φιλέω μέγαν στρατηγὸν οὐδὲ διαπεπλιγμένον
οὐδὲ βοστρύχοισι γαῦρον οὐδ᾽ ὑπεξυρημένον,
ἀλλά μοι σμικρός τις εἴη καὶ περὶ κνήμας ἰδεῖν
ῥοικός, ἀσφαλέως βεβηκὼς ποσσί, καρδίης πλέως.

I don't want a towering general, the kind that poses
With legs apart, preening with his curls and artful shave.
Give me a little guy, bandy legs and all – but solid
On his feet, and gutsy through and through.[29]

Archilochus himself apparently was forced to emigrate on account of his poverty.[30] We are also told that his mother was a slave woman, whose name was Enipo ("Blame").[31] Thus he was "degraded" by his mother. A figure embodying lowly status, feminine gender, and a harsh discourse formed an essential part of his identity.

How did the magical, woman-centered egalitarianism of the *Hymn's* joking produce a genre marked by such virulent and persistent misogyny? The answer in part lies in the crucial role women played within the aristocratic cultures targeted by iambic. A primary marker and obligation of élite status was intermarriage with other aristocratic families. Women constituted the currency of exchange within this closed circle. Thus élite wives betokened both the privileged class, and its means of perpetuating itself and excluding others. It is no coincidence that the defining story of the life of the famous iambicist Archilochus concerns a promised marriage, subsequently revoked.[32] His response is to drag the girl down in his verse. Whereas élitist poets, such as Homer, could depict noble Penelope, shining amid her (mostly) discreditable maids, the iambic poet sneers that women are all the same.[33] Thus iambic was seen paradoxically, both as a potent instrument of social control (especially, though not exclusively) of women, and as a catalyst of upheaval and revolution.[34] Iambe was felt to represent a feminine "mocking" prototype, yet she seemed to have few or no female successors in iambic literature.

The figure of Iambe tracks the sociological and cultic tides and currents flowing beneath the surface of iambic. She features in narratives and scholarly commentaries, appearing after the *Hymn*. Her narrative "fate" measures women's freedom to speak out, mockingly. Sometimes she jokes with impunity. But there are also stories depicting Iambe as a girl who experiences a savage iambic rebuke – as punishment for outspokenness – causing her to commit suicide.

Following discussion of Iambe, I turn to the iambic poets – Archilochus, Semonides, and Hipponax – and the women who appear as their targets, either in the extant poems or in the (pseudo)biographies. At least some of these women, I suggest, began their existence engaged in traditional exchanges within the cult of Demeter. In other words, one may imagine these women as agents in the production of protoiambic, not merely the targets that they seem to be in the extant poems. During the transition from cult to literature they experienced harsh efforts to silence them. Indeed the mark of a successful iambic poet was to silence his enemies forever – hence a series of suicide stories associated with the iambic tradition. Nonetheless, I suggest that the genre's bitter vituperation and the suicide stories do not demonstrate a battle lost and won, but rather a site of ongoing contestation. Far more radical even than the challenges to aristocratic privilege articulated by the genre was the simmering possibility of women's sexualized, critical, irrepressible, voices – cultic or literary – speaking from a perspective of indifference to patriarchal mores.

This brings me to the question: did women themselves ever produce iambic literature or something approximating it? In Chapter 4 a discussion of poems of Sappho and Corinna brings us closer to an answer.

The Post-*Hymn* Iambe Stories[35]

Most evidence on Iambe is Hellenistic or later, but the number and variety of the stories suggest that the traditions go back into the classical period.[36] Later Iambe stories sometimes explicitly expressed connections with Demeter-cult, as the *Hymn* had done implicitly. For example, Apollodorus says that her jesting was the precedent for the ritual joking at the Thesmophoria. Diodorus Siculus also connects the (Sicilian) ritual joking of the Thesmophoria to the time "it made Demeter laugh when she was grieving over the rape of Kore."[37] It is fair to say that, at some level, all of these stories formed part of a religious experience of Demeter. They range in type from celebratory (of women's cultic voices) to minatory. Thus one may see Iambe as a "sign," whose meaning and value were contested. She is a transgressor, triumphant, or crushed by powerful cultural norms: two sides of the same coin.

A story from Choiroboscus shows how the figure of Iambe could authorize one of the famous exponents of the genre, the sixth-century B.C.E. iambicist, Hipponax.[38] After referring to the Iambe story of the *Hymn*, this ancient scholar offers an alternative etymology for the word "iambos":

ἢ ἀπὸ Ἰάμβης τινὸς ἑτέρας γραὸς, ἣ Ἱππώνακτι παρὰ θάλασσαν ἔρια πλυνούσῃ συντυχὼν ἤκουσε τῆς σκάφης ἐφαψάμενος, ἐφ' ἧς ἔπλυνεν ἡ γραῦς, "ἄνθρωπ', ἄπελθε, τὴν σκάφην ἀνατρέπεις." καὶ συλλαβὼν τὸ ῥηθὲν ὠνόμασε τὸ μέτρον. ἄλλοι δὲ περὶ τοῦ χωλιάμβου τὴν ἱστορίαν ταύτην ἀναφέρουσι, γράφοντες τὸ τέλος τοῦ στίχου "τὴν σκάφην ἀνατρέψεις."

Or it is from some other Iambe, an old woman, whom the iambic poet Hipponax encountered by the sea, as she was washing wool. As he brushed against the basin in which the old woman was washing, he heard her say: "go away sir, you are overturning the basin [τὴν σκάφην ἀνατρέπεις]!"[39] And having heard what she said [an iambic utterance] he thus named the meter. Others relate this story regarding the choliambic meter, writing the end of the line "you'll overturn the basin" [τὴν σκάφην ἀνατρέψεις].

A variant of the story, set in Eleusis, features Iambe speaking abusively
to Hipponax, calling him "disagreeable" (ἀκαταθύμιος), someone who has
done a stupid thing).⁴⁰ The story bears the stamp of a generic aetiology,
establishing his raison d'être as an iambic poet. Whereas in the Homeric
Hymn Demeter merely laughs at the mockery, Iambe here inspires her
auditor to institute the meter – if not the genre as well.⁴¹

Iambos began in exchange; people assailed each other in cultic encounters – as Aristotle observed in the *Poetics*.⁴² As the eponymous representative of cultic mockery it was to be expected that Iambe would receive, as
well as express, mockery. Iambe was thought by some to be the daughter
of Echo and Pan, parents who might account for, or reflect, both her ribald
nature (Pan) and her participation in exchange. Surely no daughter of Echo
could speak without expecting a reply.⁴³

Photius includes iambos in a discussion of literary genres and their
origins.⁴⁴ The author says that iambos was a dialect form for "abuse." Then
he gives the story of Iambe:

οἱ δὲ ἀπό τινος Ἰάμβης θεραπαινίδος, Θρᾴττης τὸ γένος· ταύτην φασί, τῆς
Δήμητρος ἀνιωμένης ἐπὶ τῇ τῆς θυγατρὸς ἁρπαγῇ, προσελθεῖν περὶ τὸν
Ἐλευσῖνα ἐπὶ τῇ νῦν Ἀγελάστῳ καλομένῃ πέτρᾳ καθημένην καὶ διά τινῶν
χλευασμάτων εἰς γέλωτα προαγαγέσθαι τὴν θεόν. ἔοικε δὲ ὁ ἴαμβος τὸ μὲν
παλαιὸν ἐπὶ τῶν εἰς ψόγον καὶ ἔπαινον γραφομένων ὁμοίως λέγεσθαι, ἐπεὶ δέ
τινες ἐπλεόνασαν ἐν ταῖς κακολογίαις τὸ μέτρον, ἐκεῖθεν τὸ ἰαμβίζειν εἰς
τὸ ὑβρίζειν ὑπὸ τῆς συνηθείας ἐκπεσεῖν....

Others say that [iambos] derives from a certain maidservant, Iambe, Thracian by race. This woman, they say, when Demeter was angry because of
the rape of her daughter, in the vicinity of Eleusis went to the goddess who
was sitting on the rock that is now called Mirthless, and by means of certain
jokes she caused the goddess to laugh. Seemingly iambos in the old days
was a name equally given to pieces written for blame and praise (ἔπαινος),
when certain individuals exceeded the norm in their abuse. From then on
composing iambic traditionally degenerated into violence....

Photius argues that the earliest *iambos* had embraced both mockery and
praise, perhaps combining the two in ironic praise. I suggest that neither
mockery nor praise was so extreme as to drown out the other, but both
flowed back and forth between cultic participants in an ongoing exchange.
Over time and as the cultic penumbra receded, the increasingly devastating
impact of the mockery and blame had created an imbalance. Women's

cultic voices, raised in safe and sanctioned mockery and jest, had shaped a genre from which they seemed exiled.

Hellenistic writers also describe Iambe as an old woman.[45] Her immunity from a harsh response to, her aggressive joking may be explained by the relative freedom granted to old women in archaic and classical Greece. Young girls and women of childbearing years were more constrained in what they could do or say. As we shall see, if Iambe was imagined as a girl, the ricocheting jokes endangered her.

Death and the Maiden

In some stories Iambe commited suicide. An ancient account says that iambic was named

> ἢ ἀπὸ Ἰάμβης οὕτω καλουμένης κόρης, ἥτις αἰσχρῶς ὑβρισθεῖσα ἀγχόνη κατέλυσε τὸν βίον, ὅπερ καὶ αἱ Λυκαμβίδες ἐπὶ τοῖς Ἀρχιλόχου ποιήμασιν.

or from the girl called Iambe, who, having been shamefully abused (ὑβρισθεῖσα), ended her life, just as the daughters of Lycambes did because of the poems of Archilochus.[46]

The participle ὑβρισθεῖσα, a term that I translated as "abused," has a range of meanings; ὑβρίζειν means to attack – physically or verbally – or to indulge in excess: to be guilty of anything from impertinence to sexual wantonness to rape. It could appropriately describe both Iambe's (sexual) joking and some reciprocal excess on the part of another individual. What do these suicide stories mean?[47] There is more than one way to approach an answer.

One way is to consider her death as reflecting cultic polarities.[48] Iambe, the crone near death, or the unwed girl embracing death, is like the situation she confronts in the *Hymn*: an old woman and a prematurely dying girl. Iambe is the antitype of the mature female, and yet she restores wholeness to the mother goddess. She conjures life through women's speech, revealing fertility – their own or the fertility they induce in another – in women who seem least fruitful. In its very incongruity the miracle is all the more uncanny and wonderful. As we have seen in the discussion of the Thesmophoria, dead piglets – a fusion of the unripe and the overripe – form an essential part of the magical "compost" placed by the women-celebrants on the unploughed fields. There are, in Greek tradition, several myths of girls hanging themselves. These stories are associated with, and indeed usually function as, etiological "explanations" for fertility rituals, featuring figurines or images of deities hanging from trees.[49] It is therefore quite possible that "Iambe as hanging suicide" symbolizes, paradoxically, hope and new life, when viewed from a cultic perspective.[50]

Another approach is to see the suicide stories as marking the socially fraught transition from cult to literature, or at least reflecting the perspective of the noncultic world. Women might – and should – joke within certain cults of Demeter, but the suicide stories communicated that they could not transfer those jokes to a wider, literary world without being judged, isolated, and humiliated. We should remember here that the male iambicist often uttered his abusive taunts from the position of a lone outsider. The Mnesiepes Inscription on Paros, described later, tells us that Archilochus was tried and punished by the Parians for singing "too iambically" a song (probably obscene) in honor of Dionysus. According to another source the poet suffered exile. The iambic poet was linked with the lone wolf, the solitary and sneaky predator always hoping to attack the homestead from without. But whereas a man could exist and maintain a credible identity as a wolfish outsider, or a "trickster" figure, living a picaresque life, a woman could not. Outside of cult women, especially marriageable girls or those of childbearing age, faced annihilation if they drew attention to themselves by joking or laughing.

Let me offer an analogue here, to illuminate the ideological forces that could have prompted Iambe's paradoxical fates. *Genesis* 18 describes how, upon discovering that Sarah would bear a son in her ninetieth year, first Abraham, and later Sarah herself laughed. God heard Sarah's laughter (there is no mention of a reaction to Abraham's) and asked Abraham if anything was too hard for the Lord. Clearly he has interpreted her laughter as that of a skeptic. Sarah denied that she had laughed – but God insisted that indeed she had. When later Sarah bore a son, she made two observations: "God has made laughter for me; every one who hears will laugh over me."

Sarah's words illustrate two interpretations of her laughter, one in which it is the joyful expression of unexpected fertility – and eroticism, because the name Isaac is linked both with laughter and with erotic pleasure; and one in which she is the butt of God's joke, because Jaweh has proved her wrong and made her look foolish in her old age. Jaweh does not criticize Abraham, but confines his rebuke to Sarah. The story as a whole may reflect a shift to monotheism, which caused the exclusion of women from many religious practices, the ending of sexual rituals and the cultic, erotic laughter that accompanied them.[51] The two "readings" of laughter that end the story illustrate the old world of women's laughing voices, and the new in which they become the target of male laughter.

Although in archaic Greece women's cults were not superseded as they had been in ancient Israel, there was tension between different perspectives on women's – generally sexualized – laughter. The *Odyssey's* famous contrast between Penelope's tears (and decorum) and the maidservants' mockery and laughter – and sexual misbehavior – illustrates the suspicion attached to women's joking. As city-states developed, and with them a civic life and overwhelmingly male "public" culture, women's public conduct came under a more critical scrutiny. And from the vantage point of this more segregated world, harsh criticism and admonitory stories emerged in the new genre of iambic.

Eustathius linked the suicidal "Lycambides" (Daughters of Lycambes) – the victims of Archilochus' iambic attacks – to Iambe.[52] She was a maiden (*kore*) who ended her life after she had been insulted (*hybristheisa*). This is how his story begins:

Ἰστέον δὲ ὅτι πολλῶν προσώπων ἀψαμένων βρόχους ἐπὶ λύπαις ἔπαθον οὕτω κατὰ τὴν παλαιὰν ἱστορίαν καὶ οἱ Λυκαμβίδαι ἐπὶ τοῖς Ἀρχιλόχου ποιήμασι, μὴ φέροντες τὴν ἐπιφορὰν τῶν ἐκείνου σκωμμάτων. ἦν γὰρ ὁ ἀνὴρ δεινὸς ὑβρίζειν. ὅθεν καὶ παροιμία ἐπὶ τῶν οὕτω σκώπτειν εὐφυῶν τὸ Ἀρχίλοχον πεπτάτηκας· ὡς εἴ τις εἴπη σκορπίον ἢ ὄφιν ἢ κακὴν ἄκανθην. καὶ κόρη δέ τις φασὶν Ἰάμβη αἰσχρῶς ὑβρισθεῖσα κατέλυσε τὸν βίον ἀγχόνη.

One must realize that many individuals, having tied nooses around their necks on account of their griefs, had suffered as did also the Lycambides (οἱ Λυκαμβίδαι) according to the ancient story, because of the poems of Archilochus, being unable to bear the onslaught of his jests. For the man was terrible in his attacks (δεινὸς ὑβρίζειν). Whence comes the proverb regarding those who are in this way clever at joking: "you have trodden on Archilochus," as if one were to say "you have stepped on a scorpion or snake or prickly acanthus." And they say that a certain maiden, Iambe, having been shamefully insulted (ὑβρισθεῖσα), ended her life in a noose.

Eustathius then notes the disproportion between the severe iambic "response" and its "cause" – hence the iambic foot: short followed by long.

Women in Iambic Literature

When one casts an eye over iambic literature as a whole, it is quickly apparent how narrow in range is the portrayal of women. Women tend to be intemperate in every respect, especially sexually. Whether attractive or (more commonly) ugly, one has the sense of viewing "them" through the wrong end of a telescope. One's male co-drinkers may be close at hand, but the women mostly seem (thankfully) far away, seen only through the contemptuous eyes of the narrator-poet. There is irony in contemplating iambic's roots in women's own cultic joking.

Sexual jokes and encounters – often unconventional – insults and invective, eating and drinking – often excessive – poverty, animal fables, ugly people, and lowlife characters characterize many of the extant fragments. The poet-narrator himself often appears as a colorful and undignified character in his burlesque tales. Hipponax describes a scene in which he is beaten by a woman, spatters himself with his own excrement, and thus attracts a horde of dung beetles.[53] Sexual intercourse takes place on the ground in another Hipponactean fragment; both he and Archilochus describe fellatio performed by a woman on a man. In one Semonidean fragment a prostitute prepares to annoint herself before the arrival of a sailor (16), and in a snippet of Archilochus (34) unnamed women announce that they will not provide a ferry service without payment.[54] This is probably a sexual double entendre, and the speakers probably are prostitutes negotiating their fee (possibly the infamous daughters of Lycambes, of whom more later).[55] Hipponax names Arete, the mistress (and sister perhaps?) of his enemy and target, Bupalus, who is also called a motherfucker.

It is difficult to say anything with certainty about these poems' overall structures, given the fragmentary state of the corpus. In some cases, such as the famous Cologne Epode, a dialogue between a man and a woman is framed by a narrator's first-person introduction. In others he addresses his target or some other imagined interlocutor directly; sometimes he just rants in a generalized way.

Women in iambic were sometimes lecherous, ill favored but made up to look younger than they really are, and shameless in their sexual practices (fellatio was regarded as a degrading sexual service, for example).[56] As we shall see most clearly in the Semonidean diatribe against women, their generally degraded appearance and conduct rendered them animalistic rather than human, fitting denizens of iambic's sordid world.[57] Yet sometimes the representation of women seems less contemptuous. For example, what are we to make of the lovely fragments 30 and 31 in West/Gerber?

ἔχουσα θαλλὸν μυρσίνης ἐτέρπετο
ῥοδῆς τε καλὸν ἄνθος.

She rejoiced in having the bloom of myrtle
and the lovely flower of a rose.

ἡ δέ οἱ κόμη
ὤμους κατεσκίαζε καὶ μετάφρενα.

...her hair
shadowed her shoulders and back.[58]

Similarly, Hipponax wishes for a beautiful and delicate girl in a poetic line that is itself delicate and lovely.[59] Without more it is impossible to decide on the tone here – yet there is a grace in these allusions that jars with the ribald contempt elsewhere.[60] Perhaps these fragments derive from complex iambic narratives, where the tone and mood can shift suddenly.[61]

The Cologne Epode shows that iambic mockery could be nuanced and complex.[62] The narrator describes a meeting in a remote spot. The fragment picks up in the midst of his negotiation with a girl; the girl recommends self-control on both their parts; if he is really driven by his desires – then she recommends (seriously or disingenuously?) a lovely tender girl in her own household as a substitute. The man replies with a respectful address: Daughter of Amphimedo; he urges what seems to be coitus interruptus – but repudiates the girl's offer of another lover.[63] He now names the proffered substitute as Neobule – a woman infamous since antiquity for having been so savagely lampooned by Archilochus that she killed herself. The tone of the discourse shifts from courteous to vicious as he describes Neobule as "overripe" (πεπείρα) and notoriously lecherous. Anyone who weds her will be a neighborhood joke; he wishes her gone with violent emphasis. Having concluded his remarks, the poem again seems to shift as the narrator describes his tender sexual approaches to the timid girl, and his own emission of his "force" (μένος), as he touched her fair (pubic) hair.

At first glance one might say that Archilochus's verbal treatment of his lover (as opposed to Neobule) is as restrained and gentle as their physical encounter, although such a story – if purveyed to a group of his male friends – will injure the younger girl, given what we know about ancient

notions of womanly virtue.[64] There was a belief in archaic and classical
Greece that women's sexuality – if not contained by marriage – had a dangerous and destructive effect.[65] Instant aging and decay of the woman
followed an unsanctioned liaison. Thus it seems possible, if not likely, that
Neobule's metamophosis from nubile ingenue to rabid hag awaits this tender girl also – as a result of the very encounter described here.[66] Perhaps she
is the sister of Neobule mentioned by the "biographies" of the Archilochian
tradition. Both girls, daughters of Lycambes (the "Lycambides"), committed suicide as a result of the disgrace brought upon them by Archilochus,
in some accounts.[67]

The cause of the quarrel between Archilochus and the Lycambids, when
specified by our sources, was Lycambes's breaking of the betrothal between Archilochus and his daughter Neobule. As a result of Archilochus's
vituperative response, members of the family committed suicide; the two
daughters only in earlier accounts – Lycambes also in later. It is possible
that this tale of the jilted lover is not a biographical datum but rather an
expression of a more complex relationship between Archilochus and the
Lycambids.[68] The name "Lycambes" suggests an archetypal iambicist, with
its "wolfish" first element, and the "amb" syllable, present also in Iambe's
name.[69] His patronymic, Dot-ades, possibly connects him with Demeter
(Do-mater in Aeolic, Doso in the *Hymn*).[70] West concludes that Lycambes
and his daughters were "stock characters in a traditional entertainment
with some (perhaps forgotten) ritual basis." I argue later that the Lycambids were more than stock characters, although I agree with West that there
is no need to imagine personal enmity as inspiring the poems.

The poetry's outcome, death, is shocking. The Hipponactean corpus provides comparable scenarios, in which the sculptors Bupalus and Athenis
killed themselves after attacks by Hipponax.[71] Iambic convention credited
the tradition with a deadly power, and belief in this power was an important element of the genre and surely constituted a powerful form of social
constraint.

Thus although iambic shared many themes with what developed
as old comedy, its social impact was markedly different. In old comedy
the ribaldry and shameless disorder, the focus on the lower body and the
belly, the insults and cast of disreputable characters bespoke an unserious,
permissive world. We hear of only one possible victim of comic mockery
driven to suicide, an exception to prove the rule.[72] Conversely, iambic functioned as a form of social repression; the mutual ribaldry of cult gave way to

narratives in which a preliminary insult or injury was punished so as to pre-clude further exchange. This was the essence of literary iambic, as we know it – a supreme attack to which no response was possible: a joke to silence all further exchanges, to shut the door on harmless (cultic) reciprocity. The "righteous" or successful iambic poet (and if he was successful he defined righteousness and vice) silenced all who would oppose or offend him and thereby maintained a social hierarchy – or created a new one.

It was a measure of an iambicist's effectiveness and matter of honor to respond to attack or insult with an attack of greater ferocity. As Archilochus says:

> One thing I know – a great one:
> To respond to him who has wronged me with terrible wrongs.

> ἓν δ᾽ ἐπίσταμαι μέγα
> τὸν κακῶς ⟨μ᾽⟩ ἔρδοντα δεινοῖς ἀνταμείβεσθαι κακοῖς.[73]

The repetition of the κακ-root ("wronged … wrongs") with an intensifying adjective (terrible) illustrates how the poet prides himself on escalating the conflict. Indeed, as is evident from Eustathius's comments on iambic cited earlier, this excess was felt to be intrinsic to the genre. The themes of exchange, excess, and the establishment of a (new) social order, appear in a story by Aristotle, cited by Athenaeus.[74]

Ἀριστοτέλης ἐν τῇ Ναξίων πολιτείᾳ περὶ τῆς παροιμίας (ὅτι οὐδεὶς κακὸς μέγας ἰχθύς) οὕτω γράφει· τῶν παρὰ Ναξίοις εὐπόρων οἱ μὲν πολλοὶ τὸ ἄστυ ᾤκουν, οἱ δὲ ἄλλοι διεσπαρμένοι κατὰ κώμας. ἐν οὖν δή τινι τῶν κωμῶν, ᾗ ὄνομα ἦν Ληστάδαι, Τελεσταγόρας ᾤκει πλούσιός τε σφόδρα καὶ εὐδοκιμῶν καὶ τιμώμενος παρὰ τῷ δήμῳ τοῖς τ᾽ ἄλλοις ἅπασι καὶ τοῖς καθ᾽ ἡμέραν πεμπομένοις. καὶ ὅτε καταβάντες ἐκ τῆς πόλεως δυσωνοῖντό τι τῶν πωλουμένων, ἔθος ἦν τοῖς πωλοῦσι λέγειν ὅτι μᾶλλον ἂν προέλοιντο Τελεσταγόρᾳ δοῦναι ἢ τοσούτου ἀναδόσθαι. νεανίσκοι οὖν τινες ὠνούμενοι μέγαν ἰχθύν, εἰπόντος τοῦ ἁλιέως τὰ αὐτά, λυπηθέντες τῷ πολλάκις ἀκούειν, ὑποπιόντες ἐκώμασαν πρὸς αὐτόν. δεξαμένου δὲ τοῦ Τελεσταγόρου φιλοφρόνως αὐτούς, οἱ νεανίσκοι αὐτόν τε ὕβρισαν καὶ δύο θυγατέρας αὐτοῦ ἐπιγάμους, ἐφ᾽ οἷς ἀγανακτήσαντες οἱ Νάξιοι καὶ τὰ ὅπλα ἀναλαβόντες ἐπῆλθον τοῖς νεανίσκοις· καὶ μεγίστη τότε στάσις ἐγένετο, προστατοῦντος τῶν Ναξίων Λυγδάμιδος, ὃς ἀπὸ ταύτης τῆς στρατηγίας τύραννος ἀνεφάνη τῆς πατρίδος.

Aristotle in the *Constitution of the Naxians* writes as follows regarding the proverb[75] (that a poor nobody makes a big fish). Of the affluent peo-ple among the Naxians, the majority dwelt in the town, but others were scattered throughout the villages. In one of the villages, whose name was

Lestadai there lived a man who was very rich, and well reputed and honored by the people – in all other ways, but particularly by daily gifts. And
whenever those coming from the town drove down the price of something
in the hands of merchants, it was customary for the sellers to say that they
would rather give it to Telestagoras than sell it for so little. So when the
fisherman had said this same thing to some youths buying a big fish, they,
fed up at hearing it so often, got drunk and made their way in a procession
to his house. Telestagoras welcomed them graciously, but they insulted
him and his two marriageable daughters. The Naxians were enraged by
these events, and they took up arms and marched against the youths. A
massive standoff occurred, with Lygdamis representing the Naxians. As a
result of this leadership role he emerged as tyrant of his native land.

West observes the familiar cast of characters here: an eminent citizen
and his two unwed daughters, targets of abuse. The story links dietary and
sumptuary privileges with sexual and class privilege: a metaphorical big
fish with a literal one. Indeed one might argue that the acquisition of the
fish is a metaphor for marriage into the class represented by this family.
The nameless youths are attempting to acquire an élite, luxury item –
as fish, especially large or rare fish were regarded.[76] They are refused,
and they respond by attacking a man whose place within the élite class
is assured. They do so by degrading his definitive currency: his daughters.
The story shows a contestation of value, meaning, and access to privilege. One also sees signs of struggle between a patronage system to a
more market-driven economy. The passage from oligarchy-aristocracy to
tyranny is marked by the devaluation of the women who embody traditional privilege.[77] The youths' drunken excess is the antithesis of the aristocratic symposium's decorum. Their ὕβρις – and I argue that it is an iambic
ὕβρις – causes a change in the political order – and evinces a menacing
posture toward women of rank. From the point of view of an iambicist all
women are equal(ly low). No one is beyond his hybristic reach, and no
luxury evades his contemptuous and indiscriminate consumption. The
marriageable girls, like the fish, have faded out of significance at the tale's
end.

The Poet and the Women

That the iambic poet's relationship with women was fundamental and aggressive is suggested by a tale concerning iambic's best-known exponent,
perhaps its inventor.[78] One may see here how the cult of Archilochus on

Paros reflects certain basic premises of the genre that he embodied. The poet's encounter with his "Muses" turns that traditional relationship on its head. No longer is the male poet the humble and indebted recipient of a female divinity. Instead he evinces a cheeky and aggressive stance to all females, from divinities down.

The "Mnesiepes Inscription," linked with a shrine of Archilochus on Paros, records how he embarked on his career of mockery.[79] I quote from Gerber's text and translation of the passage, beginning with the second column, which includes the beginning of continuous text[80]:

Μνησιέπει ὁ θεὸς ἔχρησε λῶιον καὶ ἄμεινον εἶμεν
ἐν τῶι τεμένει, ὃ κατασκευάζει, ἱδρυσαμένωι
βωμὸν καὶ θύοντι ἐπὶ τούτου Μούσαις καὶ Ἀπόλλ[ω]ν[ι]
Μουσαγέται καὶ Μνημοσύνει· θύειν δὲ καὶ καλλιερεῖν Διὶ Ὑπερδεξίωι, Ἀθάναι Ὑπερδεξίαι,
Ποσειδῶνι Ἀσφαλείωι, Ἡρακλεῖ, Ἀρτέμιδι Εὐκλείαι.
Πυθῶδε τῶι Ἀπόλλωνι σωτήρια πέμπειν.
Μνησιέπει ὁ θεὸς ἔχρησε λῶιον καὶ ἄμεινον εἶμεν
ἐν τῶι τεμένει, ὃ κατασκευάζει, ἱδρυσαμένωι
βωμὸν καὶ θύοντι ἐπὶ τούτου Διονύσωι καὶ Νύμφαις
καὶ Ὥραις· θύειν δὲ καὶ καλλιερεῖν Ἀπόλλωνι
Προστατηρίωι, Ποσειδῶνι Ἀσφαλείωι, Ἡρακλεῖ.
Πυθῶδε τῶι Ἀπόλλωνι σωτήρια πέμπειν.
Μνησιέπει ὁ θεὸς ἔχρησε λῶιον καὶ ἄμεινον εἶμεν
τιμῶντι Ἀρχίλοχον τὸμ ποιητάν, καθ' ἃ ἐπινοεῖ.
  χρήσαντος δὲ τοῦ Ἀπόλλωνος ταῦτα τόν τε τόπον
  καλοῦμεν Ἀρχιλόχειον καὶ τοὺς βωμοὺς ἱδρύμεθα
  καὶ θύομεν καὶ τοῖς θεοῖς καὶ Ἀρχιλόχωι καὶ
  τιμῶμεν αὐτόν, καθ' ἃ ὁ θεὸς ἐθέσπισεν ἡμῖν.
  περὶ δὲ ὧν ἠβουλήθημεν ἀναγράψαι, τάδε παρα-
  δέδοταί τε ἡμῖν ὑπὸ τῶν ἀρχαίων καὶ αὐτοὶ πεπρα-
  γματεύμεθα. λέγουσι γὰρ Ἀρχίλοχον ἔτι νεώτερον
  ὄντα πεμφθέντα ὑπὸ τοῦ πατρὸς Τελεσικλέους
  εἰς ἀγρόν, εἰς τὸν δῆμον, ὃς καλεῖται Λειμῶνες,
  ὥστε βοῦν καταγαγεῖν εἰς πρᾶσιν, ἀναστάντα
  πρωίτερον τῆς νυκτός, σελήνης λαμπούσης,
  [ἄ]γειν τὴμ βοῦν εἰς πόλιν. ὡς δ' ἐγένετο κατὰ τὸν
  τόπον, ὃς καλεῖται Λισσίδες, δόξαι γυναῖκας
  [ἰ]δεῖν ἀθρόας. νομίσαντα δ' ἀπὸ τῶν ἔργων ἀπιέναι
  αὐτὰς εἰς πόλιν προσελθόντα σκώπτειν, τὰς δὲ
  δέξασθαι αὐτὸν μετὰ παιδιᾶς καὶ γέλωτος καὶ
  [ἐ]περωτῆσαι, εἰ πωλήσων ἄγει τὴμ βοῦν· φήσαντος δὲ
  [εἰ]πεῖν, ὅτι αὐταὶ δώσουσιν αὐτῶι τιμὴν ἀξίαν.

[ρη]θέντων δὲ τούτων αὐτὰς μὲν οὐδὲ τὴμ βοῦν οὐκέτι
[φ]ανερὰς εἶναι, πρὸ τῶν ποδῶν δὲ λύραν ὁρᾶν αὐτόν.
καταπλαγέντα δὲ καὶ μετά τινα χρόνον ἔννουν
[γ]ενόμενον ὑπολαβεῖν τὰς Μούσας εἶναι τὰς φανείσας
[καὶ] τὴν λύραν αὐτῶι δωρησαμένας· καὶ ἀνελό-
[μ]ενον αὐτὴν πορεύεσθαι εἰς πόλιν καὶ τῶι πατρὶ
[τὰ] γενόμενα δηλῶσαι. τὸν δὲ Τελεσικλῆν ἀκού-
[σ]αντα καὶ τὴν λύραν ἰδόντα θαυμάσαι· καὶ πρῶτομ
μὲν ζήτησιν ποιήσασθαι τῆς βοὸς κατὰ πᾶσαν
[τ]ὴν νῆσον καὶ οὐ δύνασθαι εὑρεῖν· ἔπειθ᾽ ὑπὸ τῶν
[π]ολιτῶν θεοπρόπον εἰς Δελφοὺς εἰρημένον μετὰ
[Λυ]κάμβου χρησόμενον ὑπὲρ τῆς πόλεως προθυμό-
[τ]ερον ἀποδημῆσαι, βουλόμενον καὶ περὶ τῶν
[α]ὑτοῖς συμβεβηκότων πυθέσθαι· ἀφικομένων δὲ
[κ]αὶ εἰσιόντων αὐτῶν εἰς τὸ μαντεῖον τὸν θεὸν
εἰπεῖν Τελεσικλεῖ τὸν χρησμὸν τόνδε·
[Ἀ]θάνατός σοι παῖς καὶ ἀοίδιμος, ὦ Τελεσίκλεις,
ἔσται ἐν ἀνθρώποισιν, ὃς ἂμ πρῶτός σε προσείπει
νηὸς ἀποθρώισκοντα φίλην εἰς πατρίδα γαῖαν.
    παραγενομένων δ᾽ αὐτῶν εἰς Πάρον τοῖς Ἀρτε-
μισίοις πρῶτον τῶν παίδων Ἀρχίλοχον ἀπαν-
τήσαντα προσειπεῖν τὸμ πατέρα·

The god declared to Mnesiepes that it was preferable and better to set up an altar in the precinct which he was constructing and to sacrifice on it to the Muses and Apollo Mousagetes and Mnemosyne, and also to sacrifice and obtain favourable omens from Zeus Hyperdexios, Athena Hyperdexia, Poseidon Asphaleios, Heracles, and Artemis Eukleia, and to send thank-offerings to Apollo at Pytho.

The god declared to Mnesiepes that it was preferable and better to set up an altar in the precinct which he was constructing and to sacrifice on it to Dionysus and the Nymphs and the Seasons, and also to sacrifice and obtain favourable omens from Apollo Prostaterios, Poseidon Asphaleios, and Heracles, and to send thank-offerings to Apollo at Pytho.

The god declared to Mnesiepes that it was preferable and better to honour the poet Archilochus in accordance with his intentions.

Since Apollo declared these things, we call the place the Archilocheion and we set up altars and we sacrifice both to the gods and to Archilochus and we honour him in accordance with the god's oracular response to us. Concerning the matters which we wished to inscribe, these have both been handed down to us by men of old and we have elaborated on them ourselves. They say that when Archilochus was still a young man he had been sent by his father Telesicles into the country, to the district which is called Leimones, to bring a cow for sale. He got up before the end of night, while the moon was shining, and was bringing the cow to town, and when he was at a place which is called Lissides, he thought he saw a group of women. Believing that they were on their way from their work to the town, he approached and bantered with them. They received him with jesting and laughter and asked if he was bringing the cow to sell it. When he said that he was, they replied that they would themselves give him a fitting price. After these words were spoken, neither they nor the cow were any longer visible, but before his feet he saw a lyre. He was astounded and when he recovered his senses after a while he assumed that it was the Muses who had appeared to him and that they had given him the lyre. He picked it up, went to the town, and revealed to his father what had happened. When Telesicles heard the story and saw the lyre he was amazed. First he conducted a search for the cow through the whole island and was unable to find it. Then, having been chosen by the citizens to go with Lycambes to Delphi to consult the oracle on behalf of the city, he was more eager to make the trip because he wanted to inquire about what had happened to them. After their arrival and entrance to the oracular seat the god gave Telesicles the following response:

> Immortal and renowned in song among men, Telesicles, will be whichever son of yours first speaks to you as you leap from your ship onto your beloved homeland.

> When they arrived in Paros at the festival of Artemis, Archilochus was the first of the sons to meet and speak to his father [the text, which becomes more fragmentary shortly after this point, continues, speaking of the Parians' judgment against Archilochus, and their punishment by Dionysus].

The "trade" of the cow for the lyre made Archilochus's apparently random jesting into the first moment of a literary career. His first audience took what he said both seriously and lightly; they were not insulted, but they recognized his authority as a singer of iambic,[81] Archilochus originally believed himself to be directing his banter against an unidentified throng of women (γυναῖκας...ἀθρόας, 28–9). Although his target turned out to be supernatural women, the story suggests that iambic poetry would direct itself frequently and comprehensively against women in the future. An epitaph for the Lycambids in the *Palatine Anthology* accuses Archilochus of using his fine speech for a "war with women."[82] Plutarch also accuses Archilochus of coarse and indecorous attacks "against women."[83]

A curious feature of the Mnesiepes passage is its use of the verb ὑπολαβεῖν to describe Archilochus's belief that he had encountered the Muses. The verb often denotes a false or unexamined belief, hence Gerber's translation as "assumed." The women whom Archilochus meets are described as coming ἀπὸ τῶν ἔργων ("out of the tilled fields"), an expression that suggests they were linked with Demeter and her agrarian world. Some scholars have identified them with the Hours or Graces, deities who would fit in Demeter's world.[84] The inscription as a whole, with its emphatic references to Apollo, and its use of Apollo's oracle to authorize Archilochus, suggests a transition from a feminine, agrarian world to a Panhellenic and patriarchal realm, where the poet must establish himself.

Semonides on Women

I introduce this famous poem to show, as in the case of the Homeric *Hymn to Demeter*, how elements of women's Demetrian cults lie buried in a text that comes from a strongly masculinist perspective. In this case, of course, the poem displays the virulent misogyny, characteristic of the iambic genre generally. Poem 7 of Semonides attacked wives in a prolonged broadside, in iambic trimeters.[85] This poem is important both for its ambitious scope and for the evidence it presents of the context – agrarian and cultic – for iambic poems. This pageant of horrible wives initially gives the impression of being a dour monologue, emanating from a single perspective. Yet if one reads between the lines, there are traces of a complex and interactive discourse: iambic's cultic birthplace. This is what I intend here.

The poem begins with the telling word "apart": it was apart – from men presumably – that god made the mind of women in the beginning.[86] The poem is premised on a sense of women as profoundly alien. The distinction that matters is gender; it slices through every other category, including class. The verses that follow divided this "foreign matter" into its constituents. The female mind sprang from the pig, vixen, dog, mud, the sea, a donkey, weasel, mare, monkey. These "types" were hatefully and consistently verbal: the dog woman was gossipy and loud (12–20); the vixen uttered an unpredictable mixture of bad and good things (7–11); nearly all women liked to gossip about sex (90–1); all wives picked fights at home (103–5). Despite this accusation, however, we do not hear the women's actual voices, of course, only the poem's hostile characterization of them. Yet how incessantly they seem to have rung in the poet's ears. I note that the dog-woman's husband is described as being unable to silence her *even if he knocks out her teeth with a stone* (17–18): a form of violence especially apt in iambic contexts, where blaming and verbal assault evokes the carnivorous bite of an animal.[87] In other words, the dog woman's threatened teeth suggest a female iambic voice responding to male rebukes and insults.

Homeliness was also a recurring theme; the pig woman was fat and squalid; the weasel was also ill-favored and evil smelling; the monkey was ugliest of all. A wife's ugliness made a man a laughing stock – and rendered odious his need to beget the new generation of workers on the farm. One senses an almost neurotic revulsion in fact. Women are not just "other" but nightmarishly repellant.[88]

Two of the group were sexually voracious: the donkey and the weasel. Two were unreliable and unpredictable: the vixen and the sea woman. Three were notably lazy: the mud woman, the donkey, and the mare. Three were consumers: the mud woman and donkey ate their husbands out of house and home; the mare spent her husband's income adorning herself. There was one thief (the weasel), one nosy gossip (the dog), one fool (the mud woman), and one trouble maker and trickster (the monkey).

The poet's iambic rage is fueled by the exigencies of Demeter's demanding work. Men needed reliable and competent companions to eke a living from the soil, and they required healthy and not-too-repellent partners on whom to beget children. Begetting children within a marriage was itself regarded as a kind of work analogous to that of the fields (*ergon*).[89] A wife was necessary, but her flaws could injure her husband by humiliating him within his community, or even driving him to starve: social or literal death.

The list reflects the perspective of someone directly dependent on land cultivation.[90] Moreover, it is a tough, subsistence life. Such a man needed his wife to perform like a productive work and breeding animal. Thus the mare woman was annoyingly fastidious because she disliked soot and sweeping animal dung from the dwelling. The mare is the type of an aristocratic woman – just as only kings or tyrants could afford horses – and the poet implies that such a wife is just as undesirable as the rest.[91]

The bee is the last creature on Semonides' list, and it is she who brings us back most clearly to the world of Demeter's cult:

τὴν δ᾽ ἐκ μελίσσης· τήν τις εὐτυχεῖ λαβών·
κείνη γὰρ οἴη μῶμος οὐ προσίζάνει,
θάλλει δ᾽ ὑπ᾽ αὐτῆς κἀπαέξεται βίος,
φίλη δὲ σὺν φιλέοντι γηράσκει πόσει
τεκοῦσα καλὸν κὠνομάκλυτον γένος.
κἀριπρεπὴς μὲν ἐν γυναιξὶ γίνεται
πάσῃσι, θείη δ᾽ ἀμφιδέδρομεν χάρις.

οὐδ᾿ ἐν γυναιξὶν ἥδεται καθημένη
ὅκου λέγουσιν ἀφροδισίους λόγους
τοίας γυναῖκας ἀνδράσιν χαρίζεται
Ζεὺς τὰς ἀρίστας καὶ πολυφραδεστάτας·

And one kind of woman (he made) from a bee; in getting her
a man is lucky;
on her alone blame does not alight
At her hands life blooms and grows.
In affection she grows old with her loving spouse
having borne a fair and glorious family.
She is distinguished among all women,
and a divine grace encircles her.
She takes no joy in sitting among women,
where they speak of sexual things.
Wives such as this Zeus gives as a grace to men,
the best and the most resourceful. (83–93)

As with the others, the bee woman's nature is judged from a utilitarian, male perspective. An incongruous metaphor describes the bee's unique freedom from iambic blame: a negative compliment, immediately rescinded. On the bee woman alone blame does not alight; the verb προσίζάνει suggests that iambic blame is itself an insect; the bee woman, like all women, is susceptible to its cruel sting.[92] In fact her appearance in this poem shows that even the bee cannot escape iambic's venom.

Although each woman's appearance and conduct declares which beast or substance forms the basis for her disposition – her husband often fails to see the relationship between her exterior and her interior, or chooses to praise her in public so as to protect his own dignity. Foolish or conniving husbands constitute iambic targets corresponding to these hateful women. A husband is especially gullible in the case of a woman who seems particularly self-controlled: a preliminary warning that any appearance of virtue is probably fake.

The bee's final epithet – πολυφραδεστάτη – is ambiguous, meaning "most resourceful," "most eloquent," "most talked of," or "most intelligent." The word combines notions of cleverness, speech – and notoriety. In the *Theogony*, in one of its two appearances in extant epic, the adjective describes the deceitful words of Gaia, which enabled Zeus to trick Cronos and usurp his throne.[93] The bee cannot escape calumny; the poet's very language is freighted with the misogyny permeating the Greek literary tradition as a whole.

The bee woman caused life to flourish nevertheless. The words θάλλει (blooms) and ἐπαέξεται (grows) evoked Demeter's patronage of human and agrarian fertility. An ancient scholar noted that the name μέλισσαι (bees) was given to priestesses of Demeter, and by extension to priestesses of other divinities were (inaccurately) called bees "because of the creature's purity."[94] The historian Apollodorus of Athens observed that priestesses of Demeter were known as μέλισσαι, explaining that the goddess Demeter had taken refuge with king Melissos and his sixty daughters on Paros, an iambic island, following the rape of Persephone. She gave the girls the cloth that Persephone had been weaving and told them first of Persephone's fate and about the mysteries. Whence comes the name μέλισσαι for those women who celebrate the Thesmophoria.[95]

Bees constituted an apt emblem for women, as perceived from the standpoint of the Thesmophoria. They lived in a house, populated it with new generations, and filled it with honey. They constituted a community that transcended the "nuclear" family, headed by a single patriarch. And their contributions to the common weal required a freedom of movement that came into conflict with the ideology of "containment" of women.

Ideally Greek women stayed home, prepared and preserved household stores, and avoided public notice and speech – literary or political. *Aidos* (αἰδώς) – a sense of one's "place" – was the moral dimension of this thrift and reticence. In reality, however, women needed to move in an out of the house, like bees, whose accumulation of nectar required them repeatedly to cross the threshold of their home.[96] Most of all, religious cults required women to engage in public speech and responsibility – activities vital to the community but necessarily compromising the perfect self-containment of the *oikos* and the women in it. A story told by Servius exemplifies this tension between containment and useful interaction with the world.[97] An old woman living at the Isthmus, Melissa, refused to divulge the secrets of Demeter's rites, entrusted to her by the goddess. The local women, enraged when she refused to tell them, tore her apart. Demeter sent a plague to the neighborhood and caused bees to be born from Melissa's body. Her body, emblem of courageous reticence and extreme disclosure, became a hive (the first?) in this account.

Semonides railed against women from the standpoint of the single household, where one woman was both necessary (for children, above all) and a constant bane. Yet in fact bees were the only truly communal animal on his list. Their usefulness to man depended on their cooperation with each other outside their individual homes. The poem also shows how their supposed sexuality was fraught with contradiction. Semonides commended "bee women" as superior because they did not gossip about sex (*ta aphrodisia*), yet sex was a major topic among women in Demeter's cults, while sexual abstinence was also required of cult participants, evoking the bee's supposed chastity.[98] Overall, the poem's recognition of women as agents and speakers within the vital cult that inspired iambic is perceptible as a faint outline beneath the vivid iambic cartoons. And the muffled sounds of women's cultic voices – acerbic, sexual, mocking – emerge from the caricatures of this male respondent.

Conclusion: Women as Agents

Literary iambic came to function as an instrument of social control in the hands of men. In one sense the suicide stories (regarding Iambe and Lycambids) speak the truth; women's joking-iambic voices have been virtually eradicated from the literary record. Yet there is no reason to assume that women submitted to the "rules" implicit in iambic or that they acquiesced in iambic's characterization of women. A vivid weave of fear and stress runs throughout iambic tradition, as we have seen. The bonds between men, and a man's standing within a society were fragile, especially in the tight and volatile island societies that incubated the genre. Iambic poems imply that social and (especially) sexual rules could be a matter of life and death. The insistent, even neurotic, bombast of the tradition suggests not compliance but contestation of those rules and the categories they implied. Women in their cultic roles experienced the exhilaration of a joking and mockery, which joined them in a community. They recognized bonds that transcended class, the ranks of gods and mortals, the living and the dead. These bonds challenged the strategy of Zeus and Hades to assign Persephone as Hades' bride, isolating her from her female companions and her mother. In its mythic origin and essence women's cultic laughter defied male authority. I suggest that in actual celebration it did so also and that male iambic responded – with interest – to the challenge.

　　An important question remains: were women's voices confined to cultic or domestic contexts? Were their jibes ever organized as poetry, with an existence beyond a single, cultic context? Women could and did curse or revile, just as they could make private or cultic jokes, and indeed in the Hellenistic period the woman Myro or Moiro wrote a collection of poems called *Arai* or *Curses*.[99] Cursing was linked to literary *iambos*.[100] Archilochus (or Hipponax) in a famous fragment wishes a ghastly shipwreck on a man who has betrayed him, and Horace's Fifth *Epode* culminates in a curse of a young boy on the women who are about to murder him in a diabolical rite. There is also a reference by the late mythographer Conon to the famous tale of Tereus and Procne. Following the rape of Philomela, Tereus cut out her tongue δεδιὼς τὸν ἐκ λόγων θρίαμβον, "fearing the *thriambos* from her words." Brown suggests that Tereus was intent on preventing his victim from uttering an articulate curse.[101] The word *thriambos* is disputed in meaning, but ancient sources associate it with the *iambos*.[102] If Brown is correct, we see here an extreme example of a woman's access to abusive, retaliatory speech (iambic, or some variant thereof) being denied.

Plutarch notes in his *Life of Lycourgos* the remarkable degree to which Spartan girls lived their lives in the public eye, exercising and dancing and singing at certain festivals. Such songs might include praise of young men present in their audience and mockery of individuals whose faults or inadequacies merited censure. Plutarch observes that even lighthearted taunts carried weight, because they were uttered in the presence of the kings and elders.[103] Such mockery by women may be particularly linked with highly militarized contexts; one may recall Hector's anxiety in *Iliad* 6 about the shame he would feel before Trojan men *and* women, if he were not to engage in battle on the plain of Troy but instead defend the city's ramparts, as Andromache advises.[104]

As discussed in Chapter 1, women's choruses, expert in insult, took part in various cults. At the Argive Hybristica men and women exchanged clothes and fought; the fight commemorated a victory by the women of Argos, led by Telesilla, against the Spartans.[105] The fact that Telesilla was a woman and a poet, whose victory was reenacted every year, is most interesting. Cultic authority and poetic voice seem to have united in the mysterious figure of this Argive woman.

Formally constituted, and even trained, choruses might have represented an early step on the road from cult to "literature." In such situations the question of authorship is difficult.[106] Whose voice are we hearing? Alcman's seventh-century *Partheneion* or *Maiden Song*, the text of which reflects a contest between two or more choruses of young girls in honor of the Spartan goddess (Artemis) Orthia, has seemed to some scholars to contain elements of mutual mockery or jest, although it is notoriously obscure and debated in meaning.[107] In this case the (male) poet claimed authorship of the entire work, which might have grown out of an ancient female interchoral exchange, possibly directed by a male chorus leader or leaders.

Ancient lyric affords evidence for individual or choral dialogue, probably deriving from ritual origins. A careful examination is necessary because "petrified" dialogue is easily mistaken for the work of a single poet. What were once separate voices may no longer be distinguishable in a written text; a god addressed may have been felt to be actually "present," perhaps represented by a human actor. As Adrados observes, "We are entitled to suppose, on the evidence of Literary Lyric, that the role of the word in the archaic rituals was greater than the direct evidences might give us to believe. And this applied even to rituals of *agon* type – chorus confronting chorus; one individual confronting another, each in principle at the head of a chorus; individual or chorus confronting the citizens. For the themes of persuasion, aggression, and ridicule are all central to Greek Lyric."[108]

With this in mind, let us (re)consider the Archilochean corpus, and in particular the supposedly biographical material regarding his relations with the family of Lycambes.[109] What has survived as the solo literary attacks of Archilochus may have originated in an acerbic exchange connected with the cult of Demeter.[110] Thus when we read in Eustathius: "Archilochus – the one they say was the first to use the meter – employed the iambos in response to the *hybris* (πρὸϛ ὕβριν) of the Lycambids," that word *hybris* may refer to institutionalized hostility, not the social humiliation of a broken betrothal.[111] Unfortunately for the Lycambids, Archilochus went on to define the genre of iambic by "escalating" the exchange; his response was so devastating as to destroy them. Eustathius sees the iambic meter itself, with its long syllable following the short, as reflecting this ancient aggression – a response out of proportion to the initial offense.[112]

This conventional hostility on the part of the Lycambids was perhaps not purely cultic. It also may have had a literary dimension. The terms for Lycambes' family – Lycambides, Lycambiades, Lycambidai – recall that of the Homeridai of Chios: a "school" of individuals responsibile for a cult of the poet Homer and also for the transmission of a poetic tradition, and in this sense claiming to be the (intellectual) "sons" of Homer.[113] The Lycambids, in contrast, are feminine in all but one (questionable) account.[114] I suggest that the Lycambids originally were associated with cultic mockery, given and taken. Like the Deliades of the Homeric *Hymn to Apollo*, they additionally may have had public status as singers.[115] These "daughters of Delos" were charged with singing hymns to Apollo, Leto, and Artemis, tales of heroic men and women of old – and they could also speak the part of others so well as to convince onlookers. The Lycambides, as singers within the iambic tradition, might have mocked Archilochus in sexual terms, using narratives featuring dialogue just as Archilochus himself did. The kind of insult they could have uttered (directly or in narrative form) is the premise for the *Eighth Epode* of Horace: "You are an impotent nobody – as a man, and as an iambic poet."[116] (The poem is an extended and [of course] insulting rebuttal; the addressee's overwhelming ugliness make sexual overtures all but impossible). Horace's putative Greek model, I suggest, was inspired either by the insults that women (were known to have) joked about in cultic contexts – or by actual poems, in circulation. Thus many of the Greek iambic fragments commenting on women's repellant ugliness and sexual voraciousness derive from dialogue – cultic, literary, or both.

The women recorded by male iambicists can give back as good as they get. Fragment 25 of Hipponax appears to be a vigorous cursing exchange between a man and a woman:

"'ἀπό σ' ὀλέσειεν Ἄρτεμις." "σὲ δὲ κὠπόλλων."

"May Artemis destroy you!" "And may Apollo destroy you!"

And what do we make of the Archilochean line:

τῇ μὲν ὕδωρ ἐφόρει
δολοφρονέουσα χειρί, θἠτέρῃ δὲ πῦρ.

With deceitful thoughts she was carrying water in one hand,
Fire in the other?[117]

This accomplished trickster evinces a hostile agenda, with a strategy veering from one extreme to another. Her weaponry recalls the battle between the old men and old women in the opening of Aristophanes' *Lysistrata*. These women douse the old men's (f)ire – literally and metaphorically – with a mixture of threat, cajolery, and mockery. Here the combatant seems less than pacifist in her ultimate intention. She plans to extinguish the narrator's iambic or rapacious fire, but she herself also has the power – and intention – to inflict lasting scars.

◈ 4 ◈

WOMEN'S IAMBIC VOICES

P LUTARCH LEAVES US THE FOLLOWING snippet of a women's song in his
account of one of the Seven Sages, Thales of Miletus.[1] When Thales
was in Eresos he heard his hostess singing to her handmill:

ἄλει μύλα ἄλει
καὶ γὰρ Πίττακος ἄλει
μεγάλας Μυτιλήνας βασιλεύων.

Grind mill, grind;
For Pittacus used to grind (or grinds)
As he ruled mighty Mytilene.

The little poem makes a political joke – probably an obscene one, if
ἄλει means more than "oppress" or "bear down upon."[2] Its perspective is
anti-élite, obviously, given that Pittacus was tyrant in Mytilene. The song
is meant to accompany the process of grinding (by hand) barley or similar grain in a pestle – a job usually done by a woman before baking. This
poem, taken together with the Sapphic corpus, may attest to a woman's
tradition on Lesbos, which included satire, obscenity, and the other elements that we associate with iambos. Clearly this is a "work song" intended to relieve the effort and monotony of pounding grain: a humble
task and an appropriately satirical song for Demeter.[3] We know from the
old comic fragments that there were many such songs, sung by women as
they ground barley or kneaded dough.[4] Athenaeus mentions that the mill
song was known as a *himaios*. There was also the *ailinos*, or loom song;
the *ioulos* or song of wool-spinners; and *Demetrouloi* or *calliouloi*, "sheaf"
songs for Demeter. Women specialized in the lullaby or *oatabaulooio*, the
winnowing song.[5] They performed funeral songs, both intimate and formal (*gooi* and *threnoi*), wedding songs (*hymenaioi*), and (again Athenaeus
mentions this) participated in competitions lamenting a suicidal maiden
Harpalyce, who had been spurned by her beloved. In some of these and

other songs, formal and informal, we may imagine hilarity, mockery, and obscenity, sometimes mingling with more serious or lyrical passages.

Alas, these humble work songs have not survived, although one may speculate that some at least may have displayed the vigor, "working-class" perspective, and saltiness of extant iambic. How working women's songs might have differed from men's, as surely they did, we cannot say. In this chapter I survey briefly the material within the Sapphic corpus (with a glimpse also at Corinna's work) in order to assess these remnants of élite women's poetic traditions for material that might be subsumed under the heading of iambic.

The most substantial evidence for literary joking by women derives from Sappho. Sappho was indeed said to have composed *iamboi* by a number of ancient sources.[6] We cannot be sure what any of these sources meant by the term; was she merely composing in the iambic meter, or was she creating poems of invective? The observation by the Emperor Julian implies that Sappho composed iamboi – but in a manner different from Callimachus, one of the classic exponents of the genre.[7] The scholar Philodemus, ascribes to Pausimachus of Miletus (c. 200 B.C.E.) the radical theory that great poets were great by virtue of their use of sound, not by some affinity with a particular genre. Thus Sappho composed ἰαμβικῶς (in the iambic manner), just as Archilochus was capable of composing *not* in the iambic manner.[8] Given the nature of his argument, it is wise, perhaps, not to rely too heavily on this claim.

I suggest nonetheless that Sappho's venture into *iambos* denoted more than a metrical experiment. There was something in her style and subject matter that drew her into the orbit of Archilochus and the others. Sappho is called "*mascula*" by Horace in a context that suggests he considered her to be a sole female iambicist, the exception that proved the rule[9]:

> Qui sibi fidet,
> Dux reget examen. Parios ego primus iambos
> Ostendi Latio, numeros animosque secutus
> Archilochi, non res et agentia verba Lycamben.
> Ac ne me foliis ideo brevioribus ornes,
> Quod timui mutare modos et carminis artem:
> Temperat Archilochi Musam pede mascula Sappho,
> temperat Alcaeus, sed rebus et ordine dispar,
> nec socerum quaerit, quem versibus oblinat atris,
> nec sponsae laqueum famoso carmine nectit.

> He who thinks for himself
> Will lead the swarm. I was the first to display
> Parian iambics to Latium, following the meter
> And spirit of Archilochus, but not his subject matter, the words
> Harrying Lycambes. But don't wreath me with
> Proportionately littler leaves, on the grounds that I
> Feared to transform the rhythms and structure of the song.
> Masculine Sappho tempers her Muse with Archilochus' meter.
> Alcaeus does also – but differs (from Archilochus) in subject matter and
>   line order.
> He does not track a father in law to smear with dark verses,
> Nor does he tie a noose to his betrothed because of his notorious song.

Horace's focus in this epistle is the literary tradition, and the room it leaves for originality. Thus Porphyry ad loc. speculates that "mascula" occurs "because she was famous in the craft of poetry, in which men are more often famous – or because she is defamed as having been a tribad" [i.e., "lesbian," more or less, in the modern sense of the word]." I suggest, rather, that Sappho, a lone woman in Horace's list, participates in a tradition built by Archilochus and inherited by Alcaeus – and eventually Horace himself.[10] In fact Horace's words may better sustain the meaning that iambic (rather than poetry in general) is a medium without a place for "normal" women. Sappho is *mascula* in Horace's eyes probably because she participated in what had developed as an assertively "male" genre. Like Alcaeus, she does not go to the extremes of an Archilochus, but like Alcaeus, and later Horace himself, she is capable of satirical and abusive poems. It is likely that she used the meter (although no iambic meters of hers have survived), but I believe that there is more at stake here, for Horace, than just a metrical choice. Archilochus's name inevitably leaches iambic venom into the context.

The pieces I have selected for analysis range in tone. Some resemble Archilochus at his most virulent, some are like cultic banter, that is, they seem to be less contemptuous, focused primarily on women within her circle.[11]

Aloni notes that Lesbos was a fitting context for the production of iambic poetry:

> In fact at Lesbos all the cultural modes of the iambic performance are present: (a) the cult of Dionysus is important to the point that the god is included in the triad of the political gods of Mytilene, together with Zeus the "Protector" and Hera the "Aeolian" (Alc. 129 V.; Sappho 17 V.);

(b) a widespread symposial institution (as a locus of communication) meant to characterize positively and negatively its participants; (c) finally, a production of wine remarkable both in quantity and quality, such as to be exported to overseas markets. Not to mention the quarrelsome disposition of the political and poetic leaders of the island.[12]

Unlike Archilochus, Hipponax, and Semonides, however, the extant fragments of Sappho show no signs of a connection with Demeter's cult. Lesbos may have been unusual in emphasizing the Dionysian over the Demetrian, but as Aloni observes, conditions were generally favorable toward the genre.

Maximus of Tyre speaks of Gorgo and Andromeda as Sappho's ἀντίτεχνοι ("technical rivals"), drawing an analogy with Socrates' relationship to Prodicus and other Sophists:

ὁ δὲ τῆς Λεσβίας (sc. ἔρως)...τί ἂν εἴη ἄλλο ἢ αὐτό, ἡ Σωκράτους τέχνη ἐρωτική; δοκοῦσι γάρ μοι τὴν καθ᾽ αὑτὸν ἑκάτερος φιλίαν, ἡ μὲν γυναικῶν, ὁ δὲ ἀρρένων, ἐπιτηδεῦσαι. καὶ γὰρ πολλῶν ἐρᾶν ἔλεγον καὶ ὑπὸ πάντων ἁλίσκεσθαι τῶν καλῶν· ὅ τι γὰρ ἐκείνῳ Ἀλκιβιάδης καὶ Χαρμίδης καὶ Φαῖδρος, τοῦτο τῇ Λεσβίᾳ Γυρίννα καὶ Ἀτθὶς καὶ Ἀνακτορία· καὶ ὅ τι περ Σωκράτει οἱ ἀντίτεχνοι Πρόδικος καὶ Γοργίας καὶ Θρασύμαχος καὶ Πρωταγόρας, τοῦτο τῇ Σαπφοῖ Γοργὼ καὶ Ἀνδρομέδα· νῦν μὲν ἐπιτιμᾷ ταύταις, νῦν δὲ ἐλέγχει καὶ εἰρωνεύεται αὐτὰ ἐκεῖνα τὰ Σωκράτους.

The love of the Lesbian Woman – what else could it be than Socrates' art of love? For each of them seems to have practiced affection in their own manner; she engaged in the love of women and he of men. For they said that they loved many and that they were captivated by the beautiful. Whatever Alcibiades and Charmides and Phaedrus were to him, in the same way Gyrinna and Atthis and Anactoria were to the Lesbian woman. And whatever the rival experts Prodicus and Gorgias and Thrasymachus meant to Socrates, Gorgo and Andromeda meant this same thing to Sappho. At one time she rebukes them, at another she refutes and uses irony – just like Socrates.[13]

In each case the complex of affectionate relationships on the one hand and adversarial relationships on the other defines the figure at the center of the literary, social, philosophical web. The formalized adversarial relationships recall Archilochus's relationship with the Lycambids. The passage suggests the existence of a women's world parallel to the male one, likewise literary and erotic in nature. This feminine coterie perhaps established the model for Socrates to follow.

Sappho was said to be short and ugly, according to a papyrus fragment.[14] It seems likely that this "biographical" datum derives from some aspect of the now-lost corpus, as is often the case with such apocrypha. Hipponax also was (we are told) ugly and misleadingly contemptible in appearance, as suited his role of malcontent and underdog. Of course being underestimated by his opponents as a feeble and undersized combatant only enhanced his dangerous potency.[15] His contemptible appearance is part of the blame poet's persona; he seems like easy prey to his unwitting detractors. In the case of Sappho also this notion of powers misunderstood or underestimated seems apt. Her "ugliness" might have been a trope dissembling formidable poetic powers – a disarming device, not a physical reality.[16]

Similarly, Sappho's legendary death, jumping from the "White Rock" of Leucas (supposedly out of unrequited love for a ferryman) suggests a "scapegoat" or *pharmakos* role, analogous to that of Aesop and others. Aesop threw himself to his death following an episode in which he insulted the people of Delphi.[17] Aesop himself previously had caused his adopted son to throw himself off a cliff because of vituperative criticism. Compton has argued that episodes in which an abusive or potentially abusive poet is tried and punished (with death or exile) by an outraged or ungrateful community form a tradition that included Archilochus, Aesop, Homer, and even Socrates.[18] Such a "scapegoat" created for herself or himself a "place apart", and a role both sacred and polluted. Like Archilochus, whose voice had been raised "too iambically" in a lewd song for the god Dionysus, and who was exiled as a result, Sappho may have had a double effect: injuring others, and injuring or alienating herself from her community to an equivalent degree.[19]

Another thematic similarity between Sappho and a known blame poet, Archilochus, is constituted by a series of satirical fragments addressed to girls who had left her, or to the women to whom they had turned. The nature of the broken and newly formed alliances is not always clear, but there are hints of both amatory and literary elements.

Fragment 57 addresses a woman.[20] The passage derives from Athenaeus, *Deipnosophistae* I, 21 bc, "Sappho derides [your/her?] Andromeda thus." The verb used by Athenaeus, σκώπτει, is a classic iambic indicator.[21]

† τίς δ' ἀγροΐωτις θέλγει νόον...
ἀγροΐωτιν ἐπεμμένα στόλαν †...
οὐκ ἐπισταμένα τὰ βράκε' ἔλκην ἐπὶ τῶν σφύρων;

What bumpkin lass bewitches your mind,
dressed in bumpkin clothes,
ignorant of how to cover her ankles with her rags?

Sappho mocks her for succumbing to the charms of an unsophisticated
rustic girl. It seems likely to me that the clumsy clothing mocked by Sappho
may be a metaphor for a style of literary expression antithetical to Sappho's
own, with its persistent sophisticated references to imported fabrics, perfumes, and other elegancies. Here one may observe an important distinction between Sappho's worldview and that of Archilochus or Hipponax.
She speaks not from the perspective of an anti-élite outsider, but rather
as a self-conscious and proud member of the aristocracy. This refinement
disdains the peasant style and preferences of some of her contemporaries.

Fragment 71 – a very fragmentary piece – rebukes a certain Mica for
chosing the friendship (φιλότ[ατ]) of the Penthelid house. In the next line
Sappho mentions a "sweet song," suggesting that this "choice" had literary
implications as well as amatory ones.

In 131 she laments to Atthis:

Ἄτθι, σοὶ δ ἔμεθεν μὲν ἀπήχθετο
φροντίσδην, ἐπὶ δ Ἀνδρομέδαν πότη

Atthis it has become hateful to you
To think of me; instead you fly to Andromeda.

Betrayal, and the poet's deep consciousness of injury, is a famous theme
in Archilochus and finds echoes in Sappho fragment 26:

     ]θαμέω[
     ..ὄ]ττινα[ς γὰρ
εὖ θέω, κῆ]νοί με μά]λιστα πά[ντων
   σίνοντα]ι
       ]ἀλεμάτ᾽
     ]αν, ἔγω δ᾽ ἔμ᾽ [αὔται
τοῦτο σύ]νοιδα

For those whom I treat well harm me most of all...
   and I am conscious of this....[22]

Fragments 37 and 55 seem unequivocally hostile; unfortunately, without context or any hint of what was in the rest of the poems, it is difficult to assess them further. The first is a curse, reminiscent of similar
"revenge" curses by Archilochus and Hipponax:[23]

τὸν δ᾽ ἐπιπλάζοντ᾽ ἄνεμοι φέροιεν
καὶ μελέδωναι.

May winds and sufferings sweep away
the one who rebukes me!

Fragment 55, unlike the preceding, is addressed to a woman; Sappho makes a contemptuous prophecy. Stobaeus, who cites the passage, says that it was addressed to an uneducated woman; this may be based on nothing more than the poem's contents; it seems to me plausible to read it in the context of an exchange among rival poets:

κατθάνοισα δὲ κείσῃ οὐδέ ποτα μναμοσύνα σέθεν
ἔσσετ᾽ οὐδὲ πόθα εἰς ὕστερον· οὐ γὰρ πεδέχῃς βρόδων
τὼν ἐκ Πιερίας, ἀλλ᾽ ἀφάνης κἀν Ἀίδα δόμῳ
φοιτάσῃς πεδ᾽ ἀμαύρων νεκύων ἐκπεποταμένα.

When you die you will lie still.
There will be no memory of you, nor
any longing thereafter. For you
know nothing of Pieria's roses.
Unseen in Hell also, having flitted hence
You will wander among the dim spirits.

Not all poetic assaults by women seem quite so deadly, but, as always, tone is difficult to assess. Sappho was not the only woman poet to mock a rival. What do we make of Corinna's famous rebuke to Pindar "sow with your hand, not the whole sack!" supposedly uttered in response to his exuberant and indiscriminate use of myth?[24] Corinna laughed, we are told, as she uttered this put-down. Her caustic critique apparently had begun with the sneer that he was ἄμουσον – "no poet" (in Campbell's translation) because he indulged in verbal eccentricities instead of *mythoi* or narratives. Pindar's overzealous reaction inspired her mocking "advice." These admonitions evoke a spirited poetic personality, defining itself in part by excoriating others.

Was Corinna speaking from the perspective of a single authoritative tradition in which she believed she herself and Pindar equally participated? Or was she condemning a tradition that she saw as alien to herself? The portrayal of Corinna as Pindar's teacher, rather than an acerbic and indifferent diva, may reflect androcentric reluctance on the part of her "biographers" to accord her the distinctive and separate place that she in fact occupied.

Corinna (frag. 664) blames a rival, in a snippet that interestingly speaks of "contention" (ἔρις) between Myrtis and Pindar. Corinna condemns this ἔρις between a male and a female poet:

μέμφομη δὲ κὴ λιγουρὰν
Μουρτίδ᾽ ἰώνγ᾽ ὅτι βανὰ φοῦ-
σ᾽ ἔβα Πινδάροι πὸτ ἔριν.

I also blame Myrtis, clear voiced,
Because, as a woman, she entered
A quarrel with Pindar.

Corinna herself is supposed to have defeated Pindar in competition five times, so it is difficult to know what to make of this rebuke.[25] She was from Boeotia, so I suggest that she may be repudiating the famous injunction of her other fellow countryman Hesiod, who advocates a productive rivalry or quarrel (ἔρις) between poets as between other professionals in lines 24–6 of the *Works and Days*. Possibly Corinna viewed women's poetry as most properly concerned with women as its audience, and so, she condemned an intergender rivalry that might compromise the woman poet's distinctive voice.[26] Myrtis was guilty not of temerity (a "mere" woman competing with great Pindar) but of being false to herself by honing her voice against that of a man. Corinna's own excellence (arguably) was perfected without reference to the famous male poets of her birthplace.[27]

To return to Sappho, we can also find among her works evidence of a broader, coarser humor, more in the line of male iambicists. Both of the following Sapphic fragments (110a, 111) derive from epithalamia or wedding songs, sung by a chorus of women[28]:

θυρώρῳ πόδες ἑπτορόγυιοι
τὰ δὲ σάμβαλα πεμπεβόηα,
πίσσυγγοι δὲ δέκ᾽ ἐξεπόναισαν.

The doorman's feet are seven cubits long.
His sandals are made from five ox-hides.
Ten cobblers worked on them!

Hesychius and Pollux remark that the "doorman" was the equivalent of our "best man," a friend of the bridegroom who prevented the bride's attendants from coming to her rescue. Demetrius characterizes her stance with iambic language: "Sappho mocks (σκώπτει) the rustic bridegroom and his doorman at the wedding most disparagingly, and in prosaic rather than poetic language."[29]

Fr. 111 is on the same lines:

ἴψοι δὴ τὸ μέλαθρον
ὑμήναον,
ἀέρρετε, τέκτονες ἄνδρες·
ὑμήναον.
γάμβρος † (εἰσ)έρχεται ἶσος † Ἄρευι,
ἄνδρος μεγάλω πόλυ μέσδων.

Lift high the roof!
Hymenaeus!
Lift it high you carpenters
Hymenaeus!
The bridegroom approaches, like Ares
Much larger than a large man!

Once again, the overawed reference to the "size" of the man may contain an obscene double entendre. As Apte remarks of several modern societies, "Marriage also seems to be a rite of passage that frees women from social-restraints with respect to humor. One collective humorous activity of women involves singing songs that ridicule male sexual activity, especially at rites of passage. Women seem to derive much amusement from such songs, and in some cases the practice has developed into a social institution."[30]

Even the following charming couplet, fragment 115, may also bear a mocking meaning:

τίῳ σ᾿, ὦ φίλε γάμβρε, καλῶς ἐικάσδω;
ὄρπακι βραδίνῳ σε μάλιστ᾿ἐικάσδω.

To what should I compare you, dear bridegroom?
I liken you to a tender shoot above all.

The Greek that I translate "tender shoot" is ὄρπαξ βράδινος. ὄρπαξ has roughly the same semantic range as ἔρνος (scion), the word that Thetis uses of her son Achilles at *Iliad* 18, 56 in anticipation of his premature death. As Winkler has shown, women's laments at the festival of Adonis the young but prematurely slain youth beloved of Aphrodite, might have been laden with mockery, not easily traceable now[31]: an implicit comparison between the short-lived potted "gardens" of Adonis (lettuce seedlings etc.), forced and then allowed to perish in the hot July sun, and the short life of Adonis. Winkler further suggests that the women may be mocking the evanescent sexual energy of the male and his relatively brief participation in a reproductive process that is largely the responsibility of women. The "Adonis" seedlings grow for eight days, whereas Mother Earth nourishes (real) harvests for eight months. Thus Sappho's comparison of the bridegroom to a young shoot may not be simply flattering commentary on his graceful youth. One of the possible meanings of (β)ράδινος, εὐκίνητός, was flexible, mobile, or pliant.[32] The couplet may mock the groom's untested and dubious sexual potency. Whether the mockery was recognized as such by everyone at the time of its performance we cannot say. It may have been intended to amuse only women.[33] Alternatively, it may have formed part of an openly adversarial exchange between male and female attendants at the wedding; the mood will have been festive and lighthearted, rather than cruel or destructive.

In a harsher sexual vein, there is the fragmentary and disputed fragment 99, which contains a possible reference to "those receiving the *olisbos*" or dildo. A later line in the poem contains the threat: "I wish to expose the mad one" (Campbell's translation). As Aloni has noted, editors beginning with Voigt have attributed this passage to Alcaeus on the grounds that the word *olisbos* is too crude for Sappho to have used. West has preferred to translate *olisbos* as "plectrum."[34] Here one may see how modern – and ancient – preconceptions about Sappho may have affected the very survival, and certainly the understanding, of her corpus. If a poem or word seemed too vulgar for Sappho to have uttered, then it could be shorn from the canon or ascribed to a poet perceived as more disposed to rude poetic assaults.

A number of sources charge Sappho with having assailed a courtesan, Rhodopis or Doricha, upon whom her brother, Charaxus, supposedly spent large sums of money. Athenaeus describes Sappho as attacking (διαβάλλει) Doricha in her poetry.[35] It is a strong term. This amatory "situation" (the kind of thing that the comic poets later exploited to the full) would have afforded opportunity for caustic, even crude, characterizations of Rhodopis. We should not assume that family dignity and graceful reticence were the poet's priorities. Nor should we assume that this was a "real" family embarrassment any more than Archilochus' famous jilting by the Lycambid family. It may have served as the kind of generic *hubris* that formed the premise for a spirited "rejoinder."

I close with fragment 31 L.P., the poem in which she comments on the "godlike" powers of a man who can sit, miraculously unshaken, opposite her beloved and listen to her "speak sweetly and … laugh seductively":

φαίνεταί μοι κῆνος ἴσος θέοισιν
ἔμμεν' ὤνηρ, ὄττις ἐνάντιός τοι
ἰσδάνει καὶ πλάσιον ἆδυ φωνεί-
σας ὑπακούει

καὶ γελαίσας ἰμέροεν, τό μ' ἦ μὰν
καρδίαν ἐν στήθεσιν ἐπτόαισεν·
ὡς γὰρ ἔς σ' ἴδω βρόχε', ὥς με φώναι-
σ' οὐδ' ἓν ἔτ' εἴκει

ἀλλὰ κὰμ μὲν γλῶσσᾳ ⟨μ'⟩ ἔαγε, λέπτον
δ' αὔτικα χρῷ πῦρ ὑπαδεδρόμηκεν,
ὀππάτεσσι δ' οὐδ' ἓν ὄρημμ' ἐπιρρόμ-
βεισι δ' ἄκουαι,

κὰδ δέ μ' ἴδρως κακχέεται, τρόμος δὲ
παῖσαν ἄγρει. χλωροτέρα δὲ ποίας
ἔμμι, τεθνάκην δ' ὀλίγω 'πιδεύης
φαίνομ' ἔμ αὔτ[ᾳ

ἀλλὰ πὰν τόλματον, ἐπεὶ † καὶ πένητα †

It seems to me that he is like the gods,
the man who sits before you
and – as you speak sweetly –
listens

as you laugh gracefully. Which
sets the heart trembling in my breast.
For when I see you – even briefly – speech
is mine no more

but my tongue shatters. Straight away a slender flame
runs beneath my flesh,
sight leaves my eyes, my
ears hum,

sweat pours from me, a tremor
grips me, I am paler than grass,
I seem to myself to fall little short
of death.

But all may be ventured, since ++ even the poor man++ [The text fades out]. Sappho implies that the speech and laughter of the other woman can communicate to her overpowering messages of enchantment that are (relatively) unrecognized by the man.[36] Indeed her description suggests that mere observation of her beloved can induce in her a state of orgasm – or death. The poem meanwhile executes an amatory "assault" on her beloved: a slyly dissembled attack masquerading as a description of her own helpless capitulation.[37] There is irony in the poet's clinical description of her own disintegration, beginning with the "shattering" of her tongue, like the shattering of the spear of a doomed Homeric warrior.[38] A volley of images miraculously succeeds this purported loss – a ruinous one for an oral poet – as the amatory warrior details her own collapse on the battlefield.

Sappho speaks, of course, as a woman in love, but the imaginary vignette suggests to us, its readers, that women's voices may communicate on more than one level. Poem 31 concerns a woman communicating with another woman; the man in its opening line is the rhetorical means of allowing Sappho's own ironic and seductive voice to reach her beloved; he is not an object of interest in his own right. In the same way, perhaps, these bridal hymns may communicate, slyly and mockingly, among the women who sing them, even as they seem to direct themselves flatteringly to the bridegroom. The mockery unites the women even as they face the "loss" of one of their number to marriage; aggression is lightly blended with a joyful camaraderie.[39]

In conclusion, poems incorporating everything from abuse to mild mockery seem to have flourished within the Sapphic corpus, just as, conversely, the Archilochean tradition included "anomalous" fragments of tender, elegiac poems. In each case the principal mode of the poetry's survival – quotation by later authors – has probably distorted the picture. Once a poet's reputation was established – elegant and tender, or coarse and abusive – this image will have determined which passages most likely to be selected. If one wanted an example of vituperation, it was natural to cull the Archilochean corpus, not the Sapphic.

❖ 5 ❖

COMEDY AND WOMEN

I N CHAPTER 3 I TRACED the "bones" of cult beneath the surface of extant iambic. The poetry that we now call iambic presents itself as a single, opinionated voice, decrying some other, or group of others, or presenting an amusingly unedifying story or playlet in first person narrative. I suggest that iambic's seemingly unequivocal broadsides, its scurrilous tales, had evolved in a milieu of contestation, however. We may visualize women mocking other women in their segregated cults, and women and men exchanging insults in mixed cults of Demeter and Dionysus. In "proto-iambic" songs, generated in contexts (semi)independent of cult, men and women sometimes engaged in mocking and blaming exchanges. A pattern of intergender hostility often marks societies as segregated as those of archaic Greece. Predictably, however, women singers of blame in noncultic contexts were especially susceptible to censure and suppression. The long-term result is a genre for which most the surviving works are those male practitioners – and emphatically hostile to women.

I have argued that iambic literature developed out of the spirited cultic exchanges begun by Iambe, exchanges either among women or in some cases between groups of men and women. As the genre developed, however, it fell largely into the hands of men. Iambic's extraordinary misogyny thus reflected one voice, selected from earlier confrontations or melées. Women as a topic in iambic literature are refracted through the lens of male (mock) rage and hostility. They are voracious, parasitic, draining, false – as viewed from the perspective of the individual male (usually a husband) who hopes to reap some benefit from them, in the form of pleasure, children, or a prosperous home. When we view women's own cultic behaviors, however, we see a different set of values and priorities. Women acted in concert, and paid significant attention to each other. They spoke freely, even impertinently, and gloried in the grotesque.

Classical Greek culture's dominant model of the female was the traitor, beguiling or tormenting her husband, who thereupon became society's laughing stock. Hesiod's Pandora, the ruinous deceiver in the guise of a sweet young girl, although not an iambic figure, embodies the type. Iambe and Baubo, the prototypes for women's own cultic activities, are the antithesis of Pandora. They are unprepossessing or insignificant on the outside. They inspire no desire among men. Yet from a deathly situation and within a circle of women, they can generate ribald laughter, energy, hope. Over the next two chapters I examine the women of Greek old comedy to see (among other things) whether occasionally they resonate with these cultic models. Could one expect Aristophanes to do other than draw on male experience, male traditions?

Here in Chapter 5 I turn to the relationship between women's cultic joking and Attic old comedy. I consider the development of old comedy, with its diversifying roles for women. The evolution of Attic old comedy, in turn, forms part of a larger story of the development of Athens itself as a polis. By exploring this three-way relationship – cults, comedy, and the growing civic institutions of Athens generally – one can begin to appreciate the implications of women as speakers and agents on the stage of old comedy. This is what I attempt in this chapter.

The Athenian polis in the course of the sixth and early fifth centuries B.C.E. developed cultural institutions that aired – and regulated – social conflicts or tensions. Of course new social tensions developed along with the polis' growth and concomitant encroachment upon what had been private matters. Others had long existed, in some form or other. Religious cults, among their many functions, long had constituted a means of confronting (if not resolving) such tensions. Greek tragedy, for example, grew out of preexisting cultic rituals, but its real impetus and determinative context was formed by the stresses, anxieties, and changing social perceptions that accompanied sixth- and early-fifth-century political shifts at Athens. It was a civic and religious institution, as well as part of a literary tradition stretching back to Homer.

As with tragedy, so also, I argue, with comedy. The changing landscape affected men and women, in all aspects of their lives. It shaped a new vista of "public" and "private," which featured men and women in roles more divided between these two realms than before. Comedy, like tragedy, spanned – and was driven by – these tumultuous times. Like tragedy it presented "women" (among others) to the city, and like tragedy it was a civic and religious institution that aspired to speak for them and with their traditional social and cultic authority.

Loraux and Holst-Warhaft have traced in detail the efforts of the growing polis of Athens to appropriate the traditional women's duty of lament.

The institutions of tragedy and funeral oration enshrined those aspects of lament and commemoration that served the polis, and we know of legislation attributed to Solon limiting the extravagance and expressiveness of individual funerals; this legislation paid special attention to the public conduct of women.[1] Thus by the mid–sixth century in Athens there had been a twofold initiative: to separate women from their ancient charge of lament and communication with the dead and to replace them with male spokesmen, working under rigorously controlled conditions. This is not to say that women ceased from having powers and responsibilities regarding the dead, but in its public aspect mourning became a state phenomenon, divided between the funeral oration and tragedy.

I believe that a similar development took place with regard to comedy and cultic worship – not a substitution but a significant shift in emphasis and visibility. In fact the Plutarch passage that describes Solon's funerary restrictions includes women's festivals under the same law:

Ἐπέστησε δὲ καὶ ταῖς ἐξόδοις τῶν γυναικῶν καὶ τοῖς πένθεσι καὶ ταῖς ἑορταῖς νόμον ἀπείργοντα τὸ ἄτακτον καὶ ἀκόλαστον.

He also imposed a law on the public appearances of women, both their lamentations and their festivals, limiting the disorderly and the licentious (τὸ ἄτακτον καὶ ἀκόλαστον).

The language here suggests that Demeter's festivals were included in these practices targeted by Solon. Whether or not Solon was primarily responsible, substantial societal changes were taking place in late archaic and early classical Athens, and they had a particular impact on women. Indeed Greece as a whole from the sixth century on saw legislation curbing women's roles in funeral laments.[2]

Comedy and tragedy grew out of a shared heritage of cult and ritual, but they had separated by the sixth century.[3] As Aristotle reminds us, comedy as a state *agon* was a relative latecomer on the Athenian scene (*Poetics* 1449b). I suggest that as it developed, it took a path parallel to tragedy, appropriating and regulating some of the functions and powers of ancient cultic rites. The ancient cults continued, but the new form of Dionysus worship became a magnet of attention and accrued a rich mixture of powers, implicit and explicit.

It is not surprising that the state's encroachment on women's ancient prerogative of lament has received more attention among modern scholars than the state's partial appropriation of their joking and obscene rites.

Because women's laughter and ribald joking tended to take place out of the public eye, among women only, the state did not need to invest as much energy banishing it to the private realm, as in the case of funerary practice. Such joking was already practiced in relative privacy, despite the communal implications of festivals such as the Thesmophoria. In everyday life, social convention made it unwise for respectable women to engage in public mockery or mirth. This is no doubt why we encounter strictures directed by rhetoricians and philosophers only at male jokers; it was (rightly) assumed that none were necessary for (respectable) women.[4]

By the fourth century Aristotle, our most important theorist on ancient drama, was calling for censorship of certain rituals, and for the removal of women from them altogether:

ἐπιμελὲς μὲν οὖν ἔστω τοῖς ἄρχουσι μηθὲν μήτε ἄγαλμα μήτε γραφὴν εἶναι τοιούτων πράξεων μίμησιν, εἰ μὴ παρά τισι θεοῖς τοιούτοις οἷς καὶ τὸν τωθασμὸν ἀποδίδωσιν ὁ νόμος. πρὸς δὲ τούτοις ἀφίησιν ὁ νόμος τοὺς τὴν ἡλικίαν ἔχοντες [ἔτι] τὴν ἱκνουμένην καὶ ὑπὲρ αὐτῶν καὶ τέκνων καὶ γυναικῶν τιμαλφεῖν τοὺς θεούς.

It should be a duty of the rulers that there be no statue or painting representing this sort [i.e., obscene] of action. An exception may apply regarding such deities [in whose worship] the law allows even obscenity (τωθασμός). In such cases the law may allow to men who have reached maturity to attend in place of their wives and children and worship the gods.[5]

The fourth century witnessed a change in attitude toward humor, as the gradual shift from old to new comedy, and Aristotle's comments in the *Poetics* and *Nichomachean Ethics* about the changing nature of comedy attest.[6] I suggest that Aristotle was articulating an opinion generally held by Athenian élites – and even by many ordinary attendees of the theater of Dionysus. It was the outcome of a gradual shift in notions of public decorum and in the perceived role of women within the state, which had begun in the sixth century. At the same time, although there were substantial changes in comedy as the fourth century progressed, ancient cultic rituals remained in existence, and Aristotle's very desire for their curtailment testifies to the continuing power of this type of joking.

The old comedy from which Aristotle was already distant in time and sympathy flourished during a period of ideological shift, and it functioned in part to mediate the tensions engendered by that shifting. It drew from a complex of cultic activities associated with fertility and the agricultural year.[7] The playwrights were creative artists, responding to popular tastes, but they also drew on ancient cultic practices, and their audiences were alive to the cultic strands woven into the dramas.[8] The principal dramatic festival, the newly (re)invented City Dionysia, itself included elements of ancient practices. Its scale and brilliance, its admission of non-Athenians to the audience, its civic and religious pomp, seemed to make the City Dionysia a voice for the city as a whole; of course in reality slaves, metics, and women could not play an active part, just as they were excluded from Athenian political life.

Connor describes the City Dionysia, with its complex roots, inclusive range, and contradictory claims. The dramatic festivals – especially the City Dionysia – celebrated civic order and Athenian power, even as they dealt with tensions and disorder:[9]

> The festival integrates old forms of festivity, such as rural fertility cults in honor of Dionysus, with dithyrambic choruses, the *komos*, celebratory patterns used for athletic victors, and practices derived from other Greek cities. Although its origin is complex and its functions multiple, the City Dionysia reflects the tensions and civic realities of early Athens – it is an urban festival with rural elements and roots, a time of relaxation and release combined with a representation of civic order, and of the strength, success and prosperity, that the Athenians associated with freedom and democratic institutions.

Connor's argument about the eclecticism of the festival rings true. I suggest that Demeter's cults in particular, naturally akin to Dionysus's, were significant in the mix. The worship of Dionysus and that of Demeter were always connected: a predictable affinity for deities of wine and grain.[10] In both cults obscene mockery was a characteristic feature, as we have seen. Apparently such crude songs survived into Aristotle's day, and so he was well placed to observe the relationship between them and the old comedy that he disdained.[11]

Despite the more extensive use of *aischrologia* in the cult of Demeter, it is not surprising that Dionysus, not Demeter, came to embody the Attic genre that performed *aischrologia* in the most public and systematic way.[12] Athenaeus noted that Athens had always favored Dionysus when it came to public performances, observing that the Athenians tended to prefer Dionysian choruses and circular dances, whereas the Syracusans particularly honored proponents of iambic.[13] Moreover the other dramatic genres already belonged to Dionysus, so the assimilation of obscene and lighthearted practices to his comic drama was a natural step. Reckford's point regarding the rapid growth of Dionysus' cult in sixth-century Athens is relevant here[14]: "even the women's Demetrian rites, when they took on a carnival intensity, tended to be associated with Dionysus, if not drawn into his sphere."[15]

Comedy's Origins: Aristotle – The Visual Evidence

Iambic was an Ionian phenomenon, flourishing in the Aegean islands and on the eastern shores of the Aegean. When we turn to comedy, we have overwhelmingly Attic representatives, although comedy had roots in the Peloponnese and Sicily as well as Athens. Athenian old comedy survives in eleven complete plays of Aristophanes and thousands of fragments and references to lost plays by playwrights of the latter half of the fifth century and the first decades of the fourth. It was thus both a localized and a short-lived phenomenon, the product of a remarkable place and cultural moment.

While broadly similar in subject matter, iambic and comedy differed from each other in form.[16] As we have seen, the Ionian iambus tended to be a monologue or reported dialogue, mostly in iambic trimeters or trochaic tetrameters. According to Aristotle, Athenian tragedy began as improvisational choral songs, which were subsequently interspersed by passages of iambic dialogue – between chorus and individual, and then between individuals as well. Aristotle noted that the origins of comedy were far less well known, but he suggested a parallel with tragedy, however, in comedy's improvisational origin. Whereas tragedy had grown out of the dithyramb, comedy had come from the makers of *phallika*, "phallic songs" that he described as still being performed in many Greek cities. I suggest that Aristotle's austere reference to the "makers of the *phallika*" and his observation that little was known about the origins of comedy (by comparison with those of tragedy) may partly be explained by the fact that he disapproved of such coarse humor and especially disliked the fact that women (as well as men) were involved in making it.[17]

The name "comedy" derives from κῶμος, a term for a rowdy chorus in procession.[18] The evidence for comedy's choral precursors is substantially visual, in the form of sixth-century vase paintings of *komoi* or precomic choruses. Vase evidence, from sixth-century Corinth and sixth- and fifth-century Athens depict padded (or grotesquely fat) dancers or komasts, often at banquets, mingling with élite men at a symposium.[19] These komasts were everything a "true" symposiast was not: clumsy, indecorous, ill formed, and with large genitals. At the same time, they give the impression of being an organized group. Scholars have speculated about the connections between such padded komasts and the actors of old comedy, who also were padded and depicted with grotesquely large genitals. Scenes of women solemnizing a religious occasion were sometimes combined with these komast-symposium scenes.[20]

Padded komasts seemed to fade as a vase motif about 550, to be replaced by more realistic-looking komasts, subject to no obvious choral discipline, and by hairy satyrs. There is no agreement about what, if anything, this gradual change in iconographic fashion meant in the real world. By the end of the sixth century Athenian vases combined human dancers with satyrs and female companions. Depictions of a ship festival of Dionysus and satyrs (disguised citizens) also appear in the late sixth century and are thought to reflect a ritual in which Dionysus was restored to the people after winter.[21] This ritual is known to have existed in many cities. The *komos* of padded dancers was especially linked with Dionysus in Attica, but a lighthearted chorus of padded komasts could serve other divinities as well and perhaps could even be imported from one cult to another.[22]

A series of about twenty vases, dating from 560 to 480, depicted men disguised as animals, on stilts, or riding dolphins. These figures may be basically the same chorus that had long been appearing in komast scenes, now wearing an additional disguise.[23] Representations of drinkers wearing Scythian caps on the so-called Anacreontic cups, depicting mock-Lydians, probably belong to the same category.

Questions remain as to how and when individuals began to detach from the chorus and to interact with the chorus and each other. According to Aristotle, Crates invented plots, moving from personal lampoons to something more general in theme and plot. Yet Crates supposedly was an actor, and one cannot imagine an actor without a plot. No doubt the institution of the comic competition speeded innovations such as increasing and developing the role of individuals, yet it seems likely that in the early decades individual characters were employed in a somewhat ad hoc manner. Perhaps Crates formalized or breathed new vigor into what had been embryonic and casually contrived plots.

The Growing Polis

Athens established comic contests at the City Dionysia in 486, many years after the tragic competitions.[24] Thus old comedy flowered in Athens following the Persian Wars, during the self-confident years in which the Delian

League, formed as an Athenian-led alliance to thwart Persian expansion in the Aegean, became an Athenian empire of subject states paying tribute directly into Athenian coffers. Comedy's greatest years were during the Peloponnesian War (432–404), which began and continued in this spirit of pride and assurance but ended in the city's ruinous defeat by Sparta.

Old comedy thus flourished at a watershed moment in international terms and also from the perspective of the city's own rapid political and social evolution. The introduction of comic contests at the City Dionysia followed a century of internal tumult and reform, out of which emerged the wealthy and aggressive democracy of the fifth century. The lawgiver Solon had attempted to reduce factionalism among the powerful and enslavement for debt among the poor at the beginning of the sixth century. Attempts to reduce fighting among powerful families and local factions failed, and the mid–sixth century saw the accession of the tyrant Pisistratus. It was only following the regime of Pisistratus's sons that the reformer Cleisthenes, in a series of ingenious (but still debated) moves, devised a political system that broke up large localized power blocs, relying instead on a tight interconnection between city decision making and that of the deme, or small local unit. Athenian identity – for Athenian citizen males at any rate – was rooted in the Attic countryside; only in the world outside Attics would a man describe himself as "Athenian"; within the city he defined himself, and acquired his citizen identity, through his father and his father's deme.[25]

Reforms did not end with Cleisthenes, and indeed, as with Solon, it is difficult to distinguish between what he achieved personally and what was merely credited to him. No matter. Shortly after 490 Athenians began to appoint by lot their senior magistrates, the archons, from among a larger group that had been previously elected. Probably this measure was intended to curb the tendency of influential individuals to monopolize the highest offices of state or to wrangle over it. At the same time ostracism, the process whereby a single prominent individual could be required to go into a ten-year exile, following a vote of the people, was introduced. The first three men to be ostracized, in 487, 486, and 485, respectively, were all connected with the tyrants who had ruled Athens at the end of the sixth century. Again, the new institution appears to have been designed to curtail factional strife.

This was the Athens into which the comic competitions were introduced. The coincidence of these reforms with the institution of the comic competitions in 486 may have significance.[26] If one imagines that individual aristocrats had perhaps used certain types of festival joking, formally or

informally constituted choruses or *komoi*, to malign and belittle their political rivals (one thinks of Aristotle's tale of the *komos* on Naxos, which
led to the installation of Lygdamis as tyrant), one may easily see why a
reforming statesman or statesmen might wish instead to deploy potentially divisive laughter in the city's service. With the Persians menacing
their gates, Athenians could laugh together and curb internal hostilities.
Political rivalries would be displaced by the harmless rivalries of poets
seeking to win the approval of the *demos*. Élite women as well as men had
participated to some extent in the conflicts between political factions, and
their voices were firmly silenced as a succession of Athenian statesmen
broadened the domain of the polis. Of course what the institution of old
comedy went on to become – in many cases a savage critic of individual
politicians and of individual policies – need not reflect how it was intended
to function by whoever established the competitions.

How did the city's women fit and consider themselves to fit within the
newly designed and rapidly evolving city? How did they form their identity
in this new world? In general, as the city moved to broaden the scope of
its political institutions and curtail the power of individuals and individual families, to neutralize discord, to create a collective identity within the
public sphere, women found themselves in an increasingly confined place.
Women's sphere always had been and would continue to be the home and
family (*oikos*), and they played and would continue to play a significant
role in many religious cults, but as the overall sociopolitical configuration
shifted, so did their world. In addition to his land reforms, Solon was credited with legislation curbing the public role of women in lamentation and in
certain cults. Certainly the state – and perhaps its most famous legislator –
deliberately mediated the boundaries between the public sphere and the
private world of the *oikos*, or the home, with its network of connections
and responsibilities. Women, especially those belonging to powerful families, were required to efface themselves from the public sphere, the focus
of ever-increasing energy and activity.

Like men, women belonged to many classes and groups: slave, resident
foreigner, women born of marriages contracted between Attic parents,
rich, poor. Some legal and political disabilities were common to all women,
however. No woman could belong to a deme, vote, or engage in lawsuits.
A woman's identity, as a political and civic cipher, was conferred by her
father and later by her husband. In 451–50 Pericles introduced legislation,
the intention of which is not understood, requiring that a male citizen
be born of a marriage between a native-born Athenian man and woman.

Hitherto it had been sufficient grounds for citizenship that a man's father be Athenian. This law, whatever its intent, had the result of making a woman's "Athenianness" a matter of public concern, rendering her status as a (passive) citizen something that could be investigated in a court of law.

Whether this legislation increased a sense of privilege among "true" Athenian women, and sharpened distinctions between them and noncitizen women we cannot tell. I suggest that the picture was a contradictory one. On the one hand women of varied status routinely worked together in the home, helped each other in childbirth and child rearing, and participated in cults, many of which were not confined to the freeborn or privileged. Thus women felt solidarity with each other and shared the experience of being outside the world in which decisions were made – by men. This solidarity mingled a kind of humorous acceptance of the status quo and resentment at their exclusion, especially when men made political decisions that affected everyone adversely. On the other hand, women certainly felt distinctions among themselves. The chorus leader in the *Thesmophoriazousae*, half in earnest, proposes that women who have borne cowardly or unworthy sons should yield their seats at women's festivals to the mothers of heroes.[27]

An Attic woman's civic identity was closely bound with that of the family she formed with her husband, out of which came the new generation of Athenian women and men. At the beginning of book 9 of his *Histories*, Herodotus tells a story, set in 479, the end of the Persian Wars.[28] The Persian general Mardonius was attempting to break the alliance of Greek states against him by detaching Athens. As the people of Athens watched, from their temporary exile on the island of Salamis, he sacked their city again, then sent an embassador named Mourychides to offer terms. The Council of the Athenians met on Salamis, and one man, Lycides, suggested that they should go ahead and submit the Persian proposals to the Assembly for approval. The other Council members were so angered that they stoned him to death on the spot. They allowed Mourychides to depart. Meanwhile the women of the Athenians found out what had happened and, without any encouragement from the men, went to the house of Lycides and stoned his wife and children.

The story suggests that the *oikos* and its inhabitants were strongly identified with the citizen male at its head, and that belonging to an Athenian family meant also participating in, and being responsible to, the Athenian totality. Athenian women knew that by bearing sons within a legitimately established household and by participating in their particular religious practices, they contributed to the common good – and they felt pride in this, whatever else they might have felt about Athens and Athenian men.

As I have noted, Dionysus worship became the city's premier site for the communal expression of cultic joking and abusive speech. This was, of course, old comedy, because Greek drama separated what had been mingled in cult: grief and laughter. Mingled grief and hilarity characterized women's cultic speech especially, for cultic lamentation (such as that for Adonis or Persephone) was traditionally a woman's prerogative, as was lamentation for dead family members.[29] Loraux and Holst-Warhaft uncovered the appropriating moves made by the city with regard to this traditional woman's function. Tragedy and funerary orations became the city's communal expression of grief, displacing to an extent (though not replacing) private mourning traditions. I argued that a parallel appropriation of women's voices took place as comedy evolved.

Now I examine women within the genre of old comedy – the fragments in Chapter 5 and the plays of Aristophanes in Chapter 6. I show, as much as possible given the fragmentary remains, the evolution of female parts within the comic tradition. It is important to do so because it makes it easier to assess how Aristophanes responded to women and how he appropriated their cultic voices. More significantly I find traces of what I have identified as a "different," nondominant worldview, limitedly in the fragments, more substantially in the Aristophanic plays. Certainly one finds many familiar slurs against women, collectively and individually. But there are also scenes of the positive collective energy found within women's groups, hearty disregard for male notions of propriety and limit, and a recognition that a woman's value, potential or due, is not necessarily perceptible from her surface.

First let us look at what remains of the larger tradition to which Aristophanes belonged. Following this brief overview I conclude this chapter with a question that has a significant impact on how we view these fragmentary plays and those of Aristophanes: whether women formed part of the audience at the theater of Dionysus. I maintain that they did, and that the playwrights wrote in the knowledge that their work would be viewed by women. Even if one maintains that the plays were written primarily for citizen males, the presence of others – slaves, women, foreigners – in the theater of Dionysus complicated this question of "audience." Women will have brought their own experience of outspoken, vulgar insult and jest to the city's Dionysian feast.

We know little of the first thirty years of comedy's formal existence at Athens. Tragic competitions had existed for more than half a century before comedies also were awarded prizes in the City Dionysia. The first famous name of comedy in this period, Epicharmus, was a Sicilian who composed dramas in the 480s. There are about forty Epicharmian play titles extant, and they cover a range, with mythical themes predominating.[30] In Athens, comedies were being written by Magnes and others, about whom almost nothing is known. Both Sicilian comedy and early tragedy doubtless shaped the evolution of Attic comedy in the crucial matter of plot. By midcentury Sophron, the Syracusan composer of prose mimes, was writing. These mimes will have influenced subsequent comic poets in their portrayal of women, because some of them portrayed women engaged in domestic tasks and in cult.

By the 450s Cratinus was the most successful comic playwright in Athens, writing comedies on mythical and other themes.[31] He was succeeded by a third generation: Pherecrates, Aristophanes, Eupolis, Hermippus, Plato Comicus, Theopompus, and many others who flourished in the last three decades of the fifth century, and, in some cases, into the fourth. The fragments and titles of lost plays by these men and their contemporaries reveal that women's roles underwent a rapid expansion and development within the rapid development of comedy itself. From mythic themes, the mockery of the female relatives of political notables, and female personifications of abstractions or grammatically feminine nouns (ships, islands, cities) the comic poets turned to plays featuring choruses of "real" Athenians. These tended to be lower-class women, whose commercial activity (including prostitution) made them officially visible in ways that respectable women could not be. Old women and women engaged in cultic activities had a similar official visibility and comic potential and constituted popular targets. Finally, as the genre evolved the playwrights sometimes portrayed "respectable" younger housewives – a risqué choice, given the ideology of containment and privacy that pertained to women. Not all of the women portrayed, whether "respectable" or not, were disparaging caricatures. There are sympathetic and nuanced portrayals, resembling those of tragedy, anticipating the heroines of Menander.

Iambic Mockery: Comic Plots

Aristotle viewed old comedy and iambic as linked through their shared origin in obscene cultic exchanges.[32] He described an ancient fissure of the

literary tradition into serious and light or mocking poetry. The practitioners of the latter, the "earliest creators of blame," assailed each other in the
iambic meter (Aristotle uses the verb ἰάμβιζον).[33] Homer, with his *Margites*,
was the first maker of blame to become famous; he invented comedy by
"making drama not out of blame, but out of the laughable."[34] Thus Aristotle distinguished between the blame of satire and the more lighthearted
phenomenon of comedy. At the same time, in his view they belonged together, as facetious representations of less worthy men; comedy was the
medium for those who would have used iambic in an earlier period. Subsequently, in speaking of the development of comedy in Attica, he said that
plots came from Sicily and that it was Crates (a mid-fifth-century comic
actor and playwright) who gave up the iambic form in favor of dialogue
and plots "of a general nature."[35]

THE MOCKERY OF GREEK OLD COMEDY WAS INDEED LINKED TO THE IAMBIC
tradition; it shared some of the personnel, themes, and conventions with
the iambic of Archilochus and Hipponax.[36] On a spectrum of ancient genres, comedy and iambic merged. In book 4 of the *Ethics* (1128a ff) Aristotle
drew a line, this time not between iambic and comedy, but between old
comedy and new comedy, the latter having purged itself of the *aischrologia*
that marred – and linked – old comedy and iambic.

Iambic could present scenes of the low life, including simple narratives,
or engage in diatribes, but it did not create highly complex and fanciful
plots, as comedy eventually did.[37] As one scholar puts it:

> . . . though many archaic poets tell what we may reasonably assume to be
> made-up stories in the first person about a character bearing the poet's
> name who is otherwise as fictional a character as Margites or Dicaeopolis,
> there is still no clear instance in archaic literature of narrative or dramatic
> poetry about wholly-invented human characters in a contemporary set-
> ting. The closest contenders are the *Margites* (whose setting may never-
> theless have been heroic or historical); Archilochus' Charon the carpenter
> (fr. 19 West), who seems to have spoken the poem in fictive character; Al-
> caeus fr. 10B Lobel-Page, with its opening first-person feminine; and the
> sub-literary genre of fable. . . .[38]

Iambic's coarse language describing sexual encounters, its terminology
of abuse, and some of its misogynistic themes fed into the old comic tradition, but comedy could take its portrayal of women further, and the

fifth-century playwrights used their medium to full advantage. Old comedy's sprightly female characters not only anticipated Menander's sympathetic heroines, they also started down other developmental roads that comedy could have taken, if the poets had chosen, turning comedy more and more toward the parody of tragedy and sentimental and domestic themes: lost heiresses, babies of unknown or falsified parentage, mistaken identities.

Women in Comedy

There are four strands in the early comic portraits of women: mythical tales, fantastic or utopian tales, women characters portraying concepts or entities such as cities or islands, and mockery of historical women (relatives of Athenian politicians and notables).[39] I begin with this last strand.

Cimon's sister and Callias's wife Elpinice; Pericles' mistress, Aspasia; Lycon's wife and Autolycus's mother, Rhodia; Hyperbolus's mother; Cleophon's mother; Philonides' mother; Euripides' wife; Euripides' mother; and the courtesan Lais were comic targets.[40] Some well-connected women, perhaps without being explicitly named, appeared as ludicrous characters on the stage.[41] The most commonly invoked explanation for the insults and satirical portraits is that they were a means of attacking the honor and integrity of their male relative(s). Undoubtedly such thinking drove much of this humor and made audiences laugh when they heard the jokes. Following Pericles' citizenship legislation of 451–0, smears about the foreign birth or sexual promiscuity of a politician's mother had implications beyond his family honor, serious enough in itself.[42] Only a man born of a marriage between two free- and native-born Athenians could himself be an Athenian citizen. Thus the joke that Cleophon's mother was an old whore with a Thracian accent was barbed with the double threat of family dishonor and disenfranchisement.

At the same time these women did not merely function as weapons against their male relatives in the comic plays. Forces older and deeper than the current political configuration contributed to the lampooning of powerful women. A woman's real or perceived proximity to power inspired a battery of charges – of being a meddler, a troublemaker, sexually exploitative or opportunistic (like Helen), or domineering (like Omphale, who held Heracles captive and made him perform demeaning [women's] tasks). Aspasia may have been likened to Omphale in the *Cheirons* of Cratinus, in the *Friends* of Eupolis, or both.[43] Callias claimed that Aspasia coached Pericles in public-speaking in his Πεδῆται (*Men in Fetters*).[44] Cratinus compared Aspasia to Hera, born of Time and Anal-Intercourse, in the *Cheirons*, a jibe that implies a nasty temperament *and* undue influence, the result of her own sexual versatility, and her conniving at his affairs with others. Aspasia's tolerance of Pericles' excesses was believed to have given her undesirable political power over him and the city.[45] According to Aristophanes' *Acharnians*, three whores (Aspasia and two of the women she ran) were the cause of the Peloponnesian War.[46]

The *Demes* of Eupolis, probably datable to 412, illustrates Aspasia's role as whipping post for the comic poets. It depicts Pericles, together with other now-dead heroes of Athens (Solon, Miltiades, and Aristides), returning from the grave to advise the city once more.[47] Pericles asks a certain Pyronides about his son, born to Aspasia.[48]

(Πε.) ὁ νόθος δέ μοι ζῆι; (Πυ.) καὶ πάλαι γ᾽ ἂν ἦν ἀνήρ,
εἰ μὴ τὸ τῆς πόρνης ὑπωρρώδει κακόν.

(Per.) Does my illegitimate son still live? (Pyr.) Sure. He would have
    become a man long before now
But he's a little afraid about the embarrassment of having
    a whore for a mother.

Unlike the *Odyssey*'s underworld scene upon which this seems to be modeled, the dead hero is not gratified by hearing of his son's heroic manhood.[49] Aspasia, a foreign-born woman, could not bear a new Pericles to save Athens.[50] This harsh term (*porne*) is particularly striking in that Aspasia is now dead. Doubtless the attack was motivated by the political ambitions of the younger Pericles, yet we should also consider the comic "Aspasia" as a target in her own right, the antithesis of an ideal citizen woman: independent, influential – and foreign born.[51] Similarly the *Phaon* of Plato Comicus (produced in 391) refers to the dead Lais.[52]

A woman's involvement or alleged involvement in politics was invariably sexualized by the comic poets. Elpinice's concern for her brother Cimon's welfare, and the belief (justified or not) that she interceded with Pericles when Cimon was charged with treason in 463 and later to arrange Cimon's return from exile, may have given rise to the joke that she had an incestuous relationship with her brother.[53] Plutarch records the slanders, broadcast by the comic poets, as forming part of a propaganda campaign waged by Cimon's enemies to discredit his efforts to restore the powers of the Areopagus. Such comic inventions became part of the fabric of Athenian politics.

It is clear, however, that Elpinice herself was a political force to be reckoned with and therefore a target in her own right.[54] Another Elpinice story, spans the political and socioliterary spheres. Pericles returned to Athens after his conquest of Samos (440) and praised the war dead in a state funeral.[55] As he finished his speech, most of the women present clasped his hand and placed wreaths and ribbons on his head. Only Elpinice, sister of Cimon, rebuked him with an ironic compliment for losing so many citizens in a war against a kindred people. Pericles, we are told, smiled gently and quoted a line of Archilochus:

οὐκ ἂν μύροισι γρηῦς ἐοῦσ᾽ ἠλείφεο

As an old woman you should not anoint yourself with perfumes.

The line – far from gentle in implication – puts a woman in her place, politically and socially. As we have seen, the very power to define female aging was itself a weapon of the iambic genre. Pericles implied that political opinions and sexual initiatives were equally inappropriate for this "old woman." As a woman Elpinice had no subjectivity, and as an old woman she did not even have the indirect power of being an object of desire. Wearing perfume in one's golden years becomes a metaphor for misappropriating male prerogatives. Pericles also may be referring to Elpinice's supposed sexual relationship with her brother. If he has conducted himself with undue severity toward kin, she has been guilty of undue intimacy.

One of the remarkable aspects of Plutarch's recorded exchange between Pericles and Elpinice over Samos is that she was making a public joke, during an official event. The Athenian campaign against Samos occurred in a year that saw the enactment of legislation "against joking."[56] Thus not only was Elpinice criticizing public policy, she was also joking at a time so sensitive that laws curtailed the freedoms of the city's licensed jokers. Like the Iambe of later tradition she was punished – with iambic – for her temerity. This public funeral was a site of contestation – not only between political factions in Athens but also regarding whether this powerful woman was to have a public voice at all. Elpinice, like Iambe, chooses joking to make her point in the midst of someone else's somber memorialization. The anecdote is also interesting because of the fact that other women also responded publicly to Pericles' speech; it was their positive response that distinguished them from Elpinice. But even this limited role for women was diminishing, according to Thucydides' characterization of Pericles's subsequent funeral oration, after the first year of the Peloponnesian War.

At the end of this speech he urges the grieving women to withdraw in silence, taking comfort in past glory or future hopes.[57]

Myth

Aside from explicit references to well-connected women of Athens, the poets mocked them in mythical plays through parodic evocations of their lives and circumstances. The *Dionysusalexander* of Cratinus (430) told how Dionysus carried off Helen to Troy, where the lovers were discovered by Paris: Dionysus disguised as a ram, Helen hidden in a chicken coop. Paris kept Helen for himself but sent Dionysus off to the enemy. We are told that the play satirized Pericles by innuendo (δι᾽ ἐμφάσεως) very persuasively for involving Athens in the war. It is very likely, then, that Aspasia also featured in the play, perhaps as Helen, as she was often known.

Mythical stories, whether or not they hinted at contemporary notables, had a long and successful history in comedy. From Epicharmus's day to the mid–fourth century – nearly a century and a half – mythical themes flourished within the comic repertoire. Both the comedies of Epicharmus and the flourishing tragic tradition in Athens contributed ideas and situations. With so little information about the dates and details of lost plays, one cannot be certain, but the treatment by the comic poets Diocles, Lysippus, and Antiphanes of the Bacchae theme, for example, probably derived at least in part from a comic tradition going back to Epicharmus, as well as the many fifth-century tragic versions of the theme.

Usually it is impossible to pinpoint a particular source of inspiration for a comic poet's treatment of a mythical theme. Epicharmus wrote a *Medea*, and he was followed, in the comic tradition, by Cantharus and Strattis among others, in the fifth century. We know little of the versions by Epicharmus and Strattis, but in a fragment of the Strattis version Medea boasted of the first-rate unguent she was sending to a woman (Creusa?) via an intermediary.[58] Strattis seems to have to focused on the Corinthian element of Medea's story, her murder of Creusa (as opposed to events in Colchis or the tricking of Pelias). Judging by the iconographic record alone, the Euripidean play had a big impact in 431, and so Strattis might have been parodying that version of the tragedy.[59] Similarly the *Lemnian Women* of Aristophanes, which contained notable parody of the tragic style, followed tragedies on the same theme by Aeschylus and Euripides.[60] As Lowe has suggested, "most of the apparent renaissance of mythological comedy at the end of the century is actually a flowering of tragic parody."[61] Mockery and parodies of tragedies and the tragedians became a cottage industry among the Athenian comic playwrights.[62] Euripides was an especially popular target. His own unsparing treatment of legendary situations brought the contemporary implications of ancient stories into focus. This willingness on his part to emphasize the tawdriness of human suffering, and to strip the grandeur from ancient myths, made Euripides irresistible to the comic poets. In a play called the *Women Grabbing the Tents* (αἱ Σκηνὰς Καταλαμβανοῦσαι) Aristophanes (perhaps in the Parabasis?) comments on his relationship with Euripides. Apparently Aristophanes was ridiculed for simultaneously mocking and imitating the tragic poet:

χρῶμαι γὰρ αὐτοῦ τοῦ στόματος τῷ στρογγύλῳ
τοὺς νοῦς δ'ἀγοραίους ἧττον ἢ'κεῖνος ποιῶ.

I use his clipped verbal style, sure!
But I'm much less vulgar in my choice of topics![63]

The story of Auge illustrates the common ground between the different traditions. It became the subject of a tragedy (by Euripides), a satyr play, and a comedy, by the late-fifth-, and fourth-century poet Philyllius. The *Auge*'s plot probably followed the lines we know from a late mythographer.[64] Auge, the daughter of Aleos, was a priestess of Athena in a city of Arcadia. During a ritual midnight dance she was raped by Heracles, who left her a ring as token. She bore a son, Telephus. Her father, in a rage, ordered the baby to be exposed and Auge to be drowned. Telephus was suckled by a doe, however, and so saved. Heracles returned in time to save Auge as well. She became the wife of Teuthras, following the instructions of an oracle by Apollo. One can see how some of the elements of this traditional tale would later predominate in new comedy: the rape at a festival of a respectable woman, child of an unknown father, token of identification, and last minute resolution. Similarly the *Cocalus* of Aristophanes (387), which told of the murder of Minos by the Sicilian King Cocalus and his daughters so as to prevent his (re)capture by Minos, was noted by the author of the ancient *Life* of Aristophanes as the first example of what was to become new comedy, written, as the biographer believed, when it was no longer possible to engage in political critiques. Apparently its plot included "rape, recognition, and all the other elements imitated by Menander."[65]

In addition to comically incongruous use of tragedy's high-flown language, comedy's treatment of mythical themes emphasized humdrum domestic arrangements that tragedy or epic typically ignored.[66] Thus for example in the *Lemnian Women* just mentioned, a nurse or servant exclaims that she or he has "just left Hypsipyle washing herself, in the bath."[67] The *Aeolosicon* of Aristophanes reduced the grandeur of Aeolus's Homeric palace to frowsty overcrowding: "one bedroom and one bath will do for all these women!" somebody insists, presumably of Aeolus's daughters, who probably constituted one of two choruses in the play, the other being his sons.[68] In Strattis's version of the *Phoenician Women* Jocasta (in a parody of the solemn advice to her warring sons in Euripides' version) tells them how to make pease pudding.[69] In the *Callisto* of Alcaeus someone, probably Artemis herself, advises one of her companions to bring along ground coriander to keep fresh the meat that they will get in hunting.[70] In the *Auge* of Philyllius, mentioned earlier, somebody gives instruction for clearing up and sweeping after the women's dinner and giving them scent, to freshen up.[71]

In essence, of course, comedy's use of myth was profoundly different from tragedy's, in accordance with its very different purposes.[72] If tragedy turned to myth to ponder the history of the community and its institutions, comedy tended to value the individual above all. The individual "little guy" (or gal) might achieve his dreams through the creation of some communal utopia, but the focus was still on the individual, and not the community, with its tensions and complex responsibilities. Tragedy dwelled on the stresses within the body politic. Like the equally sober genre of epic, it contemplated the body's pain and vulnerability. Comedy thought about pain too, and it reveled in indignities – but emphasized comforts and animal pleasures. Whereas in the embassy scene in the *Iliad* Achilles repudiates Agamemnon's attempt to appease him with offers of a princely marriage, land, and skilled slave women, in the *Cheiron* of Pherecrates he has a different reaction:

(A.) δώσει δέ σοι γυναῖκας ἑπτὰ Λεσβίδας
(B.) καλόν γε δῶρον, ἐπτ᾽ ἔχειν λαικαστρίας.

(Odysseus [?]) And he'll give you seven women of Lesbos
(Achilles [?]) What a great present! To have seven trollops![73]

Predictably then, the selfsame myth, whether generated as an independent comic creation or as a parody of some tragedy, would seem entirely different in each genre.

Fantasies and Utopias

These plays, constituting a fairly small category as far as one can tell, are of particular interest because of the trio of great Aristophanic plays, which derive from the same tradition: the *Lysistrata*, *Thesmophoriazousae*, and *Ecclesiazousae*. The *Miners* (οἱ Μεταλλῆς) of Pherecrates included a substantial passage in which a woman describes, to an unknown audience, a Hades filled with sumptuous food, fully prepared, into which they might "dive" (through a mine shaft?). Pherecrates also wrote a play called the Τυρραννίς, or *Woman Tyrant* (?), about which there is some controversy. Was this a fantasy in the style of Aristophanes' *Ecclesiazousae*, in which a woman or women actually took over the state? Or was it a humorous account of how women already ruled the roost? I'm inclined to the former view, on the grounds of the following passage:

εἶτ᾽ ἐκεραμεύσαντο τοῖς μὲν ἀνδράσιν ποτήρια
πλατέα, τοίχους οὐκ ἔχοντ᾽ ἀλλ᾽ αὐτὸ τοὔδαφος μόνον,
κοὐχὶ χωροῦντ᾽ οὐδὲ κόγχην, ἐμφερῆ γευστηρίοις·
σφίσι δέ ⟨γ᾽⟩ αὐταῖσιν βαθείας κύλικας ὥσπερ ὁλκάδας
οἰναγωγούς, περιφερεῖς, λεπτάς, μέσας γαστροίδας,
οὐκ ἀβούλως, ἀλλὰ πόρρωθεν κατεσκευασμέναι
αὖθ᾽, ὅπως ἀνεκλογίστως πλεῖστος οἶνος ἐκποθῆι.
εἶθ᾽ ὅταν τὸν οἶνον αὐτὰς αἰτιώμεθ᾽ ἐκπιεῖν,
λοιδοροῦνται κὠμνύμουσι μὴ πιεῖν ἀλλ᾽ ἢ μίαν.
ἡ δὲ κρείττων ἡμί᾽ ἐστὶ χιλίων ποτηρίων.

Then they had made for their husbands flat drinking cups,
Not having any sides, just a bottom,
And they hardly hold even a few drops, just like tasting spoons really.
But for themselves! Deep goblets like cargo barges,
Wine freighters, roly-poly, with shallow walls, pot bellied!
Not without advance planning! They calculated it all ahead of time,
So that as much wine as possible might get slugged,
And then when we accuse them of drinking the lot,
They abuse us, and swear they've "just had one."
But that "one" is more than a thousand normal drinks.[74]

If this play (the date of which, unfortunately, we do not know) did indeed present a fantasy of women taking over the state, then it is possible that the line

ἡγούμεθα τῆς πόλεως εἶναι ταύτας σωτῆρας ∪ – –.

We think that these women are the saviors of the city

also derives from this play. This solitary line of Pherecrates, whatever its source, certainly suggests a plot analogous to that of the *Lysistrata* or *Ecclesiazousae*.[75]

The Στρατιώτιδες (*Women at Arms*) of Theopompus, composed some time before 414, featured women serving in the army, one of whom complains about the awkwardness of the drinking canteens.[76] "Mrs. Thrasymachus" (the name means "Strong Fighter") is said to be a fine tactician.[77] And the income for families is now increased, because both husband and wife are on the payroll.[78] Thus the Athenian audience had encountered a zany plot with some resemblence to the *Lysistrata* in the years before 411.

Personification

Personification constituted another major early "feminine" strand in old comedy.[79] This was a long-lived tradition that survived well into new comedy and its Roman successors – as Plautus attests, one of whose prologues was spoken by the star Arcturus and another by the embodiment of the family's household spirit, the Lar Familiaris (both male figures).[80] The goddess Fortune spoke the prologue in Menander's *Aspis*. In old comedy, Dorpia, or the female personification of Foretaster's Day, the first day of the Apatouria, announced herself at the beginning of the *Heracles* of Philyllius.[81] Calligeneia (the feminine Feast of Fair Offspring, and the third day in the festival of the Thesmophoria) pronounced the prologue in the second *Thesmophoriazousae* of Aristophanes.[82] As we go further back in the tradition, especially in the political comedies of Eupolis and Aristophanes, animated concepts and political entities could carry the weight of the entire play. As early as Epicharmus, a play titled *Logos and Logina* (*Mr. and Mrs. Logic*) no doubt pitted these two characters against each other in a contest. Epicharmus also wrote an *Islands*, the title of subsequent plays by Aristophanes and Plato Comicus. The *Islands* of Aristophanes introduced a chorus of "women" representing islands.[83] Someone on stage identified them as they made their entrance. One of them was "downcast, hanging her head low," perhaps the result of harsh treatment at the hands of the Athenians.[84]

The practice of animating abstract nouns was not original to comedy. Hesiod's *Theogony* depicted primordial forces that drove and directed events in the human sphere. The *Theogony*'s effect is massive, formidable, often somber. When the comic poets animated the gendered nouns of classical Greek, the result was an unruly and surreal world, where cartoon characters interacted freely and unself-consciously with the humans. Although these cartoon characters and choruses could be male, they were more often female.[85]

◇

NAMING SOMETHING IN GREEK USUALLY GENDERED IT.[86] As early as Hesiod this grammatical gendering inspired fantasies of animate beings, capable of biological reproduction. In the *Theogony* Gaia and Uranus, the "male" and "female" representations of earth and sky, produced offspring as a result of a sexual union. Indeed in an earlier generation the feminine noun Night lay in love with the neuter Erebus and gave birth to Aether and to Day. A feminine noun could always mimic real women and give birth.

Predictably, when an abstraction was animated in feminine form, the comic poets emphasized sexuality. (Male) desires were personified in the female form and desires were invariably sexualized. Thus, for example, Fullfruit or Harvest (Ὀπώρα) in Aristophanes' *Peace* was a nubile and attractive woman, whose attractions are detailed during her appearance on stage and who is wed to Trygaeus at the end. She is one of the two desirable companions of the goddess Peace, the other being Festival (Θεωρία). The Queen (Βασίλεια) in *Birds* is also a lovely woman, marrried to Peisetairus at that play's end. The *Knights* features two attractive Treaties (Σπονδαί), in whom Demos expresses immediate sexual interest. The end of the *Lysistrata* featured Reconciliation (Διαλλγή) as a woman, ogled by the Athenians and Spartans. As they rushed to come to terms, they agreed to divide Greek territory, which they described in terms of the woman's body they saw before them. There also seems to have been an implicit equation between territorial acquisitiveness and sexual desire in the *Cities* of Eupolis (422), where a certain Philinus is rebuked for ogling one of the chorus cities.[87] The speaker seems to be making a distinction between a woman-city who deserves respect and one who may more appropriately satisfy his lusts.

> ὁ φιλῖνος οὗτος, τί ἄρα πρὸς ταύτην βλέπεις;
> οὐκ ἀπολιβάξεις εἰς ἀποικίαν τινά;

> Hey! Philinos, why are you gawking at her?
> Get lost to a colony can't you?

Each city was introduced individually in what must have been a spectacular parade and her vices or virtues commented on. Thus Tenos was adorned with scorpions and vipers; Chios, who never refused men or ships to Athens, was like a biddable horse that needed no spur; Cyzicus, described as wealthy and venal came out probably attired as a prostitute.[88] One ludicrous swaggerer affects to remember the bargain basement sexual escapades he enjoyed at Cyzicus, when stationed there in his youth:

ἡ δὲ ὑστάτη ποῦ 'σθ'; ἥδε Κύζικος πλέα στατήρων.
ἐν τῆδε τοίνυν τῇ πόλει φρουρῶν ⟨ἐγώ⟩ ποτ' αὐτὸς
γυναῖκ' ἐκίνουν κολλύβου καὶ παῖδα καὶ γέροντα,
κἀξῆν ὅλην τὴν ἡμέραν τὸν κύσθον ἐκκορίζειν

So where's the last one? Here she is! Ah, Cyzicus, just full of cash!
One time I was stationed in this city, guard duty,
And I got to screw a woman, a boy and an old guy – all for a dime!
I could spend the whole day just trawling for pussy!

As Rosen has argued recently, however, Eupolis's *Cities* seems to have advocated a more responsible (if no less proprietory) relationship between Athenians and their subject allies: that of a kindly husband toward his wife. The chorus of subject cities may have been individually married to Athenians at the play's end.[89]

The "Talkies"

Eupolis's appealing "cities" seem to have had little or nothing to say, although the fragmentary remains do not permit certainty.[90] The characters of Peace, Fullfruit, and Festival are notoriously silent in the *Peace*. Similarly, the *Lysistrata*'s Reconciliation is silent during the scene in which she appears. Once the feminine personifications really begin to speak as independent entities, they no longer can function as the embodiments of male lust. The relatively late play, the *Cities* of Heniochus, to judge from a probable fragment of its prologue, presented a different version of "cities as women" – not desired bodies but talkative troublemakers.[91] The women-cities have gathered to give thanks for their newfound freedom from tribute to Athens:

ἐγὼ δ' ὄνομα τὸ μὲν καθ' ἑκάστην αὐτίκα
λέξω· συνάπασαι δ' εἰσὶ παντοδαπαὶ πόλεις,
αἳ νῦν ἀνοηταίνουσι πολὺν ἤδη χρόνον.
τάχ' ἄν τις ὑποκρούσειεν ὅ τι ποτ' ἐνθάδε
νῦν εἰσι κἀνέροιτο· παρ' ἐμοῦ πεύσεται.
τὸ χωρίον μὲν γὰρ τόδ' ἐστὶ πᾶν κύκλωι
Ὀλυμπία, τηνδὶ δὲ τὴν σκηνὴν ἐκεῖ

σκηνὴν ὁρᾶν θεωρικὴν νομίζετε.
εἶέν· τί οὖν ἐνταῦθα δρῶσιν αἱ πόλεις;
ἐλευθέρι᾽ ἀφίκοντο θύσουσαί ποτε,
ὅτε τῶν φόρων ἐγένοντ᾽ ἐλεύθεραι σχεδόν.
κἄπειτ᾽ ἀπ᾽ ἐκείνης τῆς θυσίας διέφθορεν
αὐτὰς ξενίζουσ᾽ ἡμέραν ἐξ ἡμέρας
ἀβουλία κατέχουσα πολὺν ἤδη χρόνον.
γυναῖκε δ᾽ αὐτὰς δύο ταράττετόν τινε
ἀεὶ συνοῦσαι· Δημοκρατία θατέραι
ὄνομ᾽ ἐστί, τῆι δ᾽ Ἀριστοκρατία θατέραι,
δι᾽ ἃς πεπαρωινήκασιν ἤδη πολλάκις

I'll give you the name of each one right away.
They're all cities, of every kind.
They've been foolish now for ages.
Perhaps you might break in and ask
why they're here. I'll tell you.
The country here all around us is Olympia,
and this structure here, think of it as a festival tent.
What are the cities doing here?
They arrived to sacrifice to Liberty
as soon as they became freed of tribute responsibilities.
Then once the sacrifice was done, indecision changed them
and day after day has ruined them for a long time now.
Two women are always with them and set them
in turmoil. One's called Democratia,
the other Aristocratia. It's been continual
drunken brawling because of them.

Similarly, in the *Knights* of Aristophanes personified ships, speaking as women, refused to sail to Carthage under the admiral Hyperbolus.[92] These feisty triremes represented a world that did not submit quietly to the disposition of its would-be masters.

No one carried the idea of the "dangerously talkative female" to more ludicrous lengths than the comic poets, but they did not invent the practice. Both aspects of the comic poets' conceptual women had existed at least since Hesiod: the lovely object of desire and the talkative bane of man's existence. Pandora was the embodiment of self-destructive male desire. Her acquisition and use of a deceitful mind and speech detached male desire from men themselves, and she became a fully autonomous and culpable enemy, plotting against them. The anecdote, described in Chapter 1, featuring Lais trapping and humiliating Euripides with his own words may have been inspired in part by the feeling that Euripides had irresponsibly created monstrous female word spinners and deserved to be hoist with his own petard. As Aristophanes imagined it in the *Thesmophoriazousae*, the "real" women of Athens (or their comic equivalents) pursue and silence the playwright who animated their all-too-articulate tragic doubles. Diphilus and Menander, the renowned new comic playwrights, were both featured in anecdotes depicting their verbal conquest at the hands of comic courtesans.[93]

Again and again, Greek playwrights reenacted the invention of Pandora, breathing into a feminine concept unruly life – and speech.[94] Cratinus apparently wrote a song, popular at symposia if we are to believe Aristophanes, beginning with the line "[Goddess] Bribery, shod in figs!"[95]

The notion that the female represented something fake and frivolous manifested itself clearly in the characters or choruses of certain plays. The *Games* of Crates may have had a chorus consisting of different children's games. I suspect that they were women, corresponding to the feminine noun (Παιδιαί) of the title. We hear of one woman who danced with men, playing "kiss in the ring" with the handsome ones.[96] The *Fripperies* (Κραπάταλοι) of Pherecrates also probably featured a chorus of women loaded with frivolities, such as "a purple headband, a bra, a decorative edging for a dress, a comb."[97] In the second *Thesmophoriazousae* of Aristophanes a slave complains about a heavy pack containing (Agathon's?) makeup and feminine accessories.[98] The *Mockeries* or *Curses* (Καταχῆναι) of Lysippus similarly may have featured a feminine chorus, embodying this feminine noun for the "curse" tablets sometimes affixed to buildings in antiquity.

Women and feminine signifiers could signify not only fakery and deceit, but, paradoxically, also the essential, something akin to the Platonic Form: abstraction made flesh. The word ὄνομα meant both "name" and "noun," as Aristophanes illustrated in the *Clouds*, where Strepsiades tried to learn from Socrates a logical system of gendering Greek nouns.[99] Whereas individual men could make famous or notorious their own name, and that of their family, women ideally did not become known at all. With the exception of a few wives and mothers of politicians, or especially glorious priestesses, there were no public women in classical Greece and in Athens in particular. As I have noted, naming women in public was very rare, amounting to a taboo. It was thus possible for Cratinus to write a play in which he (as a character) was married to a grumpy and neglected woman called "Comedy." From the point of view of the world at large his real wife did not exist.

It was easier to conceptualize a universal or transcendant quality or practice under a feminine name than a masculine one. Women's names existed, to a greater extent at least, in a vacuum. They could be (just) nouns. At *Thesmophoriazousae* 802 ff the chorus of women proclaimed that Nausimache (Naval Victory), Aristomache (Excellence in Battle), Euboule (Good Counsel), and Stratonice (Military Victory) – all female names epitomizing excellence – outclassed actual Athenian male soldiers and politicians, such as Cleophon or Charminus. A woman's name (ὄνομα) would defeat a man's any day, because the man was freighted by the particular choices, weaknesses, and failures of his own public career.

The notion that "women" represented abstraction – the (literally) nebulous and manipulable world of ideas, words, and theories – manifested itself clearly in the "feminine" intellectual chorus of Aristophanes' *Clouds*. In the eyes of the comic poets the city was a feminized place, run by men who practiced the meretricious art of pleasing the demos and seducing them with wily language.[100]

A connection between language and the female was long established in drama.[101] A poet named Callias (probably not the comic poet of that name) produced a *Grammatical Show* (or *Grammatical Tragedy*) featuring a chorus of women who actually represented letters of the alphabet or syllables.[102] We are told nothing of the *Cleobulinas* of Cratinus beyond its title (Alexis later also wrote a *Cleobulina*), but we hear that Cleobulus of Lindus, one of the seven sages of Greece, had a daughter, Cleobulina, who composed riddles in hexameter verse.[103] The play probably featured riddles being proposed within a gathering of women.[104] Cratinus may have invented her, but nonetheless the link between women and clever, poetic ambiguous speech is significant. The *Sappho* of Antiphanes, one of six comedies named for this poet, featured Sappho herself as a character asking riddles:[105]

(Σα.) ἔστι φύσις θήλεια βρέφη σώιζουσ᾽ ὑπὸ κόλποις
αὑτῆς, ὄντα δ᾽ ἄφονα βοὴν ἵστησι γεγωνὸν
καὶ διὰ πόντιον οἶδμα καὶ ἠπείρου διὰ πάσης
οἷς ἐθέλει θνητῶν, τοῖς δ᾽ οὐδὲ παροῦσιν ἀκούειν
ἔξεστιν· κωφὴν δ᾽ ἀκοῆς αἴσθησιν ἔχουσιν.

***

(Β) ἡ μὲν φύσις γὰρ ἦν λέγεις ἐστὶν πόλις,
βρέφη δ᾽ ἐν αὐτῆι διατρέφει τοὺς ῥήτορας.
οὗτοι κεκραγότες δὲ τὰ διαπόντια
τὰκ τῆς Ἀσίας καὶ τἀπὸ Θράικης λήμματα

ἕλκουσι δεῦρο. νενομένων δὲ πλησίον
αὐτῶν κάθηται λοιδορουμένων τ᾽ ἀεὶ
ὁ δῆμος οὐδὲν οὔτ᾽ ἀκούων οὔθ᾽ ὁρῶν.
(Σα.) U̅ – U – πῶς γὰρ γένοιτ᾽ ἄν, ὦ πάτερ,
ῥήτωρ ἄφωνος; (Β.) ἢν ἁλῶι τρὶς παρανόμων.
U̅ – U – καὶ μὴν ἀκριβῶς ᾠόμην
ἐγνωκέναι τὸ ῥηθέν. ἀλλὰ δὴ λέγε.
(Σα.) θήλεια μέν νυν ἐστὶ φύσις ἐπιστολή,
βρέφη δ᾽ ἐν αὐτῆι περιφέρει τὰ γράμματα·
ἄφωνα δ᾽ ὄντα ⟨ταῦτα⟩ τοῖς πόρρω λαλεῖ
οἷς βούλεθ᾽· ἕτερος δ᾽ ἂν τύχηι τις πλησίον
ἑστὼς ἀναγιγνώσκοντος οὐκ ἀκούσεται

(Sa.) There exists a creature feminine in nature, keeping her babies
   safe in her bosom.
They, being voiceless, establish a loud cry.
Through the swell of the sea, and through all of the land
For those mortals they desire to address. It is possible for those
Who are not present to hear them. They have a mute sense of sound.

(B). The being you describe is a city.
She nourishes orators as her babies within her.
These, babbling noisily, drag here their arguments here
From Asia and from Thrace.
With these characters dwelling nearby, and brawling constantly,
The people sits by, seeing and hearing nothing.
(Sa). . . . How could it be, sir.
That an orator could be voiceless?
(B). If he's been convicted three times of breaking the law!
      . . . Well I thought that I had indeed
Understood the riddle correctly. But give me the answer.
(Sa.) The feminine being is a letter.
She bears letters as babies within her.
They are voiceless, but they address those who are far away,
Whom they wish. But if someone happens to stand near
The person reading the letter, he will not hear them.

The passage may be said to function as a metaphor for the Sapphic
tradition itself.[106] The Sapphic poetic tradition, oral in origin, famously
reflected on the notion of presence – to lovers, to a poet's audience – and
on the anguish of distance. In this comic passage the distant move from
the face-to-face culture of oral poetry to the encoding of a far-flung literary
tradition is expressed as maternity. The poet "herself" here, animated as a
dramatic character, describes the way in which a writer's "offspring" may

confront and communicate with people far from her and, alternatively, how they may reveal nothing to a person in their very presence. Ultimately and ironically "Sappho," both in antiquity and in modern times, has existed only as a text that eludes all of our efforts to give it voice and face.

Little else is known about the comic Sappho plays. Athenaeus informs us that Diphilus made Archilochus and Hipponax Sappho's lovers in his play.[107] The "biographical" tradition on Sappho also linked her romantically with Anacreon, Alcaeus, and the ferryman Phaon (her unrequited love for whom caused her to fling herself from the Leucadian rock). We also hear that she was married to the wealthy Cercylas ("tail" or "penis") from Andros ("Isle of Man"). Many of these details about *Sappho*'s hectic (and anachronistic) love life probably derive from the comic tradition's lurid fantasies.[108] There are a number of comedies entitled *Sappho* known to have existed.[109] It is also likely that the *Phaon* of Plato Comicus and Antiphanes and the *Leucadian* of Menander and Diphilus also featured Sappho as a character.[110]

In a famous article Zeitlin demonstrated how the theater had feminine connotations within Greek thought and how theatricality was conceived of as essentially feminine.[111] Many comedies featured representations of drama itself as feminine.[112] Beginning with Epicharmus, several comic playwrights wrote plays entitled the *Muses* or *Birth of the Muses*.[113] The *Poetry* of Aristophanes depicted a group of individuals in search of the lady Poetry, who had disappeared and taken refuge with someone.[114] The *Cheiron* of Pherecrates included a scene in which Music complained of her violent mistreatment (with many sexual double entendres) at the hands of recent poets.[115] Cratinus' *Wineflask* (Πυτίνη) (423), following Aristophanes' harsh mockery of Cratinus as a washed-up old drunk in the *Knights*, brilliantly turned the joke around. In the play, Cratinus' wife, Comedy, sued him for cruelty and neglect because of his alcoholism.[116] The play probably featured a set-to between Comedy and Miss Wine Flask. At one point in the play Comedy (almost certainly) exclaimed of her straying husband:

νῦν δ᾽ ἢν ἴδηι Μενδαῖον ἡβῶντ᾽ ἀρτίως
οἰνίσκον, ἕπεται κἀκολουθεῖ καὶ λέγει
"οἴμ᾽ ὡς ἁπαλὸς καὶ λευκός· ἆρ᾽ οἴσει τρία;"

Now as soon as ever he sees a ripe little flask of Mendian (wine)
he's off in pursuit, saying "Look at that! How tender and delicate
she is! Will she be able to handle a three to one?"[117]

The double reference to a pale and delicate wine and a fine young girl may extend into the third line, where a sexual double entendre underlay the reference to customary dilution of wine.

Another feminine embodiment of an author's output appears in the *Rehearsals* (Διδασκαλίαι) of Cratinus, which may have featured a chorus of the individual plays that the poet had produced. Some interlocutor sympathizes with a woman, either the poet's Muse or one of his plays:

ὅτε σὺ τοὺς καλοὺς θριάμβους ἀναρύτουσ' ἀπηχθάνου

You were hated when you reached for pretty Bacchic hymns![118]

The metaphor (drawing water from a well) perhaps also mocks a "female" vocalist for straining to make the high notes.[119]

Poets as well as their works or Muses could be feminized. Aside from jibes at politicians' supposedly promiscuous or low-life mothers, old comedy tended in general not to be interested in maternity per se, except in the matter of motherhood as a metaphor for literary production.[120] The most famous example of this is the passage from the parabasis of *Clouds*, in which Aristophanes describes his earliest dramatic successes:

ἐξ ὅτου γὰρ ἐνθάδ' ὑπ' ἀνδρῶν, οὓς ἡδὺ καὶ λέγειν,
ὁ σώφρων τε χὠ καταπύγων ἄριστ' ἠκουσάτην,
κἀγώ, παρθένος γὰρ ἔτ' ἦ κοὐκ ἐξῆν πώ μοι τεκεῖν,
ἐξέθηκα, παῖς δ' ἑτέρα τις λαβοῦσ' ἀνείλετο,
ὑμεῖς δ' ἐξεθρέψατε γενναίως κἀπαιδεύσατε.
ἐκ τούτου μοι πιστὰ παρ' ὑμῶν γνώμης ἔσθ' ὅρκια. (528–33)

From the time when my plays the *Temperate Man* and the *Bugger*
Got the best of receptions here, by men of whom I love to speak,
And I, being still a slip of a girl, and not yet permitted to bear a child,
Exposed my baby, and another lass took it up,
And you reared and taught it nobly,
From that time have I held trusty pledges of your favor.[121]

More often tragedy (especially Euripidean tragedy) was ridiculed as the work of emasculated poets. The tragedian Agathon appeared as an effeminate in Aristophanes' *Thesmophoriazousae*. Euripides featured in the comic poets as an impotent and cuckolded husband – and father of "bastard" offspring, literary and biological – or as a woman whose promiscuous behavior resulted in progeny of dubious paternity. One fragment of Aristophanes "compliments" Cephisophon, a slave born in Euripides' house and accused of having slept with the playwright's wife:

Κηφισοφῶν ἄριστε καὶ μελάντετε,
σὺ γὰρ συνέζης ὡς τὰ πόλλ᾽ Εὐριπίδηι
καὶ συνεποίεις, ὥς φασι, τὴν μελωιδίαν

Best and blackest of men, Cephisophon!
you lived with Euripides in many ways,
and, they say, you made song music together with him.[122]

Callias's *Men in Fetters* featured either Euripides himself as a woman or the feminine embodiment of his Tragedy boasting of collaboration with Socrates.[123] Most famously, the *Thesmophoriazousae* depicted Euripides disguised as an old procuress in its final scene. Through this representation Euripides was mocked not merely as a woman, but one who satisfied "low" appetites with disreputable merchandise.[124] Aristophanes himself, on the contrary, boasted that he has never used *his* Muse as a procuress at *Knights* 1025 ff.

The Developing Tradition

Mythical women and personifications of abstract entities were present in the comic tradition from the outset, and certain well-connected real Athenian women were mocked, but not directly represented, on the Athenian stage by the middle of the fifth century. These subject choices continued through the fifth century, and the mythical stories continued to be extremely popular into new comedy and beyond. But what types of "real" woman could be portrayed on the Athenian stage? There was no tradition of portraying individual Athenian citizen women as comic protagonists – the female equivalent of Trygaeus, Dicaeopolis, or Strepsiades. Instead we see how the playwrights strove to broaden their range of characters by introducing groups of women engaged in certain activities or types of women whose respectability was not an issue.

Certain types of commercial activities, such as selling produce on the streets, were regarded as belonging to the lowest class in society. The poets thus felt free to portray such déclassé women on the comic stage. To be accused of belonging to such a group was in itself a comic insult, as we have seen in the case of Euripides' mother. The comic chorus of women street vendors goes back to the earliest days of comedy at Athens, apparently. Magnes, who flourished in the 470s, wrote the *Woman Weeder* or *Herbwife* (Ποάστρια), and much later in the century Phrynichus produced a play with a similar title. The *Women Bartenders* (Καπήλιδες) of

Theopompus included someone vigorously threatening a woman with a young lover: "I'll punish you and your Attis!"[125] Eupolis's *Marikas* (421 B.C.E.) and Hermippus's *Bread Women* (Ἀρτοπώλιδες) (420–19 B.C.E.), which may have portrayed a (thinly disguised) version of Hyperbolus's mother as a bread seller, continued this tradition.[126] We also see occasional cameos of such women in Aristophanes: the old bread woman whose loaves have been stolen by the newly youthful men in the *Old Age* or the widowed seller of wreaths in the *Thesmophoriazousae* who complains that Euripides has ruined her business because he has done away with belief in the gods.[127]

Prostitutes

The commercial activity with the most comic potential, and which may have begun the practice of depicting scenes from within Athenian houses, was prostitution. Beginning with Pherecrates, who was known for being inventive in his narratives and who was winning victories in the early 430s, a steady stream developed of plays named for hetairai or with signifi-cant roles for hetairai. These women varied in rank (and price) from the unskilled "heifer infantry" (πεζὰς μόσχους) mentioned by Eupolis, to edu-cated and wealthy women, renowned for their wit.[128] It would be wonderful to know more of the *Antilais* or *Double-Lais* that Cephisodorus produced in Athens, perhaps between 395 and 390.[129] Did the famously witty Sicilian courtesan encounter a rival, or was there a plot involving a substitute for her?

Hetairai may have been introduced into comedy as symbols of (male) self-indulgence and folly. In 421 the *Flatterers* of Eupolis mocked Callias, son of Hipponicus, for wasting his patrimony.[130] But their potential as sub-jects of humor in their own right was recognized early on. Pherecrates seems to have been the pioneer in this regard.[131] In his *Corianno*, named for a hetaira, we have substantial fragments of a scene or scenes, between (it seems) two or more adults, at least one of whom is a woman (Glyce), and a child, who mixes wine and serves it to them. The person knowledge-able about foreign words for dried figs may be a swaggering soldier – or Glyce, apologizing for her servant. Corianno herself probably is the one to complain of terrible thirst, having just returned from the baths.[132] Around the familiar old comic theme of women drinkers, a slur apparently intro-duced by the comic tradition, Pherecrates built a nuanced scene, with what seems to be an irascible older woman, Glyce; a courtesan who is used to being waited on; a non-Greek-speaking slave or servant child of Glyce.[133] The assignment of lines and identity of the speakers is uncertain.

73

φέρε δὴ κατακλινῶ· σὺ δὲ τράπεζαν ⟨ἔκ⟩ φέρε
καὶ κύλικα κἀντραγεῖν, ἵνα ἥδιον πίω.
(Β.) ἰδοῦ κύλιξ σοι καὶ τράπεζα καὶ φακοί.
(Α.) μή μοι φακούς, μὰ τὸν Δί’, οὐ γὰρ ἥδομαι·
ἢν γὰρ τράγηι τις, τοῦ στόματος ὄζει κακόν

74

ἀλλ’ ἰσχάδας μοι πρόελε τῶν πεφωγμένων
οὐκ ἰσχάδας οἴσεις; τῶν μελαινῶν· μανθάνεις;
ἐν τοῖς Μαριανδυνοῖς ἐκείνοις βαρβάροις
χύτρας καλοῦσι τὰς μαλαίνας ἰσχάδας

75

ἐκ τοῦ βαλανείου γὰρ διέφθος ἔρχομαι
ξηρὰν ἔχομαι τὴν φάρυγα. (Β.) δώσω πιεῖν.
(Α.) γλίσχρον γέ μούστι τὸ σίαλον νὴ τὼ θεώ.
(Β.) † ἐι λάβω κυρισοι † τὴν κοτυλίσκην. (Α.) μηδαμῶς
μικράν γε. κινεῖται γὰρ εὐθύς μοι χολή,
ἐξ οὗπερ ἔπιον ἐκ τοιαύτης φάρμακον.
ἐς τὴν ἐμὴν νῦν ἔγχεον τὴν μείζονα

76

                    (Α.) ἄποτος, ὦ Γλύκη.
(Γλ.) ὑδαρῆ ’νέχεέν σοι; (Α.) παντάπασι μὲν οὖν ὕδωρ.
(Γλ.) τί ἠργάσω; πῶς ὦ κατάρατε ⟨δ’⟩ ἐνέχεας;
(Β.) δύ’ ὕδατος, ὦ μάμμη. (Γλ.) τί δ’ οἴνου; (Β.) τέτταρας.
(Γλ.) ἔρρ’ ἐς κόρακας. Βατράχοισιν οἰνοχοεῖν σ’ ἔδει.

73

Let me sit down!. You, bring a table
and a cup and something to nibble on, to go with the wine.
(B.) Here is your cup and table, and some lentils.
(A.) Not lentils for god's sake! I detest them.
If you munch on them your breath smells.

74

Won't you bring me some dried figs, the roasted ones?
Can't you bring the dried figs? The black ones? Do you understand?
(Aside) They call black figs "chutra" in that barbarian Mariandyna.

75

I've just come back from the baths and I'm boiled!
My throat's completely dry.
                    I'll give you something to drink.
(A) By the Holy Twain![134] My mouth is all sticky inside!
(B) <Can I bring you> the little glass?
                    (A) No way!

It's tiny. I can feel myself getting nauseous.
I used to drink my medicine out of this little glass.
Pour it into this big cup of mine!

76

(A) It's undrinkable Glyce.
(Gl.) Did she mix a watery drink?
(A) It's all water!
(Gl.) What did you do? How did you mix it you stupid child?
(B) Two parts water Ma!
(Gl.) And how much of wine?
(B) Four.
(Gl.) To hell with you! You should be mixing drinks for frogs![135]

Another fragment from the same play introduces someone (a young man perhaps, addressing his father about the woman with whom they are both in love?) who declares:

ἀπαρτὶ μὲν οὖν ἐμοὶ μὲν εἰκός ἐστ᾽ ἐρᾶν,
σοὶ δ᾽ οὐκέθ᾽ ὥρα

On the contrary! It's OK for me to be in love.
You're past it.[136]

If this is indeed a father and son fighting over a courtesan, it is an early version of a theme that was also to appear in new comedy.

Comedies that focused on single households ultimately drove a new interest in the characters of individual women. The scanty evidence does not allow us to survey the characterization of the hetairai of old comedy, and there is little to suggest nuance. Nonetheless, especially in those cases where a hetaira had a sustained relationship with a single man, it was possible to depict her as a more sympathetic and subtle figure. In the *Seasons* (Ὧραι) of Cratinus someone exclaims of the absent Dionysus, for whom his mistress (*pallake*) is pining:

μακάριος τῶν παιδικῶν

Fortunate guy! To have a lover like this![137]

The word I have translated "lover" is παιδικά, the term generally used to describe the boy beloved of an Athenian man. It was replete with notions of desire and deep romantic attachment – and indeed the ancient lexicographers singled out the passage precisely because of the unusual application of the word to a woman here.

In the *Thalatta* of Pherecrates someone, perhaps Thalatta herself, complains of a male companion who is impossible to please:

κἂν μὲν σιωπῶ, † φέρεται †, πνίγεται
καί φησι "τί σιωπᾶις;" ἐὰν δέ ⟨γ'⟩ ἀποκριθῶ
"οἴμοι τάλας," φησίν, "χαράδρα κατελήλυθεν."

If I am quiet . . . he gets all heated up
and says 'Why are you saying nothing?' But if I answer him
he says 'Give me a break! I'm drowning in the flood!'[138]

This complaint suggests a relationship that transcends sex and evokes a human being with emotional depth. The complaint about not being allowed to speak shows up later, in the *Lysistrata*, where the play's eponymous heroine describes a typical encounter between a married Athenian woman and her husband, who tells her to shut up when she inquires into the decisions at the Assembly. But it also had appeared much earlier, in tragedy in the 440s, when Sophocles' Tecmessa described her anguish over Ajax, exacerbated by his refusal to allow her to talk to him about what has happened. The concubine Tecmessa, with her knowledge of her own real worth, independent of her servile status, anticipates the understated dignity and courage of some of Menander's famous courtesans, like Chrysis, the woman of Samos.[139] Already in old comedy we can see the ironic interplay between men's expectation of prostitutes (a purchaseable amenity) and the reality: an "amenity" that talks back and has its own expectations.

"Respectable" Women

Unlike prostitutes and street vendors, respectable women officially did not appear in public. The exception to this rule was provided by religious festivals, which routinely required women to make public appearances, formally sanctioned by the community. Thus religious cults afforded the comic poets a chance to expand their repertoire of feminine targets. In this they may have been inspired by the related tradition of Italian Mime, whose practitioners seem to have taken a great interest in women and their social and religious lives. The mid-fifth-century composer of prose Mimes (both of men and of women), Sophron, composed a piece called Ταὶ γυναῖκες αἳ τὰν θεόν φαντι ἐξελᾶν (*The Women Who Say They'll Drive out the Goddess*), a substantial piece of which has survived in a papyrus fragment. In it someone is giving detailed instructions to another regarding a ritual offering.[140]

As early as Magnes' Λυδοί (*Lydians*) there were references to ὀνειροκρίταισιν and ἀναλύταις, (female) "dream readers" and "saviors from spells." Cratinus wrote a *Trophonios*, a play somehow based on the famous oracle in Boeotia whose visitors had to descend through a narrow crevice into an underground cavern. Cratinus was followed by Cephisodorus and later by Alexis and Menander. The Cratinus version includes a fragment of three lines in which somone appears to be summoning a Muse to dance. In Cephisodorus's *Trophonios* someone receives an indignant reply from a certain Xanthia (a *pallake*, or "live in girlfriend"?), when he requests therapeutic oils for massaging his feet and body:

ἔπειτ᾽ ἀλείφεσθαι τὸ σῶμά μοι πρίω
μύρον ἴρινον καὶ ῥόδινον, ἄγαμαι, Ξανθία·
καὶ τοῖς ποσὶν χωρὶς πρίω μοι βάκχαριν.
(Ξα.) ὦ λακκόπρωκτε, βάκχαριν τοῖς σοῖς ποσὶν
ἐγὼ πρίωμαι; λαικάσομ᾽ ἆρα. Βάκχαριν;

Then please buy some ointment, scented with iris and rose
To massage into my body, Xanthia,
And a separate container of cyclamen perfume for my feet.
(Xanthia.) You big asshole! I'm to get cyclamen perfume
    for your feet?

I'd sooner turn tricks for a living. Cyclamen![141]

Is it perhaps the same woman, so touchy about her less than secure status, who utters the following lines?

σανδάλιά τε τῶν λεπτοσχιδῶν,
ἐφ᾽ οἷς τὰ χρυσᾶ ταῦτα ἔπεστιν ἄνθεμα.
νῦν δ᾽, ὥσπερ ἡ θεράπαιν᾽, ἔχω περιβαρίδας.

Sandals with the most delicate cutwork,
And on top, these golden decorations.
But *now* I have plain old slippers, just like the maid.[142]

Cratinus's *Delian Women*, probably datable to 424 and referring to the Delian rites celebrated by the Athenians in the previous year, seems to have included some kind of beauty contest, to judge from one fragment.[143] Plato Comicus wrote *The Women Returning from Sacrifice* (Αἱ ἀφ᾽ ἱερῶν) about which little is known beyond its title, and the *Adonis*, which may have treated the women's rites or the myth. A fragment of Pherecrates "It's the Adonia! We weep for Adonis!" describes (if it does not actually depict) the rites, just as the *Lysistrata*'s magistrate describes them in 411.[144] The Διονυσιάζουσαι or *Women at the Dionysia* of Timocles has left us an extended passage showing how tragedy portrays people whose misfortunes make our own seem small by comparison.[145]

Often cults were portrayed – rightly or wrongly – as recently infiltrating the city from abroad.[146] Strabo explains that the Athenians always welcomed whatever is strange, including new gods. This happened to such an extent that they were ridiculed for it by the comic poets.[147] Cicero observes that Aristophanes in one of his plays depicted Sabazius and other new gods with their all-night rites being tried, condemned, and deported from the city.[148] The play in question may have been the *Seasons*.

Since Hesiod and Semonides "women" had been depicted as a race apart, and so perhaps it was natural to see them as the "carriers" of foreign, or radically new and often corrupting, practices. Thus in some "cultic" plays women were presented as a "foreign" element in the city, not a subsection of the Athenian population. The *Thracian Women* of Cratinus, datable to c. 430, probably included a chorus of women from Thrace, responsible for the rites of the goddess Bendis.[149] The *Dippers* (Βάπται) of Eupolis seems to have portrayed Athenian (male) cititzens, disguised as women, and dancing in supplication to a lyre girl. The real Dippers were worshippers of Cotyto, the Thracian Artemis, whose orgiastic rites lent themselves to this burlesque treatment by Eupolis.[150] As I argue in the next chapter, the *Thesmophoriazousae* departed from this pattern of portraying women's cults as alien and new.

Old woman expanded the category of women who could engage in comically uninhibited behavior on the stage. In archaic and classical Greece old women enjoyed greater freedom than those of childbearing age.[151] Aristophanes represented older women as more assertive, effective, and responsible than their younger counterparts.[152] The sexuality of older women inspired many jibes. Pherecrates wrote a play entitled the *Old Women* (Γρᾶες), and it is perhaps from this play that we inherit the line:

πάλιν αὖθις ἀναθυῶσιν αἱ γεραίτεραι

the older women are in heat again

using a verb that typically describes swine.[153] The expression Ἀθηναίαις αὐταῖς τε καὶ ταῖς ξυμμάχοις ("the Athenian women and their allies") certainly does derive from the *Old Women* and perhaps suggests a situation like that of the *Lysistrata*.[154] Another fragment refers to a visit to Agra, a

district outside Athens where the Little Mysteries of Demeter were celebrated, so it is likely that these old women were represented as participating in cult.[155] In the *Lysistrata* Aristophanes represented the chorus of
old women as rudely and successfully defying their male counterparts and
defending the acropolis.

Hermippus provides a solitary line of insult directed against an old
woman: ὦ σαπρὰ καὶ πασιπόρνη καὶ κάπραινα: "you rotten whore and
sow!"[156] Aristophanes, *Clouds* (554–5) described how Eupolis stole the idea
of a drunken old hag dancing the obscene kordax from Phrynichus, who
had depicted such a woman being devoured by a sea monster. Perhaps
Theopompus also refers to a kordax dancer: (πρεσβῦτις φίλοινος, μεθύση,
οἰνομάχλη, κοχώνη) ("a bibulous, drunken, wine-lusty bottom of an old
woman").[157]

A fragment of the *Nemea* of Theopompus, a play named for a hetaira,
gives a more nuanced portrayal of an old woman on stage.[158] Spinther, a
house slave, mock-heroically addresses a "Thericlean" cup of wine and
then flirts with a fellow slave, the old woman Theolyte:

(Σπ.) χώρει σὺ δεῦρο, Θηρικλέους πιστὸν τέκνον,
γενναῖον εἶδος· ὄνομα σοι τί θώμεθα;
ἆρ᾽ εἶ κάτοπτρον φύσεος, ἢν πλῆρες δοθῆις;
οὐδέν ποτ᾽ ἄλλο. δεῦρο δή, γεμίσω σ᾽ ἐγώ.
γραῦ Θεολύτη, γραῦ. (Θε.) τί με καλεῖς σύ; (Σπ.) φιλτάτη,
ἵν᾽ ἀσπάσωμαι. δεῦρω παρ᾽ ἐμέ, Θεολύτη,
παρὰ τὸν νέον ξύνδουλον. οὑτωσὶ καλῶς.
(Θε.) Σπινθὴρ τάλας, πειρᾶις με; (Σπ.) ναί, τοιοῦτό τι·
φιλοτησίαν δὲ ⟨τήνδε⟩ σοι προπίομαι.
δέξαι· πιοῦσα δ᾽ ὁπόσον ἄν σοι θυμὸς ἦι
ἐμοὶ παράδος τὸ πρῶτον

(Sp.) Come here thou faithful child of Thericles[159]
Noble shape. How shall I address thee?
Art thou a Mirror of Nature? If thou be given, filled,
Thou art indeed. Come, let me fill thee.

[*He fills it, then addresses the old slave woman*].

Yo! Theolyte! Old Timer!
(Th.) Why are you calling me, darling?
(Sp.) So I can greet you fondly. Here – sit next to me Theolyte,
Next to your new fellow slave. That's right. [*She sits*].
(Th.) Oh please. Spinther. Are you coming on to me?
(Sp.) You bet. I will drink <this> loving cup to you.

Take it. Drink as much as you like,
Then give me what's left.

Theolyte responds to his facetious flattery with cynical composure; obviously she is not about to become anyone's dupe. One wonders what plot the two are about to hatch between them. In addition to this and other fragmentary references, there are two complete "old women" scenes extant in the *Ecclesiazousae* and *Plutus*. I discuss them in the next chapter, as I consider how women themselves might have responded to them.

Finally, some poets of old comedy took the bold step of representing younger Athenian women, not hetairai, within their homes, sometimes in sexual situations. Alcaeus wrote a play called the *Sisters Who Fooled Around* (αἱ Ἀδελφαὶ Μοιχευόμεναι), and Ameipsias, Antiphanes, and Philemon wrote plays called the *Adulterer*(s) (Μοιχός or Μοιχοί). The *Slave-trainer* (Δουλοδιδάσκαλος) of Pherecrates contains a scene in which a group of women (the chorus perhaps) announce that they should take down some colored fabrics from their looms.[160] Another moment in the same play has someone consulting a woman, perhaps an old soothsayer, about the meaning of a dream in which he became a fish and traveled about the city.[161] Although such fragments and titles do not allow the reconstruction of the lost plays, they do tell us that in old comedy the household intrigues and scenes of domestic life which were to characterize new comedy were already beginning to appear.

The Composition of the Audience

Did women actually see the plays in the theater of Dionysus?[162] The evidence is contradictory, reflecting a situation that was itself paradoxical or unclear. Ancient drama was written by men, with a male audience in mind, produced by men, and acted by men. Yet drama included people and interests not normally considered part of the sovereign *demos*: slaves, foreigners, children, and, most significantly, women. Tragedies and comedies provided an opportunity to debate issues pertinent to this larger community – at least to the extent that the élite members of the *demos* who wrote the plays perceived and understood the tensions between the "official" city and its interests and the actual population of Attica.

Priestesses of major cults attended during Hadrian's reign, when they had inscribed seats at the front, and no doubt they, together with functionaries in Dionysus' cult such as the basket carrier, attended the plays in the fifth century. But what of ordinary women? The chorus in the *Lysistrata* says the following:[163]

Χορός
οὐ παρασκευαζόμεσθα
τῶν πολιτῶν οὐδέν᾿ ὦνδρες
φλαῦρον εἰπεῖν οὐδὲ ἕν.
ἀλλὰ πολὺ τοὔμπαλιν
πάντ᾿ ἀγαθὰ καὶ λέγειν καὶ
δρᾶν· ἱκανὰ γὰρ τὰ κακὰ
καὶ τὰ παρακείμενα.
ἀλλ᾿ ἐπαγγελλέτω πᾶς ἀνὴρ καὶ γυνή,
εἴ τις ἀργυρίδιον
δεῖται λαβεῖν, μνᾶς ἢ δύ᾿ ἢ τρεῖς· ὡς ἔσω
᾿στὶν κᾄχομεν βαλλάντια.

We are not prepared, gentlemen of the audience, to say even one
disparaging thing about any fellow citizen, but quite the contrary,
to say and do only good things, because your present troubles are
enough. So let every man and woman notify us, whoever needs
some small change – two or three minas – because it's in our homes, and
we've purses to put it in.

Although these women borrowing money may be imagined as participating in local festivities rather than the City Dionysia, their inclusion in
the offer made at the city festival suggests that some women were actually
there to hear it. As Henderson notes, however, the chorus formally address
ἄνδρες (gentlemen of the audience), yet include women among those they
wish to invite.[164] This discrepancy between the notional audience and the
actual audience may account for the confusion about women's presence in
the theater. Some were there, but they were not part of the official group.
Thus at *Peace* 50–3 the servant addressed the audience as consisting of
"children and youths, and men of rank, and men of the highest status."
Similarly Menander called upon the different age groups of men to ap-
plaud at the end of the *Dyskolos* (965–7). It would be unwise to see these
passages as evidence that no women were present.

Three passages in Plato tend to be cited in the dispute about women in
the theater. None is a simple description of what existed at Athens; obviously if this were the case there would be no dispute, at least with regard to
the fourth century. Rather, each forms part of an argument about the problematic impact of tragedy on people. One passage from the *Laws* deals with
the (un)desirability of troupes of actors setting up tents in the agora and

"offering demagoguery for children and women and the whole crowd." Rather the Laws themselves should teach wisdom to the inhabitants of this city governed by a good constitution.[165] In another passage from the *Laws* the Athenian Stranger imagines a competition in which representatives of all conceivable literary genres and forms of popular entertainment compete.[166] How would the prize be awarded? And on what basis would the prize *rightfully* be awarded? The answer to the first question is that it depends on who you ask. Small children would choose a puppeteer; bigger boys would pick a comic poet; educated women (αἱ πεπαιδευμέναι τῶν γυναικῶν) and the general public would pick tragedy. (Older men such as the Athenian Stranger himself would pick epic recitations, and this, although not the majority opinion, would be the answer to the question about the correct award of the prize). Again, the hypothetical nature of this competition means that one cannot be confident that actual women in Athens were present at the dramatic competitions, but nonetheless to me the passage suggests that educated women attended plays (in addition to reading them, perhaps). Would the Athenian Stranger speak so sweepingly about the reading habits of a group of women he has never met, and so predict the women's judgment between different types of entertainment, literary and nonliterary? Perhaps, but I think on balance, he did not.

Finally, in the *Gorgias* Socrates treats tragic poetry as a species of rhetoric.[167] It is addressed to "children and women and men, slaves and free" (i.e., a wildly diverse audience) and is nothing more than flattery of them. Socrates goes on to compare this rhetoric, addressed to this broadly conceived *demos*, with the political rhetoric addressed to the *demos* of citizens, at Athens and elsewhere. (Such rhetoric also seems to aim low, in his opinion, flattering and treating even this more select audience as if they were children.) Here again, although Socrates does not mention the theater of Dionysus, his argument would lose its point if all women, children, and slaves were actually excluded from tragedy's audience, making it virtually indistinguishable from the select audience of the *Ecclesia*.

Theatrical anecdotes, such as the tale that Aeschylus's *Eumenides* terrified pregnant women into miscarrying, although likely to be themselves apocryphal, indicate that women traditionally were assumed to be present in the theater of Dionysus.[168]

In conclusion, without new evidence we cannot arrive at certainty on this difficult question. On balance, however, such evidence as we have – ambiguous in nature – suggests an ambiguous situation. Some women, free and slave, "respectable" women, foreigners and – often educated – hetairai (Athenian and foreign born) did attend the plays. They were not a conspicuous presence – indeed a fragment of Alexis' *Gynaikokratia* suggests that all women, except certain priestesses presumably, sat at the back, in the last wedge of seats – but they were there[169]: "Here we women have to sit in the very last wedge of seats (περὶ τὴν ἐσχάτην κερκίδα) to watch (θεωρεῖν), just like foreign women (ὡς ξένας)."

The premise that the audience included women transforms how we understand all ancient drama, because it means that the playwrights wrote in the knowledge that women saw their plays, even if they did not formally acknowledge the fact. Euripides' *Medea*, for example, with its ironic chorus on women's place in the literary tradition and its interactions between Greek women and a foreigner, assumes a greater poignancy if women, Athenian and foreign, were there to see it. Similarly, Aristophanes' *Thesmophoriazousae*, with its ludicrous portrayal of Euripides' disgruntled female critics, has a sharper, more confrontational edge when we imagine it playing before an audience of women as well as men.

Women as Spectacle; Men as Spectators

To argue that women were present in the audience is, of course, not to suggest that the notion of female spectators was an easy or natural one for Aristophanes or his (male) audience. On the contrary. The *Women Grabbing the Tents* of Aristophanes treated a struggle between men and women over tents at some festival, probably a theater festival to judge from the following fragment and others. A woman speaks the following lines[170]:

> λήκυθον
> τὴν ἑπτακότυλον, τὴν χυτρείαν, τὴν καλήν,
> ἣν ἐφερόμην ἵν᾽ ἔχοιμι συνθεάτριαν

> The half gallon flask, the lovely one made of clay
> Which I carried off as prize so that I could
> take it (her) to see the play with me

The passage recalls a scene from the *Thesmophoriazousae* in which a woman brings her beloved bottle (disguised as a baby) to the Thesmophoria. The comic coinage συνθεάτρια or "fellow-theatergoer-ess" of this "companion bottle" illumines Aristophanes' sense of comic incongruity in formally considering a female as a watcher of plays. συνθεάτρια is structurally

equivalent to ἐράστριαι – "women-lovers," a word that appears in a fragment of Eupolis.[171] Indeed both words suggest a monstrous inversion of
"normal" behavior; women are officially passive in lovemaking; they are
(supposed to be) watched, not watchers.

There has been work on the "pornographic" nature of ancient drama.
Rabinowitz, for example, argues that "tragedy participates in a pornographic structure of representation, accomplishing the solidification of
the male subject at the expense of and through the construction of the
female as object."[172] Indeed one of the major roles of the "women" on
the stage of old comedy was to serve – or be served up – as delectable
sex objects for an audience conceptualized as male. Many of the mute
female characters in the pre-*Lysistrata* plays of Aristophanes functioned
in this way.[173] Sometimes the language used both of plays and especially
of women in them, is dietary or culinary, evoking a literally consumerist
model.[174] We have already seen the "woman as wine" metaphor realized
in Cratinus's *Wineflask*. Aristophanes spoke of having "served up" the first
edition of the *Clouds* for the Athenians to taste (πρώτους ἠξίωσ᾽ ἀναγεῦσ᾽
ὑμᾶς", 523). Plato Comicus wrote a *Europa* in which someone compared the
amount of use and pleasure to be had from a sleeping woman (none) to a
waking one. "When she's awake, even her side dishes are delicious."[175] Two
passages compare the small, firm breasts of a young woman to quinces.[176]
Someone in a play by Theopompus says, "she has become softer to me
than a ripe cucumber."[177] A fragment of the *Old Age* of Aristophanes, a play
that depicts the magical rejuvenation of a group of old men contains the
following lines:

ὦ πρεσβῦτα, πότερα φιλεῖς τὰς δρυπεπεῖς ἑταίρας
ἢ τὰς ὑποπαρθένους ἁλμάδας ὡς ἐλαίας
στιφράς;

Well gramps, do you like your hetairai ripened on the vine
Or barely mature, firm to the touch like salted olives?[178]

Trygaeus in the *Peace* asked Hermes if he would be made sick by "in-
dulging in" (the Greek is κατελάσας, which means to "thrust up") the attractive girl, Fullfruit (709–11). Hermes' answer was that he would feel all right
if he first took the *cyceon* with some pennyroyal in it. Hermes' pharmacological advice embraced both aspects of Trygaeus's planned indulgence:
sexual and alimentary. The *cyceon* would facilitate his transition from
abstinence to indulgence of both sorts.[179]

Yet women were more than passive "dishes" both in Aristophanes and in the comic tradition generally, as the fifth century came to an end. The comic poets, notably Aristophanes, debated the reaction(s) plays should elicit from their audiences. Women characters played a crucial part in this debate – precisely because of their longstanding identification with pleasure. Later, Plato's famous discussions of poetry's function were to establish a polarity between pleasure on the one hand and education toward responsible citizenship on the other. Yet years before Plato published his opinions, Aristophanes had deliberately reconciled the genre's attentiveness to the body and its interests with concern for their city. In his view, concern for the physical realities and homely pleasures of Athenians should be central to political judgments, and comedy should invite its audience to make political judgments. But a pleasurable spectacle that did not educate its audience to make intelligent political judgments was simply pandering. Aristophanes used women – and criticized Euripides' use of women – in making these arguments.

Like his contemporaries Eupolis and Plato Comicus, Aristophanes preferred political comedy, and in this he differed from men such as Pherecrates and Theopompus, who focused more on domestic stories, the forerunners of new comedy. Thus, for example, in the parabasis of the *Peace*, Aristophanes proudly distinguished himself from poets who portray lice-infested people in rags, Heracles enslaved, or runaway slaves. Neither did he "mock the little guys and their wives in private life" (751) but instead, like Heracles himself, he took on a monster – Cleon, in this case.

Even allowing for his usual playful irony (Aristophanes is not above condemning vulgar jests right before making a few himself) he is making a serious point here. If he portrayed people in private life (like Strepsiades and his dysfunctional family in the *Clouds*) it was because they manifested problems of concern to the city as a whole. In surveying the ways in which the old comic poets assessed their own work and that of others, Aristophanes alone boasts of *nouthesia*, concern to make better citizens of his audience.[180] He does so repeatedly, in six of the eight surviving parabases. Even allowing of the disproportional survival rate of Aristophanean verses compared with those of other comic poets, this pattern seems significant.

Thus when Aristophanes did turn to women as protagonists, in the plays of 411 and later in the *Ecclesiazousae* of 393, he treated them as a political bloc within the state, the "shadow" counterparts to male citizens, not as individuals with interesting private concerns or domestic situations.[181] He did not want his audience to respond to these women as individuals but rather to see them as emblems of political questions and as representing issues in their own right. His call for thoughtful rationality and the ability to think abstractly, beyond bright images anticipated Plato's stance on education, an ironic precedent.

Aristophanes' persistent attacks on Euripides reflected his own preferences about the kind of drama most useful to the city. In the *Thesmophoriazousae*, after a series of futile stagings of Euripidean plays to convince his jailors to release him, Mnesilochus was helped to escape by Euripides himself, disguised as an old madam who brought on an erotic dancer and so distracted the guard. With the scene and in the play as a whole Aristophanes implied that Euripides had worked throughout his career as a procuress who distracted her clients from their responsibilities – and he was not even good at it. His own tarts (Helen, Andromeda) were unconvincing, and he has to borrow a burlesque dancer from comedy to succeed. Similarly, during their contest to select which was better fit to guide Athens, the character Aeschylus in the *Frogs* accused Euripides of "creating whores."[182] The charge was a semiserious one, even though the accuser, as portrayed by Aristophanes, was himself a bombastic warmongering fool, who would be hardly any better at guiding the city than his rival.[183]

The category of Euripidean "whores" might be said to include many women in addition to the adulterous Phaedras or Stheneboias mentioned by the comic Aeschylus in this scene. As the comic Euripides himself boasted at *Frogs* 947-9, he "democratically" gave a voice to "the adult woman and the slave no less / and the master and the maiden and the old woman." All categories of female and slaves as well as free men spoke with equal freedom on the Euripidean stage.[184]

Yet, as I believe Aristophanes to be saying, this babel of individual voices did not benefit the city. The audience might be seduced into sympathizing with these imaginary people and taking a kind of pleasure from becoming engrossed in their situations, but the intense spotlight on individuals distracted them from thinking about collectivities and the common weal. And for Aristophanes women more than any other group came to represent collectivity.[185] In his view, to portray them as interesting and complex individuals was to pander to the audience. Aristophanes certainly was not above titillating his audience with dancing girls – indeed the dancing prostitute introduced by "Euripides" at the end of the *Thesmophoriazousae* no doubt served this function, among others. But such scenes were not at the heart of his plays.

Thinking about women as a collective unit was traditional, in some respects. After all it was a truism of iambic that "they're all the same." But other factors made it natural and desirable for Aristophanes to treat them as an entity. Pericles' legislation of 451–0 had focused attention on women as makers – and unmakers – of legitimate Athenian citizens. Every citizen now had to think of his Athenian identity and that of his sons as constituted by the women in his family equally with the men. Athenian wives and mothers formed the negative film from which citizens were printed: a shadow polis. These "Atheniennes" could readily function as a jokey counterpart state for Aristophanes.

It was easier to elide differences in class, status, and perspective that actually divided real women than to ignore divisions among men. Much labor at Athens was shared by free people and slaves working side by side, but this was especially true in the case of women's work in the home: child care, food preparation, and textile production. Because even free women did not wield power in public as men did, it was easier to maintain the fiction that women constituted a single population, riven only by the pettiest of concerns.[186] Thus while the comic Euripides of the *Frogs*, in boasting of the "democratic" diversity of his speaking characters, distinguished between master and (male) slave, he tellingly divided women into the three major age categories, not according to status. Plays in which women's behavior parodied men's (such as the *Ecclesiazousae*) displayed women distinguishing among themselves but without the shadow of murderous ideological or political divisions.

Spectator Spectatus

Thinking about ancient spectacles – however sexualized – in terms of modern theories of pornography can mislead. Athenaeus tells a story about the Athenian audience at a comic recitation during the Peloponnesian War. Whether or not it is true, it expresses something of the difference between the one-sided experience of modern screen or theater audience (viewing anonymously from a darkened room) and ancient audiences viewing masked actors in the theater of Dionysus, in a hemicircular space, in broad daylight, probably in seats designated for different groups.

ἐν δὲ τῇ Γιγαντομαχίᾳ οὕτω σφόδρα τοὺς Ἀθηναίους ἐκήλησεν,
ὡς ἐν ἐκείνῃ τῇ ἡμέρᾳ πλεῖστα αὐτοὺς γελάσαι, καίτοι ἀγγελθέντων
αὐτοῖς ἐν τῇ θεάτρῳ τῶν γενομένων περὶ Σικελίαν ἀτυχημάτων.
οὐδεὶς οὖν ἀνέστη καίτοι σχεδὸν πᾶσι τῶν οἰκείων ἀπολωλότων. ἔκλαιον
οὖν ἐγκαλυψάμενοι, οὐκ ἀνέστησαν δ', ἵνα μὴ γένωνται
διαφανεῖς τοῖς ἀπὸ τῶν ἄλλων πόλεων θεωροῦσιν ἀχθόμενοι τῇ συμφορᾷ·
διέμειναν δ' ἀκροώμενοι καίτοι καὶ αὐτοῦ τοῦ Ἡγήμονος,
ὡς ἤκουσε, σιωπᾶν διεγνωκότος.

Hegemon's parodic [recitation] *Battle of the Giants* was such a success
that the audience laughed more than ever before on that day,
even though they heard of the Sicilian disaster in the theater.
When the news came no one got up to leave, even though almost
everyone had lost members of their household. They covered their faces
and wept, but they did not get up, lest they display their pain at the
disaster to the spectators from other cities. Yet as soon as Hegemon
himself heard the news he had decided that he must stop.[187]

The story that Socrates laughed when he was made fun of by the comic
poets whereas Poliager, cruelly mocked for pimping his wife, committed
suicide, bears witness to the same phenomenon. Showing vulnerability
publicly was not a desirable thing to do.[188] In 426 Cleon prosecuted Aristophanes for slandering the magistrates, councillors, and Athenian people
before an audience that included foreign allies. He dragged Aristophanes
before the Council (which apparently did not take up the case).[189]

The very elegance of the Hegemon story renders it suspect, alas. The
poem being recited was the battle waged by giants against the gods – a
fitting commentary on the hybristic Sicilian expedition. A comedy was interrupted by a tragic messenger! The audience metaphorically assumed
comic masks, becoming themselves part of the spectacle for their foreign visitors! Yet this "reversal" of audience and spectacle alerts us to real
complexities in ancient theater dynamics, even if it was itself fictional.
The anecdote assumes what is demonstrably true of all but tragic theater
(which maintained a detached relationship with the audience): that the
spectators were part of the spectacle, acknowledged by the performers,
and able to be mirrored as individuals in the performance, either by por-
traiture or topical reference.

If we take the Alexis fragment regarding women's theater seating at face
value and assume that some Athenian women of all ranks and foreign
women (barring a few priestesses) sat at the back, a complex situation

appears. Whoever was performing was being watched by the audience, but the audience themselves, especially those of higher status nearer the front, were also part of the spectacle. At the City Dionysia citizens of other states were present in the mix. And at both festivals women, being at the back, could have seen and judged the audience reaction as well as the show.[190]

◈ 6 ◈

WOMEN AT CENTER STAGE

T HE ONLY COMPLETE OLD COMEDIES, all by Aristophanes, date to the
Peloponnesian War and its grievous aftermath. The conflict threw
the city into a turmoil from which it never fully recovered, and
there were times when everyone within the walls experienced enormous
hardship.[1] Thus it is misleading to conceive of the plays' fantasy worlds
as the voice of an anarchic, "carnival" season in an otherwise orderly
universe.[2] There were generations of Athenian women and men whose
notion of "normality" was profoundly skewed. The comic topsy-turviness
of the plays did not undermine an ordered world, but they benevolently
reimagined a frighteningly disordered one.

This chapter attempts two things. One is to analyze the function and
impact of the "woman" theme in Aristophanes' plays, drawing primarily
on the *Thesmophoriazousae*, *Ecclesiazousae*, and *Lysistrata*.[3] My attention
is directed at the poet, insofar as one may imagine Aristophanes as an
educated man, writing for a public, in an extraordinary political and civic
context about which we know a good deal. Aristophanes' literary use of
women indicates preoccupations and tensions within his work: preoccupations peculiar to him and to the time of writing *and* themes with a
history in Attic comedy and in iambic.[4] Locating his work within a broader
history of Greek old comedy and iambic renders this look at "women in
Aristophanes" useful and revealing.

MY OTHER OBJECTIVE IS MORE RADICAL. Rather than just considering Aristophanes as a poet within a (male) poetic tradition, I want to think of him as
an individual inhabiting a face-to-face, oral world in which women as well
as men spoke, criticized, and made jokes and judgments.[5] Some of what
they said he could hear; some, uttered in all-female contexts, he could only
guess at or know about through the accounts of family and other female
acquaintance. His output has made it obvious that women's voices were
of interest to him, if only, as some scholars would have it, as a convenient

way of expressing his own, male élite concerns and winning prizes at the City Dionysia. I believe, however, that Aristophanes' interest in women was not just a matter of comic convenience. It is true that "women" or the "women of Athens," imagined as a group, could serve as a metaphor for political issues – questions that Athenian citizen males would have seen as relevant primarily to themselves. It is also true that as the constructed "other" the women of ancient drama served to define the "self" that was the citizen male.[6] But this does not preclude the possibility that the women of Athens, as real and eloquent people, inspired Aristophanes to write some of his plays – to answer them, among other things.[7] We can conceive of the *Lysistrata*, for example, as a response to things Aristophanes and men of his circle heard, rather than as entirely self-generated. I suggest that his domestic knowledge of women's conversation, his knowledge of the cultic exchanges in which women participated and, conceivably, his witnessing of men and women in Dionysiac cultic exchanges all contributed to an au- thorial experience that was more interactive, less self-referential, than we have imagined. This was a poet whose parabases and dialogue responded to – facetiously and seriously – his audience, the judges, his literary rivals, and political, military, and intellectual notables of his day.[8] I proceed on the premise that he regarded the women of Athens also as having a stake in the city and its poets' representations of it, as indeed his works playfully suggest, and that his plays about them can be seen as the surviving part of an ongoing dialogue, albeit an unequal one.

411 B.C.E. The Year of the *Lysistrata* and *Thesmophoriazousae*

The "Athens" of fifth-century soldiers and politicians, an imaginary city, had served the complex purposes of its inventors. In the earliest decades of the century Themistocles had advised the Athenians to look to their "wooden walls," meaning the navy. Thucydides' Nicias addressed the doomed Athenian troops in Sicily, suggesting that they themselves em- bodied the city: "Reflect that you yourselves, wherever you settle down, are a city already."[9] Pericles' funeral oration described a city bequeathed by fathers to be the heart of an empire, an inheritance both substantial and ideological.[10] This utopian "Athens" of Pericles defied the territorial encroachment of foreign armies; it functioned as a vision and inspiration in the minds of its soldiers and citizens. Above all, such speeches were de- signed to bring people together, to create the impression that the speaker and his audience shared one mind, and that the speaker was merely voicing what any citizen might say for himself. This sense of a shared mentality, a common set of transparent metaphors, linked Athenians, even more than blood.

Yet Athens was also a physical place, with citizens who needed to eat, fields that could be ruined by foreign armies, and women who were needed to produce the next generation of citizens. Athens needed the grain, grapes, and olives of Attica to feed its people, but crop production, animal husbandry, and human reproduction were slowed.[11] Everyone felt the impact of the war on agrarian and cultic life in the hungry city, shorn of its fields. By 411 it had become difficult to draw attention away from the ravaged city to the transcendent calm of conceptual Athens.

The Spartans occupied Deceleia again in 413, this time year-round, with the result that the city was cut off from its adjacent farmland by a resident enemy force. The population lived behind the city walls in a state of siege. Thucydides describes the end of farming in Attica – for the first extended period since the war had begun.[12] Most Athenians owned and farmed land, often in scattered parcels, and when they could no longer farm, they lost livelihood and identity together.[13] Recent work on the relationship between the "city "of Athens and the "countryside" has shown how interconnected they were, how deme responsibilities and allegiance on the one hand and participation in city politics on the other combined to define what it meant to be an Athenian citizen. The city and its territory complemented each other and defined each other's sovereignty. Thus the Spartan occupation of Deceleia was not a peripheral loss; it struck at the city's heart.

Processions from the city to boundary shrines mediated between the city's center and its periphery.[14] Cults created communities linking women and men from different parts of the city, sometimes including noncitizens. The Spartan occupation of Deceleia curtailed the celebration of the Eleusinian Mysteries of Demeter because participants could no longer process fifteen miles out of the city – a major blow to Athenian international prestige and to its sense of integrity. Moreover it is likely that many other cultic processions and activities were threatened, by the exigencies of the war as a whole and by the invasions and occupation of Attic territory.[15] Thus, for example, at *Acharnians* 195–202 (a play of 425 B.C.E.) the comic hero Dicaeopolis had planned to celebrate the rural Dionysia – for the first time in six years – having concluded his private peace treaty with the Spartans.

The Sicilian disaster of 415 meant the destruction of the Athenian navy. This loss had broad implications, psychological and political, even though the fleet itself was rebuilt within a few years. The Athenian empire had depended on its fleet, and the fleet in turn had required the active participation of a broad section of the Athenian population. As Raaflaub puts it, "by rowing the fleet, the lower class citizens *permanently* assumed a military role that was crucial for the security and power of their city."[16] Thus the Athenian thalassocracy had provided the context needed to develop the Athenian constitution, revised by Cleisthenes, to the full democracy of the later fifth century. Now with that sea power and its advantages lost or in grave peril, some men sought rule by a few.[17]

In 411 some Athenians, led by Pisander, were negotiating with the exiled Alcibiades in the hope of undoing the democratic constitution of the city and replacing it with an oligarchy and then enlisting the king of Persia against their Spartan enemies.[18] Pisander's proposal, made before the people, aroused angry opposition from Alcibiades' enemies and those who disdained an alliance with a foreign tyrant. Meanwhile Phrynichus, an Athenian general and particular enemy of Alcibiades, communicated with a Spartan admiral near Miletus, telling him of Alcibiades' efforts to detach Tissaphernes from Sparta and induce him to support Athens instead. Thus, as often in this period, private enmities compromised Athenian interests. Moreover, as Thucydides had said of Corcyra's comparable plight at the outset of the war, civic common ground had disappeared, and with it the possibility of rational discourse.[19]

Later that same spring of 411 the bloody oligarchic coup occurred, resulting in the rule of the 400 (far fewer with real power), lasting several months into the summer. All those who spoke publicly against the oligarchic junta died swiftly, and many of the killers never met justice. Private criticism of the new government also became potentially lethal, because no one knew who might betray a friend's confidence.[20] Here, in Warner's translation, is Thucydides' account of the mentality induced among the majority by the coup and its aftermath:

> ἐνῆσαν γὰρ καὶ οὓς οὐκ ἄν ποτέ τις ᾤετο ἐς ὀλιγαρχίαν τραπέσθαι, καὶ τὸ ἄπιστον οὗτοι μέγιστον πρὸς τοὺς πολλοὺς ἐποίησαν, καὶ πλεῖστα ἐς τὴν τῶν ὀλίγων ἀσφάλειαν ὠφέλησαν, βέβαιον τὴν ἀπιστίαν τῷ δήμῳ πρὸς ἑαυτὸν καταστήσαντες.

And there were in fact among the revolutionaries some people whom no one could ever have imagined would have joined in an oligarchy. It was these who were mainly responsible for making the general mass of people so mistrustful of each other and who were of the greatest help in keeping the minority safe, since they made mutual suspicion an established thing in the popular assemblies.[21]

Euripides *Ion*, datable to some time after 415, perhaps 412, contains a speech by its eponymous hero, which reflects the city's dark mood and the alienation of the élite from the political arena:

ἢν δ᾽ ἐς τὸ πρῶτον πόλεος ὁρμηθεὶς ζυγὸν
ζητῶ τις εἶναι, τῶν μὲν ἀδυνάτων ὕπο
μισησόμεθα· λυπρὰ γὰρ τὰ κρείσσονα.
ὅσοι δέ, χρηστοὶ δυνάμενοί τ᾽ εἶναι σοφοί,
σιγῶσι κοὐ σπεύδουσιν ἐς τὰ πράγματα,
γέλωτ᾽ ἐν αὐτοῖς μωρίαν τε λήψομαι
οὐχ ἡσυχάζων ἐν πόλει φόβου πλέᾳ.

If I make an effort to be in the first rank of the city and to be somebody, I'll be hated by those of no ability. For superiority always rankles. But the upper classes (*chrestoi*) and those who are capable of being *sophoi*, who keep quiet and do not hasten into public life, will treat me as a laughing stock and fool if I don't mind my own business in a city filled with fear. (*Ion* 595–602).[22]

Scholars have debated possible allusions to particular events within the texts of the *Thesmophoriazousae* and *Lysistrata*.[23] Because it is not possible to pinpoint when either play was written or produced, I consider the entire year as context for the plays.[24] Some version of the plays would have been submitted to the archon in the preceding summer to get on the program, so arguments dependent on the relative timing of the plays, the Lenaia, and City Dionysia, and the developing political crisis are problematic. Moreover, although the paranoia induced by the coup was extreme, fear, recrimination for recent failures and resentment had permeated the atmosphere within the city before matters reached a crisis. All in all, 411 began as a particularly frightening year in a series of difficult years. Bitterly hostile groups tried to ally Athens with Persia on the one hand or Sparta on the other. With men lost or away on campaign, the visibility and influence of women in the crowded city was high and was augmented and refracted by the powerful voices of tragic heroines.

The plays of 411 especially, the *Lysistrata* and *Thesmophoriazousae* indicate a profound interest in, and a knowledge of, women as jokers, cultic celebrants, as makers – and unmakers – of meaning. Aristophanes turned to them as a group that could be conceptualized as a unit and whose speech within domestic and cultic contexts retained authority precisely because it was not contending within the now seismic political sphere.[25]

The *Thesmophoriazousae*: Whose Critical Gaze?

According to the *Thesmophoriazousae*, Euripides had heard that the women of Athens were planning vengeance on him for his exposé of their peccadilloes. He needed an agent to infiltrate their festival, the Thesmophoria, to find out what they had in mind. Having failed to persuade the effeminate tragic playwright, Agathon, to take the job, Euripides talked his hirsute relative, Mnesilochus, into dressing as a woman and spying on the Thesmophorians.[26] Once exposed as a fraud, Mnesilochus attempted to escape, using as his guide the scripts of Euripidean tragedies: the *Palamedes*, *Helen*, *Telephus*, and *Andromeda*. He played an innocent woman, rescued through her own resourcefulness (Helen) or through the agency of another (Andromeda); a desperate soldier, attempting to send an emergency message back to his "homeland" (Palamedes) and seizing an infant as hostage (Telephus). Clearly the incongruity of the unprepossessing old man playing these famous beauties or young hero was highly comic. The character of Euripides, meanwhile, appeared as a bumbler, unwilling to fight his own literary battles openly and unable to fight them vicariously. For all that he armed himself with these plays, Mnesilochus failed to enchant his "audience" – either the outraged Thesmophorian women or the Scythian guard appointed to watch him. Eventually Euripides was forced to come to terms, promising never again to speak ill of women in his plays (1160–71). The Scythian guard was diverted in a separate action, by means of a "nude" dancing girl provided by Euripides (appearing on stage disguised as an old madam), and Mnesilochus escaped. This dancer appeared as a comic dea ex machina, a contrivance that, by its very extraordinariness, drew attention to the impasse wrought by the plot.

IN CREATING HIS CARICATURE OF EURIPIDES' OEUVRE, Aristophanes focused on a series of recent plays. In 412, Euripides, responding to the dark Athenian mood, produced as tragedies the *Helen*, *Andromeda*, and perhaps also the *Ion*.[27] These plays embody many of the features that later would characterize new comedy: blocking characters, intrigue, mistaken identity, recognition, happy (marital) ending. Doubtless Euripides' tragedies of 412 aimed to reinvigorate the city, just as the comedies of that year aspired to the same goal. The *Demes* of Eupolis, also arguably datable to 412, tells of resurrected heroes, Miltiades, Solon, Aristides, and Pericles, returning from the grave to advise Athens in its hour of peril.[28] It contains the following line:

ἀμβλυστονῆσαι καὶ χλοῆσαι τὴν πόλιν

make the city gush and bloom.[29]

Obviously, Aristophanes' parodic portrait of Euripides did not paint a representative picture – of the poet's output or of the roles he assigned women. For example, in 415 the *Trojan Women* had constituted a powerful lament, sung entirely by women, decrying the impact of war on noncombatants.[30] But in selecting the plays he did, Aristophanes was perhaps making a point about tragedy as a whole. However incisive its mythical allegories, it was removed from contemporary reality – irrelevant, if not downright escapist. Euripidean women "gratified" their audience (and thus his final appearance as a purveyor of whores was apposite), but they did not speak directly to the present political crises. The *Helen, Andromeda*, and *Telephus* thus could serve as a caustic metaphor for tragedy as a whole.

As shown in Chapter 5, old comedy had joked about women's cults before 411, because religious practices permitted women to take part in the public life of the city and because "exotic" or orgiastic rites afforded plenty of scope for comic elaboration. Cultic women typically had appeared as "outsiders," developing a long-standing link between women and foreignness. Their "exotic" rites supposedly infiltrated the city from abroad and disrupted the orderly lives of its citizens. Aristophanes' surviving portrayal of women's cult, the *Thesmophoriazousae*, did not portray the participants as bizarre outsiders or superstitious hysterics but rather as (comically) "concerned" citizens, so that the play may have marked a watershed.[31] The cultic women theme was turned to a political purpose. Worshipping women now constituted their own "shadow" city of Athens, praying on its behalf, policing its boundaries, and censuring its discourse. The Thesmophoria lent itself to such a use, because, as we have seen, in some respects the Thesmophoria actually seems to have taken on the forms of a political assembly. Of course in Aristophanes, this was ludicrously (over)elaborated. Bowie well observes the following:

> The early part [of the play] has a strong political flavour. The festival is referred to as an "Assembly" (84, 277 etc.) in which "orators" (292) address the

demos of the women (335, 353, 1145) to discuss *psephismata* ("proposals") and *nomoi* ("laws," 361). This lengthy scene in the Assembly opens in an elaborately formal manner (which contrasts with the haste in the opening Assembly in *Acharnians*), with prose and verse prayers for the city. In 373–9 there is a parody of the actual form of the minutes of the Boule. There is also a parody of the *Arai* ("Comminations") which were formally recited at the start of an Assembly or Boule meeting (332ff.).[32]

The "Comminations" or ritual curses following the opening prayer incongruously mingled comic women's concerns and (deathly) serious political issues. Thus anyone who betrayed a woman for passing off a suppositious infant as her own, any bartender who cheated his clientele with short measures, any go-between slave who betrayed a cheating woman to her husband, anyone who negotiated with Euripides – these wrongdoers were to be cursed together with those who attempted to install tyrants or negotiate with the Medes.

One may read this catalog in different ways. On the one hand it can be seen to make the women look silly and self-absorbed. Their self-indulgence and peccadilloes hardly rate against the monstrous crime of betraying the city to a tyrant or to the Persian enemy. Yet the women's personal concerns, while laughable, are not portrayed as contemptible. If one compares the overall tone of this portrait of women's "traditional" flaws with that of Semonides' diatribe against women, for example, one can see a huge difference. In Aristophanes the Thesmophorian women represented the values and characteristics traditionally embodied by his "heroes": earthy pleasures, private freedoms, defiance of officious authority. These girls just want to have fun. And why not, if no one is the wiser? When Mnesilochus, disguised as a woman but still speaking like a male critic about what "we women" get up to, elaborated the list of women's marital outrages, the women were shocked, not at the behavior, but at "her" willingness to speak of it (520–39). The women's gathering, therefore, ridiculous as it was, was a comic haven, a place worth defending by Aristophanes, the comic advocate of earthy pleasures and their flawed practitioners, the "little" people ignored by the high-faluting purveyors of official *logoi*.

The women's most explicit response to the misogyny of the literary tradition (including iambic as well as tragedy and epic) came in the Parabasis of 785 ff:[33]

Χορός
ἡμεῖς τοίνυν ἡμᾶς αὐτὰς εὖ λέξωμεν παραβᾶσαι,
καίτοι πᾶς τις τὸ γυναικεῖον φῦλον κακὰ πόλλ᾽ ἀγορεύει,

ὡς πᾶν ἐσμὲν κακὸν ἀνθρώποις κἀξ ἡμῶν ἐστιν ἅπαντα,
ἔριδες, νείκη, στάσις ἀργαλέα, λύπη, πόλεμος. φέρε δή νυν,
εἰ κακόν ἐσμεν, τί γαμεῖθ᾽ ἡμᾶς, εἴπερ ἀληθῶς κακόν ἐσμεν,
κἀπαγορεύετε μήτ᾽ ἐξελθεῖν μήτ᾽ ἐκκύψασαν ἁλῶναι,
ἀλλ᾽ οὑτωσὶ πολλῇ σπουδῇ τὸ κακὸν βούλεσθε φυλάττειν;
κἂν ἐξέλθῃ τὸ γύναιόν ποι, κᾆθ᾽ εὕρῃτ᾽ αὐτὸ θύρασιν,
μανίας μαίνεσθ᾽, οὓς χρῆν σπένδειν καὶ χαίρειν, εἴπερ ἀληθῶς
ἔνδοθεν ηὕρετε φροῦδον τὸ κακὸν καὶ μὴ κατελαμβάνετ᾽ ἔνδον.
κἂν καταδάρθωμεν ἐν ἀλλοτρίων παίζουσαι καὶ κοπιῶσαι,
πᾶς τις τὸ κακὸν τοῦτο ζητεῖ περὶ τὰς κλίνας περινοστῶν.
κἂν ἐκ θυρίδος παρακύπτωμεν, ζητεῖ τὸ κακὸν τεθεᾶσθαι·
κἂν αἰσχυνθεῖσ᾽ ἀναχωρήσῃ, πολὺ μᾶλλον πᾶς ἐπιθυμεῖ
αὖθις τὸ κακὸν παρακύψαν ἰδεῖν. οὕτως ἡμεῖς ἐπιδήλως
ὑμῶν ἐσμεν πολὺ βελτίους, βάσανός τε πάρεστιν ἰδέθαι.
βάσανον δῶμεν πότεροι χείρους. ἡμεῖς μὲν γάρ φαμεν ὑμᾶς,
ὑμεῖς δ᾽ ἡμᾶς. σκεψώμεθα δὴ κἀντιτιθῶμεν πρὸς ἕκαστον,
παραβάλλουσαι τῆς τε γυναικὸς καὶ τἀνδρὸς τοὔνομ᾽ ἑκάστου.
Ναυσιμάχης μέν γ᾽ ἥττων ἐστὶν Χαρμῖνος· δῆλα δὲ τἄργα.
καὶ μὲν δὴ καὶ Κλεοφῶν χείρων πάντως δήπου Σαλαβακχοῦς.
πρὸς Ἀριστομάχην δὲ χρόνου πολλοῦ, πρὸς ἐκείνην τὴν
   Μαραθῶνι,
καὶ Στρατονίκην ὑμῶν οὐδεὶς οὐδ᾽ ἐγχειρεῖ πολεμίζειν.
ἀλλ᾽ Εὐβούλης τῶν πέρυσίν τις βουλευτής ἐστιν ἀμείνων
παραδοὺς ἑτέρῳ τὴν βουλείαν; οὐδ᾽ αὐτὸς τοῦτό γε φήσεις.
οὕτως ἡμεῖς πολὺ βελτίους τῶν ἀνδρῶν εὐχόμεθ᾽ εἶναι.
οὐδ᾽ ἂν κλέψασα γυνὴ ζεύγει κατὰ πεντήκοντα τάλαντα
ἐς πόλιν ἔλθοι τῶν δημοσίων· ἀλλ᾽ ἢν τὰ μέγισθ᾽ ὑφέληται
φορμὸν πυρῶν τἀνδρὸς κλέψασ᾽, αὐθημερὸν ἀνταπέδωκεν.

   ἀλλ᾽ ἡμεῖς ἂν πολλοὺς τούτων
   ἀποδείξαιμεν ταῦτα ποιοῦντας.
   καὶ πρὸς τούτοις γάστριδας ἡμῶν
   ὄντας μᾶλλον καὶ λωποδύτας
   καὶ βωμολόχους κἀνδραποδιστάς.
   καὶ μὲν δήπου καὶ τὰ πατρῷά γε
   χείρους ἡμῶν εἰσιν σῴζειν·
   ἡμῖν μὲν γὰρ σῶν ἔτι καὶ νῦν
   τἀντίον, ὁ κανὼν, οἱ καλαθίσκοι,
   τὸ σκιάδειον·
   τοῖς δ᾽ ἡμετέροις ἀνδράσι τούτοις
   ἀπόλωλεν μὲν πολλοῖς ὁ κανὼν
   ἐκ τῶν οἴκων αὐτῇ λόγχῃ,
   πολλοῖς δ᾽ ἑτέροις ἀπὸ τῶν ὤμων
   ἐν ταῖς στρατιαῖς
   ἔρριπται τὸ σκιάδειον.

πόλλ' ἂν αἱ γυναῖκες ἡμεῖς ἐν δίκῃ μεμψαίμεθ' ἂν
τοῖσιν ἀνδράσιν δικαίως, ἓν δ' ὑπερφυέστατον.
χρῆν γάρ, ἡμῶν εἰ τέκοι τις ἄνδρα χρηστὸν τῇ πόλει,
ταξίαρχον ἢ στρατηγόν, λαμβάνειν τιμήν τινα,
προεδρίαν τ' αὐτῇ δίδοσθαι Στηνίοισι καὶ Σκίροις
ἔν τε ταῖς ἄλλαις ἑορταῖς αἷσιν ἡμεῖς ἤγομεν·
εἰ δὲ δειλὸν καὶ πονηρὸν ἄνδρα τις τέκοι γυνή,
ἢ τριήραρχον πονηρὸν ἢ κυβερνήτην κακόν,
ὑστέραν αὐτὴν καθῆσθαι σκάφιον ἀποκεκαρμένην
τῆς τὸν ἀνδρεῖον τεκούσης. τῷ γὰρ εἰκὸς ὦ πόλις
τὴν Ὑπερβόλου καθῆσθαι μητέρ' ἠμφιεσμένην
λευκὰ καὶ κόμας καθεῖσαν πλησίον τῆς Λαμάχου,
καὶ δανείζειν χρήμαθ', ᾗ χρῆν, εἰ δανείσειέν τινι
καὶ τόκον πράττοιτο, διδόναι μηδέν' ἀνθρώπων τόκον,
ἀλλ' ἀφαιρεῖσθαι βίᾳ τὰ χρήματ' εἰπόντας τοδί,
"ἀξία γοῦν εἶ τόκου τεκοῦσα τοιοῦτον τόκον."

CHORUS:
Let us step up and praise ourselves,
Since every man says so many bad things about the "race of women"
How we are all a "problem" to men, and how from us
Come all Strifes, Quarrels, Standoffs, Painful Griefs, War. Come on!
If we are a "problem," why marry us? If we really are a "problem"
Why tell us never to leave the house, or get caught peeping out
   the window?
But why do you need to guard your "problem" so fanatically?
And if your little wife goes out somewhere, and you find her outside
You go nuts, when you should be toasting the gods and rejoicing
If indeed you found the household "problem" gone, and not available
   within.
And if we get tired out partying, and fall asleep at someone else's house,
Every man tracks down his "problem," inspecting all the couches.
And if we peep out of the window everyone tries to glimpse the
   "problem."
And if we back away in embarrassment everyone tries to
See the "problem" all the more, when it peeps out again.
So obviously we are far better than you. Here's proof.
Let's run a test to see which sex is worst.
Since we say that you are and you say that it's us.
Let's direct our attention to the question, and juxtapose the name of
An individual man with that of an individual women.
Charminus is worse than Nausimache. The facts speak for themselves.
And Cleophon obviously can't compete with Salabaccho!
And for ages not one of you has even tried to compete with
Aristomache – the Marathon girl – and with Stratonike.[34]

So is that councillor of last year – the one who surrendered his
    authority to
Someone else – better than Euboule? Even you couldn't argue that!
And so we maintain that we are way better than men.
A woman would not help herself to funds from the public treasury – fifty
    talents a dip –
And then yoke her chariot team and cruise downtown Athens.
If – at the most – she pilfers a cup of flour from her hubby
She pays him back the next day.
But we could show that many of these men do just that –
And moreover they are more likely than us to sport huge bellies,
Pinch other people's stuff, nick altar offerings, deal in slaves.
And even when it comes to their inheritance
They are worse than us at saving.
We still keep safe our loom, weaving rod, baskets, parasol.
But as for those husbands of ours, many have lost their spear, point and
    all, from the house.
Many others have thrown off their parasol from their shoulders during
    military service.
We women could rightly bring many charges against our husbands,
And one that is especially heinous.
If a woman bears a son who is useful to the city,
A taxiarch or general, she should receive some honor –
A front row seat at the Stenia or Skira, or in the other festivals that we
    celebrate.
But if a woman bears some coward or scoundrel, a rotten ship's captain
    or bungling pilot
She should sit behind the one who mothered a brave son
With her hair clipped round a pudding bowl.
How is it fitting, City, that the mother of Hyperbolus, wearing white, her
    hair flowing down her back,
Should sit near Lamachus's mother, and lend money? If she lends money
    at interest,
And profits from the growth of her investment, no one should pay her
    interest, but seize her cash by force and say:
"What makes you fit to charge interest, after bearing an offspring like
    this?"[35]

Here they made three main points, speaking directly to the audience in
their own behalf (not for the poet, as often in the parabasis):

1. If we're as terrible as you say, why do you haunt us; why not leave us
   alone? (785–99).
2. We may indulge in minor dishonesty, but none of us has the effrontery
   to embezzle the State Treasury and then swank about in a chariot, in

full view. We are less destructive to the city than men, less wasteful and careless. We could point out any number of gluttons, thugs, slave traders here in the audience – *but we won't,* is the unspoken coda (810–29).

3. We bear sons to serve the state. Yet this is not acknowledged, and indeed the mothers of wretched public figures like Hyperbolus are given no less standing than the women who have produced heroes, such as Lamachus's mother (830–47).

The parabasis is followed by Mnesilochus's failed attempt to pass himself off as Helen and escape with Euripides/Menelaus, and then the chorus sing an interlude, in honor of Demeter, Persephone, and other divinities at 947–1000. Here they explicitly undertake to refrain from abuse of men (κακῶς ἐρεῖν...ἄνδρας, 963–5). It was customary in the latter part of old comedy for the chorus to engage in specific attacks on individuals, and both the *Lysistrata* and the *Thesmophoriazousae* were unusual in refraining.[36] But their earlier generalized attacks on men's destructiveness combined with men's hypocritical condemnation of women who display their own faults, but to an infinitely lesser degree, still ring in our ears. Their voices participate in a true quid pro quo, launched from within a cultic context and in keeping with the spirit of the festival.

The Unmasked Imposter

Near the end of the play Euripidean fictions have failed to extricate Mnesilochus. Although he is self-evidently a comic protagonist with many characteristic traits, Mnesilochus leaps into tragic plots to save himself from punishment at the hands of the women. His exposure, capture, and failure to escape – until by means of the virtually extradramatic expedient of a dancing girl – could be said to constitute failure. Is this a failure of tragedy (to effect "real-life" solutions by means of its mythic paradigms) or a failure of comedy? Both, perhaps. But comedy's failure is different from tragedy's. Let me explain by means of a critic who, like Aristophanes, juxtaposed tragic and comic spokesmen for his own purposes

The *Symposium* was a fourth-century Platonic dialogue purportedly describing a late-fifth-century party to celebrate a victory by the tragic poet Agathon (also featured as a ludicrous character in the *Thesmophoriazousae*). It comprised speeches on the nature of erotic desire by a number of famous Athenians, including Agathon himself, Aristophanes, Alcibiades, and Socrates. Plato ascribed to his character Aristophanes a fable. Original four-legged humans, doubly featured and genitaled, were split in two by Zeus, who was angry because of their wickedness. In a postlapsarian world each of us seeks the complementary "half" of whom we were shorn. Some of the primordial creatures had combined male and female parts, some included only male or only female; thus we are predisposed either to heterosexual or homosexual union. Whichever is the case, the point that Plato attributed to Aristophanes is that none of us is whole or at peace. Our sexual desire springs from nostalgia for a lost completeness.[37]

Comedy required the poet to represent Athens' actual population in order to create the illusion of erotic union, magical completeness. The citizens of this theatrical Athens were female as well as male, old and ugly as well as young and comely. As its cultic origins and its happy (often marital) endings indicate, old comedy aspired to a kind of erotic magic: uniting mortals in joyful congress. In so doing it often created an imaginary Golden Age harmony and plenitude. Yet conversely, much of comedy's essential power lay in the dismantling of illusions and pretense: the exposure of animal realities that the polite world masks or dissembles. Just as the myth Plato credited to Aristophanes showed that authentic union with our "lost half" is impossible and that a makeshift substitution (sex) is all we have, so old comedy sounded the themes of inauthenticity, disguise, dissolution, and incompleteness – in the midst of its miracle working. Indeed, as I argue here, failure and demonstrated inauthenticity lay at the heart of its miracle working.

In the *Thesmophoriazousae*'s opening scene (Aristophanes' version of) the tragic poet Agathon discussed his adoption of a feminine bearing and accoutrements – a necessary preliminary to writing tragic parts for women, he believed:

ἐγὼ δὲ τὴν ἐσθῆθ' ἅμα ⟨τῇ⟩ γνώμῃ φορῶ.
χρὴ γὰρ ποιητὴν ἄνδρα πρὸς τὰ δράματα
ἃ δεῖ ποιεῖν, πρὸς ταῦτα τοὺς τρόπους ἔχειν.
αὐτίκα γυναικεῖ' ἢν ποιῇ τις δράματα,
μετουσίαν δεῖ τῶν τρόπων τὸ σῶμ' ἔχειν... (148–52)

ἀνδρεῖα δ' ἢν ποιῇ τις, ἐν τῷ σώματι
ἔνεσθ' ὑπάρχον τοῦθ'. ἃ δ' οὐ κεκτήμεθα,
μίμησις ἤδη ταῦτα συνθηρεύεται. (153–5)

I wear clothes to suit my frame of mind.
For it is necessary for the male poet to assume the manner

appropriate for the plays he must write.
When someone composes womanly plays
He must change his ways with respect to his body....

But if someone writes manly plays, he has this
quality already established in his body. What we *don't* have
we will pursue through imitation.

Aristophanes showed this (tragic) poet as "method" actor, creating something almost indistinguishable from reality by thinking himself into the part: a process inspired by female dress. The verb συνθηρεύεται ("gather," "quest after," "gather up"), which I here translate "pursue," suggests a hunter, focused on his prey. Tragic playwriting, like acting female tragic parts, dissembled physical reality as it "closed in on" a convincing similacrum.

Unfortunately for Euripides, the proficient mimic and real-life tragic poet Agathon, as portrayed by Aristophanes, refused to disguise himself as a woman and spy on the celebrants of the Thesmophoria on Euripides' behalf; he claimed that he would be a target for their rage, being so convincingly female and therefore capable of poaching their sexual pleasures.[38]

Instead Euripides is forced to send a clumsy imposter, destined for rapid exposure: the hairy and outspoken Mnesilochus. The Thesmophorian women, warned by Clesithenes (an effeminate and therefore "legitimately" present at the women's festival) of an interloper and rendered suspicious by Mnesilochus's imprudent catalog of women's tricks and deceptions and his failure to produce on demand a credible identity as an Athenian woman, look under Mnesilochus's dress. Certainly one may see this exposure as a strategic and dramatic failure; Mnesilochus failed as a woman and was revealed as an imposter. But there is another way to view the collapse of his effort. Like his character Agathon, Aristophanes "pursues the female through imitation," but unlike the tragic poet he deliberately avoids the seamless metaphor, the perfect disguise; instead the comic poet embraces inauthenticity, outrage, failure – and thereby expressed a different kind of truth and invoked a different kind of power.

Mnesilochus participated in a distorted ritual for Demeter. In a sense he corrupted the women's rite, of course, but in the inverted world of Aristophanic parody he also perfected it. The stories of Demeter and Iambe or Baubo, which accompanied the Thesmophoria, display the same motifs – the outsider who infiltrates the circle, the bawdy "iambic" comments, the revelation of genitals – inspiring laughter. Both dramas embody sexual fluidity, extreme indecorousness, unpredictable possibilities. When cornered by the suspicious Thesmophorians, Mnesilochus, confused and panicked, claims to be a mother of nine – *and* a childless widow – a contradiction that renders his inquisitors justifiably suspicious.[39] In this contradiction he recalls (parodically) the great Demeter herself, the eternal Mother of all, bitterly bereft of her only child, and so de-mothered. I submit that Mnesilochus functions not as a failed woman but as a grotesque and transgressive combination of male and female, reminiscent of the hybrids attributed to Aristophanes by Plato. He wears the woman's gown and accoutrements until the play's end, together with the oversized phallos.

As a play in the Dionysian theater, the *Thesmophoriazousae* was a formal offering to Dionysus and a bid for first prize in the competition. It was also a joke, certainly, a mocking critique of Euripides and of Athenian stupidity. It also had another purpose. The unusual choral song and dance of 947–1000 addresses and honors the two Thesmophoroi, Apollo, Artemis, Hera, Hermes, Pan, and Dionysus.[40] The last choral ode (1136–59) calls passionately and beautifully upon Pallas Athena and "the gracious and blessed queens": the respectfully unnamed Demeter and Persephone. In the play's final lines, it explicitly offers itself as an address to Demeter.[41] The play's "women" ask for a "gracious response to us" (ἡμῖν ἀγαθὴν τούτων χάριν) regarding "these things" from the two Thesmophoroi (Demeter and Persephone), suggesting that the play has addressed itself to them at least as much as to drama's patron, Dionysus. Bowie notes that as the prayer called upon the two Thesmophoroi to appear, the audience would see ludicrous doubles on the stage: Demeter, as played by Euripides, disguised as an old madam, and Persephone, the imprisoned girl, as doubly represented by the dancing girl and by Mnesilochus, still garbed as a woman.[42]

Much of the action echoed (albeit ludicrously) actual cultic themes and practices. Ambiguity, mingling, and conflation of the "ideally" separate categories of male and female, (mock) antagonism – these themes were also present in the cult and the myths of the Thesmophoria. The story of women discovering an imposter was traditional. The kinds of jokes and accusations leveled by Mnesilochus against women, in his clumsy efforts to "reason with" the Thesmophorians, epitomized traditional iambic insults: ["Euripides hasn't told half of what really goes on!" (466–519; 555–65)]. The scene in which Mnesilochus snatched a "baby" girl from one of the Thesmophorians, discovering it to be a swaddled wine flask whose "throat" he then cut, causing its "mother" dismay – and simultaneous desire to draw off some of her child's "blood" (689–764) – also echoes the deadly schism between mother and child at the heart of the Thesmophoria, the serious and mock anguish of cult; the bizarre consolation by a presumptuous intruder. Thus Aristophanes' play, although not an accurate enactment of the Thesmophoria, made a real claim on the goddess Demeter: help our hungry and divided city recover itself. It was an act of iambic hubris on Aristophanes' part and on the part of his comic surrogate, Mnesilochus, with appropriate punishment of the latter.[43] It was a public offering to the goddess that was both mocking and serious.[44]

In conclusion, I believe that one can see the *Thesmophoriazousae* as both an earnest and a mocking response in an ongoing dialogue between Aristophanes and the women of Athens.[45] It is of course likely that the things his women characters say about Euripides were criticisms that Aristophanes himself wished to make for his own reasons. Yet the play also illustrates how the women's cults functioned as a focal point of resistance to (certain types of) hegemonic discourse. The Thesmophorian women denied tragedy's truth, resisted its power, and unmade its meanings. Tragedy, with its intensely negative portrait of women, was characterized by Aristophanes' Thesmophorians as intrusive, divisive, and irrelevant. Who is to say that many Athenian women did not find it so, and say so? Comedy, in the meantime, was cleverly recast in the likeness of women's own cultic dramas. Aristophanes' Thesmophorian women mingled rage with raucous laughter, reverence with irreverence, alienation with negotiation, just as their cultic counterparts.

Lysistrata[46]

The *Lysistrata* could be said to be about women's voices, cultic and domestic. It famously featured a plan by its eponymous heroine to stop the Peloponnesian War. The young women of Athens and Sparta were to stop sleeping with their husbands, and the older women of Athens simultaneously seized the acropolis. At the end of the play (following much comic distress on the part of Greece's menfolk) they capitulated, came to terms, and all joined in a celebration feast.

As far as we know, women's perspectives never had been wholeheartedly imagined in comedy before, and so this play marked a turning point. The audience had the opportunity both to hear their voices at close range, as if – as in the *Thesmophoriazousae* – they were unseen eavesdroppers on a female conspiracy. At the same time, by hearing the angry reaction of various male characters to this plot, and of men to women's voices generally, either directly or as reported, the audience also could perceive how, from the public point of view, Athenian women's voices murmured in a distant (and discordant) continuo beneath the louder voices of citizen males. The play also ironically showed how men's reporting of women's activities and comments did not necessarily correspond with reality. For example, the first man to arrive on the scene following the women's takeover of the acropolis was a magistrate, huffing outrage at their temerity.

ἆρ' ἐξέλαμψε τῶν γυναικῶν ἡ τρυφὴ
χὠ τυμπανισμὸς χοἰ πυκνοὶ Σαβάζιοι,
ὅ τ' Ἀδωνιασμὸς οὗτος οὑπὶ τῶν τεγῶν,
οὗ 'γώ ποτ' ὢν ἤκουον ἐν τἠκκλησίᾳ·
ἔλεγε δ' ὁ μὴ ὥρασι μὲν Δημόστρατος
πλεῖν ἐς Σικελίαν, ἡ γυνὴ δ' ὀρχουμένη
"αἰαῖ Ἄδωνιν" φησίν, ὁ δὲ Δημόστρατος
ἔλεγεν ὁπλίτας καταλέγειν Ζακυνθίων,
ἡ δ' ὑποπεπωκυῖ' ἡ γυνὴ 'πὶ τοῦ τέγους
"κόπτεσθ' Ἄδωνιν" φησίν· ὁ δ' ἐβιάζετο
ὁ θεοῖσιν ἐχθρὸς καὶ μιαρὸς Χολοζύγης.
τοιαῦτ' ἀπ' αὐτῶν ἐστιν ἀκολαστάσματα. (387–98)

So the women's wantonness is erupting again!
The drums! Those incessant "Sabazios" chants,
And this "Adonisizing" on the roofs!
I once heard it in the Assembly.
Demostratus (bad luck to him!) was advocating that we
    sail to Sicily,
And his wife was prancing about and saying "Woe for Adonis!"
Then Demostratus said that we should levy troops from
    Zakynthus,
While his wife on the roof was drunk and proclaiming
"Beat your breasts for Adonis!"
But he droned on anyway, that cursed man,
That stinking Right Honorable Mr. Rant!
This is the kind of permissiveness you get from women![47]

The magistrate claimed to recognize in their meeting a "typical" women's debauch, with drums and yelling for Sabazios and Adonis. Yet, as Henderson has observed, in the play itself the old women of the chorus expressed devotion only to the city's official gods (not the foreign "imports" like Adonis and Sabazius).[48] (Ironically Aristophanes himself had written a play in which Sabazius and other "immigrant" gods were tried and deported from the city).[49] Similarly Lysistrata herself, as she fretted over the late arrival of the younger women in the play's opening lines, said that although they were cavalier regarding a "serious" meeting, they would race out at the drop of a hat to celebrate Pan, Bacchus, or Genetyllis at Colias (bona fide Athenian gods, incidentally).

The magistrate apparently remembered how a group of women on the rooftop keened and yelled drunkenly for Adonis at the very time that Demostratus, whose wife was one of the Adonis worshippers, was proposing troops for the Sicilian expedition in the Assembly.[50] This "jinxing" of the Sicilian expedition by women's voices probably was contrived by Aristophanes and not historical.[51] Yet if Aristophanes/the magistrate invented the connection, it is all the more suggestive. The Adonia, a festival that was celebrated by unofficial groups of women every summer, featured Athenian women lamenting the death of a youth in a public, indeed exhibitionist, way. The women also joked, thus engaging in a characteristic cultic mix of bawdy laughter and lamentation.[52] How disturbingly fierce and compelling their mingled grief and angry laughter must have been in the war-worn city.[53] The eerie rooftop wailing and laughter, evoked or imagined, during a crucial session of the assembly suggested that women's voices, whether raised in cultic cries or in (veiled) political commentary, were becoming more audible at this time.

I note in passing how this "Adonis" scene (leaving aside the question of its historicity) illustrates how women could be both present and not present in a public situation; how their voices could be audible while not officially on a public agenda. The "liminality" had been illustrated also in the *Acharnians* of 425, in which Dicaeopolis celebrated his personal Dionysia, complete with a phallic procession, joined by his wife, who was on the roof of their house (262).

In her conversation with the magistrate explaining the situation Lysistrata produced an insight into life for Athenian women. She pointed to a woman's discourse that never became explicitly public, and indeed she showed how women could not even raise certain issues in private with impunity:

Λυ.
ἡμεῖς τὸν μὲν πρότερόν γε χρόνον (σιγῇ γ᾽) ἠνειχόμεθ᾽ ⟨ὑμῶν⟩
ὑπὸ σωφροσύνης τῆς ἡμετέρας τῶν ἀνδρῶν ἅττ᾽ ἐποιεῖτε·

οὐ γὰρ γρύζειν εἰᾶθ᾽ ἡμᾶς· καί τοὐκ ἠρέσκετέ γ᾽ ἡμᾶς.
ἀλλ᾽ ᾐσθανόμεθα καλῶς ὑμῶν, καὶ πολλάκις ἔνδον ἂν οὖσαι
ἠκούσαμεν ἄν τι κακῶς ὑμᾶς βουλευσαμένους μέγα πρᾶγμα·
εἶτ᾽ ἀλγοῦσαι τἄνδοθεν ὑμᾶς ἐπανηρόμεθ᾽ ἂν γελάσασαι·
"τί βεβούλευται περὶ τῶν σπονδῶν ἐν τῇ στήλῃ παραγράψαι
ἐν τῷ δήμῳ τήμερον ὑμῖν;" "τί δὲ σοὶ τοῦτ᾽;" ἦ δ᾽ ὃς ἂν ἀνήρ·
"οὐ σιγήσει;" κἀγὼ ᾽σίγων.

Γρ.
                          ἀλλ᾽ οὐκ ἂν ἐγώ ποτ᾽ ἐσίγων.

Πρ.
κἂν ᾤμωζές γ᾽, εἰ μὴ ᾽σίγας.

Λυ.
                          τοίγαρ ⟨ἐγὼ⟩ μὲν τότ᾽ ἐσίγων.
⟨αὖθις δ᾽⟩ ἕτερόν τι πονηρότερον βούλευμ᾽ ἐπεπύσμεθ᾽ ἂν ὑμῶν·
εἶτ᾽ ἠρόμεθ᾽ ἄν· "πῶς ταῦτ᾽, ὦνερ, διαπράττεσθ᾽ ὧδ᾽ ἀνοήτως;"
ὁ δέ μ᾽ εὐθὺς ὑποβλέψας ⟨ἂν⟩ ἔφασκ᾽, εἰ μὴ τὸν στήμονα νήσω,
ὀτοτύξεσθαι μακρὰ τὴν κεφαλήν· "πόλεμος δ᾽ ἄνδρεσσι μελήσει."
    (507–20)[54]

LYS:
Previously we women endured <in silence> whatever
You men did, because of our self restraint;
You didn't let us utter a word. But you didn't please us!
No – we knew well what you were about, and often, being at home
as we were we would hear that you had made some terrible decision
on an important matter. Then, grieving inside we would laughingly
    ask you
"What did you decide to inscribe on the stele regarding the truce
today, in the assembly?" "What's it got to do with you!" he'd say
Or "Shut up!" And so I shut up.

OLD WOMAN:
    I would not have shut up!

MAGISTRATE:
And you would have been groaning if you hadn't!

LYS:
    That's why I said nothing at the time.
<But later> we would hear about some even worse decision that you
had made, and then we would ask: "Husband, how could you do
something so stupid?" And he'd immediately look daggers and say
    "If you don't

spin your thread you'll be howling with a sore head! War is men's business."

This "War is men's business" is a famous quote from the *Iliad*. In the battlement scene at 6, 390–493, Andromache pleaded with Hector not to expose himself unnecessarily to the collective onslaught of the Achaeans, but to remain on the rampart and direct his men to defend the wall where it was most broachable. Hector's response bespoke tenderness and pity for her future (inevitable) fate at the hands of the Achaeans. Nonetheless, as he observed, he felt tremendous pressure from the watchful eyes of Trojan men *and* women (6, 442) and could not quit the foremost ranks to save his life. His consolation would be not having to witness the day of enslavement for his wife, having died long before. His speech continued with an illogical hope that his baby son would grow up to lead the Trojans and smite their enemies. Finally, his death, like everyone's, was determined by fate. So he enjoined Andromache see to her loom and distaff, because πόλεμος δ᾽ ἄνδρεσσι μελήσει. The Greek is ambiguous, meaning something like: "War will be a concern to men" or "War will be something for men to take care of." In the second sense, he is of course right; warfare was waged by men only; it was their business, just as textile production was women's business. In the first sense, he is wrong.[55] As Andromache eloquently pointed out, Hector was all she had precisely because the warring Greeks (notably Achilles) had wiped out her family. And she has further misery to look forward to, beyond even what either was willing to imagine, as they tenderly nourished hopes for the son who would not live to be a man.

Lysistrata's modern "Hector" is a loutish counterpart to this tragic figure. And if the expression πόλεμος δ᾽ ἄνδρεσσι μελήσει. was not entirely true for Hector, it is truly jarring in the mouth of this modern husband. In fifth-century Athens, there was no need or place for solitary heroes; decision making was collective, and warfare was necessarily cooperative and civic, not the virtual preserve of an élite class, conducted independently of proletarian wishes. Why should a citizen woman not even hear about the decisions upon which her future life and welfare might depend? Indeed, shadowed by the epic scene and grimly recontextualized in this sordid spat, the aphorism begs for a response, even as he threatens her to shut up. (*War is for men – who use violence as a form of communication. If war concerns men, then peace and reconciliation concern women*).[56] In fact, following a scene in which the women dressed the magistrate as a woman because he refused to take orders from anyone in a veil, Lysistrata cries πόλεμος δὲ γυναιξὶ μελήσει ("War will be something for *women* to take care of!" 538). Meanwhile the magistrate, like Mnesilochus in the *Thesmophoriazousae*, has joined a women's ritual circle.

One of the striking features of Lysistrata's account of the modern connubial conversation are the modulations of this "Everywoman's" tone of voice. First she masks the seriousness of her question and her own grief with laughter. Her husband silences her anyway. A second, more harshly worded rebuke for follies committed in the Assembly earns her a threat of a beating. Lysistrata's archetypal Athenian wife tried a comic and then a more frankly iambic tone, but in each case she is roughly cut off. Having described how her alter ego failed to persuade with jokes and abuse, little wonder that Lysistrata evolved into a tragic character. In her Aristophanes created a woman with the presence, resolve, and moral authority of a Sophoclean protagonist.

Lysistrata's message, as well as her bearing, had a somber tinge, for all that it expresses a "comic" priority.[57] The city's women are aging; young girls will die unwed if the war continues, because their time of marriageability is particularly short (591–7).[58] In comedy old men may grow young again – metaphorically like the irrepressible Philocleon, at the end of the *Wasps*, or literally, as in the *Old Age* or *Snakeskin* of Aristophanes. This option is not open to women, even in comedy's fantasy world, as far as I can tell.[59]

Nonetheless the *Lysistrata* comes as close as any play to celebrating the vigor and power of old women. In the *Lysistrata* the old men express the need to become young again in order to attack the acropolis and dislodge the old women, who have occupied it (664–71). In fact these doddering old men seem trapped in their own rhetoric of heroic history, claiming to have participated in the ousting of the Pisistratid tyrants, the expulsion of the Spartan Cleomenes, who took over the acropolis briefly in 508, and the battle of Marathon in 490.[60] Obviously to have had a military career spanning these events and extending into 411 would make these old soldiers incredibly ancient.

The old women occupying the acropolis evince a greater liveliness and resourcefulness than their male counterparts. The men attempt to storm the acropolis with fire but are handily rebuffed by the women, who douse them with water. The women describe their watery assault as a bath for a bridegroom and a watering of a plant to make it bloom (378, 384), suggesting that they have within them rejuvenating powers, even if they themselves are no longer young. Later the woman's leader forcibly kisses the men's leader (having removed the "gnat" that was making his eyes water),

and persuades the old men – still grumbling – to form a single chorus with
their female counterparts (1035–42).

κορυφαία

καὶ φιλήσω.

κορυφαῖος

μὴ φιλήσῃς.

κορυφαία

ἤν τε βούλῃ γ᾽ ἤν τε μή.

κορυφαῖος

ἀλλὰ μὴ ὥρασ᾽ ἵκοισθ᾽· ὡς ἐστὲ θωπικαὶ φύσει,
κᾆστ᾽ ἐκεῖνο τοὔπος ὀρθῶς κοὐ κακῶς εἰρημένον,
οὔτε σὺν πανωλέθροισιν οὔτ᾽ ἄνευ πανωλέθρων.
ἀλλὰ νυνὶ σπένδομαί σοι, καὶ τὸ λοιπὸν οὐκέτι
οὔτε δράσω φλαῦρον οὐδὲν οὔθ᾽ ὑφ᾽ ὑμῶν πείσομαι.
ἀλλὰ κοινῇ συσταλέντες τοῦ μέλους ἀρξώμεθα.

WOMEN'S CHORUS LEADER
And I'll kiss you!

MEN'S CHORUS LEADER
Don't kiss me!

WOMEN'S CHORUS LEADER
Whether you like it or not!

MEN'S CHORUS LEADER
Bad luck to you! You are born sweet talkers,
And that old saying is exactly right:
"You can't live with the plagues or without 'em."
But now I'll make a truce, and in the future
I will not do you ill, or suffer ill at your hands,
But let's form a single group and begin our song

This sexual-martial capitulation follows directly upon that of Cinesias,
who has been teased into a state of raging priapism by his scantily clad
wife, Myrrhine. The old women may not have Myrrhine's allure, but they
still maintain a certain pride in their appearance and clearly have not
abandoned sex entirely.[61] This sexuality seems linked with their overall
vigor, resourcefulness, and effectiveness. They make better soldiers because somehow they are not as old as the old men, and certainly not as
old as the old men accuse them of being.[62] Indeed the old women, when

they look to *their* laurels, do not and cannot link themselves to any particular historical event. Instead they boast of having participated in the Arrhephoria of Athena Polias; grinding ritual cakes, probably for Demeter at Eleusis; dressing in yellow for Brauronian Artemis; carrying ritual baskets (probably in the procession for the Panathenaia; 638–47). These cultic honors tie them to the city but to no particular time. They are cultic, recurring events and belong to the special "time out of time" of cult.[63] In this sense the women have a "timeless" youthfulness denied their male peers.

In the play's final scene, Lysistrata instructs the comely female figure of Reconciliation to take by the hand (by the penis, if they object) the male representatives of each city. I suggest that the figure of Reconciliation was larger than life, hence Lysistrata's direction to her to lead the Athenians and Spartans gently, not in a rough and overbearing way as a man might (1115–19). The gesture of leading by the hand, as vase painting amply testifies in marriage and similar scenes, typically belonged to the male and indicated authority (over a woman) if not ownership (as of a female slave). Thus the scene would have presented a sharply inverted norm to its audience.

Lysistrata simultaneously urges the men to remember their common Greek culture: the sacrifices, worship, oracles, athletic contests. She reminds each side of past military assistance offered by their current enemy.[64] The rival ambassadors respond in the only way they knew how: with sexualized aggression toward a desirable prize. Athenian and Spartan ambassadors contend for pieces of Reconciliation, predictably focusing on her genitalia and legs. For them, so long embroiled in war, Greek commonality no longer exists. They cannot see Reconciliation for who she is, in Lysistrata's dream. Reconciliation literally embodies Greece in their eyes, and their claims on individual parts of her evoke the grotesquerie of civil war. In an astounding *legerdemain* Lysistrata redirects their sexual desire away from destructive dreams of territorial monopoly toward the legitimate sexual monopolies of the marriage bed. It is a miracle: getting the male combatants to revisualize their limited claims on the public world from the woman's perspective of the household. Bounded in their individual nutshells, they can jointly rule as kings of infinite space. The play ends in the customary magical banquet.

Taaffe and others have observed that the scene plays to a retrograde version of the male gaze and the objectified female.[65] I would like to qualify this position, however. Reconciliation was a powerful image: not a symbol of powerlessness. While she remained silent, her (probably large and exaggerated) body symbolizes bounty and plenitude. I offer the second half of Sophocles' *Ajax* by way of comparison. Following his suicide, Ajax's body becomes a focus of debate and a source of power. At the end, surrounded by his family and friends, with his wounds still miraculously flowing, his body seems as "eloquent" as any speaking actor. And like Reconciliation here, his body brings together men of opposing political views.

But I want to end my discussion of the *Lysistrata* with the heroine's voice, as I believe Aristophanes intended. In the closing lines of the play it is she who directs the now reunited husbands and wives to dance and sing together – in a most unusual way. Men and women typically did not dance together.[66]

> ἄγε νυν ἐπειδὴ τἄλλα πεποίηται καλῶς,
> ἀπάγεσθε ταύτας ὦ Λάκωνες, τάσδε δὶ
> ὑμεῖς· ἀνὴρ δὲ παρὰ γυναῖκα καὶ γυνὴ
> στήτω παρ' ἄνδρα, κᾆτ' ἐπ' ἀγαθαῖς συμφοραῖς
> ὀρχησάμενοι θεοῖσιν εὐλαβώμεθα
> τὸ λοιπὸν αὖθις μὴ 'ξαμαρτάνειν ἔτι. (1273–78)

Come now, now that everything else has been fixed so well
You Spartans, take your partners, and you Athenian men, take yours!
Each man must stand by his wife, and each woman by her husband,
And then let's dance for these happy circumstances!
And let's take care never to make mistakes in the future!

The scene, like the previous one featuring reconciliation, must have had a powerful visual impact. Lysistrata, like the city's goddess whose double she was, presided over a previously unimagined harmony of private rapture and public restraint.

Change and Changelessness: The *Ecclesiazousae*

Old comedy was topical, fast paced. In winning the right to put on plays, the poets became public officials, engaged in a competitive display before the *demos*. They often spoke to political decisions, mocked Athenian institutions, and ridiculed politicians, by implication questioning the judgment of the citizens who had elected such men to office.[67] The comic poet addressed the fickle and unreliable citizens who elected Cleon and Cleophon, who voted for war. He did so with a mixture of old jokes, new jokes – and new plots. There was pressure to innovate, to excel and win the prize.

Whether his material was new or traditional, Aristophanes consistently expressed the ironic opinion that novelty was what the Athenians prized above all else and in all contexts.[68] The parabasis of the *Clouds* 541 ff boasted about the (now rewritten) play's avoidance of old jokes and characters, its use of sparkling new jokes. *Wasps* 57 promises novelty and avoidance of stale obscenity. At *Clouds* 896–8, the Just Logic declares that the innovative ideas proposed by the Unjust Logic will succeed with the thoughtless people in the audience. Dionysus sternly rebuked Xanthias for attempting to invoke tired old (scatological) jests at *Frogs* 8. Nowhere did Aristophanes express a deeper sense of the competing allure of an idealized, unchanging past on the one hand and of exciting change on the other than in the third great extant "women's" play, the *Ecclesiazousae*, possibly datable to 393.[69] As one might expect, Aristophanes' "women" were symbols of this ideal cultic stability, albeit flawed ones.

The *Ecclesiazousae* depicted a woman's revolution, ironically justified on the grounds that women were more conservative, less given to rash innovation, than men. The women of Athens disguised themselves as men, appeared in the Assembly and decreed women as the city's new leaders. This ambitious plan, we are told twice in the opening lines of the play, was first thought out at the Scira, a transition ritual that took place during the Greek new year, in midsummer, as described in Chapter 1.[70] Thus the play from the outset sketches a cultic framework for its plot. Women gathered apart from men, formed their own society, as in the Thesmophoria, and ate garlic, a ritual anaphrodisiac. There is no explicit evidence for *aischrologia*, but it is consonant with other features of this festival. We also lack clear evidence for cross dressing, although such behavior was characteristic of some transition rites, such as the Argive Hybristica.[71]

Here is the passage in which Praxagora, the ringleader, established that women, by virtue of their innate conservatism, were reliable guides for the city. She rebuked the men of the city for their changeable politics, their failure to act as a group and their pursuit of private gain at the expense of the city:

ὡς δ᾽ εἰσὶν ἡμῶν τοὺς τρόπους βελτίονες
ἐγὼ διδάξω. πρῶτα μὲν γὰρ τἄρια
βάπτουσι θερμῷ κατὰ τὸν ἀρχαῖον νόμον
ἁπαξάπασαι, κοὐχὶ μεταπειρωμένας
ἴδιοις ἂν αὐτάς. ἡ δ᾽ Ἀθηναίων πόλις
εἰ τοῦτο χρηστῶς εἶχεν, οὐκ ἂν ἐσῴζετο,

εἰ μὴ τι καινὸν ⟨γ'⟩ ἄλλο περιηργάζετο.
καθήμεναι φρύγουσιν ὥσπερ καὶ πρὸ τοῦ·
ἐπὶ τῆς κεφαλῆς φέρουσιν ὥσπερ καὶ πρὸ τοῦ·
τὰ Θεσμοφόρι' ἄγουσιν ὥσπερ καὶ πρὸ τοῦ·
πέττουσι τοὺς πλακοῦντας ὥσπερ καὶ πρὸ τοῦ·
τοὺς ἄνδρας ἐπιτρίβουσιν ὥσπερ καὶ πρὸ τοῦ·
μοιχοὺς ἔχουσιν ἔνδον ὥσπερ καὶ πρὸ τοῦ·
αὑταῖς παροψωνοῦσιν ὥσπερ καὶ πρὸ τοῦ·
οἶνον φιλοῦσ' εὔζωρον ὥσπερ καὶ πρὸ τοῦ·
βινούμεναι χαίρουσιν ὥσπερ καὶ πρὸ τοῦ·

I will explain to you how our ways (τρόποι)
Are better [than yours]. First, women dye their wool
In warm water, according to the ancient manner,
Every one of them. You wouldn't find
them experimenting. But as for Athens,
If the old way worked fine, the city would not choose salvation
Unless it involved wasting time on some novelty.
They sit and roast barley, as before.
They bear (vessels) on their heads, as before.
They keep the Thesmophoria, as before.
They cook their flat cakes, as before.
They wear out their husbands, as before.
They hide their lovers, as before.
They buy themselves goodies, as before.
They like their wine unmixed, as before.
They love to get laid, as before. (214–28)

The speech had an incantatory quality, which itself evoked women's cults and their recurring patterns. Phrynichus's *Mystai* uses the same expression: ἐβούλομην ἂν ἡμῖν ὥσπερ καὶ πρὸ τοῦ. ("I wish we could have things as before").[72] Cults, such as the Thesmophoria, rooted the city in its stable past and reminded the people of what should not change. Such cults did not need to justify themselves in each new political context, to please the caprices of the demos or its leaders. They knitted people together as a genuine community, ideally transcending the selfish and competing desires of individuals.

The speech begins well, with women's key role in textiles, food preparation, and cult, but its latter half descends to familiar iambic jibes. Despite the change in tone, however, women throughout are treated as a tight community, a group whose cohesion is emphasized by the chiming verb endings. Obviously this notion of group activity particularly applied to cult, and to a lesser extent, to textile and food preparation. The fact that adultery and the pilfering of household resources appear seamlessly in the list gives the impression, familiar from iambic, that women as a whole have always formed a tightly knit conspiracy against men, a fifth column within men's ordered universe. The play quickly unravels this traditional illusion of a woman's conspiracy, however. Once Praxagora's decree was passed, once the city's distinction between public and private was eradicated and the women's world became the only world, women's competing sexual interests threatened their community, reminding us how the polis previously had been shattered by competing male interests. The play suggests that women's voices had unique value precisely because of the constraints upon them. Bound by the cults they celebrated, prevented from practicing politics, they could speak to communal interests and on behalf of ancient loyalties. Once admitted to the contentious "public" world, their voices and opinions fragmented, like those of men.

Following urgent invitations to innovate by her coconspirators (571–87), Praxagora complied, with her radical plan for a "city as one giant household" with sexual access to all. The old and ugly would have first claim, however, and the young and comely would not be able to enjoy each other until all others are satisfied. The play concluded with scenes depicting the comic chaos that ensued. The first depicted a citizen in the process of bringing his property to the communal depot and debating with a dissident who refused to sell his property but who still wanted to join in the common feasting. The scene raised interesting questions but ended inconclusively. There is no indication as to whether the "dissident" will manage to have it both ways or be punished. It was immediately followed by a second scene, far more disturbing to modern audiences, involving a young man whose sexual services were being quarreled over by three hags and a girl.

There is much debate over how to read these closing scenes, which means that the play as a whole has been subject to very different readings. Saïd, Hubbard, and Zeitlin see the play as depicting a failed Utopia, and thus the final scenes are ironic.[73] Henderson, Konstan and Dillon, Rothwell and Sommerstein view the play's satire as directed, not at the communist ideas themselves but at those who rejected them out of selfishness or greed.[74] Saxonhouse sees the play as an exercise in breaking down inadequate old dichotomies, but introducing an unnatural and unmanageable new society as a result.[75] Slater is, I believe, closer to the mark.[76] He observes, "The notion that the *Ecclesiazousae* is an indictment of a value system based on individual selfishness has always seemed dubious, since self-gratification is the goal of every Aristophanic hero. Food, wine, and sex are *the* comic goods. . . . We should not therefore let modern sentimentality betray us into an undeserved sympathy for the young man in this play." Quite right. Indeed I would go further and say that the young man's wishes didn't rise to the level of an issue, at least in the minds of some audience members.

The ultimate scene yields insights into women's roles within Aristophanes and women's readings of his plays. I suggest that they might have been read differently by men and by women. Thus I now treat the old hag scene in more detail.

How Did Women See Drama?

Did women have a sense of solidarity as a group? And, if so, would this have colored their response to the plays? Although there is no direct evidence bearing on these questions, what we know generally about women's lives suggests that the answer to the first question must be yes – at least to an extent. Actual wives, slaves, mistresses, and mothers in fifth-century Athens responded to the plays as individuals, but they also routinely assembled with other women to work or to shape the city's future in their dealings with the gods. Their sense(s) of humor would have been shaped by their lives and by their collective experiences – so different from men's in each case – so, taken as a whole, their reaction to the plays differed in some respects from men's.

How would old comedy have looked to women in Athens? Throughout the plays women characters functioned as emblems of human sexuality and as targets of misogynistic humor. No doubt to an extent the women of Athens had absorbed the perspective of the dominant culture and found misogynistic humor funny, as some women do today.[77] But their vision of themselves and of their sexuality was complicated by their cultic experiences, some of which took place at a remove from the dominant culture. These cultic experiences did not necessarily re-create the misogynistic perspective of the male polis – or at least the misogyny was balanced by what was probably equally virulent antimale humor among women. Did women's rude ripostes to Aristophanes silently reverberate between the iambic lines of the *Thesmophoriazousae* and *Ecclesiazousae* at least in the minds of some members of the audience? We should be alert to such possibilities.

I conclude this chapter with two comic – and cultic – themes: sexual old women and sexual prepubescent girls. These topics have inspired discomfort in modern scholars, men and women alike. How might they have looked to Athenian women?

The *Acharnians* (425) contains a scene in which a Megarian man persuades his two preadolescent daughters to be sold as piglets to Dicaeopolis, a renegade Athenian who has made a private peace with the Peloponnesians. In return the Megarian will receive garlic and salt, and his daughters themselves will be able to fill their starving bellies. To this end he encourages them to make piglet noises, which they do. The audience probably viewed the scene as a whole as a "Megarian scheme" (Μεγαρικά ... μαχανά), a characteristic piece of bawdy humor purveyed by a city that claimed to have been comedy's birthplace.[78] It is not surprising to find in it features of fertility cult, and the joking associated with it. The Megarian asks his girls to apply their γαστήρ (rather than their νοῦς or mind) to his proposition that they sell themselves to Diceopolis. The γαστήρ was both the belly – a hungry and importunate inner voice for the war-weary Megarians – and the womb. Thus the girls are invoked as empty vessels, which can be "full" in two ways. This double meaning runs throughout the scene, which is rife with sexual double entendres.

One of the most striking elements of the exchange as a whole is the girls' extreme youth. The girls are sucking pigs (χοιρία) capable of being tucked into a sack. When Diceopolis objects that they are not piglets, the Megarian replies, punning on the double use of χοῖρος as piglet and (immature) female genitalia:[79]

> νῦν γε χοῖρος φαίνεται,
> ἀτὰρ ἐκτραφείς γε κύσθος ἔσται (781–2)

Now she looks like a piglet
But all grown up she will be a fully grown pussy!

Given the early date at which most Athenian women married, usually not long after their first menstruation, these are young children indeed.

This is not refined humor, even by old comedy's standards. Indeed Aristophanes seems to disown the scene by causing a Megarian to instigate it; elsewhere, in the *Wasps*, he (half jokingly) repudiates Megarian jokes as too coarse. Yet it is more than just coarseness. To be sure, these piglet girls are to be consumed – and consuming – both in the sexual and in the alimentary sense. They embody animal pleasures in the most basic (and perhaps to the modern eye, degrading) way, reflecting a society that routinely treated women – and children and men – as commodities.[80] But they also epitomize something basic in women's fertility cults: the power of the unexpected; the potential of a seemingly unpreposessing or insignificant body. This uncanny power was most powerfully expressed not through the mature female, but through her antitypes: the unripe girl – and the crone, close to death, and already showing signs of decay. We recall the piglets tossed to die and to decay in pits from which they were retrieved at the Thesmophoria. They symbolized what was not yet and what had been, brought together in violence and in hope, and serving as catalyst for next year's generation of crops and of babies.

A late play, the *Plutus* (388) also presents images of the female, which communicate complex messages, not immediately accessible to the modern reader. The play falls into two major parts, each of which contains a significant female figure.[81] In the first sequence of acts, the play's impoverished hero, Chremylus, following the advice of Delphi, attaches himself to an elderly, blind old man, whom he discovers to be none other than the god Wealth (Plutus). He takes Plutus back to his house. He and his neighbor Blepsidamus decide that they will arrange for the god to see again, through a visit to the shrine of the physician god, Asclepius. As a result of this they expect that Plutus will change his ways, confining his visits to the homes of good men, and abandoning the wicked, with whom he used to consort, because of his blindness. Before they can do this, however, they are interrupted by the figure of Penia (Poverty), with whom they engage in a spirited "debate" before driving her from the stage. Following an entr'acte we hear of the cure of Plutus. The effect of this miracle is not quite as the characters had predicted: widespread wealth, rather than monetary rewards for virtue. The play does make it clear, however, that the new system will produce a redistribution of wealth, and that the old rules no longer apply. There are new winners and new losers, and some individuals (whose characters could not be described as "good" or "bad" in any obvious way) accommodate themselves to, or are permitted to share in, the new arrangements. They also belong in the revolutionary utopia.

The second part of the play contains a series of scenes depicting the effect of universal wealth on the "economy," represented in the most lurid and ridiculous way imaginable. Thus a Sycophant or professional prosecutor can no longer make his living from selling information, because money has lost all meaning. His fine clothes are exchanged for the rags of a Good Man, who now becomes rich under the new regime. The Sycophant is chased off the stage with a drubbing when he refuses to repudiate his trade and indeed threatens to denounce the god Plutus himself. The Sycophant is followed by an old woman who can no longer keep her young gigolo, because he no longer needs the money and provisions with which she alone once supplied him. He has turned rude and contemptuous and has deserted her. The god Hermes also appears; he suffers under the new regime, because mortals no longer need to appease him with offerings; they have nothing to gain anymore. A priest of Zeus the Savior similarly feels the pinch, now that sacrificial offerings have fallen off. By the play's end, Hermes has talked his way into the festival of bounty inside Chremylus's house, where he is joined by the priest and where Zeus the Savior is already ensconced. The old woman reappears and agrees to carry a sacrificial vessel to the temple of Wealth. In return she is promised another night with her young man. The play ends with this promise.

The play thus presents two fundamentally different worlds: the threadbare, workaday world in the first half and a magical banquet in the second. Although the unscrupulous Sycophant undergoes punishment in the second half, its emphasis is on plenitude, a gracious excess of benefits for anyone who might lay plausible claim to Comedy's banquet. In the first half the ageless figure of Poverty is compared with a Fury: a figure more appropriate to the tragic stage. She terrifies and repels her interlocutors, as one might expect a Fury to do.

> Χρεμύλος
> σὺ δ' εἶ τίς; ὠχρὰ μὲν γὰρ εἶναί μοι δοκεῖς.
>
> Βλεψίδημος
> ἴσως Ἐρινύς ἐστιν ἐκ τραγῳδίας·
> βλέπει γέ τοι μανικόν τι καὶ τραγῳδικόν.
>
> Χρεμύλος
> ἀλλ' οὐκ ἔχει γὰρ δᾷδας. (422–4)

> CHREMYLUS:
> Who are you? You seem rather anemic.
>
> BLESPSIDAMUS:
> Perhaps she's a Fury from a tragedy. She looks a bit lunatic, and
>   tragic-like.
>
> CHREMYLUS:
> But she doesn't have any torches.

Yet, as she herself observes, she is not to be confused with utter penury; she merely embodies the order of (say) Hesiod's *Works and Days*. If you work hard, you may expect to eat and have a moderately comfortable life.

εἰ γὰρ ὁ Πλοῦτος βλέψειε πάλιν διανείμειέν τ᾽ ἴσον αὑτόν,
οὔτε τέχνην ἂν τῶν ἀνθρώπων οὔτ᾽ ἂν σοφίαν μελετῴη
οὐδείς· ἀμφοῖν δ᾽ ὑμῖν τούτοιν ἀφανισθέντοιν ἐθελήσει
τίς χαλκεύειν ἢ ναυπηγεῖν ἢ ῥάπτειν ἢ τροχοποιεῖν,
ἢ σκυτοτομεῖν ἢ πλινθουργεῖν ἢ πλύνειν ἢ σκυλοδεψεῖν,
ἢ γῆς ἀρότροις ῥήξας δάπεδον καρπὸν Δηοῦς θερίσασθαι,
ἢν ἐξῇ ζῆν ἀργοῖς ὑμῖν τούτων πάντων ἀμελοῦσιν; (510–17)

If Wealth gets his sight back, and shares himself out equally,
No one will practice any human art or craft.
And with these gone who will want to work as a smith,
A shipbuilder, a tailor, a wheelwright,
A shoemaker, a bricklayer, a launderer, a tanner.
Who will break the soil with the plough,
To harvest the fruits of Demeter,
If you can live a life of leisure, and ignore all of these things?

As she notes, again with impeccable logic, she is the driving force behind all human endeavor, all crafts. It is she who makes available the gifts of Demeter, because men work the fields so as to feed their families. Poverty epitomizes the spirit of the play's first half, where actions have predictable consequences and where it is easy to understand the characters' expectation that bestowing sight on Plutus will result in a wave of punishment for the unworthily rich as well as rewards for the virtuous but poor.

Poverty knows that her arguments are unassailable, but Chremylus and Blepsidamus resort to violence and drive her from the stage. The world that follows Plutus's cure is one in which calculation, logic, and reason have no place. And the old woman, deserted by her gigolo, belongs in it. Like the god Plutus himself, as portrayed in the opening scene, she is old, decrepit, seemingly friendless and lost. As soon as she opens her mouth, her interlocutors notice that she presents herself as a timid young girl:

Γραῦς
ἆρ᾽ ὦ φίλοι γέροντες ἐπὶ τὴν οἰκίαν
ἀφίγμεθ᾽ ὄντως τοῦ νέου τούτου θεοῦ,
ἢ τῆς ὁδοῦ τὸ παράπαν ἡμαρτήκαμεν;

Κορυφαῖος
ἀλλ᾽ ἴσθ᾽ ἐπ᾽ αὐτὰς τὰς θύρας ἀφιγμένη
ὦ μειρακίσκη· πυνθάνει γὰρ ὡρικῶς. (959–63)

OLD WOMAN:
Please Sirs, have I really and truly come
To the house of this new god?
Or have I completely lost my way?

CHORUS LEADER:
No. You can rest assured that you're at his door, girlie,
Since you ask so girlishly.

She wears paint and conducts herself like an attractive woman but is old, grey, and (almost) toothless.[82] In the inflexible economy of the real world these are serious impediments to erotic attachments. She has managed previously thanks to her wealth, but in the new world order of the play's second half she seems displaced. Yet she is not. Her speech marks her, like the hero Chremylus, as a devotee of Demeter. She is an initiate in the Eleusinian Mysteries, and her claim to youth, vigor, and love amid the ruin of her old age reaches beyond delusional folly into the world of cult and its larger possibilities.[83] As we have seen, women's Demetrian cults allowed for simultaneous age and vigor, grace and grotesquerie. Thus, alone of the figures who demonstrate the economic revolution in the play's second half, she reappears at the end. Chremylus concludes the play with (what seems to us to be) a lame pun. This *graus* will be underneath the little pots used to furnish Plutus' altars, whereas the *graus* is usually on top. The word *graus* could mean both "old woman" and "skin" or "membrane" such as one might find on a dish of cooling soup or porridge. Thus Chremylus jokes (probably obscenely) that this (underneath) will be an unusual position for an old woman.[84] But the topsy-turvy world of comedy's banquet will indeed have a place for her. The play ends with this focus on her pleasure; the young gigolo's newfound fastidiousness rates not one whit. Old comedy so often portrayed women as "meals" for men, but this *graus* is portrayed mostly in terms of her appetite.

In the *Ecclesiazousae* we again encounter a scene with highly sexualized old women, this time with a rather different flavor to it. Praxagora's radical plan requires that a man must give sexual priority to old and unattractive women before he indulges his desires with the young and comely. In its final scene a young man finds himself the subject of a contest: first between a young girl (whom he desires) and a hag and then between two more old hags, each more unattractive and closer to death than the last. The women's language is both obscene and abusive of each other. The youth describes one of these old women as an Empousa (1056), the other as a hideous revenant (1073). Eventually he departs in despair, dragged off by his elderly admirers. I suspect that these old women may have touched off an atavistic abhorrence in some audience members, in part because of ancient cultic and mythic links between the aged female and terrible death or paralysis.[85] This was not the only possible reaction, however.

As I have noted, the *Ecclesiazousae* was tied to the Scira, the midsummer dissolution festival.[86] In the *Ecclesiazousae* the first old hag appealed to the Muses to inspire her "Ionian Song" at the beginning of her combative exchange with the young girl over the handsome youth's attentions. The term "Ionian song," with its connotations of lasciviousness, implies *aischrologia*.[87] She and the other old women perhaps had emerged from the Scira, articulating their lewd ambitions and hostile competitiveness as they approached the Eleusinian pair, Demeter and Persephone. Their proximity to death enhanced the paradoxical joke. As the players, including the old women and their captive lover, leave the stage, a drunken slave girl yells

ὦ μακάριος μὲν δῆμος, εὐδαίμων δὲ γῆ

Blessed the people, fortunate the land! (1112)

There is humor in the prayer; it is not necessarily just a bitter comment on the degradation of the city.[88] Rather, these lascivious old women do indeed embody a power to restore life and fertility, a power all the more astounding because it is belied by their aged bodies. Perhaps this was the kind of "forced or stolen love" (κλεψιγαμία) joked about by the priestesses of Demeter to the women celebrating the Haloa.[89]

The *Ecclesiazousae*'s second scene, like this, its closing, has not earned many admirers among modern readers. Following the opening episode in which Praxagora and the other women don their male disguises and depart for the Assembly, Praxagora's aging husband, Blepyrus, enters, wearing his wife's yellow slip and pumps (she has taken his clothes). He is seeking solitude in order to evacuate his blocked bowels and squats down (in center stage!) only to be interrupted by a neighbor who wants to know what's going on. Blepyrus is that well-established object of scorn, a sexually inadequate elderly man with a younger wife, and he struggles to quell his anxieties about her mysterious absence from his bed. The verbal exchange between him and his neighbor includes a series of scatalogical jests and jokes at the expense of contemporary politicians, whose well traveled (prostituted) posterior orifices are understandably free of the kind of blockage he is experiencing. Finally Blepyrus calls on Eleithuia, the goddess of childbirth, to release him from his anguish (369–71).

Henderson is not alone in regarding the scene as (just) smutty and tedious.[90] I suggest, however, that the scene activates a cultic symbol: the figure of the pregnant crone.[91] In the world of iambic poetry Blepyrus would be the target of mockery. Yet in the brave new world under construction by the women – during his "travail" – Blepyrus will be rewarded with a place at the banquet and access to young and lovely girls, as befits his status as an unattractive old man.[92] As he "gives birth," so the old segregated community of the city gives way to a new, integrated one. He appears simultaneously as an impotent and isolated old man and a bizarre, transgendered symbol of fecundity. When he finally has the chance to remonstrate with Praxagora regarding her early-morning disappearance with his clothes, he pitifully describes himself, lying in bed in his wife's clothes as laid out "with everything but a wreath and urn" like a corpse (535–8).[93]

Death occasioned and strengthened women's restorative powers, beginning with the death of Persephone, which inspired her mother to challenge Zeus – and Death himself. This in turn inspired subsequent generations of women to challenge mortality with laughter in their reenactment of Demeter's mourning and Iambe's jesting during the Thesmophoria. Whether she was represented as shameless girl or shameless hag, Iambe represented a model of femininity at odds with much of dominant Greek tradition. She challenged Hesiod's influential prototype, Pandora, the destructive incubus hidden beneath the skin of an alluring maid, ripe for marriage and childbearing. Indeed Iambe/Baubo was more akin to the Socrates wistfully described by the savant Alcibiades in the *Symposium*: an uncanny and dazzling power beneath a grotesque and laughable exterior. In the Thesmophorian stories and rituals and in these dramatic scenes of lustful hags and sexualized children, we encounter models of feminity which shock with their apparent wrongness and hopelessness. And yet, beneath the unprepossessing surface of such females, power lay hidden. The renewal of agrarian, animal, and human fertility belonged to women. At the heart of the miracle – and the women's joking – was the dissonance between women's own dying bodies and the eternal cycles that they protected and ensured. The figurines of pregnant crones, found in graves all over the Greek world, most graphically represented the paradox.

These sexual crones exerted a power over Death, belonging to those close to Death, because of their complex affinity with Persephone and Demeter, the once and future unity of child-bride and mother-crone. The hags of *Ecclesiazousae* and *Plutus* left the stage in anticipation of a night of love with their respective young men – their legitimate share in Comedy's banquet. In flouting the limits imposed by a repressive society they incurred men's mockery, it is true, but they also challenged the very notion of finitude, as they flashed their painted smiles at Death himself. The scene may have unnerved some, as it certainly unsettles modern scholars, but it may also have raised a triumphant, last laugh among women in the audience.

NOTES

Introduction

1 Interest in these areas marks me as an optimist (small case), within Richlin's (1993) classification scheme. Although I recognize the inequalities of ancient Greek legal and social systems, I prefer to think about how women managed their lives within those systems. With regard to the question of trying to recover the voices of real women, Lardinois and McClure's 2001 collection of essays has been a significant pioneer.

2 Skinner (1993 and 1996, a slightly revised version) has been key in analyzing the impact of these "new French Feminisms" on classics and their implications for "reading" women in antiquity. The work of Cixous, Irigaray, and Kristeva has been collected and translated in a handy guide by Marks and de Courtivron (1980).

3 The nature of that transgression is disputed. See Skinner 1996, 176–7, summarizing the positions of Cixous, Irigaray, and Kristeva. Skinner notes that Kristeva denies the possibility of a female identity based in biology:

> she argues instead that subversion of the rational symbolic process occurs only through irruption of a repressed linguistic core, the "semiotic" – affiliated, though not explicitly identified, with the cultural category of the feminine. Cixous, for her part, advocates the active production of *écriture féminine*, a mode of writing informed by sexual difference yet not absolutely restricted to women. Characterized by a lyric openness and a lack of conventional, logical organization – qualities also imputed to the tender utterances of the lost pre-Oedipal mother – the texts of *écriture féminine* are intended to challenge the "phallogocentric" symbolic order directly. Lastly Irigaray postulates an exclusively female discourse (*parler femme*) grounded in women's specific libidinal economy.

See Moi 1985; Jones 1981; Hekman 1990.

4 Irigaray 1985.

5 Showalter 1985.

6 Skinner (1996, 190–1) makes this claim for Sappho, as an extraordinary exception. Her poetic achievement was such that male readers also "cherished Sappho's work as a socially permissible escape from the strict constraints of masculinity."

7 See Austin 1975 and Searle 1969 for this notion of the instrumentality of language.

8 Andrisano (2001, 43) comments on the careful gradation of terms used to describe Iambe's words and Demeter's reaction in the *Hymn*. See Rosen 1988a, 54–5, for analysis of the terms ἐπισκώπτω and χλευάζω, both of which, he observes, imply a strong element of mockery.

9 Clinton 1992.

10 The relationship between myth and ritual has long been discussed by classical and anthropological scholars. I tend to agree with those who see both myth and ritual as deriving from prehistorically rooted "programs of action." See Bell 1997, especially

her first three chapters, for a history of anthropological approaches to questions of ritual. Hughes-Freeland and Crain 1998 is also useful in presenting a spectrum of modern anthropological paradigms in the analysis of ritual. Burkert 1970 was a key study in the field of classics on the question of the relationship between myth and ritual. See also Versnel 1990.

11 See Dupréel 1928, 236–8, for the distinction between the laughter of inclusion and the laughter of exclusion.

12 The early history of the relationship between cult and genre is impossible to recover. I argue in Chapter 3 that the ancient literary genres of comedy and iambic were substantially inspired by the abuse and ribaldry of certain cults, as Aristotle (*Poetics* 1449 a 10) and other sources imply. Rosen 1988a, 4: "Although the evidence for ritual abuse in festivals such as the Haloa, the Stenia and the Thesmophoria says nothing about iambic verse per se, the connection between iambs and ritual abuse is implicit in the name of Demeter's servant Iambe who, as recounted in the Homeric *Hymn to Demeter*, uses mockery to shock the goddess out of mourning for her lost daughter."

13 West 1974, 33. Bartol (1993, 7–11, 34) takes issue with the notion of a "genre," at least in a classificatory sense, at this early date. She argues for iambic as an "identifying" category.

14 McClure (1999a, 29), in the opening chapter of her book on speech and gender in Athenian drama, makes the point that our male sources indicate women's speech genres could play a significant role in the larger community, whether for good (ritual speech) or ill (gossip or seductive persuasion). I argue here that the literary genres, traditionally viewed as male preserves, themselves also were shaped by women.

15 See Skinner 1987 (introduction) on this problem of data and on how to proceed.

16 See Todd 1993 for Athenian law; Thomas 1989 for the complex orality of Greek culture.

17 Zeitlin (1982, 144–5) discusses the power of women's voices in this context: "Furthermore, if the aim of the ritual jest is to produce laughter, we might consider that laughter opens the mouth in a mimetic representation of that other orifice below, the vulva . . . provocation (obscenity, *anasyrma*) and response (laughter) both then partake of the same function, that of opening and release, an explosion of energy, whether its source is the upper or lower level of the body."

18 Henderson 1985, 9–12. Cairns (1993, 5–26) discusses the problems of defining concepts such as the English word "shame" and the Greek αἰδώς. The definition is a problem that has interested philosophers and psychologists. The Greek term partially overlaps with the English concepts of guilt and embarrassment. I follow Cairns in seeing "shame" and αἰδώς as emotions, with a cognitive, evaluative element. They are experienced also, in part, through language, the words that name them.

19 Brumfield 1996, 67.

20 This practice is not without its critics. Humphreys (1993, introduction to the second edition) warns that insufficient understanding of a field's history (and so, its limitations) can lead an untrained borrower of its methods into making unquestioned assumptions – about what's "natural," "original," and so on. One of the best statements in favor of thoughtful use of anthropological material appears in Blok (2001). Zeitlin's introduction to Vernant 1991 is also a concise history of anthropology's impact on classics. See the comments of Cohen 1991 (especially 95–6, note 5). I agree with Cohen that one should not and need not argue for continuity of culture within the Mediterranean area but that the cultural patterns shared by classical Greece and many modern cultures in that part of the world are uniquely substantial. Without insisting on a (chimerical) "homo Mediterraneus," using modern comparative material helps one "visualize" the past.

21 I do not wish to insist that women altogether left their "noncultic" identities behind when they entered the cultic world. In Aristophanes *Thesmophoriazousae* 830 ff. (for what it's worth), the women argue that bearing noble and brave sons (rather than merely being rich) should entitle a woman to a good seat at the women's festivals. What I suggest here is that a woman practicing the cults might not have felt her licentious behavior to affect her family's status.

22 I realize that the term "fertility cults" begs important questions of interpretation, to which I shall return in the course of the book. I use it as shorthand for a more complex picture, to be explored more fully in Chapter 1 in particular. For analysis of joking and laughter, I have found Apte 1985 and Halliwell 1991a especially helpful. Apte is a general anthropological survey of humor and laughter, whereas Halliwell is a study of the uses of laughter in Greek culture. See also Desclos 2000 (a series of essays on the anthropology of laughter in Greek culture) and Trédé and Hoffmann 1998.

23 Humphreys (1993, 49) makes the point well. See Gould 1980 on the question of women's power within the home. See also the work of Cohen 1991 on this distinction between the complexities and contradictions of real life and "official" accounts of it. He draws on modern anthropological insights into (roughly parallel) Mediterranean cultures. The work of Bourdieu 1977, following Geertz 1973 and Turner 1967, 1969, and 1974 regarding the manipulable nature of societal norms, is influential here.

24 Foley (1982, 3–4) makes the point in passing, speaking of the *Oeconomicus* of Xenophon: "Yet Xenophon's confinement of women to the internal space of the oikos is not historically accurate (women did act in the public sphere in religious contexts), and his model tends to obscure those areas in which male and female find common ground in public life." Ironically, men's suspicious speculation regarding the trouble concocted by women when they get together and engage in idle chatter testifies to the power of women's collective rites. They were allowed to continue – and were actively supported – year after year, male anxieties notwithstanding. For such suspicions, see Semonides 7, 90–2; Euripides *Andromache*, 936–53; Plutarch, *Moralia*, 143, E–F; Lloyd-Jones 1975, passim.

25 Davidson (1997, xxii–iii) makes this point.

26 σεμνά, τά γ᾽ οὐ πως ἔστι παρεξ[ίμ]εν οὔ[τε] πυθέσθαι
   οὔτ᾽ ἀχέειν· μέγα γάρ τι θεῶν σέβας ἰσχάνει αὐδήν

   "holy rites that are not to be transgressed, nor pried into nor divulged. For a great awe of the gods stops the voice" (478–9, in the translation of Foley 1994).

27 I do not wish to imply that if we could speak directly to the practitioners of ancient women's cults that all our problems would be solved. For example, Needham (1972) showed clearly that the notion of religious "belief," long a staple of anthropological study, is not a cross-cultural universal.

28 Reed (1995) on the question of what was known to men. Winkler (1990a, 162–209, discusses the Adonia, a festival of joking and lament for Adonis, Aphrodite's young beloved. I follow his lead. In his analysis of women's cultic joking in the Adonia, he warned against the dangers of a "masculinist" approach to ancient sources, in which modern scholars compound the evidentiary bias toward the male perspective by not thinking about women in their own right.

29 Lowe (1998, 163) discusses the extremely vexed question of how our literary sources on the Thesmophoria and Haloa reflect an opaque series of ancient witness-interpreters, intermediary-interpreters, Christian polemicists, and so on. To begin with, something of the "secret" rites presumably was passed by the female

practitioners to men. Any attempt to look for ancient "meanings" to these rituals must come to grips with the palimpsestic layering of our accounts.

30 Brumfield 1996, 73.

31 See, for example, Bourdieu 1977, 124, on how people's various "senses," including a sense of the sacred and a sense of humor, are shaped by their experience of culture. Bell 1997 has also been useful.

32 Brumfield 1996, 72.

33 After reaching my own conclusions about "iambic" Sappho, I discovered Aloni's (1997) edition of the fragments, where he comes to a similar conclusion.

34 Loraux 1986; Holst-Warhaft 1992.

35 Recent studies of women in Aristophanes include Rosellini 1979, Saïd 1979, Auger 1979, Zeitlin 1981 and 1999, Foley 1982, and Taaffe 1993.

1. Cultic Obscenity in Greece, Especially Attica

1 Versnel (1992) is wrong in thinking of the women's joking at the Thesmophoria as rightfully male – something usurped by women during the carnival atmosphere of the festival. The Thesmophoria may have had "lawless" elements, but the joking and laughter of the women was not a misappropriation of male prerogative.

2 Richardson 1974, 216–17, for the international sources. Plutarch tells of a Boeotian Hera cult (the Daedala) in which a priestess of the goddess tears the veil from a statue on an ox cart and then bursts out laughing. The mythical commentary on this, that the goddess herself was originally duped into jealous rage by Zeus's mischievous construction of a veiled statue, resembling a bride, and that her laughter was in relief at her discovery of the wooden dummy and not a real girl, does not necessarily have anything to do with the ritual or its "original" meaning(s). One may note here also the "exposure" motif (in modified form), followed by laughter. Reinach (1912) discusses the Plutarch passage, Fr. 157–8, which is found in Eusebius *PE* 3.1.6; cf. Pausanias 9.3.

3 Louis Gernet began the practice in classics. See, for example Gernet and Boulanger 1932. Zeitlin's introduction to Vernant 1991 gives a useful history. Humphreys' introduction to the 1993 edition of her book on the ancient family warns of the dangers of facile importations from other fields. Winkler's work (1990) and that of Cohen (1991) exemplify the use of anthropology by classicists at its best.

4 Gernet and Boulanger 1932, 52–4. Nilsson 1906, 184 ff, for dances with opposed choruses of men and women.

5 Loraux 1993; Boedeker and Raaflaub 1998, 32–6 (especially 35).

6 Plut. *De Virtutibus Mulierum* 4. See also Paus. 2.20, 7–8, on Telesilla's victory. Adrados (1975), 295, suggests that there were two *komoi* or representative groups, each headed by its own leader.

7 Paus. 7.27.9. See Farnell 1907, 99.

8 Burkert (1985, 244) suggests that there must have been intergender insult exchanges associated with the cults of Demeter, as well as the all-female cults. See Nilsson 1906, 175–6, for the Apollo Aigletes ritual. *IG* 12 (3) 248.8, 27, suggests that the name "Aigletes" ("The Gleamer") may derive from "Asgelatas," an obscure epithet for Apollo. Ap. Rhod. 4, 1710 ff; Apoll. 1.139.

9 Herodotus 5, 83. See Fluck 1931, 21–2, on their names and identity. He suggests that the names mean "Tamer" and "Increaser" and argues for a close parallelism, if not identity, with the Demeter–Persephone pair. Pausanias remarks at 2.32.2 that

Damia and Auxesia were worshipped also at Troezen. The local people call them the "Maidens from Crete" and hold a festival, the Λιθοβολία ("Stone-Throwing Feast"), in their honor.

10 Phot. τὰ ἐκ τῶν ἁμαξῶν, Suda τ 19 = Paus. Att τ4 Erbse: "In the festival of the Choai the people joyfully processing on the wagons used to joke at and abuse those encountering them; they would do the same thing later on in the Lenaia." See Fluck 1931, 34–51, and Burkert 1983, 229, n. 18, for a full list of citations.

11 See Henrichs 1990, 263–4, on women in the cult of Dionysus at Athens. He discusses calendars of the god's festivals with provisions for animal sacrifices "to be handed over to the women."

12 Simon 1983, 17; Harrison 1922, 272.

13 Foxhall (1995) and Humphreys (1993) have critiqued severely etiological readings of the Thesmophoria and other rites. See Bell 1997, chapters 2 and 3, which I have found useful in their concise articulation of the differences among structuralist, functionalist, cultural-symbolist, and practice theories of ritual interpretation.

14 Brumfield 1981, 80, for details. Photius, under Σήνια (sic), Kock 1880–8, vol. II, 164.

15 Hesychius under Στήνια, στηνιῶσαι.

16 Rabe (1906).

17 Lowe (1998) analyzed these passages, together with a fourth, a scholion on Lucian's *Council of the Gods*, which says nothing direct about women's festivals, but of which the wording and treatment of the myth of Icarius show clear signs of connections with the other three. Lowe's conclusion is that all four passages derive from the same ancient source.

18 Lowe (1998) shows, from a related account of the Icarius story (sch. ad Lucian, *Council of the Gods* 5), that following their murder of Icarius for what they believed was the lethal effect of the wine he had given them, Dionysus appeared among them in the form of a handsome youth. They were struck by desire for him, which did not abate until they took the advice of an oracle and made clay images in the shape of male genitals.

19 See Brumfield (1981), 128, n. 21, for interpretation of κλεψιγαμία, which can mean rape or illicit love. Lowe translates "adultery." I suppose that we tend to imagine forced or stolen love being imposed on a woman by a man (just as Hades stole Persephone). Yet the *Ecclesiazousae*'s scene in which three old hags contend for the love of a hapless young man may be just such a phenomenon.

20 Text and translation appear in Lowe 1998, 167–8.

21 Brumfield 1981, 192–207.

22 See Ar. *Frogs* 391 ff; Schol. Ar. *Plutus* 1014; Hesychius under γεφυρίς, γεφυρισταί. Strabo 9, 1.24. Fluck 1931, 57; Rusten 1977.

23 Riu 1999, 238.

24 Brumfield 1981, 156–81. Simon 1983, 22–4. Burkert 1985, 230; 1983, 143–9. Deubner 1932, 40–50. The ancient source is Lysimachus. *F.Gr.Hist*. 366 F3.

25 *IG* II/III² 1177. Ar. *Thesmophoriazousae* 834–5.

26 Philochorus *F.Gr.Hist*. 328 F89 = Photius under τρόπηλις.

27 Rosen 1988a, 30, n. 73.

28 Brumfield 1981, 150–3.

29 *IG* II² 1177, 6–8, cited by Brumfield 1996, 68, n. 7. ἡ ἑορτή τῶν Θεσμοφορίων καὶ Πληροσίᾳ καὶ Καλαμαίοις καὶ τὰ Σκίρα.

30 See Lowe 1998, passim, and Brumfield 1981, 70 ff, where she discusses the difficulties in the principal source, a scholion to Lucian's *Dialogs of the Courtesans*. Parke 1977,

82–8. See also Peredolskaya 1964, discussed later. Clinton 1992, 29–37, 59–63, is a useful discussion. See also Deubner 1932, 50–60; Versnel 1992. Prytz-Johansen (1975) disputes the connection of the festival with agrarian fertility by observing (inter alia) that on Delos and at Thebes the Thesmophoria took place two months earlier than in the rest of Greece. He prefers to see in it a kind of initiation rite. Foxhall (1995) has expanded the context in which to read the festival. She argues – persuasively – that women's relations with each other were central to the festival. Brumfield notes well the difficulties of interpretation: "Any religious rite bears many meanings, and it is pedantic to insist on a single exact equation. That the main thrust of the rite was to regenerate the powers of fertility at the time of sowing, is evident" (Brumfield (1981), 79).

    Humphreys (1993, xxiv) makes a more radical warning about the festival and our readings of it: "It should not be taken as self evident that if a ritual refers to political organization, social categories, and agricultural processes, its 'original' concern must have been agricultural." Humphreys' scepticism notwithstanding, I believe with Brumfield that the weight of evidence is in favor of an agricultural basis to the Thesmophoria, which is not the same as its having agricultural objectives.

31 This is a mistake. They were completely different festivals. Similarly the Arretophoria is mistakenly identified with the Thesmophoria by our source.

32 See Kron 1992, 617, n. 28, for discussion of this (possible) use of the *bothroi* in Priene, Agrigento, and Heracleia; see Clinton 1988 for a similar interpretation of the pits at Eleusis.

33 Theodoretus, *Therap.* 3, 84, is the source that mentions that models of female genitals also were worshipped by women at the Thesmophoria.

34 Simon (1983, 22) suggests that the epithet has to do with the Greek verb τίθημι, "I lay down," and referred to the agricultural invention of compost, which had to be "laid down" for a time before it was used on the fields.

35 Aristotle, *H.A.* 549b 25. Aristophanes wrote a play called τό Γῆρας (*Old Age*, or *The Snakeskin*(?)) datable perhaps to 412 B.C.E., and featuring a chorus of old men miraculously rejuvenated. On snakes and death, see Burkert 1985, 195.

36 Aristophanes made joking reference to the "deep destruction" (ὄλεθρον τὸν βαθὺν) and "pit" (βάραθρον) as terms for the female genitals. Aristophanes *Thesmophoriazousae* II (*PCG* 332.3) and *Plutus* 431. See Henderson 1975, 139, on βάραθρον ("pit") as a term for the female genitals. See also Brumfield 1996, 70, on the affinity between the vagina and the chasms of the Thesmophoria. Edwards (1993) discusses the paradoxical connections between filth and decay on one hand and fertility and wealth on the other in the poetics of Aristophanes.

37 Diodorus Siculus 5.4.7. On Eretria the women refrained from using fire. Plut. *Quaestiones Graecae* 298bc. See Parker 1983, 83, 144 ff, for inscriptional evidence of sacred laws regarding the Peloponnesian cult of Demeter Thesmophoros and other goddesses, banning embroidered robes, ornaments, and cosmetics.

38 Clinton 1996.

39 Henderson (1996, 92–3) argues in favor of the Pnyx, on the grounds of what the women say about their festival in the *Thesmophoriazousae* of Aristophanes. See also Bowie 1993, 205–9. MacDowell (1995) disputes the Pnyx as the cite of the "City Thesmophoria."

40 Clinton (1996, 115–16) shows how line 80 of the *Thesmophoriazousae* of Aristophanes, which seems to identify the "middle" day as the "third" may have spawned the problem. An ancient scholiast adduced the information that in the deme Halimous the Thesmophoria began one day earlier than elsewhere, on the tenth rather than the

eleventh of Pyanopsion. This in turn produced a problem, because it required two systems of reckoning, one counting the tenth, making the twelfth into the third day of the festival, one beginning (as was the custom in most places) with the eleventh. So another ancient scholar, possibly Callimachus, suggested that the festival at Halimous was joined with the "central" one, and the twelfth was grandfathered in as the "middle" day.

41 Kron 1992, 620–2.

42 Detienne 1989, 138–9. Clinton (1996) gives a full account of the epigraphic evidence, which (among other things) provides for the election of priestesses or ἄρχουσαι within the different demes.

43 See Augustine, *City of God* 18, 9, where he describes an ancient vote of the Athenian population regarding their patron deity. The women voted for Athena, the men for Poseidon. The women's vote carried the day, and Poseidon responded with a flood. This was an explanation as to why women were denied voting privileges within the Athenian state. See Zeitlin 1982, 142, for discussion of the fact that the Thesmophoria was believed to be a celebration of a prior time, mythically constructed as pre(agri)culture, and so a time of rule by women.

44 Deubner 1932, 52.

45 For the fasting at the Thesmophoria, see Plut., *Moralia* 378E, *Dem.* 30. Athenaeus, *Deipnosophistae* 307 f. See Holst-Warhaft 1995, and 1992, 101, which notes that modern Greek laments (made by women) also contain a strange mixture of elements: "The paradoxical nature of modern Greek laments, where anything from ribaldry to political satire can be woven into a dirge, remind us that Eros and Thanatos, like tears and laughter, were intimately associated in antiquity."

46 Brumfield 1981, 84–8, for a summary of the evidence. Her conclusion on 88 is as follows: "The festival was open to all women, and in a sense was the responsibility of all; the community's life depended on it." See also Prytz-Johansen 1975, 81: "There is no evidence that only married women took part in the festival" (but cf. Detienne's influential 1989 piece).

47 See Clinton 1992, 35. One might note also the Aristophanic reference to the *cyceon*, at *Peace* 712, where the *cyceon* is offered as a means of transition from abstinence (from sex and nature's bounty generally) to indulgence.

48 Cleomedes *de motu circulari corporum caelestium* 2.1 (p. 166.7 ed. Ziegler).

49 Hesychius under μόροττον.

50 Schol. Soph. *O.C.* 681; Pliny, *N.H.* 24.59. With regard to the Scira, Philochorus, a fourth-century (B.C.E.) Attidographer, mentions that the women ate garlic so as to remain chaste (Photius, under Τρόπηλις).

51 Nixon 1995.

52 Clement, *Protrepticus* 2.19.3.

53 Nixon 1995, 91–3.

54 Nixon 1995, passim.

55 Burkert 1985, 244.

56 Herodotus, 2, 171.

57 Ael. Frag. 44 Hercher = Suda α 4329, θ 272, σ 1590, 1714. Detienne (1989) talks of the bloody aspects of Demeter's rites.

58 Semus, *F.Gr.H.* 396 F21 = Suda s.v. χαλκιδικὸν δίωγμα of Delos. See also Hesychius s.v. δίωγμα.

59 Pausanias 4.17.1.

60 Detienne (1989, 135) argues for a connection between the right to blood sacrifice and political power; he believes that the violent myths associated with the

Thesmophoria express a male fear of gynocracy and the potential outcome of allowing women to carry and wield (sacrificial) knives.

61 Foxhall 1995, 106. McClure 1999a, 48, says, of the κλεψιγαμία that the priestesses at the Eleusinian Haloa supposedly advocated to the participants: "The comment that ritual obscenity may encourage women's adultery indicates the suspicions it aroused in men and its potential for challenging normal social hierarchies."

62 Kron 1992.

63 See Coldstream 1973 for Knossos; Warden 1990 for Cyrene; Rolley 1965 for Thasos. Cole (1994) has surveyed several Demeter sites and noted that the distinctive finds, including women carrying water jars and piglets, often identify the site as belonging to Demeter. Nixon (1995) discusses Demeter sites in terms of their distinctive location, architecture, and the finds.

64 Peredolskaya 1964.

65 Clinton 1992, 36, n. 110. "The terracottas, however, insofar as they do suggest a Demeter cult, really show nothing that definitely pertains to the iconography of the Mysteries; they express fertility and parody, and point therefore to the Thesmophoria."

66 Pfisterer-Haas (1989) discusses figurines that she classifies as cultic at 69–77.

67 These include Pfisterer-Haas IV, 28 (pl. 127, 128) = Athens, Kanellopoulos Museum 1457; an example from a private collection in Rome, Pfisterer-Haas IV 30 (pl. 129).

68 Peredolskaya (1964, 5) cites the finds at Argos, Olynthus, and Tarentum. Orlandini (1967) describes some terracottas of the fifth century, including women holding infants. The context (the Thesmophorion at Bitalemi, near Gela) is obviously cultic. Some scholars have interpreted the round belly as "comic fat person" padding that actors wore, padding that remained the same whether they wore a male or a female mask. Webster (1960, 1961) for example, examined terracotta masks and figurines with the intention of filling out our fragmentary picture of Attic comedy. Such artifacts may well be related to dramas, but there may be cultic references also. On Acrocorinth, see Stroud 1968; Bookides and Stroud 1997; Merker (2000) has published the Acrocorinth figurines. In the case of a female wearing a cloak and himation draped over all of her body except the face, Bieber (1961, 77) argues that she is not pregnant, merely comically padded. See also Bernabò-Brea and Cavalier 1965, where there are several figurines of old hags with swollen bellies, within a very large collection of masks and figurines from Meligunìs Lipára. As Webster notes in his introduction to the Old and Middle Comedy Collection (third edition 1978): "Another problem is of course that of drawing a line between the dramatic and the non-dramatic, a common one also in Sicily. Characters from the stage can be taken over into caricatures, just as certain common types can at times have a 'dramatic' appearance. A classic instance is that of the old nurse, where the stage type seems to fade imperceptibly into that of everyday life"(2).

69 Pfisterer-Haas (1989) classifies some naked old women figurines as *hetairai*, and many of these, together with some that she includes under a "miscellaneous" heading at 85 ff, have distended bellies.

70 Green and Handley 1995, 60.

71 Pickard-Cambridge 1968, 214.

72 Peredolskaya 1964, 17: "Der breit verzogene Mund, die parallelen Runzeln auf Stirn und Nasenwurzel und die zusammengezogenen Brauen lassen enfernt an eine traditionelle Schauspielermaske denken." She is referring to BB 164 in the State Hermitage Museum, St. Petersburg (my Plate 3; Tafel 4.2 in her article).

73 Bakhtin (1968, 25–6) discusses the aesthetic of the grotesque – the complete antithesis of classical completeness and beauty.

74 Stallybrass and White 1986, 22.

75 Nagy 1979, 255, 5 n. 1.

76 I do not agree with McClure (1999a, 52), who follows Burkert 1985, 259: "Although the Demetrian festivals of licence may have allowed their participants a momentary escape from the social constraints placed upon them, it would be difficult to maintain that these women-only gatherings offered any real opportunity for subversion, since rituals of role reversal must be viewed as ultimately reinforcing dominant ideology, as Burkert points out: 'Through such grotesque negation, a person is led to accept his or her role.'"

77 Grant 1924 is useful for ancient rhetorical theories of comedy. See also Halliwell 1991a, which discusses the ambiguities in Greek attitudes toward what was permissible "play" and what was unacceptable attack. Gilhus (1997, 43–4) briefly discusses the question of fourth-century changes in attitude.

78 *Nichomachean Ethics*, 8.6. Janko (1984) attempted to reconstruct Aristotle's comic *Poetics*, using the *Tractatus Coslinianus*, a text whose relationship to Aristotle's school is much debated, and Sutton (1994) has considered the notion of a comic catharsis on the model of Aristotle's tragic catharsis, extending the emotions "purged" or purified to include anxiety and aggression as well as pity and fear. Golden (1992), on the other hand, understands Aristotle's catharsis as an intellectual event, a recognition of the poet's mimesis of noble or ridiculous individuals, in the case of tragedy and comedy, respectively. Indignation (τὸ νεμεσᾶν) is the emotional response to a painless and nondestructive example of the ridiculous.

79 See Grant 1924. For example, Periander ("revile with the expectation of becoming a friend," Diels parag. 524, 1; Pythagoras (on avoiding excesses of mirth or gloom) in Iambl. *Vita Pythog.* 196 ff (Diels parag. 285, 2–3); Plato (serious men should understand the comic in order to appreciate the serious, but they themselves should not participate actively in the comic) *Laws* VII, 816–17; *Republic* II, 388E (the Guardians should not indulge in laughter, and worthy people and gods should not be represented as overcome with mirth). See also Aristotle, *Nichomachean Ethics* 1128a1–b11, on the need for restraint in mockery (the passage is discussed by Edwards 1991, 173–4). Aristotle contrasts *aischrologia* as old comedy's source of humor with *hyponoia* (innuendo) in new.

80 Aristotle *Nicomachean Ethics* 1176b33 cites the quote from Anacharsis.

81 Pliny, *NII* 34.70. "Dua signa, diversos adfectus exprimentia, flentis matronae et meretricis gaudentis."

82 Adrados 1975.

83 Bergren (1983) argues that in archaic Greece the female was perceived as the source of both truth and lies. This power was then appropriated by the male, who wished to demonstrate the truth of his own speech.

84 Bergren 1983. Recently Van Nortwick (2001) has also written on feminine "transgression" of boundaries and the threat that this poses for Greek masculine identity, which depended upon boundaries, upon separation.

85 Holst-Warhaft (1992) shows this mingling of hilarity and grief in modern Greek lamentation rituals, conducted by women.

86 Irigaray (1985) postulates a female discourse that is connected to women's desires. See Burke 1981, 289.

87 Brumfield (1996) argues that women's speech – characterized as shameful by the male writers who describe it – challenged male categories of proper female

behavior. It simultaneously rendered subversive the "official" silence, expected of women.

88 On distinctive aspects of women's speech in general and of women's tragic speech, see McClure 1995, 1999a, and Sommerstein 1995.

89 Henderson 1975 is the definitive study for obscenity in classical Greece. Davidson 1997, 220 cites Aeschines on Timarchus (Aes. 1.127; 84). His (unintended) double entendre revealed him for the prostitute he was.

90 See Strabo 8.6.20, where a courtesan, rebuked for neglecting women's quintessential responsibility, textile making, replies that she has "taken down three loom masts" in a short time (jokingly equating the loom support beam with the penis).

91 Eupolis 53 PCG, from the Autolycus, as cited by Pollux 10.45.

92 Ar., Thesmophoriazousae 633; see Henderson 1975, 191, for discussion.

93 Athenaeus, Deipnosophistae 582, c–d. See McClure 2003 on the power of courtesans' witticisms to destabilize class and gender hierarchies.

94 Ar. Frogs 1475.

95 On this meaning of αἰσχροποιός, see Eust. Comm. ad Homeri Il, volume 2, p. 677, line 16; Hesychius D entry 687, line 1; Sch. in Ar. Plut. 314–15; Suda σ, entry 748, line 1.

96 Plut., Mor. 33C. The audience of Euripides' Aeolus made a hubbub when it heard the line "What's shameful if the users do not think it so?" Antisthenes reportedly retorted, "Shameful is shame whether it seems so or not."

97 I believe, following Brumfield 1981, 84–8, that the evidence does not support the conclusion that the Thesmophoria was confined to well-born women. See also Menander, Samia, 35–48, where a Samian hetaira became friends with, and celebrated the Adonia together with, Athenian women.

98 The women's speech at the Thesmophoria was likened to that used in a brothel; there is no reason to assume that "respectable" women invariably saw themselves as completely different in perspective from prostitutes.

99 Sophocles, Antigone 510–11.

2. Iambe and the *Hymn to Demeter*

1 On the date see Richardson 1974, 5–11; Padgug 1972; Janko 1982, 181–3; Osborne 1989; Foley 1994, 29–30, 169–78. There are no firm external criteria for dating the Homeric *Hymn to Demeter*, as was once thought. It is no longer possible to work from arguments based on the supposedly changing political relations between Athens and the neighboring vicinity of Eleusis, where the events of the *Hymn* take place and where the famous cult of the Mysteries was celebrated throughout antiquity; scholars have long since shown that Eleusis and Athens were very closely connected for centuries before the supposed date of composition.

2 Janko 1982, 183. He has observed many Boeotian features but still believes Attica is a likely birthplace.

3 See Janko 1982 passim and Segal 1981 on the orality of the *Hymn*. Enjambment is one such feature.

4 Pucci 1987 illustrates this type of intertextuality with regard to the *Iliad* and *Odyssey*.

5 *Hymn to Demeter* 490–5.

6 Thalmann (1984) speaks to the notion of a hexameter continuum embracing Homer, Hesiod, and the *Hymns*.

7 Here and elsewhere I use Richardson's (1974) edition of the *Hymn*.

8 For the Orphic *Hymns* see Graf 1974; Burkert 1985, 296–9. These hymns, ascribed to the legendary poet Orpheus, were associated with various mystery cults and the sites of those cults. They were probably in circulation by the middle of the sixth century B.C.E., perhaps earlier.

9 Andrisano 2001, 42–3 comments on the semantic range in the passage describing Iambe's words and Demeter's reaction.

10 Nixon 1995, 86.

11 See Richardson, 1974, 245–7, on the *balletus* or ritual warfare that the men of Eleusis will fight in his honor.

12 Psychological studies of the poem's complex relationships have been plentiful. See, for example, the introduction to Foley 1994 and also Arthur 1977 (on the psychology of mother–daughter separation within a patriarchal society) reprinted in Foley.

13 Reinach 1912 (120–1) in an article on ritual laughter makes the interesting suggestion that the *Hymn* changes an "original" version of the story, in which Iambe's joking *alone* dispelled the famine, because a later age needed more substantial psychological underpinnings for the ancient nature story and ritual. Prytz–Johansen (1975) cites Eur., *Helen* 1301–52, in which Demeter is solaced by the Charites and Muses led by Aphrodite, not by Kore's return. He argues that the myth of the loss of Kore (underlying the Thesmophoria) did not generally end in Kore's return. Rather, it was associated with women's initiation into adulthood and the death (and so, permanent loss) of their young selves. Bremmer (1983b, 85–8) shows how in some cultures (including, perhaps, archaic Greece) the dead themselves and those who have come into contact with the dead are considered unable to laugh.

14 Farnell 1907, 119–20; Burkert 1979, 140 and notes; Zuntz 1971, 154 (pl. 22) discusses a two-faced bust depicting an older and younger woman from Agrigento; see also Hadzisteliou Price 1971; Kerenyi 1967, 130, 144 ff; Kerenyi and Jung 1949, 101–83; Demargne (1930) discusses a Cretan plaque in which the two goddesses seem identical, and so he argues against their being mother and daughter. See also Jost (1985, 307–12, 353), where she concludes that at certain cultic centers, such as Thelpousa, there were *twinned Demeters*, who evolved in a kind of complementary relationship. Fontenrose (1959, 366–74) and Loraux (1992, 33–5) also discuss the issue.

15 In his account of the cult sites of Arcadia, Pausanias (8.24, 5–6) describes a deity known as Demeter Erinys, with a sanctuary at Onceium. Here were located two statues: Erinys and Demeter Lousia ("the Bather"). Poseidon raped Demeter, whose anger inspired the epithet Erinys, but later she put aside her wrath and bathed in a local stream, hence her second epithet

16 Burkert (1979, 123–42 and 1985, 160) points out that the Greek tradition seems to unite *two* Near Eastern myths concerning a deity's disappearance and return, with the cessation of all vegetative growth and human reproduction in the interim. Kore's *katabasis* is accompanied by the catastrophic disappearance of her angry mother – a simultaneous *double* departure without parallel in Near Eastern tradition. The parallels are "the Sumerian-Babylonian myth of the *katabasis* of Innana-Ishtar, and the Hittite myth of Telepinu."

17 The daughters of Celeus use the term ἐκτρέφειν (166) when they speak of Demeter's role in raising the child Demophoon; Metaneira asks Demeter to nurture (τρέφειν) Demophoon, so that he might reach the ἥβης μέτρον or "marker of maturity." τρέφειν and ἐκτρέφειν refer to the early nurturance and upbringing of children, a term that includes, but is not confined to, breast-feeding. Demeter's reply, in which she claims to be taking on the responsibility "as you instruct" (226), includes a promise to place

the child beneath her breast and employs the term τιθηνή, "nurse" (227), which tends to be restricted to the sense of "wet nurse."

18 Arthur (1977, 230) in Foley 1994 notes: "In the *Hymn*, then, Demeter's laughter is an abrupt and momentary abandonment of her sorrow. But it is also a further movement toward the recreation of her identity. Because the object of her laughter is a display of sexuality in some form or other, Demeter's laughter signifies an acceptance, though an ambivalent one, of female sexuality."

19 Clay 1989, 235.

20 The expression κέδν᾽ εἰδυῖα appears in the *Odyssey*, where the question of the sexual trustworthiness of wives and maidservants is a resonant theme. It occurs at *Odyssey* 1, 428, where Laertes is accompanied by the "reliable" Eurykleia, a woman with whom he never slept; at *Odyssey* 19, 346, Odysseus requests some aged and "reliable" woman to wash his feet; at 20, 57; 23, 182; and 23, 232, it is used of Penelope. In the *Hymn to Pythian Apollo* at 313 Hera angrily reproaches Zeus for dishonoring her even though he has made her his κέδν᾽ εἰδυῖαν wife; at 44 of the *Hymn to Aphrodite* the expression is used (this time by the poet) of Hera, in her capacity as Zeus's loyal wife.

21 See Di Nola 1974, 46–52 for divine laughter. Proclus *In Plat. Remp.* 1. 127, 29 = Kern (1922) 354, sees the gods' laughter as a sign of their plenitude.

22 *Genesis* 18. See Gilhus 1997, 24–6.

23 Demeter's importance for human as well as agrarian fertility is well known. Day three of the Thesmophoria, one of her most widespread festivals, was called the Calligeneia, the feast of handsome children.

24 See Levine 1980, 19, for all the instances of Iliadic laughter. Halliwell (1991a, 282) talks about the psychological range of laughter in Homer. One conspicuous exception – to the tone of the laughter and to the tendency to male monopoly – is at *Iliad* 6, 471, where Hector and Andromache laugh tenderly at Astyanax's fear of his father's helmet.

25 Levine (1987) points out that the two recorded instances of the laughter of the unfaithful maidservants (*Odyssey* 18, 302 ff; 20, 7 ff) appear in the context of their sleeping with the suitors and of Odysseus's angry reaction. It is a symbol of their disloyalty. Penelope herself laughs twice (in contrast to numerous instances of her weeping). Levine (1983b) has discussed this laughter, which, in his view, expresses her growing confidence in Odysseus's return (17, 542) and in 18, 163, is intended to seduce the suitors and deceive them. In other words, the second of her two recorded laughs was intended to communicate what women's laughter usually did: a frivolous and unreliable disposition. Davidson (1997 xx), in speaking of the opening scene of Aristophanes' *Ecclesiazousae*, points out how women's "sexual insubordination and political insubordination could be linked in the imagination and on the stage."

26 *Odyssey* 8, 266–366.

27 Lines 107–8 suggest that this group, which has now left the palace, consists of athletes, male spectators (the best of the Phaeacians), and Demodocus.

28 See Heubeck 1965 on the meaning of the Homeric epithet φιλομμειδής vis-à-vis the Hesiodic φιλομμηδής. Heubeck concludes that Aphrodite was originally linked with an original, pre-Homeric epithet *φιλο-μηδής, meaning "lover of the genitals," "patron of the genitals" and that Homer reformed this into φιλομμειδής, following his well-known "humanizing" tendency.

29 The translation is from Lattimore 1951.

30 *Iliad* 2, 211–77.

31 Nagy 1979, 259–62.

32 Hesiod, *WD* 708–11.

33 Thalmann 1988. See also Lowry 1991 on the notion that Thersites – like others – was actually licensed to speak shamingly in public.

34 cf. Douglas 1968, 367, where she argues (a little tendentiously) that the humor of the situation resides in the fact that Thersites (momentarily) represents the real power among the Greeks; Odysseus as one of a mere handful of leaders is in the weaker position, and so his rebuke of Thersites subverts the structure of (mass) power. See also Rose, 1988, who argues that the Achaean laughter may not direct itself entirely at Thersites but that there may be irony in their hyperbolic compliment to Odysseus at 2, 272–6 that his suppression of Thersites was by far his greatest accomplishment among the Argives.

35 For discussion of Thersites as a scapegoat, see Parker 1983, 260 ff. Rosen 1988a, 21–2, shows how the blame poet Hipponax describes his target Bupalus as a *pharmakos* – a "public" enemy, not just a personal one.

36 On purification by way of *pharmakoi*, see Bremmer 1983; Burkert 1985, 82–4.

37 On the function of laughter within the *Odyssey* as a whole, see Levine 1980 and also 1982b.

38 Levine 1982a.

39 20, 345. On this scene, see especially Levine 1983a; Colakis 1986.

40 Arnould (1985) points out that laughter – often mad and excessive – can have a tragic weight and portends death in many texts.

41 Iros' loss "disarms" him as a blamer. He had himself boasted of knocking out all of Odysseus's teeth (at 18, 27–30). Having teeth knocked out is a predictable boxing injury, of course. For the carnivorous nature of blame, see Pindar, *Nemean* 8, 21–5 where Ajax is the prey of an animalistic envy. At *Pythian* 2, 55–6, Archilochus fattens himself on his own envious words. The name Lycambes – Archilochus's famous enemy – has been interpreted to mean "Wolf-Stepper" (Nagy 1979, 242–9). At *Pythian* 2, 83–5, Pindar swears to be a friend to the friends of the victor – but an enemy (*ekhthros*) to his enemies: "I will attack in secret *like a wolf*, dodging this way and that with twisted course." See fr. 132 Dg. (= fr. 73, 4–5W) of Hipponax, where an individual comments, "All of my teeth have moved in my jaws." Rosen (1990) 16 cites the line, together with fragments 121 and 122 Dg. (= 120, 121W, which refer to someone's removal of his himation and a boast of boxing prowess, respectively) to suggest a Hipponactian parallel with the Odysseus and Iros episode. See Seidensticker 1978 for parallels in the lives of Odysseus and Archilochus, the blame poet.

42 Gilhus (1997, 31) analyzes the incident as an intentional effort by Hephaestus to remind everyone of the hierarchy on Olympus.

43 The revealing parallel Alexandrian story of Ascabalus or Ambas takes the opposite tack. Ambas was the son of Ambe or Metaneira (obviously his name, like Iambe's, is making an etiological point). He jeered at Demeter as she was drinking the *kukeon*, whereupon she turned him into a lizard by pouring the remains of the broth over him. Clearly this story, with its male protagonist, conforms to the Homeric typology, unlike that of the *Hymn*. Richardson 1974, 215. Nicander frag. 56 (= Ant. Lib. 24); Schol. Nic. *Ther.* 483; Ovid, *Met.* 5, 446 ff; Lact. Plac. *Fab.* 5. 7.

44 See Horace, *Epistles* 1.19.28–3, and my discussion in Chapter 4.

45 Line 254. Clay (1989, 243) argues, citing Homeric parallels, that the participle *aspaironta* used of the child at 289 suggests his imminent death.

46 For the various Orphic tales, see Richardson 1974, 79–86; Burkert 1983, 285–6; Kern 1963, 115–30; Graf 1974, 174–5. For Baubo (and Iambe), see Di Nola 1974, 19–53; Devereux 1983; Arans 1988; Olender 1990; Gilhus 1997, 33–7. The vision of the

female genitals or a genitalized face may have sharply different effects, depending on audience or circumstance. Vernant (1991, 112–50) discusses the Gorgon Medusa as a terrifying emblem of a genitalized female face, capable of killing those who confront her. Cixous's famous 1976 essay portrays the laughing Medusa as a symbol for the open, abundant bodies of women.

47 Clay 1989, 224: "I would like to go further [than Richardson, who merely acknowledges the possibility of preexisting Orphic poetry] and suggest that the *Hymn*-poet assumes a knowledge of this common version on the part of his audience and has deliberately modified it. Moreover he draws attention to his modifications by short-circuiting the expected narrative connections and reshaping the story to his own purposes." Foley (1994, 99–100) concurs in the opinion that the Orphic tales probably predate the *Hymn*.

48 Richardson 1974, 216–17, and Di Nola 1974, 19–90, cite parallels from Egypt and Japan.

49 The *Hymn* mentions Triptolemus and Eumolpus in a list of local dignitaries given by Callidice, daughter of Celeus, to the disguised Demeter (153–5). At 477 ff Demeter instructs local leaders (including Triptolemus and Eumolpus) in her Mysteries. The *Hymn* does not mention Dysaules, Baubo, or Eubouleus. For the range of Baubo's roles see Olender 1990, 84. Baubo is a nurse (τιθήνη) in Hesychius (under Baubo); a maenad in a first-century C.E. inscription from Magnesia on the Meander (Kern 1900, 215a, 32–40); a slave in a scholion to Nicander, *Alexipharmaka* 130; a demon of the night in a fragment preserved in Psellos (Kern 1963, 52).

50 The *Hymn* prescribes the Mysteries only; agriculture already exists.

51 Hesychius s.v. Βαυβώ.

52 See Kern 1963, no. 52 (pp. 126–9). This gesture may be either positive (related to fertility) or negative (turning away an enemy with the magical potency of what is normally hidden). Gilhus (1997, 1–5) discusses the two fields of meaning (creation and joy; destruction and repression) in which laughter may be interpreted. Di Nola 1974 is (as far as I can tell) the earliest and fullest account of the ways in which the Baubo incident may be viewed. See Zeitlin 1982, 145, on Medusa, whose "genitalized" face can turn men to stone. Similar apotropaic revelations occur in Plut., *De Mulierum Virtutibus* 5, 9, Rabelais *Pantagruel: le quart livre*, 47 and the *Táin Bó Cualgne*. See Vorwahl 1933, King 1986 discusses the *anasyrmos* as a conservative gesture, used repressively by women toward men so as to establish social order and gender roles.

53 Iakkhos, the boy, also seems to have been present in some manner. Festugière (1952) understood the child's image to have been drawn on Baubo's belly. Graf (1974, 196) argues, from Diels, that the word *iakkhos* in Athenaeus was equivalent to *choiros* (cunnus), but, as Marcovich 1986 shows, this argument was based on a misunderstanding of unreliable evidence. Marcovich argues that, of the two principal texts describing the gesture, Clement, *Protrepticus* 2.20.2–21.2 and Arnobius, *Adv. Nat.* 5.25, the latter, with the details of manipulation of genitals so as to create the image of a child, has no real basis, deriving from a misunderstood and badly emended text of Clement. He amends ἦεν to ἦκεν and so maintains that Iakkhos "arrived" at this point in the narrative, following the *anasyrmos*, not that he was inscribed (or whatever) on Baubo's belly.

54 Devereux 1983 passim; Clay 1989, 234. Herod. *Mim.* 6.19 uses the term *baubon* to mean "phallos." For "dildo" as a possible explanation see Olender 1990, 84, and Devereux 1983, 70. Zeitlin (1982, 145–6) following Rohde and others, suggests the "bark of a dog, the latter animal being another term applied to the female pudenda," but

Devereux (72–4) dismisses this onomatopoeia as fanciful. See Olender 98 for references to the theory that *baubo* is a babble word, spoken by nurses to fretful infants.

55 See Karaghiorga-Stathacopoulou 1986 for details (and pictures) of both kinds of figurine. See also Pfisterer-Haas 1989, 71–3.

56 Reinach 1912, 117, suggests that in some cases the framing device may be Baubo's clothing, rolled back to reveal her face/vulva.

57 Karaghiorga-Stathacopoulou 1986, 88 (in the volume of text). The pig-riding Baubo is Berlin Staatl. Mus. TC 4875.

58 *Praktika* 1950, 280; 1954, 336; *SEG* XVI (1959) 478.

59 *IG* XII 5, 227. All three are described as χθόνιοι ("chthonic"). See Di Nola 1974, 30, where he discusses the infernal aspects of Baubo. Arans (1988) also discusses this aspect of Baubo. Like Di Nola she refers to Kenyon, 1893, 79, for a fourth-century B.C.E. Gnostic papyrus in which a funerary Hermes is called Ortho Baubo. See also the twelfth-century author, Michail Psellus (*de Graecorum hodie quorundam opinat. Orph. Fr.* 53, Kern 1963), cited by Arans 1988, 48. Di Nola (1974) suggests that the resemblence to a dog's barking heard in the name may have a funerary aspect (see Johnston 1990, 134–42). The Orphic *Hymn to Hecate* uses Baubo as an epithet of the goddess.

60 *SEG* XXII 1980, 280; cf. *SEG* XXXIV (1984) 610, where Babo seems to be the name of a woman who erected a monument to her dead husband in Lykaonia.

61 Nonnus *PG* 36, 1028. The euphemistically worded passage refers only to her "thighs," but the meaning seems obvious. See Di Nola 1974, 44.

62 Olender 1990, 99.

63 Peredolskaya (1964) argues for an identification of one of the Taman peninsula grave figurines with Iambe. I think it is reasonable to see the naked woman portrayed as carrying a phallos and sitting on an altar as fulfilling a role analogous to Iambe's, but there is no certain basis for naming her Iambe rather than (say) Baubo. There was a shrine to Echo, Iambe's mother, on the Sacred Way at Eleusis, *IG* II 470, 266.

64 Celeus is mentioned in an Attic inscription as a recipient of honors. Sokolowski 1962, Supplément X, line 72. It is likely that his wife Metaneira also existed as an Eleusinian cult figure.

65 The translation is from Foley 1994. She notes (56) the difficulties of translation.

66 Arthur, 237, in Foley 1994, notes how pomegranates might symbolize blood and death, fertility and marriage, male and female.

67 Nixon (1995, 86) notes: "Towards the end of the poem Persephone tells Demeter that Hades tricked her and forced her to spend part of the year with him in the underworld, but the may also *presumably unwittingly*, have caused Persephone to be sterile" [my italics].

68 As Clay (1989, 250) notes, the fact that Hermes, when sent to negotiate with Hades, discovers him "sitting on a bed with his revered wife" indicates that the marriage has indeed been consummated.

69 In most accounts the match between Hades and Persephone appears to have resulted in no issue. But see Arans 1988, 138. She cites the following: Euripides *Orestes* 964, where *Persephone* is called *callipais*. [This may be translated either as "a beautiful child" or "having fair children."] The scholiast ad loc. notes that Persephone bore Iakkhos. See also Clement *Protrepticus* 2.16.3: "Even Persephone bears a child with the form of a bull." See also Kern 273, 197.

70 Irwin (1998, note 24) observes the following: "that marriage implies children or the potential for children is attested in the story of the wife of Itaphernes as recorded in

Hdt. 3.119, and in Soph. *Antigone* 909–10. There are conversely numerous examples where the status of one's marriage is held to be confirmed or questioned by the presence or absence of children. See, for instance, Aesch. *Ag.* 877–8, Lysias 1.6–7, Hdt. 1.61.1–2."

71 See Foley 1994, 56, for sources. Ovid, *Met.* 5, 53 ff; Ovid, *Fasti* 4, 607–8, Persephone eats three seeds; Nicander frag. 56 and *Theriaca* 483–7, together with the scholia on 484 tells of Ascabalus's punishment; Apollodorus, *Bibliotheca* 1.33.

72 See Richardson 1974, 213, on the *cyceon*. Rosen (1987) shows a connection between a fragment of Hipponax and the drinking of the *cyceon*.

73 Delatte 1955.

74 Scarborough 1991, 144–5; Nixon 1995.

75 See Chapter 1, note 37, for the Eretrian festival of the Thesmophoria where meat is "cooked" in the sun, not on a fire.

76 Ephesus was the reputed home of Hipponax, iambic poet and (in one fragment) drinker of the *cyceon*.

77 Foley (1994, 47), suggests that Heraclitus may be referring to the Mysteries of Eleusis.

78 There is no evidence to support the argument that the *cyceon* was intoxicating, and this passage implies that it was not. At *Peace* 712 the *cyceon* is recommended to facilitate a transition from abstinence to indulgence, sexual and alimentary.

79 Hipponax 39 Gerber.

80 Clinton 1986, 1992. Brown (1997b, 18–19, n. 22) agrees, noting that "other testimonia concerning Iambe seem to point in that direction too."

81 Clinton 1992, 116–20.

82 Clinton 1992, 96–9. On 35 he argues that the *cyceon* probably was not part of the Mysteries but was confined to the Thesmophoria. See also Clinton 1993, for discussion of the relationship between the Thesmophoria and the Mysteries of Eleusis.

83 See Zeitlin 1982, 142, for discussion of the fact that the Thesmophoria was believed to be a celebration of a prior time, mythically constructed as pre-(agri)culture, and so a time of rule by women. In fact as the *Hymn* presents the story, Demeter's gift of agriculture is already in existence.

84 Brumfield (1996, 72) makes the following point: "The Eleusinian Mysteries can be seen as a public and rationalized version of the local mysteries traditionally celebrated by women. The Mysteries are an excellent example of the way in which masculine, accessible, public ideology appropriates the silent, interior magic of women."

85 On this question of the political ambitions underlying the celebration of the Mysteries, see Clinton 1994.

3. Iambic's Relationship with the Female

1 See Dover 1964; West 1974; Bowie 2001; Bartol 1993 on the problems of defining literary iambos. As Bartol notes, the notion of "genre" was not the same in the archaic and in the hellenistic periods. In the archaic period to call a poem *iambos*, or to understand it to be *iambos*, meant that its audience or target would receive it in a certain way. It was not a matter of classification until later. This Aristotle passage is from *Poetics* 1448b24–1449a5.

2 Brown 1997b, 15.

3 West 1974, 22. On the same page he gives a list of later iambographers, such as Aristoxenus of Selinus and Asopodorus of Phlius.

4 Bowie 2001, 5,

5 West 1974, 25.

6 Bowie 2001, 6.

7 As I indicated in Chapter 2, I do not agree with this hypothesis that the cultic reference was to the Eleusinian Mysteries. The Thesmophoria is more consistent with the evidence.

8 Bowie 2001, 3.

9 Brown (1997b, 24) observes the following: "From most of the *testimonia* concerning Iambe, we can infer that these utterances took the form of abuse, and that is consonant with those authorities that hold that invective was the salient feature of early ἴαμβος." A discussion of the Iambe stories in question is given later in this chapter.

10 The degree to which the connection with cult may have shaped the genre is a matter of debate. See Bartol 1992, 66, where she contrasts West 1974 with Carey 1986. As will become clear, I tend to see more, rather than less, cultic influence on the genre.

11 Archilochus frag. 215 Gerber: καί μ᾽οὖτ᾽ ἰάμβων οὖτε τερπωλέων μέλει ("neither iambics nor joyful songs concern me now"). Frag. 322 Gerber, attributed to Archilochus, celebrates Demeter and Kore, and frag. 169 Gerber refers to worship of Demeter. West 1974, 26–7: [of Lycambes] "Is it not remarkable that the same element – amb – appears in the name of a figure who plays a recurrent part in the iambi of the most celebrated exponent of the genre? More than that: he bears the patronymic Dotades (fr. 57.7), son of Dotes. That too is significant if iambus had to do with the rites of Demeter, for we think of the name Dos (or whatever it was) that the goddess assumes in *Hymn. Dem* 122 for the period before she reveals her true identity, a period during which Iambe's jesting takes place. There is also an Aeolic form of her name *Do-mater*." See also Burnett 1983, 24-5 and West 1974, 24 on Archilochus' connections with Demeter's cult. According to Pausanias 10.28.3 Archilochus' grandfather, together with the priestess Cleoboea, brought Demeter's rites to Thasos from Paros.

12 West 1974, 24.

13 Under Paros in Steph. Byz.

14 *IG* 12.5.227. I note also Hipponax fragments 135 a and b (Gerber), which cite the term ἀνασυρτόλις and ἀνασυρτό[πο]λιν. This word, meaning "self-exposer" recalls Baubo's famous gesture.

15 West 1984, 27. Zanetto 2001 cites Bonnano (1980, 81–2), who suggests that the name is "an insolent allusion to the broken marriage. Lycambes should have been given Neobule's dowry (δώς) to the poet but in fact he did not; *contra* West 1974, 27, who explains the name in relation to Δώς, an epithet of Demeter.

16 See Rosen 1987 for discussion. "I will hand over my grief-stricken soul to troubles/unless you give me a bushel of barley as soon as possible/so that I may make a barley/*kukeon* to drink, a remedy for suffering." See also frag. 84 Gerber, which mentions pennyroyal, one of the key ingredients of the *cyceon*.

17 Nagy's 1976 article, reprised and expanded in his 1979 book, builds on Detienne's notion of a fundamental opposition between principles of blame and of praise in archaic Greece. He does not include Demeter's cult in his discussion of blame poetry.

18 Fluck 1931 has collected ancient evidence on all scurrilous rites in Greek cult. See Poilloux 1963b for discussion of the rites of Demeter and Dionysus on Paros and Thasos.

19 Henrichs 1982, 138–9, makes the point that Dionysus' cult – in which men and women participated equally – was the exception rather than the rule. See also Lyons 1997,

112: "Dionysiac myth . . . presents a different model of gender-relations, one that is by turns co-operative and combative, but that is not based on sexual domination of the female by the male. In this context women appear as the nurses and companions of the god, worshipers or resisters of his cult, and figures connected with the introduction of wine." In most cults there were clearly defined patterns of gender differentiation. Thus, for example the inner circle of worshippers of Demeter and Kore was almost always feminine.

20 West (1974, 24–5) comments on the tendency within Greek religion to link Demeter and Dionysus. See also Fontenrose 1959 (1980) 396. See Zeitlin 1982 on the "correlation through opposition" of the two cults, a phrase she borrows from Chirassi-Columbo 1975, 292. Zeitlin 1993 develops her earlier theory on the broadly opposed nature of Dionysian (transgressive) and Demetrian (soteriological) modes of behavior in Greek comedy and tragedy. Athens (unlike Thebes) is a place where Demeter and Dionysus fruitfully cooperate for the benefit of the entire community.

21 Archilochus 2 Gerber.

22 There is dispute regarding the meaning of ἐν δορί. See Gerber ad loc. He translates "on board ship" although thinks that it may possibly mean "under arms."

23 See Brown 1997b, 26–38, for discussion of this passage, and other indications of Dionysian connections in iambic. See Aeschylus frag. 355 Radt., which also implies a connection between Dionysus and iambic μειξοβόαν πρέπει / διθύραμβον ὁμαρτεῖν / σύγκωμον Διονύσῳ.

24 See the introduction to Gerber 1999; Bartol 1993, 40.

25 *FGr.Hist* 396 F 24 = Athenaeus 14, 16 p. 622 A–D = Suda s.v. Σῆμος. See Brown 1997b, 31–7.

26 Schol. to Aristophanes, *Birds* 1764. The Scholiast cites a fragment of Archilochus, and then says: δοκεῖ δὲ πρῶτος Ἀρχίλοχος νικήσας ἐν Πάρῳ τὸν Δημητρος ὕμνον ἑαυτῷ [τοῦτο] ἐπιπεφωνηκέναι. Herington (1985, 164–5) observes the following: "A poetic contest, possibly in honor of Demeter, in which Archilochus was the victor, is implied by Schol. Aristophanes, *Birds* 1764. The entry is slightly corrupt, but the general drift seems certain; if its information can be trusted at all, this Parian festival must have been in existence by the mid seventh century B.C." See also a fragment of Heraclitus (12 B 42 Diels = 22 B 42 Diels-Kranz): "Homer deserves to be thrown out of the *agones* and whipped; and the same holds true for Archilochus." This suggests that the poetry of Archilochus was being performed in poetic competitions by the end of the sixth century. Herington observes (174) that Heraclitus may be punning on the word *rhapisdesthai* ("whipped") and *rhapsoideisthai* ("to be performed by rhapsodes"). Bartol 1992 presents the evidence for iambic competitions in fourth-century (and, she argues, also archaic) Greece. See Bartol 1993, 65–70, for a discussion of the context (festivals and symposia) and form (narrative, rather than dramatic presentation) of early iambic.

27 Morris 1996.

28 I am indebted to Sarah Connell for this insight. See Brown 1997b, 18.

29 Archilochus 114 Gerber.

30 Gentili 1988 193 ff. Critias 88 B 44 Diels-Krantz = Gerber test. 33.

31 Archilochus test. 33 Gerber.

32 Hipponax test. 11 Gerber on the same theme, probably derives from an analogy with Archilochus.

33 For misogyny as class based and a class marker, see Griffiths 1995a, 94.

34 Aristotle *Politics* 1303b37–1304a 17 describes how broken or unsuccessful betrothals often could lead to major political changes.

35 For a list of sources, see *RE* and Richardson 1974, 213–17.

36 Sophocles wrote a satyr play called *Iambe*, but unfortunately we know nothing else about it.

37 Diodorus Siculus 5. 4. 7. He does not name the individual who made Demeter laugh. Apollodorus 1.5.1.

38 Rosen 1988b. The source is Hipponax test. 21a Degani. See Degani 21c–d for other references to this story. Choiroboscus is one of the scholiasts on the second-century c.e. scholar of metrics, Hephaistion.

39 Who knows what she means by this. "*Skaphe*" can also mean "cradle," "chamber-pot." There may be a sexual double entendre meant. A boat, ferry, can be a term for a prostitute – see Gerber 1989, 101. Cf. Ar., *Lysistrata* 138–9 in which Lysistrata says that it is not surprising that women are the subject of tragedies because "we are nothing but Poseidon and a *skaphe*." The reference apparently is to the god's seduction of Tyro and her subsequent casting adrift of the resulting children in a boat. Henderson (1975, 165–6) suggests that "obscenely it means, we are good for nothing but childbearing and τὸ κελητίζειν" [that is, "riding" or being on top in a sexual encounter, a position regarded as especially risqué].

40 Tzetzes' commentary on Lycophron, from the fourteenth-century manuscript, cod. Pal. 356 (fol. 163ᵛ).

41 Hall 2000, 407–18 (411–12) notes that Greek nouns related to an activity tend to follow a gendered pattern. Whereas feminine nouns describe the action or sphere in which the action takes place (e.g., ποίησις), masculine nouns refer to the agent (ποιητής). The Iambe story of the *Hymn* depicts Iambe as both an autonymous agent and as the archetypal moment for a cultic activity. This Iambe of the Hipponax stories seems to cede agency to the male poet.

42 Aristotle, *Poetics* 1448 b.

43 The *Etymologicum Magnum* under Iambe, Philochorus *F.Gr.Hist.* 328 frag. 103 and the scholiast ad Nicander *Alexipharmaka* 130 mention Iambe's parents.

44 Photius, *Bibliotheca*, ed. R. Henry, Paris 1967, Tome V, 158. Photius is citing the *Grammatical Compendium* (*Chrestomathia Grammatike*) of Proclus.

45 Philicus, *Hymn to Demeter* in Page 1941, # 90; Apollodorus, 1, 30. Philicus mentions that Iambe comes from Halimous, a coastal deme near Athens. See Brumfield 1981, 82, for discussion of the celebration of the Thesmophoria at Halimous.

46 Schol. Hephaestion 281.8 Consbruch. See West 1971, 64.

47 Elegeis is another genre-naming woman associated with a "doublet" of stories: a comic obscene gesture, and a harmful outcome. See West 1974, 8–9, Lloyd-Jones 1967. The various versions of the Elegeis story appear in the *Etymologicum Magnum* under "ἀσελγαίνειν" and in Lycophron, *Alexandra* 1378–1387. See also Tzetzes on Lycophron ad loc. Elegeis, daughter of Neleus, at the time of her father's setting forth to found a colony, appeared naked, struck her vagina, and instructed it to "find a great man, who will take you to Miletus and bring troubles on the Carians." The *Et.Mag.* under "Elegeiis" (sic) tells us in addition that Elegeis was named because of her ἐλεγαίνειν or ἀκολασταίνειν (profligacy) because of which no one of the Athenians wished to marry her. On the same page (295) the *Et.Mag.* explains that "ἐλεγαίνειν" means "to be deranged."

48 "Cultic polarities" reflect a structuralist mode of interpretation. For a renowned structuralist (feminist) reading of the *Hymn*, see Arthur 1977, now in Foley 1994. Zeitlin's introduction to Vernant 1991 includes a summary of structuralist readings of ritual within classics. Detienne and Vernant 1989 is also representative of this type of approach.

49 On these cults see Cole 1998; King 1983.

50 Miralles and Pòrtulas 1983, 22–3, make this point. They cite a brief list of sources including the cult of Artemis Apanchomene (Artemis Hanged) in Pausanias 8.23.6; Erigone, the daughter of Icarius, the inventor of wine (Ael. *Var. Hist.* 7, 28; *Schol. Il.* 22, 29; Hyg. *Fab.* 130, *Astr.* 2, 4; Hsch. s.v. Αἰώρα; *P. Oxy.* XI 1362). See also Compton 1990, n. 17.

51 I am drawing here on the analysis of Gilhus 1997, 2–5.

52 Eustathius is commenting on *Odyssey* 11, 227, a passage concerning Epicaste, the suicidal mother of Oedipus. Eustathius and the scholiast to Hephaestion may share a source. Their language and details are similar, but not identical. Yet curiously, Eustathius here uses a masculine article (οἱ Λυκαμβίδαι), whereas the scholiast to Hephaestion uses the more comprehensible feminine (αἱ Λυκαμβίδες). Perhaps Eustathius included Lycambes in the suicide of his daughters, although the male-ending patronymic "Children of Lycambes" can really only refer to a group of sons, or of sons together with daughters. No sons are attested for Lycambes elsewhere, leading some scholars to amend the passage.

53 Morris (1996, 35) notes that the woman is described as "Lydizousa" – "speaking like a Lydian." The narrator targets élite pretensions, whether the woman is a real Lydian or someone aping Lydian modes of speech. The fragment is Gerber 92.

54 The numbers are those of Gerber 1999. For discussion of Archilochus speaking the part of a character (such as Charon the carpenter) see Dover 1964, 207 ff. He cites a parallel from Alcaeus (frag. 10 L.P.) in which the narrator, speaking in the first person, appears to be a woman (judging from feminine adjectives and participle).

55 Gerber 1989, following West.

56 See West 1974, 28–33, on the themes of iambus. Frag. 205 Gerber is an admonition by Archilochus to an old woman not to wear myrtle. Frag. 206 Gerber describes a lewd (μισήτη) woman with thick ankles; frag. 188 Gerber addressed to a person of unknown gender but probably a woman, speaks of the skin's soft bloom replaced by withering. Frag. 246 Gerber describes women as lewd, using the rare word λέγαι. Hipponax 135 Gerber similarly accuses a woman of being βορβορόπην (lewd).

57 Thus, for example, frags. 13–14 Gerber describe a scene in which Hipponax drinks out of a milk pail with a woman named Arete, because a slave has broken her only drinking cup.

58 Bergk 1915 suggested that the two fragments be read consecutively, and that Neobule may be the woman described.

59 εἴ μοι γένοιτο παρθένος καλή τε καὶ τέρεινα. Frag. 119 Gerber.

60 For discussion of the juxtaposition of grace and obscenity in Archilochus see Rankin 1977.

61 Bowie 2001 discusses narrative as an important element of the genre.

62 Van Sickle 1975. This poem is in iambic trimeters alternating with a hexameter half line and iambic dimeter.

63 Rankin (1977, 71) suggests that if Archilochus represents himself as refraining from complete possession, it is to ensure that the poem's focus remain on Neobule, his real target and to retain a certain distance from the family, as befits an avenger.

64 Nagy (1979) postulates the existence of a group of (all male) "friends" (*philoi*) for whom the poet composes his racy and amusing anecdotes about his targeted "enemies" – and himself.

65 Carson 1990.

66 See frag. 118 Gerber in which Archilochus expresses the wish to touch Neobule's hand. Again the tone of deferential love resembles his approach to the unknown

girl in the Cologne Epode – and we know how violently Archilochus's attitude to Neobule must have changed.

67 Lefkowitz 1981, 26–7; Tarditi 1968, frag. 155–9; West 1971, 63–4.

68 But see Carey 1986, in which he maintains that Lycambes must have been a real person, and the story of the broken engagement true. Brown (1997b, 40–2) follows Carey. Carey argues that one cannot insist upon invention, given the large number of *redende Namen* in Greek. Also the fact that Lycambes appears as one of the ambassadors to Delphi on the Mnesiepes Inscription means that he was probably a real and remembered local figure of importance. I disagree. The Mnesiepes Inscription (discussed later) was a third-century work, and so there are several centuries of local tradition intervening, with many opportunities for all kinds of misapprehension. As a "historical document" it hardly describes actual events, but rather narratives linked with the cult of Archilochus. It may be as Gentili (1988, 294, n. 50) suggests, that there were real people (conceivably with different names) behind the *redende Namen*, but I believe that the situation was shaped by the genre, and not a real-life scenario. See Calame 1995, 183–5, for a subtle treatment of the question of "speaking" names.

69 West 1974, 26–7.

70 But see Zanetto 2001, where he argues that Dotades may hint at the δώς or dowry that lay near the heart of the famous dispute. Carey (1986, 63) notes, however, that the name Dotades was borne by a (real) Messenian, who run the footrace at Olympia in 740 B.C.E. (Euseb. *Chron* i. 196).

71 See West 1971, 109 ff. West (1974, 26) suggests that Bupalus and Athenis may have been real people (citing Pliny *N.H.* 36, 12–13, Paus. 4.30.6; 9.35.6; schol. Ar. *Birds* 573). I think it unlikely.

72 This marks a distinction between iambic and comedy. At *Poetics* 1449a Aristotle says that comedy is a mimesis of men of a lower (φαυλεροτέρων) type. This is not out and out viciousness, because the ludicrous (τὸ γελοῖον) is merely a subcategory of the ugly (τοῦ αἰσχροῦ). The ludicrous is a defect or error (ἁμάρτημα) or ugliness (αἶσχος) that is not painful or destructive. Thus comic masks are ugly but do not imply pain. Ael. *Varia Hist.* 5.8: "When Socrates was mocked by the comic poets, he laughed. But Poliager hanged himself" (*PCG* (*Adespota*) 708). Poliager was (according to the tradition) a hunchback who took a fee from his wife's lovers.

73 Frag. 126 Gerber (Theophilus *ad Autolycum* 2.37).

74 Aristotle frag. 558 is cited by West 1974, 27. The translation here is mine. See also Plato, *Republic* 388c, which presents Socrates as saying: "if you indulge a violent laughter, you are seeking violent change."

75 Athenaeus, *Deipnosophistae* 348c, presents the story and the proverb: οὐδεὶς μακὸς μέγας ἰχθύς. It is first used as a put-down by the harp player Stratonicus of a fellow musician, Propis. Propis was big, but not good at playing, and so one might render the saying: "A bungling nobody, but a big fish!" Theophrastus in his treatise *On the Ridiculous* agreed that Stratonicus was the author but claimed that he was critiquing the actor Simycas and twisting the proverb: οὐδεὶς μέγας σαπρὸς ἰχθύς, meaning something like "No big man is a rotten fish!" or "no rotten fish is big!" Then Aristotle in his *Constitution of the Naxians* gives the story cited here as a commentary on the original proverb, whatever he may have taken it to mean.

76 Davidson 1997.

77 Aristotle, *Politics* 3, 3, gives several instances of betrothals to aristocratic women which, when disrupted, proved to be catalysts in major political upheavals. One of these, on Mytilene, again included a wealthy man with two daughters. When a man

named Doxander failed to win these girls as brides for his two sons he encouraged a war between the Athenians, whose consul he was, and Mytilene.

78 Archilochus was credited with inventing the iambus by Clement of Alexandria *Stromateis* 1.79.1

79 The *temenos* and altar for Archilochus and other divinities were erected by Mnesiepes in the second half of the fourth century B.C.E. For the inscription, which is third century, see *SEG* 15.517, or Archilochus *test.* 3 Gerber. *Test.* 4 is a second inscription, added by Sosthenes in the first century B.C.E. See *IG* XII 5 n. 445 (+ Suppl. pp. 212–14).

80 Reprinted by permission of the publishers and the Trustees of the Loeb Classical Library from *Greek Iambic Poetry*, Loeb Classical Library Volume L 259, translated by Douglas Gerber, Cambridge, Mass.: Harvard University Press, Copyright 1999 by the President and Fellows of Harvard College. The Loeb Classical Library is a registered trademark of the President and Fellows of Harvard College.

81 Compton (1990) shows how the ancient *Lives* of Aesop and Archilochus (and Socrates) also tell of hostile responses to their work – either from their own community or from another. I deal with the scapegoat theme in Chapter 4.

82 Gerber *test.* 21 = *Anth. Pal* 7.352.

83 Gerber *test.* 40 = Plut. *de curiositate* 10. 520 a–b.

84 Miralles and Pòrtulas 1983, 73. They argue (65–8) that the encounter has a chthonic aspect, occurring as it does at night and at a place (Lissides) that may bespeak associations with the dead, if Lissides can be identified with *lissades*, an adjective describing rocks or stones. Like the roadside cairns where travelers leave offerings for the dead, this meeting place between Archilochus and the women (arguably a crossroads) may be a passage between two worlds.

85 Semonides 7, cited by Stobaeus 4.22. 193. Hubbard (1994) argues for a late-sixth-century date. As West (1974) points out, this type of "philosophic" catalog poem is not confined to the iambic meter – indeed Phocylides' shorter poem comparing women with animals is in hexameters. Phocylides frag. 2 Diehl. See Lloyd-Jones 1975, Appendix II.

86 Lloyd-Jones (1975) explains that χώρις may mean either "apart" from men or "in discrete categories," "apart from each other" – anticipating the poem's divisions of womankind. He prefers the former meaning on the grounds that then the poem makes a more significant opening statement and also the singular genitive "of woman" makes more sense if the poet is beginning with a single category and not many.

87 See Chapter 2, n. 41.

88 Leach (1964) studies animal categories and their relationship to obscenities and verbal abuse. He notes that animals that are not fully assignable to a category, working on a grid that moves outward from the self to the distant "wild" typically are associated with food taboos in different cultures. He finds a deeply felt analogy between such taboo animals and taboo sexual partners. I am struck by how many of Semonides' animals could be said to be liminal within a Greek grid (and so, taboo). Marriage, as defined by the poem, seems repugnantly "unnatural" in the eyes of this poet.

89 Carson 1990, especially 149–53.

90 Alternatively, misogynistic *topoi* that were to feature in Attic old comedy – women as drunkards, women in league with each other, women who dealt in supposititious babies, women whose large dowries made them tyrants in their husbands' households,

socially pretentious women – these did not form part of the catalogue. We will see that women's laziness did not constitute a big theme in Attic old comedy – again reflecting a more urban perspective on labor. Furthermore, Attic comedy treated female ugliness differently. Age (and its concomitant disfigurements) in old comedy became the primary way of talking about ugliness. Female decrepitude was not a theme in Semonides, perhaps reflecting a world in which few women got to be old.

91 Kurke 1992.

92 Aristotle, *Historia Animalium* 535 a2, notes that bees *never* land on anything rotten (σαθρόν) only fragrant things; presumably the iambic wasp lands *only* on putrefying targets – like the overripe Neobule. See Oeri 1948, 11–12.

93 *Theogony* 494. The only other occurrence of the word in early epic poetry is in frag. 310 of Hesiod (ed. Merkelbach and West, 1967), where the Muses are described as making a man πολυφραδέοντα...θέσπιον αὐδήεντα.

94 See the scholion to Pindar *P.*4, 60 (106a), Drachmann 1910, 112–13. The context is Delphi, where the priestess of Apollo has been called a Bee.

> Elsewhere he (Pindar) calls those involved with divine and mystic affairs "Bees" (fr. 158); he rejoices in the sacred bees. Mnaseas from Patara (ὁ Παταρεύς) is the first to mention that they called those who perform sacred duties "Bees", since they caused flesh-eating men to cease, persuading them to turn to the fruit of trees; at this time a certain Melissa, having been the first to discover the honeycomb, ate it, and mixing it with water, drank it, and she taught the other women. She called the creatures "μελίσσαι" after her own name, and she built the greatest fortification [for them?]. They say that these things happened in the Peloponnese. For the shrine/cult of Demeter is not honored without νύμφαι (young, marriageable girls/bee-pupae) because these were the first to inform (people) about fruit and to end cannibalism and to contrive clothing from raw materials, because of their modesty; nor is any marriage celebrated without νύμφαι, but we worship these first, because of the tradition.

The scholion goes on to mention the fact that priestesses of Demeter are most properly called "Bees," even though priestesses of other divinities are named "Bees" by extension of the use.

95 Apollodorus of Athens 244 F 89 in *F.Gr.H.* Vol. IIb. Detienne (1981, 100) discusses the story without citing the source.

96 Vergil (*Georgics* 4, 33–6), describes the ideal construction of a hive; it should be made of bark or willow patched with clay, and its entrances should be as narrow as possible to preserve an even temperature within: a nice balance between containment and accessibility.

97 Servius ad *Aeneid* 1; 430.

98 Bees were reputed to reproduce asexually; see Aristaeus, *Gen. An.* 10, 759–60; Vergil *Georgics.* 4, 198–9.

99 Parthenius, *Narrationes Amatoriae* chapter 27, section N, line 1. According to the *Suda* under Myro and Homeros she was the wife of the so-called philologus Andromachus and the mother of the tragic Homeros. Parthenius cites a story from the *Arai* of a maidservant, unjustly dismissed, who cursed her mistress, Alcinoe. The mistress developed a passion for a guest of her husband's, ran away with him, and eventually killed herself in remorse.

100 Hendrickson (1925) suggests that there is a connection between the iambics of Archilochus and Hipponax and the "magical" curses recorded in Greek tragedy or on curse tablets (*defixiones*). It seems likely. See Mankin (1995, 109) for comments on the connection between iambic and magic. See also Watson (1991,

56–62). The most famous example of iambic cursing is the first Strasbourg epode, attributed both to Archilochus (frag. 193 Tarditi) and to Hipponax (Hipponax frag. 115, Gerber).

101 Brown 1997b, 30–1.

102 Photius 94.24; Naber: θρίαμβους· τοὺς ἰάμβους ἔνιοι ἔλεγον. Hesychius's entry is more diffuse: θρίαμβος· πομπή, ἐπίδειξις νίκης ἢ Διονυσιακὸς ὕμνος, ἴαμβος.

103 Plut., *Lycourgos* 14.

104 *Iliad* 6, 440–3. Cf. Chapter 2, 52, citing instances of the *anasyrmos* as a "shaming" gesture directed by women at men judged to be cowardly.

105 Plut. *Virt. Mul.* 4. See also Paus. 2.20.7–8 on Telesilla's victory. Adrados (1975, 295) suggests that there were two *komoi* or representative groups, each headed by its own leader.

106 See Nagy 1990 on this question.

107 See Page 1951; Rosenmeyer 1966; Nagy 1990 (345–65).

108 Adrados 1975, 318. See Calame 2001, 138–40, on choruses associated with Demeter.

109 Lefkowitz 1981, 26–7; Tarditi 1968, frag. 155–9; West 1971, 63–4; Van Sickle 1975.

110 Cf. West 1974, 27.

111 West (1971, 64) cites the passage from Eustathius in Hom. 1684.45. See Aristotle, *Rhet.*, 1379a, where he identifies the verb χλευάζω (jest, mock) with a kind of ὕβρις.

112 Eustathius on *Odyssey* 11, 227.

113 On the Homeridai, see Burkert 1972; Nagy 1990, 22–3. Nagy (1979, 304) observes, "the poetry of Archilochus and its transmission also are rooted in cult."

114 Alexandrian poets wrote epitaphs for the daughters of Lycambes (two or three in number) but not for Lycambes himself. See book 7 of the *Greek Anthology*, 69, 70, 71, 352. The term Λυκαμβιάδες appears in 70; 69 and 71 use the words ("the daughters of Lycambes"); in 352 the girls themselves speak, describing themselves as πάρθενοι and κόραι (maidens) on whom the Muses turned the hybristic iambics of Archilochus. The suicides are also feminine in the scholion to Hephaestion (αἱ Λυκαμβίδες). Horace (*Ep.* 1, 19.23) describes a single suicidal daughter. Eustathius uniquely speaks of "sons of Lycambes" (οἱ Λυκαμβίδαι), and Ovid (*A.P.* 53) hints, and the scholiast on Horace, *Ep.* 6, 13 specifies, that Lycambes killed himself over what happened to his daughters.

115 *Hymn to Delian Apollo* 156–7.

116 For impotence as a theme within the iambic tradition, see Archilochus 252 (Gerber).

117 Gerber 184. Plut., *de primo frig.* 14.950e.

4. Women's Iambic Voices

1 Plut., *Sept. sap. con.* 14. See Campbell 1982a, 132 (*carm. pop.* 869). The meter is lyric (choriambic).

2 Cf. *Adespota Iambica* 37 Gerber = Plut. *non posse suav viv. sec. Epic.* 21. 1101 f, where a mill woman is described as "being screwed" against the millstone.

3 Kron (1992, 636) describes the primitive stone handmills found among the votive deposits at the Thesmophorion at Bitalemi, near Gela.

4 At *Clouds*, 1353–8 ff, Strepsiades recounts how his pretentious son refused to sing a Simonidean song during dinner, saying that to sing during meals was crude and old-fashioned "like an old woman grinding corn." In a fragment from the lost Aristophanic *Plays* or the *Centaur* (*PCG* 287), there is a reference to a kneading dance or μετρισμός, performed by several women together. The second version of the *Thesmophoriazousae* of Aristophanes contains a reference to a song by women

winnowing or hulling barley (*PCG* 352). In a play by Nicophron (*PCG* 8) someone calls on a flute girl (probably) to "play a pounding song." Some of these songs were obscene in nature (see Henderson 1975) on σποδεῖν (crush) and δέρειν (flay). Pherecrates' *Savages* (*PCG* 10) describes the "good old days" before women had slaves and servants to do their housework and before dawn you could "hear the whole village re-echo the sound of their grinding." Barley (κριθή) could refer to the penis (*Peace* 962–7) and the term εὔστρα (Cratinus 409 *PCG*, citing Eustathius on the word) of ripe barley also applies in comedy to the pudenda muliebra or the loins.

5 Athenaeus *Deipnosophistae* 14, 618 ff. See McClure 1999a, 39–40.

6 *Suda* 107 Adler = test. 235 Voigt; Philodemus *de Poem* I, 117 (Janko 2000, 330-1); Julian, *Epistle to Alypius* (# 10 Bidez and Cumont 1922, parg. 403D).

7 Julian praises Alypius' *iamboi*, which are more in the style of Sappho than Callimachus: καὶ κατεμούσωσας αὐτὸ προσθεὶς τοὺς ἰάμβους, οὐ μάχην ἀείδοντας τὴν Βουπάλειον κατὰ τὸν Κυρηναῖον ποιητήν, ἀλλ᾽ οἵους ἡ καλὴ Σαπφὼ βούλεται τοῖς νόμοις ἁρμόττειν. ". . and you have embellished it [your letter] by adding iambics, not of the sort that "sing the fight with Bupalus," as the poet of Cyrene does, but such as lovely Sappho arranges for her songs." The poet of Cyrene is Callimachus, who took Hipponax (and his target, Bupalus) as a model. See Edmunds 2001.

8   ...οἱ γ[ὰρ ἰ
    αμβοποιοὶ τραγικὰ ποι-
    οῦσιν, καὶ οἱ τραγῳδοποι-
    οὶ πάλιν ἰαμβικά, καὶ Σαπ-
    φώ τινα ἰαμβικῶς ποιεῖ,
    καὶ Ἀρχίλοχος οὐκ ἰαμ-
    βικῶς. ὥστε φύσει μὲν <
    οὐ ῥ]ητέον ἰαμβοποιὸν
    ἢ ἄλλ]ο τι ποιοῦντα γένος,
    ἀλλὰ νόμωι...

    (in Janko's translation): ". . . For poets of lampoon compose tragic (verses), and conversely tragic poets compose lampoons, and Sappho composes some (verses) in the manner of lampoon, and Archilochus (some) not in the manner of lampoon. Hence one must say that a composer of iambus or some other genre (exists) not by nature, but by convention"

Brown (1997b, 28, n. 57) cites the sources and discusses the issue. He believes it unlikely that Sappho belonged to the same tradition as Archilochus, Hipponax, and Semonides. Instead he suggests that these ancient links between Sappho and iambic may have been echoing a lost comedy such as Diphilus's *Sappho*.

9 Horace, *Ep.* 1.19.28–9. I follow Bentley and most modern editors in translating 28. McClure (1999b) discusses women's blame speech in the context of Euripides' *Medea*. See also Lardinois 1989, where he analyzes some of Sappho's 'rebuke' fragments in the context of her (debated) sexuality.

10 See Andrisano 2001 for iambic motifs in Alcaeus.

11 None of the fragments that I cite is in the iambic meter. This is not an insurmountable difficulty in the light of West's observation that it was the genre of mockery that gave its name to the meter frequently used to express it, not the other way around. As Aloni (2001, 29) observes, "Iambic Sappho's aggressive performance is directed against targets which are not different from those peculiar to the iambic poets. The modalities (except for meter) as well as the aim of the aggression are also similar." Aloni and I independently arrived at the same conclusion with regard to Sappho's "iambic" nature.

12 Aloni 2001, 30.

13 Campbell 1982b, *test.* 20 = Max. Tyr. 18. 9.

14 Campbell 1982b, *test.* 1 = P. Oxy. 1800 fr. 1.

15 See Rosen 1990 on the similarities between Hipponax and the Homeric Odysseus in this regard. Rosen (1990) cites Degani 1984 on the relationship between a poet's work and his physical appearance. Aristophanes describes himself as bald in the Parodos of the *Clouds*.

16 Sappho's love poetry has a combative quality also. See Rissman 1983; O'Higgins 1996.

17 Compton 1990 (335 n. 19) "Expulsion from a cliff is of course a standard pharmakos death, cf. the leap of Sappho at Leucas, Stab. 10.2.9 ... "

18 Compton 1990 includes Aesop and Socrates within the category "poet." Following Parker 1983 and *contra* West 1985 he says (330 n. 1): "I will define the poet more broadly, as a verbal artist who broadcasts praise or blame.... Both Aesop and Archilochus use fables for blame, sometimes the same fables; Archilochus merely puts them into meter.... The fact that one wrote in prose and the other in verse is significant, but the shared fables still point up a basic unity."

19 Compton 1990, where he argues that Sappho's death falls into the *pharmakos* (scapegoat) pattern. His 1988 dissertation, argues that the poet's victimization is proportional to his power of victimizing. Nagy 1973 examines the mythical themes behind the tale of Sappho's suicide, but does not stress the *pharmakos* motif.

20 My Sappho numbers derive from Campbell 1982b.

21 Maximus of Tyre 18.9s. uses the term κωμῳδέω to characterize the same fragment when he quotes it.

22 I am using Campbell's 1982b translation. The piece is very fragmentary.

23 Archilochus Frag. 79a Diehl (or Hipponax frag. 115 West/Gerber; 194 Dg.; the attribution is uncertain) describes – with gusto – the ghastly shipwreck that Archilochus wishes on someone who has injured him by betraying a friendship.

24 Corinna *test.* 2 = Plutarch, *glor. Athen.* 4. 347f–348a (Campbell 1992).

25 Corinna in Campbell 1992, *test.* 3.

26 Rayor 1993 argues that Corinna's poetry was "women-identified." This does not necessarily mean that she shunned traditionally male themes, but rather that she appropriated them for her own use, and focused primarily on women as her audience.

27 Rabinowitz (1993, 10) cites some of the more notable scholarship in the area of classical "gynocritics" or the inquiry into the "history, themes, genres and structures of literature by women" (Showalter 1985, 128): Arthur 1980; Showalter 1985; Skinner 1989 and 1991.

28 See Campbell 1982a, 283, 284. Campbell dismisses the suggestion of Kirk 1963 that there is "indecency" in the last line of 111, suggesting "the fun may be childish." See Lloyd-Jones 1967 on Sappho 111, where he cites an (obscene) parallel for the double entendre "great man."

29 Demetrius *Eloc.* 167. I translate εὐτελέστατα as "slightingly, disparagingly" rather than "cheaply" as Campbell (1982a) does. εὐτελίζω may mean to "make disreputable," which is the point here, I believe.

30 Apte 1985, 78. See also Apte, 162, for further references. Stehle (1997, 281) discusses the passage and suggests that the double entendre seen by Killeen 1973 is "more in keeping with the wedding spirit than the flat (-footed?) humor that others, such as Page 1955, 120, find in it. Page insists that there is "no trace of that ribaldry" found in other ancient wedding songs.

31 Winkler 1990.

32 Schol. *PV* 401 suggests εὐκινητός (among others) for the epithet ῥάδινος.

33 See Bourdieu 1977, 92, where he argues that in all societies "dominated by male values" – as Greece certainly was – women's sexual talk tends to be limited by

the overwhelming concerns and priorities of male sexuality. "As for the women, it is true to say, with Erikson, that male domination tends to 'restrict their verbal consciousness' so long as this is undertaken to mean not that they are forbidden all talk of sex, but that their discourse is dominated by the male values of virility, so that all reference to specifically female sexual 'interests' is excluded from this aggressive and shame-filled cult of male potency." See Erikson 1945, Vol. I, 319–50. I believe, following Skinner 1996 and others, that women's discourse could concern itself with female sexuality per se, as well as engaging in the type of joking described here, in what is obviously a public context.

34 Aloni 2001, 30.

35 Williamson (1995, 136–9) discusses the question, and analyzes fragment 5 (Sappho's prayer for her brother's safe return) and the question of how he caused grief for his family. The passages arguably referring to Rhodopis or Doricha are *Testimonia* 1, 15, 16; frag. 15. Lidov 2002 has looked carefully at the evidence, however, and concluded that the entire biographical tradition derives not from poems of Sappho, but rather from fifth-century comic portrayals of Sappho and her circle. Lidov is correct in saying that Sappho's own extant fragmentary poems do not sustain a Doricha tradition.

36 For details on the text and its interpretation see O'Higgins 1996; Lidov 1993. Lidov suggests that the final words begin a reply by the woman addressed in the opening lines; thus the poem represents a kind of exchange between poet-lovers. Prins (1996, 46) gives a summary of interpretations and her own reading of the complicated questions of performance, voice, transmission, and translation, especially as affecting Sappho 31 L.P. "By virtue of its own prosopopoieia, fragment 31 does not lead to the discovery of the poem as 'you,' but rather, to the discovery that 'you' is the personification of an 'it' that remains mute. What we discover, in other words, is neither the death of Sappho as speaker nor the death of speaking voice as such, but dead letters that cannot be read as voice: hence tongue is broken. How is Sappho to be recuperated from that break – except, perhaps, as a name for it?"

37 Humphreys (1993, xxvii) discusses the connections between ancient love songs such as this and amatory magic.

38 Aloni (2001, 31) and passim identifies irony as one of the modalities of the iambic voice.

39 I note here, as elsewhere, that Aloni (2001 and 1997) has come to the same conclusion as I have with regard to Sappho's iambic nature, both in this poem and elsewhere. Aloni (2001) observes that the deictic κῆνος, which evokes this putative male "other" is expressly hostile in Alcaeus and elsewhere in Sappho. Furthermore he argues that the fragment 165 φαίνεται Ϝοι κῆνος can be understood as an alternative beginning to this poem, within the formulaic context of ancient oral lyric. Thus, even if the poet uses the first-person pronoun, the alternative third-person pronoun resonates in the minds of her audience, mocking the self-absorption of this strangely oblivious man.

5. Comedy and Women

1 Holst-Warhaft 1992. Loraux (1986) focuses especially on the the *epitaphios logos*. Plutarch, *Solon* 21, for the legislation. Foley (1993) argues that tragedies allowed "the politics of the past, whether real or imaginary, to re-emerge on stage, and to re-enact the sort of social scenarios that may well have led to the earlier funerary legislation" (142). In general tragedy tended to communicate that a mourning woman is dangerous. At the same time Foley suggests, following Loraux 1986, that a shift in

Athenian democratic ideology, perhaps reflecting the effects of the Peloponnesian War, is visible between the lamenting choruses of Aeschylus' *Seven Against Thebes* (467) and Euripides' *Suppliant Women* (mid-420s). The archaic assertiveness of the earlier grieving chorus contrasts with the "managed" lamentation of the latter.

2 Holst-Warhaft (1992, 114), "Legislation is passed, first by Solon at Athens, later in Ioulis on the island of Keos, then at Delphi towards the end of the fifth century, at Gambreion in Asia Minor in the third century and at a number of other places in the Greek world." See Alexiou 1974, 14–23; Humphreys 1983.

3 Carrière 1979, 26; Adrados 1975, in which he argues that tragedy developed first out of a variegated mass of cults and myths, serious and profane. Its tendency to draw chiefly on the more serious side of the tradition inspired the development of comedy from what was left; as time went by the two traditions became increasingly polarized, as they came to define each other by contrast. See also Gruber 1983, 101: "Among other things, I am proposing an evolutionary process whereby tragedy and comedy grew from a single common source, gradually and self-consciously distancing and distinguishing themselves from each other."

4 Then, as now, however, "fishwives" were the paradigm for crass shrillness and indecorous speech, thus providing the lesson in what decent women (and men) should avoid. Halliwell (1991a, 289, n. 40) cites several examples including *Il.* 20, 251–5, Chilon *apud* D.L. 1.70; Ar. *Kn* 1400, 1403; and Pl. *Rep.* 395d 6–7.

5 Aristotle *Politics* 1336b 14.

6 Gilhus 1997, 43–44. Branham (1989, 52), in discussing how Plato's Socrates and his way of problematizing the categories of serious and comic, also points to this fourth-century change in attitude toward humor.

7 Adrados (1975, 319 –65) surveys the range of agricultural festivals and fertility cults and suggests connections with theater, both tragic and comic. Most of the evidence regarding fertility related activities is for the cults of Demeter and Dionysus, but we also know of the obscene kordax being danced in honor of Artemis and the hero Pelops. See also Reckford, 1987, 443–98, for a broad discussion of cult and comedy.

8 Bowie (1993) and Bierl (2001) have both worked on issues of cult in old comedy.

9 For example, Goldhill 1990 and Winkler and Zeitlin 1990; Connor 1989 argues that the City Dionysia postdated the foundation of the Athenian democracy and that earlier figures, such as Thespis, were participating in local, not state, cult. The quote is from page 23. Sourvinou-Inwood 1994 takes a different approach to the origin and meaning of the City Dionysia. Rather than viewing the Dionysia as an integration festival, wrapping the preexisting cult of Dionysus Eleutheros into the City Dionysia, she interprets the Dionysia as a *xenismos*, celebrating the installation of the cult of Dionysus in Athens. This view of the festival also connects Dionysus' cult with Demeter's. As Sourvinou-Inwood notes (278): "Apollodorus 3. 14. 7 tells us that the two deities to receive *xenismoi*, Demeter and Dionysus, came to Attica at the same time, at the time of King Pandion; Demeter was received by Keleos, and Dionysus by Ikarios."

10 See Chapter 3's discussion of this connection.

11 Brumfield (1981) discusses all aspects of Demeter's cult, including obscenity. I found Fluck 1931 and Henderson 1975 (especially 13–20) useful, as well as Zeitlin 1982, Reckford 1987, and Burkert 1983 and 1985.

12 Gildersleeve 1889 and 1897 may have been the first to make the suggestion that comedy originated in the insult exchanges at the bridge en route to the celebration of the Mysteries at Eleusis: "The *gephurismos*, the chaffing of the *pompe*, only needed the organization of art to become the *agon* of the developed comedy" (1889, 383).

I do not feel it necessary to be so particular about a single point of origin, but Gildersleeve's belief in the relevance of Demeter's cult to comedy is well placed.

13 Athenaeus, *Deipnosophistae* 5, 181c. καθόλου δὲ διάφορος ἦν ἡ μουσικὴ παρὰ τοῖς "Ἕλλησι, τῶν μὲν Ἀθηναίων τοὺς Διονυσιακοὺς χοροὺς καὶ τοὺς κυκλίους προτιμώντων, Συρακοσίων δέ τοὺς ἰαμβιστάς, ἄλλων δ' ἄλλο τι.

14 Reckford 1987, 466.

15 Similarly, Cantarella (1967, 174–6) locates comedy's origins in a broad-spectrum: (secular) popular mime and religious ritual, including both Dionysiac and Demetrian rites and the lyric κῶμος.

16 West (1974, 32–9) discusses the relationship between the two genres. I borrow from his discussion.

17 See Aristotle, *Politics* 1336b 14, cited earlier.

18 Aristotle (*Poetics* 1448a) cites the claim made by certain Dorians of the Peloponnese that the Dorian word for village κώμη and not the verb κωμάζειν was the source of the genre's name.

19 Csapo and Slater (1994) give a good overview. I draw extensively on Seeberg's interesting 1995 summary of previous scholarship and of his own views for this brief discussion.

20 Seeberg 1971 and 1995; Amyx 1988 for examples. Jucker 1963 discusses these women scenes.

21 See Burkert 1985, 166 and n. 38, for sources.

22 See Seeberg 1995 for speculation on how such borrowing could have occurred. He cites the much-discussed masks found in the sanctuary of Artemis Orthia at Sparta (for which see Jameson 1990). Perhaps, as Graf (1985, 86 ff) has suggested, one may associate such masks (featuring ugly faces of indeterminate gender and handsome male faces) with rituals of removal and later restoration of a deity's image to its cult site. "Choruses" of individuals representing outsiders of some sort, foreigners or ugly "others" would play the role of removal, and the rescue would be effected by people representing the community. Plut. (*Aristid.* 17.8) refers to a procession of "Lydians" taking place at the shrine of Orthia.

23 Seeberg 1995 makes this suggestion.

24 The Lenaia, a festival that drew few nonresidents of the city because it took place in February/March, before sailing was safe, added comedies c. 442, see *IG* II² 2325; see Csapo and Slater 1994, 133–4.

25 Osborne 1985.

26 Seeberg 1995 makes this suggestion.

27 *Thesmophoriazousae* 830–45.

28 Patterson (1994) cites the story in her discussion of Neaira and women's civic identity at Athens.

29 Holst-Warhaft (1995) talks about the mingling of grief and hilarity in modern funerary traditions, such as those of Ireland and Greece.

30 Lowe 2000 has shown how complex this category of "mythical" can be. Comic poets preferred divine myths over heroic (tragedy's choice) and were happy to mingle the mythical and the contemporary world. Lowe argues that the generic apartheid between comedy and tragedy was one of the principal engines driving comedy's eventual development away from traditional myth and toward pure "fiction" as we might recognize the term.

31 Cratinus was also known for having instituted political comedy. *Test.* 19 *PCG* (Anon. *De com.* (*Proleg. de com.* V) 1 p. 13 Kost.). He abandoned the old ἀταξία and did not treat laughter as the only aim.

32 *Poetics* 1448b 24–1449a 5, cited in Chapter 3.

33 Horace, *Ep.* II, i, 139, traces a similar connection between the rustic Fescennine verses and Roman comedy.

34 The *Margites* was an early mock epic, attributed to Homer. A few fragments remain. It featured an idiot called Margites as its hero. It was composed in a mixture of dactylic hexameters and iambic trimeters.

35 *Poetics* 1449b.

36 Rosen (1988a) suggests that practitioners of old comedy may have been protected by the generic conventions that rendered iambic poets immune to retaliation. The evidence for legislation curbing freedom of comic speech is fragmentary, ambiguous, and debated. See Halliwell 1991b; Atkinson 1992. Henderson (1998b) concludes that drama was a form of public speech, like oratory, and that all speech was allowed in drama and oratory "as long as it did not threaten the democracy or impede its progress." Riu (1999, 11–48) reads the plays in a cultic context. He questions the notion of comedy's political "seriousness" in the light of its origins in cultic *aischrologia* (256–9).

37 See Bowie 2001, 1–27. He argues that narrative was an essential feature of ancient iambic. I distinguish here between the kind of narrative he describes and the ambitious inventiveness of old comedy.

38 Lowe 2000, 264–5.

39 J. Henderson in a 1997 paper delivered at the Maine Classicists' Association in Ogunquit, "The Women of Old Comedy," divided the roles of women in old comedy into categories, many of which I have adopted here. See now Henderson 2000a.

40 Sommerstein (1980b) argues that, with the exception of the public priestesses Lysistrata and Lysimache, respectable women were never *named* by men on the Athenian stage, a practice identical with that of oratory. Such women would be identified only as someone's wife, daughter, or mother. A courtesan such as Lais could be named by anyone in a public context.

41 Hyperbolus's mother may have been portrayed as an aged bread seller on the stage in the *Bread Women* of Hermippus (420–19) and the *Marikas* of Eupolis in 421. Bergk (1838, 314) believed that the insult "you rotten lecherous old sow!" may have been addressed to the breadwoman portraying Hyperbolus's mother (Hermippus *PCG* 9). In the parabasis of *Clouds* (551–6) Aristophanes may be implying that Hyperbolus's mother appeared as a drunken crone in the *Marikas* and that Phrynichus earlier had represented her as fodder for a sea monster in a burlesque of the Andromeda story. Rhodia in Eupolis 58 *PCG* (*Autolycus*) and 232 *PCG* (*Cities*) is mocked for her use of perfume and her sexual promiscuity, repectively; Eupolis also ridiculed Rhodia in the *Friends* (295 *PCG*); in the *Cleophon* of Plato Comicus (61 *PCG*) Cleophon's mother speaks with a foreign accent; according to Eupolis 262 *PCG* (The *Prospaltians*) Cleophon's mother was a Thracian seller of women's underwear; Aristophanes, *Thesmophoriazousae* 387, accuses Euripides' mother of being a vegetable seller; Philyllius 9a *PCG* asks if some she-camel calved Philonides, Aspasia was known as Omphale or Omphaletyrannos (Eupolis 294 *PCG*); Cratinus gives her a mock-heroic genealogy; she is the child of Anal Intercourse, Hera-Aspasia, a dog-eyed concubine (*Cheirons*, 259 *PCG*). In the *Prospaltians* (267 *PCG*) Cratinus compared Aspasia with Helen. In Aristophanes (*Acharnians* 516–39) the Peloponnesian War is said to have begun because of the seizure by Megara of two of Aspasia's prostitutes. See Henry 1995, 19–28, for Aspasia in the comic poets. See also Powell 1995, 245–70. The building program on the acropolis was decried by Pericles' enemies as if it were

the meretricious adornment of a pretentious woman, according to Chapters 12 and 14 of Plutarch's *Pericles*. Powell argues that Plutarch's remarks derive from a real fifth-century dispute, and further: "There seems a chance that Pericles' link with Aspasia, the most conspicuous female intruder of the age, was meant to come to mind when Athens was likened to a 'pretentious woman.'" (260).

42 MacDowell (1993) discusses the theme of foreign parentage in Athenian old comedy and concludes it was only in those relatively rare cases that there must have been some justification for the slur.

43 Powell 1995, 259. The source is a scholion to the *Menexenus* of Plato (Schol. TW) Plat. *Menex.* p. 235E. See Cratinus *PCG* * 259.

44 Callias *PCG* 21 (Schol. (TW) Plato *Menex.* p. 235E).

45 The story recounted by Plutarch (*Life of Pericles* 32.1) that Aspasia was prosecuted for impiety by the comic poet Hermippus for (inter alia) procuring freeborn women for Pericles is likely to derive from a joke or series of jokes by Hermippus.

46 *Acharnians* 516–39.

47 Storey 1990 dates the *Demes* to 416.

48 Eupolis 110 *PCG*.

49 *Odyssey* 11, 491–540. Odysseus tells Achilles that Neoptolemus excels in different types of fighting and in counsel. Perhaps this news is not exactly what Achilles wants to hear (he himself epitomizes a very particular type of combat and might be expected to hope for his son to do the same), but Odysseus, the narrator, tells us that he was gratified.

50 Pericles' own legislation of 451–0 had denied citizenship to the son of an Athenian father and a noncitizen mother.

51 See Davies 1971, 458 ff, for Aspasia's actual status.

52 Plato 196 *PCG*.

53 Eupolis 221 *PCG* (from Plut. *Cimon* 15, 3) "He was no coward, but fond of drink and careless / Sometimes he would spend the night in Sparta / and leave Elpinice here, alone." See also Plut., *Pericles*, on Elpinice's assistance to Cimon.

54 A fifth-century ostrakhon writes that Cimon should "get out and take his sister with him." Powell 1985, 262; Mattingly 1971, 284.

55 Plut., *Life of Pericles* 28 = Archilochus 205 Gerber.

56 See Csapo and Slater 1994, 165–85. A scholiast to Ar., *Acharnians* 67, describes the law μὴ κωμῳδεῖν, which was rescinded two years later. Thucydides 1.115–17 describes the action at Samos. The decree limiting comic freedom of criticism lasted until 437–6.

57 Thucydides 2, 46.

58 Strattis *PCG* 34.

59 See Sourvinou-Inwood 1997b.

60 Its mockery of Euripides' account of the etymology of the name Thoas (*Iphigenia in Tauris* 32) suggests that Aristophanes' *Lemnian Women* is datable to the last decade of the fifth century (see *PCG* ad loc.).

61 Lowe 2000, 267.

62 Foley 1993, 134, n. 8: "When the Peloponnesian war led the city to reduce the number of comedies at the City Dionysia from five to three ... to produce them at the conclusion of each of three days following the production of a tragic poet, the changed structure of the festival may have sparked a new kind of confrontation and even rivalry between the genres." Cf. Pickard-Cambridge 1968, 82–3.

63 Aristophanes 488 *PCG*. Schol. Areth. (B) Plato. *Apol.* parag. 19 C (p. 241 Gr.) "Aristophanes was made fun of for mocking Euripides, and for imitating him also."

64 Moses Chorenensis *Progymn.* 3.3.

65 *Vit. Ar.* lines 45–51 *PCG*.

66 In the *Frogs* of Aristophanes the character of Aeschylus charges Euripides with portraying seedy domestic scenes, inappropriate to the dignity of tragedy.

67 Ar. 376 *PCG*.

68 Ar. 6 *PCG*. Kock observes the contrast between *Odyssey* 10, 8–9, and this scene. Euripides wrote a tragedy called *Aeolus*, which Aristophanes is parodying here.

69 Strattis 47 *PCG*. Cf. Euripides, *Phoinissai* 460 ff.

70 Alcaeus 17 *PCG*.

71 Philyllius 3 *PCG*.

72 Lowe (2000, 264) was most helpful to me in thinking through these questions.

73 Pherecrates 159 *PCG*.

74 Pherecrates 152 *PCG*.

75 Pherecrates 200 *PCG*.

76 Theopompus 55 *PCG*.

77 Theopompus 57 *PCG*.

78 Theopompus 56 *PCG*.

79 Hall (2000) discusses personification in old comedy. See also Olson (1992) on Aristophanes' use of personifications, especially 313–14. He notes that the poet tended to make his male symbolic figures (like Demos in the *Knights*, War in the *Peace*) more concrete, talkative, and substantial, whereas female personifications tended to be mutes, with little personality.

80 The *Lar Familiaris* introduces the *Pot of Gold*, and Arcturus speaks the prologue to the *Rope*.

81 Philyllius 7 *PCG*.

82 Ar. 331 *PCG*.

83 Ar. 403 *PCG*.

84 Ar. 410 *PCG*.

85 Examples of male characters include Demos in the *Cities* of Eupolis and the *Knights* of Aristophanes; War in Aristophanes' *Peace*. The *Laws* and *Ploutoi* of Cratinus probably featured male choruses embodying their titles.

86 Rosen (1997, 151–2) discusses this question of the linguistic gendering of nouns and how it forms but the starting point of a portrayal, which reveals much about ancient concepts of gender and of the entity being depicted.

87 Eupolis 223 *PCG*. Rosen (1997) argues that the choice of women to represent allied cities was very deliberate on Eupolis's part and that the kind of relationship Athens was supposed to have with its subject allies was akin to a marriage, with Athenian men in the role of husband.

88 Tenos = Eupolis *PCG* 245; Chios is *PCG* 246 and Cyzicus is *PCG* 247.

89 Rosen 1997.

90 Rosen (1997, 174, n. 49) discusses a passage (Eupolis 229 *PCG*) that may be one of the allied cities herself speaking of harsh treatment at the hands of her "protectors."

91 Heniochus 5 *PCG*. Meineke (1839–57) attributes the lines to the *Cities*. Nesselrath (1997, 274) discusses the play's date. He tentatively assigns it to a period between 380 and 350 B.C.E. The Suda (η 392) says that Heniochus is a middle comic poet. There is no clue as to how the *Islands* of Epicharmus may have appeared or acted.

92 *Knights* 1288–1315. Eupolis may have helped in the composition of the *Knights*. The *Merchant Ships* of Aristophanes (423) featured a chorus of "feminine" ships, describing the difficulty of importing supplies to the city during wartime. Cratinus' *Wineflask* also had a parabasis containing a personification of triremes, echoing

Aristophanes (210 *PCG*) and containing a counterattack on him for plagiarism (213 *PCG*).

93 See McClure 2003. See Athenaeus 13.579e; 13.580a; 13.583f; 13.585c.

94 The comic poet Nicophon actually wrote a play entitled *Pandora*, which is also the title of a satyr play by Sophocles.

95 Cratinus 70 *PCG* (Aristophanes *Knights* 529). The reference to figs is because of the Greek noun συκοφαντής, "informer" (literally "one who shows figs," a word whose history has been variously guessed at).

96 Crates *PCG* 27. Bergk (1838, 131) suggests that the chorus comprised representatives of different kinds of games. See Davidson 2000, 41–64, on the relationship between old comedy and the παίγνιον, or erotic mime. This was a tradition of quasi-literary playlets, often erotic and sentimental in nature, and performed in private contexts such as symposia. Educated women such as *hetairai* could compose *paignia*.

97 Pherecrates 106 *PCG*.

98 Aristophanes 332 *PCG*.

99 *Clouds* 658–93.

100 See Ar. *Eccl.* 110–14.

101 Bergren 1983, especially 93 on the emasculization of poets. See Zeitlin 1981 on the feminization of Greek culture.

102 See *PCG*. *7 under Callias. It is called a γραμματικὴ τραγωιδία or γραμματικὴ θεωρία.

103 Diogenes Laertius, *Life of Cleobulus of Lindus*. See *PCG*, 91 ii under Cratinus. See also Plutarch, *Moralia* 150E.

104 The suggestion of Meineke (1839–57). Alexis' *Hypnos* features a mother and daughter riddling about sleep. See *PCG* 242 under Alexis.

105 The other poets who wrote Sappho plays were Ameipsias, Amphis, Timocles, Ephippus, and Diphilus. Antiphanes was a middle comic poet, according to the *Suda*,α 2735.

106 Prins (1996) discusses questions of performance, voice, transmission, and translation, in Sappho. See Chapter four, n. 36.

107 Athenaeus, *Deipnosophistae* 13, 599cd.

108 See Most 1996. See also Lidov 2002. Campbell (1982b, 27, n. 1, on *Testimonia* 26) handily provides all the known information on the comic tradition on Sappho. See Henderson 1975, 128, for the word κέρκος.

109 There was a *Sappho* by Ameipsias, Amphis, Antiphanes, Diphilos, Ephippus, and Timocles.

110 The *Phaon* of Platon Comicus can be dated to 391. A substantial fragment survives, in which Aphrodite lists offerings that she expects from a group of women who all want a glimpse of Phaon, now rendered irresistible to women because of the potion given him by the goddess.

111 Zeitlin 1985.

112 Hall (2000) surveys the ways in which old comic poets staged plays featuring female personifications of poetry in one form or another or included references to plays or other literary entities as feminine beings. As she notes on page 415, "... studies both of gender in Old Comedy and of literary criticism in the fifth century should perhaps take more serious note of these feminine literary abstractions, who demonstrate more clearly than any other feature of the genre its ability to meditate upon its own poetics."

113 In addition to Epicharmus, Phrynichus, Ophelion and Euphanes, and Euphron wrote versions of the *Muses*. Polyzelus wrote a *Birth of the Muses*.

114 Aristophanes 466 *PCG*.

115 Pherecrates 155 *PCG*. See Dobrov and Urios-Aparisi 1995, and Hall 2000.
116 For the plot, see Heath 1990.
117 Cratinus 195 *PCG*.
118 Cratinus 38 *PCG*. There may be some corruption in the title of this play.
119 Meineke 1839–57, cited by *PCG* ad loc., makes this suggestion.
120 Athens is the predictable exception in the case of conceptual women. In Aristophanes 112 *PCG* (from the *Farmers*) datable to 424, 423, or 422, the chorus exclaims: "O Attic city beloved of Cecrops, self-engendered, / Hail shining land, breast of the good earth!" The lines, probably a parody of some tragedy, refer to the famous myth of autochthony, which became important in Athens following the Persian Wars. See Rosivach 1987.
121 *Clouds* 528–33.
122 Aristophanes *PCG* 596. The *Life* of Euripides 6, parag. 6, 2 cites the passage as part of its explanation of Euripides' (supposed) hostility to women. He caught Cephisophon in bed with his wife. Eventually he abandoned her to Cephisophon altogether.
123 Callias *PCG* 15.
124 In the *Frogs* also "Aeschylus" compares "Euripides" with the famous courtesan, Cyrene, at 1325–8.
125 Theopompus *PCG* 28.
126 At *Odyssey* 18, 26–7 Iros contemptuously compares Odysseus (disguised as a beggar) to a garrulous old women at the oven.
127 Ar. 125 *PCG*. *Thesmophoriazousae* 443–58.
128 Eupolis 184 *PCG*, from the *Flatterers* (Κόλακες). Theopompus 22 *PCG* describes "middle range" hetairai costing a stater (οὗ φησιν εἶναι τῶν ἑταιρῶν τὰς μέσας/ στατηριαίας).
129 Geissler 1969 suggests the date. Lais also appeared on stage in the *Macedonians* or *Pausanias* of Strattis (27 *PCG*).
130 Eupolis *Kolakes* Testimonia iii *PCG* = Sch. ad Ar. *Av*. 283. Eupolis 50 *PCG*, from the *Autolycus*, quotes Leogoras (the father of Andocides and a well-known rake) saying to Myrrhina, ὁτιὴ τὰ πατρῷα πρὸς σὲ καταδιέφθορα. ("I've squandered all my patrimony on you.") The Suda notes that Myrrhina was a prostitute.
131 Henderson (2000a) makes this suggestion.
132 Bergk (1838, 299) believed that the party was being prepared for women. Kaibel (1899) argued that the person asking for breakfast and dropping references to his experiences in Asia is a conceited man (a swaggering soldier) just back from Asia. The fragments are *PCG* 73, 74, 75, and 76. The theme of a desperately thirsty woman returning from the baths appears in Juvenal, *Satire* 6, 419–33.
133 The only possible exception I can find to iambic's neglect of the women drinkers theme is Hipponax, 13–14 Gerber, in which the narrator and Arete drink out of a milking pail, because her drinking cup is broken. The point is likely to be squalor (as often in such scenes) rather than – necessarily – overindulgence in liquor. On women drinkers in comedy, see Pherecrates 152 *PCG* (the *Tyrannis*), which describes how women give shallow drinking cups to their husbands and keep the big ones for themselves. Pherecrates 186 *PCG*, a solitary line of abuse, calls some woman a "sow, a drunk and a pharmakis" – all standard accusations. Fragments 41 and 42 *PCG* from the *Pamphile* of Theopompus, a play named for a hetaira, describes a woman who has drunk heavily and is now making a public disturbance "singing like a cricket." The *Thesmophoriazousae* of Aristophanes maintains that drinking is the real activity of the women at the Thesmophoria.

134 Swearing by "the Two" (Demeter and Persephone) was a woman's oath.

135 Pherecrates 73, 74, 75, 76 *PCG*.

136 Pherecrates 77 *PCG*.

137 Cratinus *PCG* 278. Photius 369, 4 = Sud. π 858. Eupolis 356 *PCG* cites an example of παιδικά being used of a flute girl.

138 Pherecrates 56 *PCG*. The *Thalatta* or *Forgetful One* was perhaps one of the earliest plays named after a prostitute. Diocles later also wrote a *Thalatta*. Athenaeus *Deipnosophistae* 13, 567c lists some of the many dramas that derived their names from hetairai: "*Thalatta* by Diocles, *Corianno* by Pherecrates, *Anteia* by Eunicus or Philyllius, *Thaïs* and *Phanion* by Menander, *Opora* by Alexis, *Clepsydra* by Eubulus. This last hetaira got her name because she timed her sexual encounters by the waterclock."

139 Nesselrath (1990 318 ff) discusses the development of the *hetaira-porne* as old comedy gave way to middle and new. See Henry 1985 and Konstan 1993 on the courtesans in Menander.

140 Sophron 4 *PCG*.

141 Cephisodorus 3 *PCG*.

142 Cephisodorus 4 *PCG*.

143 Cratinus 30 *PCG*.

144 Pherecrates 181 *PCG*. The old comic poets Plato Comicus and Nicophon wrote about Adonis and the Adonia, and it continued to be a popular theme in middle and new comedy. A scholiast to Aristophanes, *Lysistrata* 389, disputes the claim that the *Adoniazousae* was an alternate title for that play in antiquity.

145 Timocles *PCG* 6.

146 Bowie (2000, 327) notes "how many of the plays concern cults with unusual rituals, often with actual or claimed foreign connections." He goes on to note that the distinction between "Greek" and "foreign" is often perceived rather than real.

147 Strabo 10.471.18.

148 Cicero, *Laws* 2, 15.

149 Mention of Euathlus and the younger Callias suggests the date of c. 430. Bergk (1838, 91) was the first to suggest that the chorus comprised female votaries of Bendis.

150 Schol. (π) Juvenal 2, 92. Schol. ζ (ibid.)

151 Bremmer 1987 suggests that postmenopausal women were less of a risk in a system that placed such high value on legitimate children.

152 Henderson 1987a, Oeri 1948; Pratt 2000.

153 Pherecrates 185 *PCG*. Diogenianus Paroemiographus 3.74: γραῦς βακχεύει ἐπὶ τῶν παρ' ὥραν τι ποιούντων· καὶ Ἀριστοφάνης· γραῦς καπρῶσα καὶ βακχεύουσα. Diogenianus Paroemiographus 4.10: γραῦς ἀναθυᾷ· ἀντὶ τοῦ καπρᾷ· ἐπὶ τῶν παρ' ἡλικίαν γυναικιζομένων. ὡς καὶ τὸ "γραῦς ἀναβακχεύει." At *Plutus* 1024 the old woman who is enamoured of the mercenary youth is described as γραὸς καπρώσης. Aristotle, *Historia Animalium* 572 b24, uses καπρῶ (of a sow) in the sense of "want the boar."

154 Pherecrates 39 *PCG*.

155 Pherecrates 40 *PCG*. εὐθὺς γὰρ ὡς ἐκαθίζομεν ἐξ Ἄγρας. "As soon as we sat down outside Agra."

156 Hermippus 9 *PCG*, from the *Bread Women*. Bergk (1838, 314) suggested that the woman being insulted might be Hyperbolus's mother. Cf. Phrynichus 34 *PCG* (the *Muses*): ὦ κάπραινα καὶ περίπολις καὶ δρομάς. ("You sow, you street walker and whore").

157 Theopompus 80 *PCG*.

158 Theopompus 33 *PCG*.

159 According to Athenaeus (*Deipnosophistae* 11, 470 ff), Thericles was a potter. The language is mock-tragic.

160 Pherecrates 51 *PCG*.

161 Pherecrates 43 *PCG*.

162 Pickard-Cambridge, 1968, 263–5. Henderson 1991 judiciously discusses the evidence and concludes that (some) women were in attendance. See also Zweig 1992, 76. Goldhill (1994) argues that the consensus (that some women did attend the dramatic competitions) is based on a misconstruing of the evidence.

163 *Lysistrata* 1043–53. I'm using the translation of Henderson 1991, as cited on p. 139.

164 Henderson 1991, 140; Lévy 1976a. Pickard-Cambridge 1968 and Goldhill 1994 do not discuss this passage.

165 *Laws* 817a–c.

166 *Laws* 658a–d.

167 *Gorgias* 502b–d.

168 Pickard-Cambridge (1968, 265) cites these stories. The *Eumenides* story is from the ancient *Life* of Aeschylus 9 and Pollux iv. 110.

169 Alexis, *Gynaikokratia* 42 *PCG*. I am citing the passage as cited and translated by Henderson 1991, 140. Goldhill 1994 disputes the passage's validity on the grounds that the play's title implies a topsy-turvy world, so that no such statement can be held to reflect contemporary realities. Aristophanes' *Peace* 961–7, with its joke about thrown barley has been debated in this same context. "The women haven't got any [barley/penis]" may suggest that they were too far back for the thrown seed to reach them.

170 Aristophanes *PCG* 487. The play's title is αἱ Σκηνὰς Καταλαμβάνουσαι or *The Women Grabbing the Shelters* (*Tents*), but, as Henderson 1991, 141, explains, the fragments point in the direction of a theater festival. For example, the term τριτοστάτις or "third-row chorus woman" appears in frag. 503 *PCG*. Aristophanes, *Peace* 731 and *Thesmophoriazousae* 658 refer to temporary shelters in use in the theater of Dionysus.

171 Eupolis *PCG* 451. Similarly, ναύτριαι for women sailors (Ar. *PCG* 858).

172 Rabinowitz 1992, 51. Rabinowitz goes on to argue that Greek tragedy portrayed female agency (usually sexualized) as deeply problematic, often causing havoc.

173 Zweig 1992. Henderson (1975, 114–15, 144) gives examples of women's sexual organs being represented as food. He cites a fragment of Eubulus (Eubulus 75 *PCG*) in which "Demeter's Daughter" seems to be the name of a pastry hollowed out with a finger prior to baking. There is an obscene double entendre, with the pastry representing the woman's genitalia.

174 The apparent obsession of old comedy with food generally is not a simple matter. Much of our fragmentary evidence derives from Athenaeus' tale (c. 200 C.E.) of the conversation of learned diners (*Deipnosophistae*). Their natural interest in food and entertainments such as hetairai certainly has influenced the collection of comic fragments. Henry (1992) points out that reading Athenaeus in the light of radical feminist theory "gives us a way to see how Athenaeus constructs women and food as usable, consumable, and to be enjoyed by men in nearly identical terms" (251–2). At the same time, as we can tell from the plays of Aristophanes that have survived in toto, food *was* a hugely important theme in its own right within the genre. See Davidson 1997 for all aspects of food and of pleasure generally.

175 Plato Comicus 43 *PCG*. According to our source (Athenaeus *Deipnosophistae* 9.367c) the interlocutor goes on to enumerate these side dishes. In fact this metaphor does not apply only to women (although food imagery generally is linked with women rather than men). Frag. 191 *PCG* of Aristophanes (from the *Daidalos*) states that "every wife has a lover for a side dish" (μοιχὸς ὥσπερ παροψίς).

176 Ar., *Acharnians* 1199. Cantharus, *Tereus* 6 *PCG*.
177 Theopompus 76 *PCG*.
178 Aristophanes 148 *PCG*.
179 See my discussion of the *cyceon* in Chapter 2.
180 Sommerstein 1992, 28–30.
181 Plutarch (*Moralia* 853C–D) criticized Aristophanes for not distinguishing between the speech of different people, unlike Menander. In Aristophanes there is little intrinsic to a character's speech that renders it characteristic of a particular role in life or either gender. (Foreigners with funny accents, such as the Scythian in the *Thesmophoriazousae* or the Spartans in the *Lysistrata* are lampooned). I suggest that this relative homogeneity of speech reflects Aristophanes' different priorities.
182 *Frogs* 1043–56.
183 Heiden 1991 makes the point well. Neither Euripides nor Aeschylus is a plausible guide for the city. The contest is a joke, not a serious tribute to Aeschylus.
184 This is a lunatic version of *isegoria* or "the right of all citizens, including the poor and humble, simply to speak" (Edwards 1993, 117, n. 61).
185 Aristophanes may not have invented this way of thinking about women. Pherecrates 200 *PCG* ἡγούμεθα τῆς πόλεως εἶναι ταύτας σωτῆρας ∪--"we think these women will be the saviors of the city" suggests a plot similar to the *Ecclesiazousae*. Kock I 186 thinks that it may come from the *Tyranny* or *Woman Tyrant*. But Hoffman (1910, 34) argues that the *Τυραννίς* of Pherecrates described the supposed contemporary reality of women's control, not a fantastic dream of a political takeover by women.
186 Aristophanes trod a fine line between open criticism and tact. His care in openly rebuking Athenian (men) for the divisions among them fits with a larger picture of élite reticence on such themes. Connor 1994, 41: "In ancient Athenian practice, diversity was to a large extent masked by language, myths and rituals. The official civic ideology played down tensions and confronted diversity at the individual rather than the group level." See also Ober and Strauss 1990 on ideological tensions within Athenian society (between élitism and egalitarianism) and the tensions between enfranchised and disenfranchised inhabitants of the city, and how these tensions were dealt with in the continuum of drama and political rhetoric.
187 Athenaeus, *Deipnosophistae* 9, 407a–b.
188 Ael. *Varia.Hist.* 5.8.
189 Sch. ad *Acharnians* 378. Cleon prosecuted Aristophanes again after the *Knights*–presumably on different grounds, because the *Knights*, was produced at the Lenaia and thus no foreigners would have been present. See Csapo and Slater (1994, 176–85).
190 For men to worry about what women thought of their public bearing was nothing new. At *Iliad* 6, 440–6 Hector expresses his sense of shame before the men *and women* of Troy, should he fail to fight valiantly. See Scott 1990, 49–50, on élites "performing power" before their social and political subordinates.

6. Women at Center Stage

1 Thucydides 2, 17, (on overcrowding within the city walls). The war's privations affected everyone; indeed Thucydides observes at 8, 48 that the most powerful Athenians suffered most from the war.
2 Bakhtin (1968) interpreted Rabelais's work as the expression of a carnival, antiauthoritarian voice. His work has been influential in studies of Aristophanes. Edwards (1993) discusses Bakhtin's take on Aristophanes, which Edwards sees as distorted. Edwards himself presents the political type of old comedy as an appropriation by

(largely conservative) élites of the popular grotesque. Old comedy was originally sponsored by the demos to contain the power of its leaders but was taken over by the educated élite, who had the education to use the medium most effectively. To men such as these, democratic Athens often looked disordered, topsy-turvy.

3 Taaffe (1993) reviews scenes featuring women in Aristophanes, with particular attention to the feminine as imaginative construct and the comic fakery of men (obviously) playing women.

4 I build on Bowie 1993, especially chapter 9 on the *Thesmophoriazousae*. Bowie explains how Aristophanes' comedies reflected cultic motifs, drawing on the full range of cults to which the plays refer. I draw different conclusions from the evidence, however, because I see the *Thesmophoriazousae* as more than a critique of Euripidean tragedy. Riu (1999) emphasizes the Dionysian aspect of Aristophanes' plays. For Riu, Aristophanes' women serve as especially apt vehicles of the Dionysian move to "unfound" (and then refound) the city. He sees the "women plays" of Aristophanes as returning the city to its status quo. Bierl (2001) studies the ritual aspects of Aristophanes' choral songs, with special reference to the *Thesmophoriazousae*. He relies on performance theory and speech-act theory to derive a vision of the song-and-dance elements of old comedy as ritual performances in themselves. He argues further that comedy's links to some kind of predramatic ritual were stronger than tragedy's, largely because of comedy's shorter existence in the formal literary world of dramatic competition and correspondingly longer life in the twilight world of "ritual." It was difficult for me always to understand what Bierl means by ritual, however. In the case of the *Thesmophoriazousae* he analyzes the play's major choral passages, seeing in them evidence of the chorus' participation in two frameworks of reference: that of the play's own fictional world and that of cult. He assimilates the actions of the play's "female" chorus to the world of initiation into adulthood for both women and men. Thus the chorus in this play, as in others, he argues, functions to mediate a transition between youth and adulthood. The "relative" (or Mnesilochus) also is a liminal, initiation figure in Bierl's analysis, a position I found persuasive.

5 Thomas 1989 passim.

6 The work of Froma Zeitlin is particularly notable in this regard.

7 Henderson (1996, 29) in his introduction, has made the point that "life as lived by women" was a genuine subject of interest to Athenian playwrights.

8 See Biles 2002 for the rivalry between Cratinus and Aristophanes. Henderson (1990, 271–313) discusses the question of Aristophanes as political spokesman.

9 Thucydides 7, 77. See duBois, 1988, 85; Garlan 1973.

10 Thucydides 2, 34–46.

11 Black Sea grain imports had become necessary since the Persian Wars. See Garnsey 1989, 105–6. During the occupation of Deceleia the city had to turn entirely to imports. For grain production and imports, see Gomme 1933, 28–37. Garland (1987) describes the archaeological evidence for grain warehouses. Thucydides 8, 90.

12 See Dillon 1987. Thucydides 7, 27–8.

13 Osborne (1985, 142) argues that about 85 percent owned land, usually in scattered holdings.

14 de Polignac 1984 (revised and translated 1995) discusses the development of the Greek city state in the archaic period. Sourvinou-Inwood 1997a extends de Polignac's thesis to Athens. Osborne 1985 deals with classical Athens.

15 There were also processions for Artemis Brauronia, the Scira, the City Dionysia, and the Lenaia festival of Dionysus as well as one for the Thesmophoria (to Halimous) if

Osborne (1985, 170) is correct. The procession of the Scira festival took place along the same route as the Eleusinian Mysteries, stopping short of Eleusis at a shrine of Demeter and Kore en route. See Allen 1938. He suggests that the City Dionysia may have been shortened during the Peloponnesian War. See MacDowell 1995, 9, n. 12, for recent debate. See Meiggs and Lewis 1969 72 (cited in Parke 1977, 73, and 195 n. 76) for an inscription concerning the Proerosia or First Fruits, an offering to Demeter by the Athenians on behalf of all of Greece, to be renewed (no doubt following interruption attributable to the hostilities).

16 Raaflaub 1998, 19.

17 Forrest 1975. In fact the loss was only temporary. By 410 the fleet was back in control.

18 Thucydides 8, 45–98. For the timing of the negotiations see Avery 1999.

19 Thucydides 3, 82–5.

20 Thucydides 8, 66.

21 Warner (1954, 576).

22 Wallace (1998, 220) cites this (in his own translation) among several passages illustrating the alienation of upper-class Athenians from political life after about 430. Segal 1995 argues that 412 is a plausible date for the *Ion*.

23 Wysocki (1988) suggests that the intrigue of the *Lysistrata* reflects the tensions inspired by Pisander's negotiations. Henderson (1987b, xx–xxv), argues that Pisander's negotiations were unknown to Aristophanes at the time of writing the *Lysistrata*, because Aristophanes refers to Pisander in terms incompatible with the assumption that he knew.

24 Sommerstein (1977) argues that *Lysistrata* was produced at the Lenaia of 411 (which occurred in early February of that year) "either before or just after the 'first assembly' addressed by Peisandros" (120), while the *Thesmophoriazousae* appeared at the City Dionysia; the campaign of terror preceding the oligarchic takeover would have made overt political commentary dangerous, and so Aristophanes chose the Thesmophoria, a less obviously political subject.

25 Lévy (1976a, 110) suggested that from the year 412 onward Aristophanes replaced his myth of the timeless "good peasant" (men like Dicaeopolis and Trygaeus) with "woman" as the embodiment of simplicity, sympathy with nature, and remoteness from political intrigues. Dillon (1987) also observes that, with the *Lysistrata* (following the Spartan occupation of Deceleia), Aristophanes made women the exclusive spokespersons for fertility; farmers and their fields no longer worked as symbols of an ideal, fruitful order.

26 We are not told the name of Euripides' kinsman in the play itself. Bierl (2001, 276–82) discusses the cultic implications of the name Mnesilochus, cited in a scholiast ("He who remembers the ambush") and on the fact that the Kinsman is not named in the course of the play, as perhaps befits his "betwixt and between" status.

27 Segal (1995) makes this argument.

28 Storey (2000) dates the *Demes* to 417 on the basis of (inter alia) Eupolis 99 *PCG*, 30–2, a reference to an unnamed demagogue. Storey identifies the demagogue as Hyperbolus, who was ostracized in 426–15, and therefore not "good contemporary comic material." He argues in favor of a necromantic summoning of the four heroes, not a *katabasis*, in the manner of *Frogs*.

29 Eupolis 119 *PCG*.

30 Foley 1993 argues that the opening scenes of the *Helen*, in which Helen deceives Theoclymenus by faking maritime funeral rites and a lament for Menelaus, gave the ancient audience an uneasy reminder of the power of women's lament.

31 There are fragments of a second *Thesmophoriazousae* (date unknown) and of an Aristophanic play called *The Women Grabbing the Tents*, which probably concerned a theater festival, but we know little about these plays other than their titles.

32 Bowie 1993, 209.

33 I am using the text of Henderson 2000b. The translation is mine.

34 The men's names are those of actual Athenian generals. The women's names "Naval Victory," "Best in Battle," "Military Victory," and "Good Counsel" outclass the performance of these men in the field and in Assembly. Salabaccho was a courtesan and was better at prostituting herself than the politician Cleophon.

35 The Greek puns on the word τόκος, which means both "offspring" and "interest" (on an investment).

36 Henderson (1996, 218, n. 188) makes this point.

37 But see Saxonhouse 1984, where she points out that Plato's Aristophanes sees the best, most virile kind of citizen as one deriving from an original all-male entity.

38 See Butler 1990, 1993 on "acting" gender.

39 637–42.

40 Bierl (2001, 105–50) sees this song and dance as belonging simultaneously to two fields of reference: the extradramatic world of cult and the fictional world of the play.

41 Dover (1993, 58) makes a similar point of the *Frogs*. The *Frogs*, composed within a few months of the end of the war, also addressed itself to Demeter as well as to Dionysus. In this later play, which takes place in Hades, dead Eleusinian initiates, male and female, constituted one of the choruses. The bliss of an afterlife under the protection of Hades' queen offered a somber hope to the play's audience, even as these blessed dead *pray for the living chorus representing them* to survive. I am using the text of Henderson 2002a, with my own translation.

(στρ.) Δήμητερ, ἀγνῶν ὀργίων
ἄνασσα, συμπαραστάτει,
καὶ σῷζε τὸν σαυτῆς χορόν·
καί μ' ἀσφαλῶς πανήμερον
παῖσαί τε καὶ χορεῦσαι.

(ἀντ.) καὶ πολλὰ μὲν γέλοιά μ' εἰπεῖν, πολλὰ δὲ σπουδαῖα, καὶ
τῆς σῆς ἑορτῆς ἀξίως
παίσαντα καὶ σκώψαντα νι-
κήσαντα ταινιοῦσθαι.

Demeter, queen of holy rites,
stand by us and save your dancers.
Let me play and dance
safely and for ever.

May I speak many things both
funny and serious,
and having played and joked
worthily of the festival,
let me win and wear a victory crown. (384–93)

Moreover, Brown (1997a) argues (contra Dover 1993) that the abuse uttered by the chorus at 416–30 is indeed a dramatic version of the *gephurismos* (ritual abuse at the bridge) of the Eleusinian initiates.

42 Bowie 1993, 216. In 214–17 he details the multiple homologies among play, Thesmophorian myths, and the festival.

43 Apte (1985, 174) has described ritual clowns and their punishment.

44 Tzanetou (2002) is an elegant and layered analysis of the play, which discusses, among other things, "the intricate relationship between ritual and theatrical representation within the play's larger commentary on the nature of mimesis." (359). In many respects we have arrived independently at a similar reading of this relationship; as Tzanetou concludes: "But the performance itself, under the pretext of exposing women's ritual secrets and defeating Euripides, ironically discloses comedy's true affinity with women's rituals; for both affirm, celebrate, and promote the continuity of human life." (361).

45 Bowie (1993) sees Euripides' promise to refrain from further attacks on Athenian women as the happy outcome of the play's faux Thesmophoria. Thus a return to "normalcy" is signaled, just as the real festival ends with a return to normalcy. I find this intrepretation, following a fine analysis of the Thesmophorian motifs in the play, narrow in scope.

46 Lewis (1955) was the first to observe that the (real) priestess of Athena Polias in 411 was named Lysimache, a name close in form and meaning to Lysistrata ("Disbander of armies"). She seems to be addressed by name at *Peace* 991–2, as Henderson (1996, 208) observes. Both this remarkable coincidence and the fact that Myrrhine (one of Lysistrata's named lieutenants) was the name of a priestess of Athena Nike (see Papademetriou 1948–9) points to some interest on the part of Aristophanes in aligning his heroines with real and signifiicant religious figures. Even allowing for comic parody, the parallel gives Lysistrata a certain weight and substance—but does not altogether account for her remarkable portrayal by Aristophanes.

47 I am using the text of Henderson 2000b. The translations are mine.

48 Henderson 1996, note ad loc.

49 The play may have been the *Seasons*. Cicero, *Laws*, 2.15. 37.

50 The ten Probouloi, appointed in the emergency situation of 411, included the elderly poet Sophocles among their number.

51 Servais 1981. Plutarch (*Nicias* 13) cites the story also, but Plutarch's source may well have been Aristophanes.

52 The *Theseus* of Diphilus portrays three Samian *hetairai* joking at the Adonia about the "strongest thing in the world." The first says "iron," because it is the universal material for cutting and digging. The second claims that the smith is stronger, because he can bend iron to his will. The third trumps the others by saying "the penis" because it can penetrate even a smith. *PCG* 49 under Diphilus = Athenaeus, *Deipnosophistae* 10. 451b. The festival seems to have included both "respectable" Athenian women and prostitutes, if we can rely on Menander's *Samia*. See also Diphilus *PCG* 42 for a reference to prostitutes celebrating the Adonia.

53 Winkler 1990; Simms 1998.

54 The text is from Henderson 2000b.

55 In *Acharnians* 1062 Dicaeopolis concedes that a bride has a right to sexual pleasure when her husband is called up because "she is a woman, and not deserving of war."

56 The question of actual women's attitudes to war and fighting has been debated by scholars. Obviously Aristophanes here is postulating agreement on this topic among women in order to make his plot work. I believe that by this stage in a protracted and costly war most women in Athens probably had had enough. But see Holst-Warhaft 1992, 122: "The notion that women will not, by virtue of their nature, acquiesce with the state in its demand for men to die in its defense is one that has been the subject of much debate among feminists." She cites Ruddick 1990, arguing for a "sturdy

anti-militarist conception of the body" among women, and Berkman, from the same collection of essays, arguing a different point of view. Schaps 1982 discusses ancient Greek women's experiences of, and attitudes to, war. He concludes that, insofar as the very limited evidence allows us to infer women's attitudes, "the men and women of a city were partners in war" (212).

57 Henderson 1975, 97–8, on Lysistrata's language. She does make some obscene jokes, obviously unlike a tragic heroine.

58 Dillon 1987. In a frightening and circumscribed world, women speak for a fertility expressed in human as well as in agrarian terms.

59 There is no evidence to support the position that the *Old Women* of Pherecrates featured a rejuvenation of the chorus (contra Henderson 2000a). Henderson (1987a, note 93) cites Meineke's emendation of a line arguably from this play (Phenecrates, 185 *PCG*): πάλιν αὖθις ἀναθυῶσιν αἱ γεραίτεραι (the manuscripts read πάλιν αὖθις ἀναθύουσιν αἱ γεραίτεραι). Meineke's emendation, as Henderson notes, makes the line correspond to a traditional proverb, "The old women are in heat again," whereas the manuscripts would suggest rejuvenation. I follow Meineke 1839–57 and Henderson 1987a in thinking that Pherecrates is more likely to have exploited the joke of the horny old crone than to have rejuvenated the old women, a theme without parallel in old comedy as far as I can tell.

60 *Lysistrata* 272–85.

61 At 825–8 the old women reveal that they still depilate their pubic hair, a standard grooming practice for any Greek woman with pretensions to sexual allure.

62 At 364 an old man threatens to beat the γῆρας (hide) off an old woman; at 378 an old woman is called σαπρά, a classic insult meaning "rotten; decayed." At 506 an old man responds to a threat of violence with the insult: "Croak at yourself, you old woman!" (ὦ γραῦ).

63 Csapo and Miller (1998) discuss time, as handled by ancient writers and by modern scholars. They distinguish between archetypal and phenotypal thought. As the archaic period gave way to the classical in Athens, there was a shift from archetypal thinking, concerned with the past and with timeless truths, to phenotypal thinking, concerned more with a future that could be shaped by active intervention. The two types of thinking coexisted to a degree; cultic activities, which occurred throughout the fifth century, reflected archetypal thought.

64 1122–56.

65 Konstan 1993; Taaffe 1993.

66 Sommerstein (1990, 221–2) disputes Henderson 1987b and assigns the speech directing this final dance to Lysistrata (1273–90). I briefly summarize his arguments: Lysistrata is the proper person to bring together the groups whom she separated at the beginning; the Athenian ambassador (to whom Henderson attributes the lines) is a husband himself, and it would be awkward for him to direct and participate; the speaker addresses the Athenians and Spartans as "you," indicating a stance outside of the fray; the wives have left the acropolis, and Lysistrata is the only person who could have led them. As Sommerstein observes, contra Henderson, there is no need for Lysistrata's arrival to have been announced, as were her other entrances. She has been on stage throughout this final scene. Moulton (1981) also assigns the lines to Lysistrata.

67 Ancient sources seem agreed on the fact that there was a shift in the class from which Athenians drew their leaders in 429, the year of Pericles' death, from old propertied families to "new" men. Thuc. 2.65.10. See Connor 1971, especially 119–28; Rhodes 1981, 345. Henderson (1990, especially 292–3) argues that the sympathies of

the comic poets after 429 lay more with the old-style politicians than with the new, such as Cleon and Cleophon.

68 Antiphanes 189 *PCG* contrasts the comic poets' need to innovate with the relative ease of the tragic poets' job: recycling familiar myths.

69 The date of this play is uncertain. Ussher (1973) suggests 393, but more recently Sommerstein (1998, 7) argues for "not earlier than 391."

70 Praxagora refers to the "things agreed upon" at the Scira in lines 18 and 59.

71 Bowie 1993, 257, note 14. For vase depictions of transvestite figures possibly linked with the Scira see Deubner 1932, 49 ff; Beazley 1954, 55–61; cf. Vidal-Naquet 1981, 156–8.

72 Phrynichus, *Mystai* 38 *PCG*.

73 Saïd 1979; Hubbard 1997, (36–41). Zeitlin (1999) makes an argument that Praxagora's new society is in fact a reversion to the age of Cecrops, the first king of Athens, an age both of abundance and of disorder. In the end she argues that the last scenes demonstrate "that the cure may be worse than the ailment" (196).

74 Henderson 1996, 143–51; Konstan and Dillon 1981; Sommerstein 1998, 1–22. Rothwell (1990, 11) argues "that the play is neither an attack on communism *qua* communism nor even on the radical democrats, but instead satirizes the greedy, individualistic attitudes of certain Athenians, has of course been argued before, but without reference to the larger questions of persuasion and without a full appreciation of the extent of which participation in public life remained a poweful ideal and could offset self-interest."

75 Saxonhouse 1992, 1–19.

76 Slater 1997.

77 This misogynistic humor includes jokes about beating women, just as there are numerous jokes about slaves being beaten or fearful of being beaten. These are long established in the iambic tradition as well. For example, the Semonidean poem about women includes a reference to striking the bitch woman in the mouth (to silence her) and knocking out all her teeth. Aristophanes 9 *PCG* (the *Aeolosicon*) is a speech by a woman ("it's not without cause that we wives get beaten up by our husbands"). Plato 105 *PCG* (the *Peisander*) recommends that a woman needs to be beaten regularly, or else she will get out of hand.

78 For Megarian humor, see *Wasps* 57. Susarion of Megara is said to have invented comedy. See Pickard-Cambridge 1962 178–87; Parian Marble, ed. Jacoby (1904) 13; Clement of Alexandria, *Stromateis*. 1.16, 79 p. 366 Kaibel. For the *Acharnians*, I am using Henderson 1998a but the translations are mine. See also Sommerstein 1980a.

79 Henderson (1975 131) indicates that χοῖρος refers to the hairless genitalia of young girls.

80 Henderson (2002b) notes that at a production of the *Acharnians* at Emory University in 1991, the actresses cast to play these piggies "balked at playing these parts; their rebellion became part of the show, and a parallel routine was added in which two boys are sold as cocks" (509).

81 I do not count the minor figure of Chremylus' wife, who appears in the first part of the play and whose chief (dramatic) function seems to be to ask what happened at the shrine of Asclepius, so that Chremylus's slave, Cario, relays the story to the audience.

82 1042–3; 1057–9.

83 Chremylus swears by Demeter at 64, 364, and 555. His wife swears by Hecate at 764. The old woman swears by "the Two" (Demeter and Kore) at 1006 and mentions an incident at the Mysteries, in which she was participating, at 1013.

84 Henderson 1975, 164–6 on the notion that the (sexual) position with the woman on top was considered risqué. Thus I suggest that Chremylus's joke may hint that (like fellatio) this was a form of sexual activity to which older and less attractive *hetairai* were confined. Athenaeus, *Deipnosophistae* 13.585c also features a sexual pun on *graus* in both its senses; the elderly prostitute Glycera tells the poet Menander, who balks at drinking a cup of milk on which a skin has formed, to "use what's below." In other words, her body is still serviceable, even if her face is aged.

85 Vernant (1991) has shown that terrible death, as opposed to peaceable, sleeplike death, was conceptualized as monstrous and feminine in ancient Greece. Jameson (1990) has analyzed masks of hideous crones from the shrine of Artemis Orthia in Sparta and the shrine of Hera at Tiryns, suggesting that they reflect widespread and old ritual practices, pitting adolescent males against a monstrous female, just as Perseus took on the Gorgon. Hesychius under βρυλλιχισταί explains the term as "men who put on masks of ugly women and sing hymns," perhaps a reference to the same phenomenon. A late expression of this morbid May–December lethal-sexual encounter is Lucan's witch, Erictho, who tears the "flower" or first beard from a dead boy's face, steals a dead ephebe's virgin lock of hair, and bites the tongues of dead men. Freud (1953, 105 ff) made a connection between the Gorgon's open mouth and the female genitals. See also Burkert 1985, 104.

86 Pherecrates 265 *PCG* also mentions the Scira.

87 Rosen 1988, 30, n. 73 (in a discussion of Ionia and its relationship with the iambos and with crude humor): "Cf. *Eccl.* 883, where the old woman, in a hymnic parody, invokes the Muses for her 'Ionian song' (μελύδριον...τῶν Ἰωνικῶν), which, as is clear from the ensuing amoebean song (900–23), implies αἰσχρολογία)."

88 Henderson 1975, 104.

89 Davidson (2000) discusses the tradition of *paignia* (informal, often erotic mimes and playlets), which could be performed by educated *hetairai*, among others. He sees this scene as a literary version of such a playlet. Although I do not see it as impossible that such scenes as this featured in *paignia*, I believe that women's cults (with perhaps their own possibilities for informal skits and playlets) are a more significant point of reference.

90 Henderson 1975, 103 ff.

91 See Clay's suggestion (Clay 1989, 235) cited in Chapter 2. She suggests that Demeter's squatting position in the *Hymn* may have inspired Iambe to joke that she (Demeter, disguised as a crone) was in labor.

92 1149–50. He departs for the banquet assisted by a comely young girl.

93 Cf. *Lysistrata* 567–610 where the Magistrate is dressed up as a woman and a corpse. Bowie (1993, 259) sees both scenes as depicting the infertility and incompetence of the city's male leaders. I suggest that although both scenes obviously express the inversion of political norms, Blepyrus is not a complete "outsider" in the same sense as the Magistrate. He is more like Mnesilochus in the *Thesmophoriazousae*, a cultic "intruder," but also a part of the cultic scenario.

BIBLIOGRAPHY

Adrados, F. R. (1975) *Festival, Comedy and Tragedy: The Greek Origins of Theatre*, trans. C. Holme (Leiden, Brill).

Alcock, S. E., and Osborne, R. (eds.) (1994) *Placing the Gods: Sanctuaries and Sacred Space in Ancient Greece* (Oxford: Clarendon Press; New York: Oxford University Press).

Alexiou, M. (1974) *The Ritual Lament in Greek Tradition* (Cambridge, England: Cambridge University Press).

Allen, J. T. (1938) *On the Program of the City Dionysia during the Peloponnesian War* (Berkeley, California: University of California Press).

Aloni, A. (1997) *Saffo, Frammenti* (Florence, Giunti).

———. (2001) "What Is That Man Doing in Sappho, fr. 31 V?" in Cavarzere, Barchiesi, and Aloni, 29–40.

Amyx, D. A. (1988) *Corinthian Vase Painting of the Archaic Period*, California Studies in the History of Art 25 (Berkeley, CA).

Andrisano, A. (2001) "Iambic Motifs in Alcaeus' Lyrics," in Cavarzere, Aloni, and Barchiesi, 41–63.

Apte, M. L. (1985) *Humor and Laughter: An Anthropological Approach* (Ithaca, New York: Cornell University Press).

Arans, O. R. (1988) *Iambe and Baubo: A Study in Ritual Laughter* (Ph.D. thesis, University of Illinois at Urbana-Champaign. Photocopy. Ann Arbor, MI: UMI Dissertation Services 2002).

Arnould, D.(1985) "Mourir de rire dans *l'Odyssée*: les rapports avec le rire sardonique et le rire dément," *Bulletin de l' Association Guillaume Budé*, 177–86.

Arthur, M. (1977) "Politics and Pomegranates: An Interpretation of the Homeric *Hymn to Demeter*," *Arethusa* 6, 7–58. Republished in Foley 1994.

———. (1980) "The Tortoise and the Mirror: Erinna PSI 1090," *Classical World* 74, 53–65.

Atkinson, J. E. (1992) "Curbing the Comedians: Cleon versus Aristophanes and Syracosius' Decree," *Classical Quarterly* 42, 56–64.

Auger, D.(1979) "Le théâtre d'Aristophane: le mythe et les femmes," *les cahiers de Fontenay* 17, 71–102.

Austin, J. L.(1975) *How to Do Things with Words*, 2nd ed. (Cambridge, Massachusetts: Harvard University Press).

Avery, H. C. (1999) "The Chronology of Peisander's Mission to Athens," *Classical Philology* 94, 127–46.

Bakhtin, M. (1968) *Rabelais and His World*, trans. H. Iswolsky (Boston, M.I.T. Press).

Barber, E. W. (1994) *Women's Work, The First 20,000 Years: Women, Cloth and Society in Early Times* (New York, Norton).

Barchiesi, A. (2001) "Horace and Iambos: The Poet as Literary Historian," in Cavarzere, Aloni, and Barchiesi, 141–64.

Bartol, K. (1992) "Where Was Iambic Poetry Performed? Some Evidence from the Fourth Century B.C.," *Classical Quarterly* 42, 65–71.

————. (1993) *Greek Elegy and Iambus* (Poznán, Universytet im. Adama Mickiewicza).

Bell, C. (1997) *Ritual: Perspectives and Dimensions* (New York: Oxford University Press).

Bergk, Th. (1838) *Commentationum de reliquiis comoediae Atticae antiquae libri duo* (Leipzig, at the expense of F. Koehler).

————. (1915) *Poetae Lyrici Gracei*, vol. 2 (Leipzig: Teubner), based on the 1882 edition, with indices by J. Rubenbauer.

Bergren, A. L. T. (1983) "Language and the Female in Early Greek Thought," *Arethusa* 16, 69–95.

Berkman, J. (1990) "Feminism, War and Peace Politics," in Elshtain and Tobias, 141–62.

Bernabò-Brea, L., and Cavalier, M. (1965) *Meligunìs-Lipára Vol. II. La Necropoli Greca e Romana nella Contrada Diana* (Palermo, Flaccovio).

Bieber, M. (1961) *An Introduction to the Greek and Roman Theater* (Princeton, New Jersey: Princeton University Press).

Bierl, A. (2001) *Der Chor in Der Alten Komödie: Ritual und Performativität (unter besonderer Berücksichtigung von Aristophanes Thesmophoriazusen und der Phalloslieder fr. 851 PMG* (Munich, Saur).

Biles, Z. (2002) "Intertextual Biography in the Rivalry of Cratinus and Aristophanes," *American Journal of Philology* 123, 169–204.

Blok, J. (2001) "Towards a choreography of women's speech in classical Athens," in Lardinois and McClure, 95–116.

Blundell, S., and Williamson, M. (1998) *The Sacred and the Feminine in Ancient Greece* (London; New York: Routledge).

Boedeker, D., and Raaflaub K. A. (1998) *Democracy, Empire and the Arts in Fifth-Century Athens* (Cambridge, Massachusetts: Harvard University Press).

Boegehold, A. L., and Scafuro, A. C. (1994) *Athenian Identity and Civic Ideology* (Baltimore, Maryland: The Johns Hopkins University Press).

Bonnano, M. G. (1980) "Nomi e Soprannomi Archilochei," *Museum Helveticum* 37, 65–88.

Bookides, N., and Stroud, R. (1997) *The Sanctuary of Demeter and Kore: Topography and Architecture, Corinth* (Princeton, New Jersey: American School of Classical Studies at Athens).

Bourdieu, P. (1977) *Outline of a Theory of Practice* (Cambridge, England; New York: Cambridge University Press).

Bowie, A. M. (1993) *Aristophanes: Myth, Ritual and Comedy* (Cambridge, England; New York: Cambridge University Press).

————. (2000) "Myth and ritual in the rivals of Aristophanes," in Harvey and Wilkins, 317–39.

Bowie, E. (2001) "Early Greek Iambic Poetry: The Importance of Narrative," in Cavarzere, Aloni, and Barchiesi, 1–27.

Branham, R. (1989) *Unruly Eloquence: Lucian and the Comedy of Tradition* (Cambridge, Massachusetts: Harvard University Press).

Bremmer, J. (1983a) "Scapegoat Rituals in Ancient Greece," *Harvard Studies in Classical Philology* 87, 299–320.

————. (1983b) *The Early Greek Concept of the Soul* (Princeton, New Jersey: Princeton University Press).

————. (1987) "The Old Women of Ancient Greece," in *Sexual Asymmetry. Studies in Ancient Society*, ed. J. Blok and P. Mason, 191–215 (Amsterdam, J. C. Gieben).

————. (1989) *From Sappho to De Sade: Moments in the History of Sexuality* (London; New York: Routledge).

Brown, C. (1997a) "Politician, Pathic, Profligate: Three Targets (Aristophanes, *Frogs* 416–430)," *Eikasmos* 8, 61–9.

———. (1997b) "Iambos" in Gerber, 11–88.

Brumfield, A. C. (1981) *The Attic Festivals of Demeter and Their Relation to the Agricultural Year* (Salem, NH): Ayer Co. Reprint. Originally Published: New York: Arno Press, 1981 (Monographs in Classical Studies).

———. (1996) "Aporreta: Verbal and Ritual Obscenity in the Cults of Ancient Women," *Opuscula Atheniensa* (*Publications of the Swedish Institute at Athens*) 67–74.

Burke, C. (1981) "Irigaray through the Looking Glass," *Feminist Studies* 7, 288–306.

Burkert, W. (1970) "Iason, Hypsipyle and New Fire at Lemnos: A Study in Myth and Ritual," *Classical Quarterly* 20, 1–16.

———. (1972) "Die Leistung eines Kreophylos: Kreophyleer, Homeriden und die archaische Heraklesepik," *Museum Helveticum* 29, 74–85.

———. (1979) *Structure and History in Greek Mythology and Ritual* (Berkeley: University of California Press).

———. (1983) *Homo Necans: The Anthropology of Ancient Greek Sacrificial Ritual and Myth*, trans. P. Bing (Berkeley: University of California Press).

———. (1985) *Greek Religion*, trans. J. Raffan (Cambridge, Massachusetts: Harvard University Press).

Burnett, A. P. (1983) *Three Archaic Poets: Archilochus, Alcaeus, Sappho* (Cambridge, Massachusetts).

Butler, J. (1990) *Gender Trouble: Feminism and the Subversion of Identity* (New York: Routledge).

———. (1993) *Bodies That Matter: On the Discursive Limits of "Sex"* (New York: Routledge).

Cairns, D. L. (1993) *Aidos: The Psychology and Ethics of Honour and Shame in Ancient Greek Literature* (Oxford: Clarendon Press; New York: Oxford University Press).

Calame, C. (1995) *The Craft of Poetic Speech in Ancient Greece*, Translated from the French by Janice Orion (Ithaca: Cornell University Press).

———. (1997, 2nd edition 2001) *Choruses of Young Women in Ancient Greece: Their Morphology, Religious Role and Social Functions*, trans. D. Collins and J. Orion (Lanham, Maryland: Rowman & Littlefield).

Cameron, A., and Kuhrt, A. (1983) *Images of Woman in Antiquity* (London: Croom Helm)

Campbell, D. A. (1967, 1982a) *Greek Lyric Poetry: A Selection of Early Greek Lyric, Elegiac and Iambic Poetry* (London, Melbourne [etc.]: Macmillan; New York: St. Martin's Press). New edition published in 1982 by Bristol Classical Press.

———. (1982b) *Greek Lyric I: Sappho and Alcaeus* (Cambridge, Massachusetts: Harvard University Press). Reprinted, with corrections 1990.

———. (1992) *Greek Lyric IV: Bacchylides, Corinna, and Others* (Cambridge, Massachusetts: Harvard University Press).

Cantarella, R. (1967) *La letteratura Greca classica* (Milan, Accademia).

Carey, C. (1986) "Archilochus and Lycambes," *Classical Quarterly* 36, 60–7.

Carrière, J. C. (1979) *Le Carnaval et la Politique. Une Introduction à la Comédie Grecque: Suivie d'un choix de fragments*. Paris: Belles Lettres (Centre de recherches d'histoire anciennne, vol. 26).

Carson, A. (1990) "Putting Her in Her Place: Woman, Dirt, and Desire," in Winkler, Halperin, and Zeitlin, 135–69 (Princeton, New Jersey).

Caskey, L. D., and Beazley, J. D. (1954) *Attic Vase Paintings in the Museum of Fine Arts in Boston*, vol. I, Published for the Museum of Fine Arts by the Oxford University Press.

Cavarzere, A., Aloni, A., and Barchiesi, A. (2001) *Iambic Ideas: Essays on a Poetic Tradition from Archaic Greece to the Late Roman Empire* (Lanham, Maryland: Rowman & Littlefield).

Chirassi-Columbo, I. (1975) "I doni di Demeter: Mito e ideologia nella Grecia arcaica," in *Studi Triestini di antichità in onore di L. Stella*, 183–213 (Trieste: Università degli studi, Facoltà di lettere e filosofia).

Cixous, H. (1976) "The Laugh of the Medusa," *Signs: Journal for Women in Culture and Society* 1 (41), 875–93.

Clauss, J., and Johnston, S. I. (1997) *Medea: Essays on Medea in Myth, Literature, Philosophy and Art* (Princeton, New Jersey: Princeton University Press).

Clay, J. S. (1989) *The Politics of Olympus: Form and Meaning in the Major Homeric Hymns* (Princeton, New Jersey: Princeton University Press).

Clinton, K. (1986) "The Author of the Homeric *Hymn to Demeter*," *Opuscula Athenensia* (*Publications of the Swedish Institute of Athens*) 16, 43–9.

———. (1988) "Sacrifice at the Eleusinian Mysteries," in Hägg, Marinatos, and Nordquist, 68–80.

———. (1992) *Myth and Cult: The Iconography of the Eleusinian Mysteries: the Martin P. Nilsson lectures on Greek religion, delivered 19–21 November 1990 at the Swedish Institutet at Athens.* (Stockholm: Svenska Institutet i Athen; distributor P. Åströms Förlag).

———. (1993) "The Sanctuary of Demeter and Kore at Eleusis," in Marinatos and Hägg, 110–24.

———. (1994) "The Eleusinian Mysteries and Panhellenism in Democratic Athens," in *The Archaeology of Athens and Attica under the Democracy: proceedings of an international conference celebrating 2500 years since the birth of democracy in Greece, held at the American School of Classical Studies at Athens, December 4–6, 1992*, ed. W. Coulson, O. Palagia, T. L. Shear, Jr., H. A. Shapiro, and F. J. Frost (Oxbow Monograph 37, Oxford).

———. (1996) "The Thesmophorion in Central Athens and the Celebration of the Thesmophoria in Attica" in Hägg, 111–25.

Cohen, D. (1991) *Law, Sexuality and Society: The Enforcement of Morals in Classical Athens* (Cambridge, England; New York: Cambridge University Press).

Colakis, M. (1986) "The Laughter of the Suitors in *Odyssey* 20," *Classical World* 79, 137–41.

Coldstream, J. N. (1973) *Knossos, the Sanctuary of Demeter* (London: British School of Archaeology at Athens 8).

———. (1994) "Demeter in the ancient Greek city and its countryside" in Alcock & Osborne, 199–216.

Cole, S. G. (1998) "Domesticating Artemis," in Blundell and Williamson, 27–43.

Compton, T. (1988) "The Exile of the Poet" (Diss. University of California at Los Angeles).

———. (1990) "The Trial of the Satirist: Poetic *Vitae* (Aesop, Archilochus, Homer) as Background for Plato's *Apology*," *American Journal of Philology* 111, 330–47.

Connor, W. R. (1971) *The New Politicians of Fifth Century Athens* (Princeton, New Jersey: Princeton University Press).

———. (1989) "City Dionysia and Athenian Democracy," *Classica et Mediaevalia* 40, 7–32.

———. (1994) "The Problem of Athenian Civic Identity," in Boegehold and Scafuro, 34–44.

Csapo, E., and Miller, M. (1998) "Democracy, Empire and Art: Towards a Politics of Time and Narrative," in Boedeker and Raaflaub, 87–125.

Csapo, E., and Slater, W. J. (1994) *The Context of Ancient Drama* (Ann Arbor, Michigan: University of Michigan Press).

Davidson, J. (1997) *Courtesans and Fishcakes. The Consuming Passions of Classical Athens* (Hammersmith, London: HarperCollins).

———. (2000) "Gnesippus Paigniagraphos: The Comic Poets and the Erotic Mime," in Harvey and Wilkins, 41–64.

Davies, J. K. (1971) *Athenian Propertied Families, 600–300 b.c.* (Oxford: Clarendon Press).

Degani, H. (1983) *Hipponactis Testimonia et Fragmenta* (Leipzig: B. G. Teubner).

———. (1984) *Studi su Ipponatte* (Bari: Adriatica).

Delatte, A. (1955) *Le cycéon, breuvage rituel des Mystères d'Éleusis* Collection d'études anciennes, 5 sér., t. XL (Paris: Les Belles Lettres).

Demargne, P. (1930) "Plaquettes votives de la Crète archaïque," *Bulletin de correspondance hellénique* 54, 195–204.

De Martino, F., and Sommerstein, A. H. (1995) *Lo spettacolo della voci,* Le Rane. Studi; 14 (Bari: Levante).

de Polignac, F. (1995) *Cults, Territory and the Origins of the Greek City State,* trans. J. Lloyd (Chicago: University of Chicago Press).

Desclos, M.-L. (2000) *Le Rire des Grecs: Anthropologie du rire en Grèce ancienne* (Grenoble: Millon).

Detienne, M. (1973) *Les maîtres de vérité dans la Grèce archaïque,* 2nd ed. (Paris: F. Maspero).

———. (1981) "The myth of 'Honeyed Orpheus'" in *Myth, Religion and Society. Structuralist Essays,* ed. R. L. Gordon (Cambridge: Cambridge University Press; Paris: Editions de la Maison des Sciences de l'Homme, 95–109).

———. (1989) "The Violence of Wellborn Ladies: Women in the Thesmophoria," in *The Cuisine of Sacrifice among the Greeks,* ed. M. Detienne and J.-P. Vernant, trans. P. Wissing (Chicago: University of Chicago Press).

Deubner, L. (1932) *Attische Feste* (Berlin; reprinted Hildesheim: H. Keller 1959).

Devereux G. (1983) *Baubo, la vulve mythique,* trans. George Olms (Paris: J.-C. Godefoy).

Dillon, M. (1987) "The *Lysistrata* as a post-Dekeleian Peace Play," *Transactions of the American Philological Association* 117, 97–104.

Di Nola, A. M. (1974) *Antropologia Religiosa* (Firenze: Vallechi).

Dobrov, G. W. (1995) *Beyond Aristophanes: Transition and Diversity in Greek Comedy* (Atlanta, Georgia: Scholars Press).

———. (1997) *The City as Comedy: Society and Representation in Athenian Drama* (Chapel Hill, North Carolina: University of North Carolina Press).

Dobrov, G. W., and Urios-Aparisi, E. (1995) "The Maculate Music: Gender, Genre and the *Chiron* of Pherecrates," in Dobrov, 139–74.

Douglas, M. (1968) "The Social Control of Cognition: Some Factors in Joke Perception," *Man* 3, 361–76.

Dover, K. J. (1964) "The Poetry of Archilochus," in Poilloux, 181–227.

———. (1993) *The Frogs, Aristophanes* (Oxford, England: Clarendon Press; New York: Oxford University Press).

Drachmann, A. B. (1910) *Scholia Vetera in Pindari Carmina,* vol. II: Teubner (Leipzig).

duBois, P. (1988) *Sowing the Body: Psychoanalysis and Ancient Representations of Women* (Chicago: University of Chicago Press).

Dupréel, E. (1928) "Le problème sociologique du rire," *Revue philosophique* 106, 213–60.

Edmunds, L. (1990) *Approaches to Greek Myth* (Baltimore, Maryland: Johns Hopkins University Press).

———. (2001) "Callimachus *Iamb* 4: From Performance to Writing" in Cavarzere, Aloni, and Barchiesi, 77–98.

Edwards, A. (1991) "Aristophanes' Comic Poetics: Τρύξ, Scatology, Σκῶμμα," *Transactions of the American Philological Association* 121, 157–79.

———. (1993) "Historicizing the Popular Grotesque: Bakhtin's *Rabelais* and Attic Old Comedy" in *Theater and Society in the Classical World,* ed. R. Scodel, 89–117 (Ann Arbor, Michigan: University of Michigan Press).

Elshtain, J. B., and Tobias, S. (1990) *Women, Militarism, and War: Essays in History, Politics and Social Theory* (Savage, Maryland: Rowman & Littlefield).

Erikson, E. H. (1945) "Childhood and Tradition in Two American tribes," in *The Psycho-analytic Study of the Child* (vol I: New Haven: Yale University Press).

Faraone, C. A., and Obbink, D. (1991) *Magika Hiera* (New York: Oxford University Press).

Farnell, L. R. (1907) *The Cults of the Greek States*, volume III (Oxford: Clarendon Press).

Festugière, A. J. (1952) "Arnobiana," *Vigiliae Christianae* 6, 208–54.

Finley, M. I. (1973) *Problèmes de la terre en Grèce ancienne. Civilisations et sociétés* 33 (Paris: Mouton).

Fluck, H. (1931) *Skurrile Riten in griechischen Kulten* (Endingen: Druck von E. Wild).

Foley, H. P. (1982) "The Female Intruder Reconsidered: Women in Aristophanes' *Lysistrata* and *Eccleziazusae*," *Classical Philology* 77, 1–21.

———. (1993) "The politics of tragic lamentation," in Sommerstein, 101–43.

———. (1994) *The Homeric Hymn to Demeter: Translation, Commentary, and Interpretive Essays* (Princeton, New Jersey: Princeton University Press).

Fontenrose, J. (1959) *Python, a Study of Delphic Myth and Its Origins* (Berkeley, California: University of California Press).

Forrest, W. G. (1975) "An Athenian Generation Gap," *Yale Classical Studies* 24, 37–52.

Foxhall, L. (1995) "Women's Ritual and Men's Work in Ancient Athens," in Hawley and Levick, 97–110.

Freud, S. (1953) "Medusa's Head," in *The Complete Works of Sigmund Freud* (24 volumes), vol. 18, 273–4, ed. by James Strachey (London: Hogarth Press and the Institute of Psycho-Analysis).

Gamel, M.-K. (2002) *Performing/Transforming Aristophanes' Thesmophoriazousai*. Special issue of *American Journal of Philology* (vol. 123.3).

Garlan, Y. (1973) "La défense du territoire à l'époque classique: problèmes de la terre en Grèce ancienne," in Finley, 149–60.

Garland, R. (1987) *The Piraeus from the Fifth to the First Century B.C.*, (Ithaca, New York: Cornell University Press).

Garnsey, P. (1989) *Famine and Food Supply in the Graeco-Roman World: Responses to Risk and Crisis* (Cambridge; New York: Cambridge University Press).

Geertz, C. (1973) *The Interpretation of Cultures: Selected Essays* (New York: Basic Books).

Geissler, P. (1925) *Chronologie der altattischen Komödie*, Berlin; Weidmann, 2nd ed., Philologische Untersuchungen: 30. Heft, with additions (Dublin/Zurich 1969).

Gentili, B. (1988) *Poetry and its Public in Ancient Greece: From Homer to the Fifth Century*. Translated, with an Introduction by A. Thomas Cole (Baltimore and London: Johns Hopkins).

———. (1988) *Poetry and Its Public in Ancient Greece* (Baltimore: Maryland: Johns Hopkins University Press).

Gerber, D. E. (1989) "Archilochus Fr. 34 West: ἀμισθὶ γάρ σε πάμπαν οὐ διάξομεν," *Acta Classica* 32, 99–103.

———. (1997) *A Companion to the Greek Lyric Poets* (Leiden; New York: Köln: Brill).

———. (1999) *Greek Iambic Poetry: from the Seventh to the Fifth Centuries BC* (Cambridge, Massachusetts. Harvard University Press).

Gernet, L., and Boulanger, A. (1932) *Le Génie Grec dans la religion* (L'évolution de l'Humanité. Synthèse collective XI, Paris: La Renaissance du Livre).

Gildersleeve, B. L. (1889) *American Journal of Philology* 10, 383.

———. (1897) *American Journal of Philology* 18, 243.

Gilhus, I. S. (1997) *Laughing Gods, Weeping Virgins: Laughter in the History of Religion* (London; New York: Routledge).

Golden L. (1992) *Aristotle on Tragic and Comic Mimesis* (American Classical Studies No. 29; Atlanta, Georgia: Scholars Press).
——. (1994) "Aristotle on the Pleasure of Comedy," in *Essays on Aristotle's Poetics*, ed. A. O. Rorty (Princeton, New Jersey: Princeton University Press).
Golden, M., and Toohey, P. (1997) *Inventing Ancient Culture: Historicism, Periodization and the Ancient World* (London; New York: Routledge).
Goldhill, S. (1990) "The Great Dionysia and Civic Ideology," in *Nothing to Do with Dionysus?*, ed. J. J. Winkler and F. I. Zeitlin, 97–129 (Princeton, New Jersey: Princeton University Press).
——. (1994) "Representing Democracy: Women at the Great Dionysia," in R. Osborne and S. Hornblower, 347–69.
Gomme, A. W. (1933) *The Population of Athens in the Fifth and Fourth Centuries B.C.* (Oxford: B. Blackwell).
Gordon, R. L. (1981) *Myth, Religion and Society: Structuralist Essays by M. Detienne, L. Gernet, J.-P. Vernant and P. Vidal-Naquet* (Cambridge, England; New York: Cambridge University Press).
Gould, J. (1980) "Law, Custom and Myth: Aspects of the Social Position of Women in Classical Athens," *Journal of Hellenic Studies* 100, 38–59.
Graf, F. (1974) *Eleusis und die orphische Dichtung Athens in vorhellenistischer Zeit* (Berlin; New York: De Gruyter).
——. (1985) *Nordionische Kulte: religionsgeschichtliche und epigraphische Untersuchungen zu den Kulten von Chios, Erythrai, Klazomenai und Phokaia*, Bibliotheca Helvetica Romana 21 (Rome: Schweizerisches Institut in Rome).
Grant, M. A. (1924) *The Ancient Rhetorical Theories of the Laughable: The Greek Rhetoicians and Cicero* (Madison, Wisconsin: University of Wisconsin).
Green, J. R. (1994) *Theatre in Ancient Greek Society* (London; New York: Routledge).
Green, R., and Handley, E. (1995) *Images of the Greek Theatre* (Austin, Texas: University of Texas Press).
Greene, E. (1996) *Re-reading Sappho: Reception and Transmission* (Berkeley, California: University of California Press).
Griffiths, A. (1995a) "Non Aristocratic Elements in Archaic Poetry," in Powell, 85–103.
——. (1995b) *Stage Directions. Essays in Ancient Drama in honour of E. W. Handley, Bulletin of the Institute of Classical Studies of the University of London*. Supplement 66 (London).
Gruber, W. E. (1983) "Systematized Delirium: The Craft, Form and Meaning of Aristophanic Comedy," *Helios* n.s. 10, 97–111.
Hadzisteliou Price, T. (1971) "Double and Multiple Representations in Greek Art and Religious Thought," *Journal of Hellenic Studies* 91, 48–69.
Hägg, R. (1996) *The Role of Religion in the Early Greek Polis. Proceedings of the Third International Seminar on Ancient Greek Cult, Organized by the Swedish Institute at Athens, 16–18 October 1992* (Stockholm: Svenska Institutet i Athen: distributor P. Åströms Förlag).
Hägg, R., and Marinatos, N. (1993) *Greek Sanctuaries: New Approaches* (London; New York: Routledge).
Hägg, R., Marinatos, N., and Nordquist, G. C. (1988) *Early Greek Cult Practice. Proceedings of the Fifth International Symposium at the Swedish Institute at Athens, 26–29 June 1986* (Stockholm: Svenska Institutet i Athen; Göteborg: Distributor, P. Åströms Förlag).
Hall, E. (2000) "Female Figures and Metapoetry in Old Comedy," in Harvey and Wilkins, 407–18.

Halliwell, S. (1991a) "The Uses of Laughter in Greek Culture," *Classical Quarterly* 41, 279–296.

———. (1991b) "Comic Satire and Freedom of Speech in Classical Athens," *Journal of Hellenic Studies* 111, 48–70.

Harrison, J. E. (1922) *Prolegomena to the Study of Greek Religion* (Cambridge: Cambridge University Press).

Harvey, D., and Wilkins, J. (2000) *The Rivals of Aristophanes: Studies in Athenian Old Comedy* (London: Duckworth and the Classical Press of Wales).

Hawley, R., and Levick, B. (1995) *Women in Antiquity. New Assessments* (London; New York: Routledge).

Heath, M. (1990) "Aristophanes and His Rivals," *Greece & Rome* 37, 143–58.

Heiden. B. (1991) "Tragedy and Comedy in the Frogs of Aristophanes," *Ramus* 20, 95–110.

Hekman, S. J. (1990) *Gender and Knowledge: Elements of a Postmodern Feminism* (Boston: Northeastern University Press).

Henderson, J. (1975) *The Maculate Muse: Obscene Language in Attic Comedy* (New Haven: Yale University Press). Second edition (1991), New York: Oxford University Press.

———. (1987a) "Older Women in Attic Old Comedy," *Transactions of the American Philological Association* 117, 105–29.

———. (1987b) *Lysistrata*, edited with introduction and commentary (Oxford).

———. (1990) "The Demos and the Comic Competition," in J. J. Winkler and F. Zeitlin, 271–313.

———. (1991) "Women and the Athenian Dramatic Festivals," *Transactions of the American Philological Association* 121, 133–47.

———. (1996) *Three Plays by Aristophanes. Staging Women* (New York: Routledge).

———. (1998a) *Aristophanes, Acharnians; Knights* (Cambridge, Massachusetts; London, England: Harvard University Press).

———. (1998b) "Attic Old Comedy, Frank Speech," in Boedeker and Raaflaub, 255–73.

———. (2000a) "Pherecrates and the Women of Old Comedy," in Harvey and Wilkins, 135–50.

———. (2000b) *Aristophanes: Birds, Lysistrata, Women at the Thesmophoria* (Cambridge, Massachusetts; London, England: Harvard University Press).

———. (2002a) Aristophanes: *Frogs, Assemblywomen, Wealth* (Cambridge, Massachusetts; London, England: Harvard University Press).

———. (2002b) "Epilogue" in Gamel, 501–11.

Hendrickson, G. L. (1925) "Archilochus and the Victims of His Iambics," *American Journal of Philology* 46, 101–27.

Henrichs, A. (1982) "Changing Dionysiac Identities," in *Jewish and Christian Self-Definition*, vol. II., *Self-Definition in the Greco-Roman World*, B. F. Meyer and E. P. Sanders (London).

———. (1990) "Between Country and City: Cultic Dimensions of Dionysus in Athens and Attica," in *Cabinet of the Muses: Essays on Classical and Comparative Literature in Honor of Thomas G. Rosenmeyer*, ed. M. Griffith and D. J. Mastronarde, 257–77 (Atlanta, Georgia. Scholars Press).

Henry, M. (1985) *Menander's Courtesans and the Greek Comic Tradition* (Frankfurt am Main; New York: P. Lang).

———. (1992) "The Edible Woman: Athenaeus's Concept of the Pornographic," in Richlin, 250–68.

———. (1995) *Prisoner of History: Aspasia of Miletus and Her Biographical Tradition* (New York: Oxford University Press).

Herington, J. (1985) *Poetry into Drama: Early Tragedy and the Greek Poetic Tradition* (Berkeley, California: University of California Press).

Heubeck, A. (1965) "Aphrodite Philommedes," *Beitrage zur Namenforschung* 16, 204–6.

Hoffman, W. (1910) *Ad Antiquae Atticae comoediae historiam symbolae*, Diss. Berlin University (Berlin: A. Ebering).

Holst-Warhaft, G. (1992) *Dangerous Voices: Women's Laments and Greek Literature* (London; New York: Routledge).

———. (1995) "The Fun in the Funeral," Paper delivered at the Women's Classical Caucus Panel, APA national conference in San Diego, CA, December.

Howie, A. M. (1993) *Aristophanes: Myth, Ritual and Comedy* (Cambridge, England; New York, New York: Cambridge University Press).

Hubbard, T. H. (1994) "The Date of Semonides of Amorgos," *American Journal of Philology* 115, 175–97.

———. (1997) "Utopianism and the Sophistic City in Aristophanes," in Dobrov, 23–50.

Hughes-Freeland, F., and Crain, M. M. (1998) *Recasting Ritual: Performance, Media, Identity* (London; New York: Routledge).

Humphreys S. C. (1983) *The Family, Women and Death: Comparative Studies* (Ann Arbor, Michigan: University of Michigan Press). Second edition 1993. The first edition is London; Boston: Routledge & Kegan Paul.

Irigaray, L. (1985) *This Sex Which Is Not One*, trans. C. Porter, with C. Burke (Ithaca, New York: Cornell University Press).

Irwin, E. (1998) "Biography, Fiction, and the Archilochean *ainos*," *Journal of Hellenic Studies* 118, 177–83.

Jacoby, F. (1904) *Das Marmor Parium* (Berlin: Weidmann).

Jameson, M. H. (1990), "Perseus, the Hero of Mykenai," in *Celebrations of Death and Divinity in the Bronze Age Argolid*, ed. R. Hägg and G. C. Nordquist (Stockholm: Svenska Institutet i Athen; Göteborg: Distributor, Paul Åströms Förlag) 213–23.

Janko, R. (1982) *Homer, Hesiod and the Hymns: Diachronic Development in Epic Diction* (Cambridge; New York: Cambridge University Press).

———. (1984) *Aristotle on Comedy: Towards a Reconstruction of Poetics II* (Berkeley, California: University of California Press).

———. (2000) *Philodemus. On Poems. Book 1.* Edited with introduction, translation and commentary. (Oxford, England; New York: Oxford University Press).

Johnston, S. I. (1990) *Hekate Soteira: A Study of Hekate's Roles in the Chaldean Oracles and Related Literature* (Atlanta: Scholars Press).

Jones, A. R. (1981) "Writing the Body: Toward an Understanding of *l'écriture féminine*" *Feminist Studies* 7, 247–63.

Jost, M. (1985) *Sanctuaires et Cultes d'Arcadie* (Paris: J. Vrin).

Jucker, I. (1963) " Frauenfest in Korinth," *Antike Kunst* 6, 47–61.

Kaibel, G. (1899) *Comicorum Graecorum fragmenta* (Berlin: Weidmann).

Karaghiorga-Stathacopoulou, T. (1986) Article on Baubo in the *Lexicon Iconographicum Mythologiae Classicae*, Volume IIIi, 87–90; IIIii 67–8. (Zürich: Artemis Verlag).

Kassell, R., and Austin, C. (1983–98) *Poetae Comici Graeci* (Berlin: De Gruyter).

Kenyon, F. G. (1893) *Greek Papyri in the British Museum*, vol. I (London: British Museum).

Kerenyi, C. (1967) *Eleusis: Archetypal Image of Mother and Daughter*, trans. R. Manheim (New York: Bollingen Foundation; Bollingen series, 65: distributed by Pantheon Books).

Kerenyi, C., and Jung, C. (1949) *Essays on a Science of Mythology: The Myth of the Divine Child and the Mysteries of Eleusis*, trans. R. F. C. Hull (New York: Pantheon Books).

Kern, O. (1900) *Die Inschriften von Magnesia am Meander* (Berlin: W. Spemann).

———. (1922) *Orphicorum Fragmenta* (Berlin: Weidmann). Second Edition 1963, reprinted Berlin, De Gruyter 1967.

Killeen, K. F. (1973) "Sappho fr. 111," *Classical Quarterly* n.s. 23: 198.

King, H. (1986) "Agnodike and the profession of medicine," *Proceedings of the Cambridge Philological Society* 212 (New Series 32), 53–77.

Kirk, G. S. (1963) "A fragment of Sappho reinterpreted," *Classical Quarterly* n.s. 13, 51–2.

Knox, B. M. W. (1979) "Euripidean Comedy" in *Word and Action: Essays on the Ancient Theater*, 250–274 (Baltimore: Johns Hopkins University Press). Reprinted from Cheuse, A. and Koffler, R. eds. (1970) *The Rarer Action: Essays in Honor of Francis Fergusson* (New Brunswick, New Jersey: Rutgers University Press), 1970.

Kock, T. (1880–8) *Comicorum Atticorum Fragmenta* (3 volumes) (Leipzig: Teubner).

Konstan, D. (1993) "The Young Concubine in Menandrian Comedy," in Scodel, 139–60.

Konstan, D., and Dillon, M. (1981) "The Ideology of Aristophanes' *Wealth*," *American Journal of Philology* 102, 371–94.

Kontoleon, N. M. (1952) "ΝΕΑΙ ΕΠΙΓΡΑΦΑΙ ΠΕΡΙ ΤΟΥ ΑΡΧΙΛΟΧΟΥ ΕΚ ΠΑΡΟΥ," *Archaiologika Ephemeris*, 32–95.

Kron, U. (1992) "Frauenfeste in Demeterheiligtümern: Das Thesmophorion von Bitalemi, Eine Archäologische Fallstudie," *Archäologische Anzeiger*, 611–50.

Kurke, L. (1992) "The Politics of ἁβροσύνη in Archaic Greece," *Classical Antiquity* 11, 91–120.

Lardinois, A. (1989) "Lesbian Sappho and Sappho of Lesbos," in Bremmer, 15–35.

Lardinois, A., and McClure, L. eds. (2001) *Making Silence Speak: Women's Voices in Greek Literature and Society* (Princeton, New Jersey: Princeton University Press).

Lattimore, R. (1951) *The Iliad of Homer* (Chicago) Second edition, 1990.

Leach, E. R. (1964) "Animal Categories and Verbal Abuse," in E. H. Lenneberg, 23–63.

Lefkowitz, M. (1981) *The Lives of the Greek Poets* (Baltimore, Maryland: Johns Hopkins University Press).

Lenneberg, E. H. (1964) *New Directions in the Study of Language* (Cambridge: M.I.T. Press).

Levine, D. P. (1980) *Geloi Ekthanon: Laughter and the Demise of the Suitors*, Diss. Univ. of Cincinnati (Ann Arbor, MI: UMI Dissertation Services).

———. (1982a) "Iros as Paradigm for the Suitors," *Classical Journal* 77, 200–4.

———. (1982b) "Homeric Laughter and the Unsmiling Suitors," *Classical Journal* 78, 97–104.

———. (1983a) "Theoklymenus and the Apocalypse," *Classical Journal* 79, 1–7.

———. (1983b) "Penelope's Laugh: *Odyssey* 18.163," *American Journal of Philology* 104, 172–8.

———. (1987) "*Flens Matrona et Meretrices Gaudentes*: Penelope and Her Maids," *Classical World* 81, 23–7.

Lévy, E. (1976a) "Les femmes chez Aristophane," *Ktema* 1, 99–112.

———. (1976b) *Athènes devant la défaite de 404; histoire d'une crise idéologique* (Athens: École française d' Athènes; Paris: Dépositaire, Diffusion de Boccard).

Lewis, D. M. (1955) "Notes on Attic Inscriptions II," *Annual of the British School at Athens* 50: 1–36.

Lidov, J. (1993) "The Second Stanza of Sappho 31: Another look," *American Journal of Philology* 114, 503–37.

———. (2002) "Sappho, Herodotus, and the Hetaira," *Classical Philology* 97, 203–37.

Lloyd-Jones, H. (1967) "Sappho Fr. 111," *Classical Quarterly* 17, 168.

———. (1975) *Females of the Species: Semonides on Women* (London: Duckworth).

Loraux, N. (1978) "Sur la race des femmes et quelques-unes de ses tribus," *Arethusa* 11, 43–87.

———. (1986) *The Invention of Athens: The Funeral Oration in the Classical City*, trans. of *L'invention d'Athènes*, by A. Sheridan (Cambridge, Massachusetts: Harvard University Press).

———. (1992) "What Is a Goddess?" in *A History of Women in the West I. From Ancient Goddesses to Christian Saints*, G. Duby and M. Perrot, several editors, vol. I, ed. P. Schmitt Pantel, trans. A. Goldhammer, 11–45 (Cambridge, Massachusetts: Bellknap Press of Harvard University Press).

———. (1993) *The Children of Athena: Athenian Ideas about Citizenship and the Division between the Sexes*, trans. C. Levine (Princeton, New Jersey: Princeton University Press).

Lowe, N. J. (1998) "Thesmophoria and Haloa: Myth, Physics and Mysteries" in Blundell and Williamson, 149–173.

———. (2000) "Comic plots and the invention of fiction," in Harvey and Wilkins, 259–72.

Lowry, E. P. (1991), *Thersites: a study in comic shame* (New York: Garland Publishing).

Lyons, D. (1997) *Gender and Immortality: Heroines in Ancient Greek Myth and Cult* (Princeton, New Jersey: Princeton University Press).

MacDowell, D. M. (1993) "Foreign birth and Athenian citizenship in Aristophanes," in Sommerstein, 359–71.

———. (1995) *Aristophanes and Athens. An Introduction to the Plays* (Oxford; New York: Oxford University Press).

Mankin, D. (1995) *Horace: Epodes* (Cambridge, New York: Cambridge University Press).

Marcovich, M. (1986) "Demeter, Baubo, Iacchus – and a Redactor," *Vigiliae Christianae* 40, 294–301. Reprinted in *Studies in Graeco-Roman Religions and Gnosticism* (1988), 20–7 (Leiden; New York: E. J. Brill).

Marks, E., and de Courtivron, I., eds. (1980) *New French Feminisms* (Amherst, Massachusetts: University of Massachusetts Press).

Mattingly, H. B. (1971) "Facts and Artifacts," *The University of Leeds Review* 14, 280–7.

McClure, L. K. (1995) "Female Speech and Characterization in Euripides," in DeMartino and Sommerstein, 35–60.

———. (1999a) *Spoken Like a Woman: Speech and Gender in Athenian Drama* (Princeton, New Jersey: Princeton University Press).

———. (1999b) "'The Worst Husband': Discourses of Praise and Blame in Euripides' *Medea*," *Classical Philology* 94, 373–94.

———. (2003) "Subversive Laughter: The Sayings of Courtesans in Book 13 of Athenaeus' *Deipnosophistae*," *American Journal of Philology* 124, 259–294.

McGlew, J. (1997) "After Irony: Aristophanes' *Wealth* and Its Modern Interpreters," *American Journal of Philology* 118, 35–53.

Meiggs, R., and Lewis, D. M. (1969) *A Selection of Greek Historical Inscriptions to the End of the Fifth Century B.C.* (Oxford: Clarendon Press).

Meineke, A. (1839–57) *Fragmenta Comicorum Graecorum* (Berlin: Reimer).

Merkelbach, R., and West, M. L. (1967) *Fragmenta Hesiodea* (Oxford: Clarendon Press).

Merker, G. S. (2000) The Sanctuary of Demeter and Kore: Terra Cotta Figurines of the Classical, Hellenistic, and Roman Periods (Princeton, New Jersey: American School of Classical Studies at Athens).

Miralles, C., and Pòrtulas, J. (1983) *Archilochus and the Iambic Poetry* (Rome: Edizioni dell' Ateneo).

Moi, T. (1985) *Sexual/Textual Politics; Feminist Literary Theory* (London; New York: Methuen).

Morris, I. (1996) "The Strong Principle of Equality and the Archaic Origin of Greek Democracy," in Ober and Hedrick, 19–48.

Most, G. (1996) "Reflecting Sappho," in Greene, 11–35.

Moulton, C. (1981) *Aristophanic Poetry* (Göttingen: Vandenhoeck & Ruprecht).

Nagy, G. (1973) "Phaethon, Sappho's Phaon, and the White Rock of Leukas," *Harvard Studies in Classical Philology* 77, 137–77.

———. (1976) "Iambos: Typologies of Invective and Praise," *Arethusa* 9, 191–205.

———. (1979) *The Best of the Achaeans: Concepts of the Hero in Archaic Greek Poetry* (Baltimore: Johns Hopkins University Press).

———. (1990) *Pindar's Homer: The Lyric Possession of an Epic Past* (Baltimore: Johns Hopkins University Press).

Needham, R. (1972) *Belief, Language and Experience* (Oxford: Blackwell).

Nesselrath, H.-G. (1990) *Die attische mittlere Komödie: Ihre Stellung in der antiken Literaturkritik* (Berlin/New York: De Gruyter).

———. (1997) "The Polis of Athens in Middle Comedy," in Dobrov, 271–88.

Nilsson, M. (1906) *Griechische Feste von religiöser Bedeutung: mit Ausschluss der Attischen* (Leipzig: Teubner).

Nixon, L. (1995) "The cults of Demeter and Kore," in Hawley and Levick, 75–96.

Ober, J., and Hedrick, C. (1996) *Demokratia: A Conversation on Democracies, Ancient and Modern* (Princeton, New Jersey: Princeton University Press).

Ober, J., and Strauss, B. (1990) "Drama, Political Rhetoric and the Discourse of Athenian Democracy," in Winkler and Zeitlin, 237–70.

Oeri, H. G. (1948) *Der Typ der komischen Alten in der Griechischen Komödie, seine Nachwirkungen und seine Herkunft* (Basel: B. Schwabe).

O'Higgins, D. M. (1996) "Sappho's Splintered Tongue: Silence in Sappho 31 and Catullus 51," in Greene, 68–78.

Olender, M. (1990) "Aspects of Baubo: Ancient Texts and Contexts," in Winkler, Halpern, and Zeitlin, 83–113.

Olson, S. D. (1992) "Names and Naming in Aristophanic Comedy," *Classical Quarterly* 42, 304–19.

Orlandini, P. (1967) "Lo Scavo del Thesmophorion di Bitalemi e il Culto della Divinità Ctonie a Gela," *Kokalos* 12, 8–35.

Osborne, R., and Hornblower, S. (1994) *Ritual, Finance, Politics: Athenian Democratic Accounts Presented to David Lewis* (Oxford: Clarendon Press; New York: Oxford University Press).

Osborne, R. G. (1985) *Demos, the discovery of classical Attika* (Cambridge; New York: Cambridge University Press).

———. (1989) "A Crisis in Archaeological History? The Seventh Century in Attica," *Annual of the British School at Athens* 84, 297–322.

Padgug, R. A. (1972) "Eleusis and the Union of Attica," *Greek, Roman and Byzantine Studies* 13, 135–50.

Page, D. (1941) *Select Papyri.* Vol. III. *Literary Papyri: Poetry* (Cambridge, Massachusetts: Harvard University Press).

. (1951) *Alcman. The Partheneion* (Oxford: Clarendon Press).

———. (1955) *Sappho and Alcaeus: An Introduction to the Study of Ancient Lesbian Poetry* (Oxford: Clarendon Press).

Papademetriou, I. (1948–9) "ATTIKA I," *Arkhaiologiki Ephemeris* 86–7, 146–53.

Parke, H. W. (1977) *Festivals of the Athenians* (Ithaca, New York: Cornell University Press).

Parker, R. (1983) *Miasma: Pollution and Purification in Early Greek Religion* (Oxford: Clarendon Press; New York: Oxford University Press).

———. (1996) *Athenian Religion: A History* (Oxford: Clarendon Press; New York: Oxford University Press).

Patterson C. (1994) "The Case against Neaira and the Public Ideology of the Athenian Family," in Boegehold and Scafuro, 199–216.

Peredolskaya, A. A. (1964) *Attische Tonfiguren aus einem südrussischen Grab. Antike Kunst: Beiheft 2* (Basel).

Pfisterer-Haas, S. (1989) *Darstellungen alter Frauen in der griechischen Kunst*, European University Studies, Series XXXVIII, vol. 21 (Frankfurt am Main; New York: P. Lang).

Pickard-Cambridge, A.W. (1962) *Dithyramb, Tragedy and Comedy*, 2nd ed., revised by T. B. L. Webster (Oxford: Clarendon Press).

———. (1968) *The Dramatic Festivals of Athens*, 2nd ed., revised by J. Gould and D. M. Lewis (Oxford: Clarendon Press).

Poilloux, J. (1963a) *Archiloque: sept exposés et discussions* (Genève: Fondation Hardt).

———. (1963b) "Archiloque et Thasos: Histoire et Poesie," in Poilloux, 3–36.

Pomeroy, S. B. (1991) *Women's History and Ancient History* (Chapel Hill, North Carolina: University of North Carolina Press).

Powell, A. (1995) "Athens' Pretty Face: Anti-feminine Rhetoric and Fifth Century Controversy over the Parthenon," in *The Greek World*, 245–70 (London and New York: Routledge).

Pratt, L. (2000) "The Old Women of Ancient Greece and the Homeric *Hymn to Demeter*," *Transactions of the American Philological Association* 130, 41–65.

Prins, Y. (1996) "Sappho's Afterlife in Translation," in Greene, 36–67.

Prytz-Johansen, J. (1975) "The Thesmophoria as a Women's Festival," *Temenos* 11, 78–87.

Pucci, P. (1987) *Odysseus Polutropos: intertextual readings in the Odyssey and the Iliad* (Ithaca, New York: Cornell University Press).

Raaflaub, K. A. (1998) "The Transformation of Athens in the Fifth Century," in Boedeker and Raaflaub, 15–41.

Rabe, H. (1906) *Scholia in Lucianum* (Leipzig: Teubner).

Rabinowitz, N. S. (1992) "Tragedy and the Politics of Containment," in Richlin, 36–52.

———. (1993) "Introduction" in Rabinowitz & Richlin, 1–20.

Rabinowitz, N. S., and Richlin, A. (1993) *Feminist Theory and the Classics* (New York).

Rankin, H. D. (1977) *Archilochus of Paros* (Park Ridge, New Jersey: Noyes Press).

Rayor, D. (1993) "Korinna: Gender and the Narrative Tradition," *Arethusa* 26, 219–31.

Reckford, K. J. (1987) *Aristophanes Old-And-New Comedy, Volume 1: Six Essays in Perspective* (Chapel Hill, North Carolina: University of North Carolina Press).

Reed, J. D. (1995) "The Sexuality of Adonis," *Classical Antiquity* 14, 317–47.

Reinach, S. (1912) "Le Rire Rituel," in *Cultes, Mythes et Religions* Tome 4 (Paris: E. Leroux).

Rhodes, P. J. (1981) *A Commentary on the Aristotelian Athenaion Politeia* (Oxford: Clarendon Press; New York: Oxford University Press).

Richardson, N. J. (1974) *The Homeric Hymn to Demeter* (Oxford: Clarendon Press).

Richlin, A. (1992) *Pornography and Representation in Greece and Rome* (New York: Oxford University Press).

———. (1993) "The ethnographer's dilemma and the dream of a lost golden age," in Rabinowitz and Richlin.

Rissman, L. (1983) *Love as War: Homeric Allusion in the Poetry of Sappho* (Königstein/Ts: Hain).

Riu, X. (1999) *Dionysism and Comedy* (Lanham, Maryland: Rowman and Littlefield).

Rolley, C. (1965) "le sanctuaire des dieux Patrooi et le Thesmophorion de Thasos," *Bulletin de correspondance hellénique* 89, 441–83.

Rose, P. (1988) "Thersites and the Plural Voices of Homer," *Arethusa* 21, 5–25.

Rosellini, M. (1979) "*Lysistrata*, une mise en scène de la feminité," *Les cahiers de Fontenay* 17, 11–32.

Rosen, R. M. (1987) "Hipponax Fr. 48 DG. and the Eleusinian *Kukeon*," *American Journal of Philology* 108, 416–26.

——. (1988a) *Old Comedy and the Iambographic Tradition* (Atlanta, Georgia: Scholars Press).

——. (1988b) "A Poetic Initiation Scene in Hipponax?" *American Journal of Philology* 109, 174–9.

——. (1990) "Hipponax and the Homeric Odysseus," *Eikasmos* 1, 11–25.

——. (1997) "The Gendered Polis in Eupolis' *Cities*," in Dobrov, 149–76.

Rosenmeyer, T. G. (1966) "Alcman's *Partheneion* 1 Reconsidered," *Greek, Roman, & Byzantine Studies* 7, 321–59.

Rosivach, V. J. (1987) "Autochthony and the Athenians," *Classical Quarterly* 37, 294–306.

Rothwell, K. S. Jr. (1990) *Politics and Persuasion in Aristophanes' Ecclesiazusae* (Leiden; New York: Brill).

Ruddick, S. (1990) "The Rationality of Care," in Elshtain and Tobias (229–54).

Rusten, J. (1977) "*Wasps* 1360–1369: Philocleon's *Tothasmos*," *American Journal of Philology* 98, 157–61.

Saïd, S. (1979) L'Assemblée des femmes, l'économie et la politique," *Les cahiers de Fontenay* 17, 33–70.

Saxonhouse, A. (1984) "Eros and the Female in Greek Political Thought. An Interpretation of Plato's *Symposium*," *Political Theory* 12, 5–27.

——. (1992) *Fear of Diversity: The Birth of Political Science in Ancient Greek Thought* (Chicago: University of Chicago Press).

Scarborough, J. (1991) "The Pharmacology of Sacred Plants, Herbs and Roots," in Faraone and Obbink, 138–74.

Schaps, D. M. (1982) "The Women of Greece in Wartime," *Classical Philology* 77, 193–213.

Scodel, R. (1993) *Theater and Society in the Classical World* (Ann Arbor, Michigan: University of Michigan Press).

Scott, J. C. (1990) *Domination and the Arts of Resistance. Hidden Transcripts* (New Haven, Connecticut: Yale University Press).

Searle, J. R. (1969) *Speech Acts: An Essay in the Philology of Language* (London: Cambridge University Press).

Seeberg, A. (1971) *Corinthian Komos Vases, Bulletin of the Institute of Classical Studies* Supplement 27, London.

——. (1995) "From Padded Dancers to Comedy," in Griffiths 1995b.

Segal, C. P. (1981) "Orality, Repetition and Formulaic Artistry in the Homeric 'Hymn to Demeter,'" in *I poemi epici e rapsodici non omerici e la tradizione orale: atti del convegno di Venezia, 28–30 Settembre 1977*, ed. C. Brillante, M. Cantilena, and C. O. Pavese, 107–60 (Padua: Antenore).

Segal, E. (1995) "The Comic Catastrophe: An Essay on Euripidean Comedy," in Griffiths 1995b, 46–55.

Seidensticker, B. (1978) "Archilochus and Odysseus," *Greek, Roman & Byzantine Studies* 19, 5–22.

Servais, J. (1981) "La Date Des Adonies D'Athènes Et L'Expedition De Sicile (À Propos D'Aristophane, *Lysistrate* 387–98)," in *Adonis: aspetti orientali di un mito greco*, ed. by S. Ribichini (Rome). *Studi Semitici* 55. Pubblicazioni del centro di studio per la civiltà fenica e punica 22.

Showalter, E. (1985) "Towards a Feminist Poetics," reprinted in E. Showalter, ed., *The New Feminist Criticism: Essays on Women, Literature and Theory*, 125–43 (New York: Pantheon).

Simms, R. (1998) "Mourning and Community at the Athenian Adonia," *Classical Journal* 93, 121–41.

Simon, E. (1983) *Festivals of Attica: An Archaeological Commentary* (Madison, Wisconsin: University of Wisconsin Press).

Skinner, M. (1987) *Rescuing Creusa: New Methodological Approaches to Women in Antiquity* (Lubbock, Texas: Texas Tech.).

———. (1989) "Sapphic Nossis," *Arethusa* 22, 5–18.

———. (1991) "Nossis Thelyglossos: The Private Text and the Public Book," in Pomeroy, 20–47.

———. (1993, 1996) "Woman and Language in Archaic Greece, or, Why is Sappho a Woman?"in Rabinowitz and Richlin, 125–44. Reprinted in Greene 1996, 175–92.

Slater, W. J. (1997) "Waiting in the Wings: Aristophanes' *Ecclesiazousae*," *Arion* 3rd Series 5, 97–129.

Sokolowski, F. (1962) *Lois sacrées des cités grecques. Supplément* (Paris: E. de Boccard).

Sommerstein, A. H. (1977) "Aristophanes and the Events of 411," *Journal of Hellenic Studies* 97, 112–26.

———. (1980a) *Acharnians. English and Greek* (Warminster, Wiltshire, UK: Aris & Phillips).

———. (1980b) "The naming of women in Greek and Roman comedy," *Quaderni di storia* 11, 393–418.

———. (1984b) "Aristophanes and the Demon Poverty," *Classical Quarterly* 34, 314–33.

———. (1990) *Lysistrata. English and Greek* (Warminster, Wiltshire, UK: Aris & Phillips).

———. (1992) "Old Comedians on Old Comedy," in Zimmerman, 14–33.

———. (1993) *Tragedy, comedy and the polis: papers from the Greek drama conference: Nottingham, 18–20 July 1990* (Bari: Levante).

———. (1995) "The Language of Athenian Women," in DeMartino and Sommerstein, 61–85.

———. (1998) *Ecclesiazousae: English and Greek* (Warminster, Wiltshire, UK: Aris & Phillips).

Sourvinou-Inwood, C. (1994) "Something to do with Athens: Tragedy and Ritual" in Osborne and Hornblower, 269–90.

———. (1997a) "Reconstructing Change: Ideology and the Eleusinian Mysteries," in Golden and Toohey, 132–64.

———. (1997b) "Medea at a Shifting Distance: Images and Euripidean Tragedy" in Clauss and Johnston, 253–96.

Stallybrass, P., and White, A. (1986) *The Politics and Poetics of Transgression* (Ithaca, New York: Cornell University Press).

Stehle, E. (1997) *Performance and Gender in Ancient Greece: Non-Dramatic Poetry in Its Setting* (Princeton, New Jersey: Princeton University Press).

Storey, I. C. (1990) "Dating and Redating Eupolis," *Phoenix* 44, 1–30.

———. (2000) "Some Problems in Eupolis' *Demoi*," in Harvey and Wilkins, 173–231.

Stroud, R. (1968) "The Sanctuary of Demeter and Kore on Acrocorinth: Preliminary Report II; 1964–1965," *Hesperia* 37, 299–333 (pl. 87–99).

Sutton, D. F. (1994) *The Catharsis of Comedy* (Lanham, Maryland: Rowman and Littlefield).

Taaffe, L. (1993) *Aristophanes and Women* (London and New York: Routledge).

Tarditi, G. (1968) *Archilochus: Fragmenta* (Rome: Athenaeum).

Thalmann, W. G. (1984) *Conventions of form and Thought in Early Greek Epic Poetry* (Baltimore: Johns Hopkins University Press).

Thalmann (1988) "Thersites: Comedy, Scapegoats, and Heroic Ideology in the *Iliad*." *Transactions of the American Philological Association* 118, 1–28.

Thomas, R. (1989) *Oral Tradition and Written Record in Classical Athens* (Cambridge; New York: Cambridge University Press).

Todd, S. C.(1993) *The Shape of Athenian Law* (Oxford: Clarendon Press).

Trédé, M., and Hoffmann, P., with Auvray-Assayas, C. (1998) *Le Rire des Anciens: Actes du colloque international, Université de Rouen, École normale supérieure, 11-13 janvier 1995* (Paris: Presses de L'École normale supérieure).

Turner, V. (1974) *Dramas, Fields, and Metaphors: Symbolic Action in Human Society* (Ithaca, New York: Cornell University Press).

———. (1967) *The Forest of Symbols: Aspects of Ndembu Ritual* (Ithaca, New York: Cornell University Press).

———. (1969) *The Ritual Process: Structure and Anti-structure* (Chicago: Aldine Pub.).

Tzanetou, A (2002) "Something to Do with Demeter: Ritual and Performance in Aristophanes' *Women at the Thesmophoria*," in Gamel, 329–67.

Ussher, R. G. (1973) *Aristophanes, Ecclesiazousae. Edited with an Introduction and Notes* (Oxford: Clarendon Press).

Van Nortwick, T. (2001) "Like a Woman: Hector and the Boundaries of Masculinity," *Arethusa* 34, 221–35.

Van Sickle, J. (1975) "Archilochus: A New Fragment of an Epode," *Classical Journal* 71, 1–15.

Vernant, J.-P. (1991) "Death in the Eyes: Gorgo, Figure of the Other," in *Mortals and Immortals. Collected Essays*, ed. F. I. Zeitlin, 111–38 (Princeton, New Jersey: Princeton University Press).

———. "In the Mirror of Medusa," in *Mortals and Immortals*, 141–50.

Versnel, H. S. (1990) "What's Sauce for the Goose Is Sauce for the Gander: Myth and Ritual, Old and New," in Edmunds, 25–90.

———. (1992) "The Festival for Bona Dea and the Thesmophoria", *Greece & Rome* 1, 31–55.

Vidal-Naquet, P. (1981) "The Black Hunter and the Origins of the Athenian Ephebeia," in Gordon, 147–62.

Vorwahl, H. (1933) "Ein apotropäischer Kriegsbrauch," *Archiv für Religionwissenschaft* 30, 395–7.

Wallace, R. W. (1998) "The Sophists in Athens," in Raaflaub and Boedeker, 203–22.

Warden, P. G. (1990) *The Extramural Sanctuary of Demeter and Persephone at Cyrene, Libya: The Small Finds, Final Reports* IV part 1. University of Pennsylvania University Museum for Libyan Department of Antiquities. University Museum Monographs No. 67 (Philadelphia).

Warner, R. (1954), *Thucydides: History of the Peloponnesian War*, Harmondsworth, Middlesex and New York, New York: Penguin.

Watson, L. (1991) *Arae: The Curse Poetry of Antiquity* (Leeds: Cairns).

Webster, T. B. L. (1960) *Monuments Illustrating Old and Middle Comedy*, London, Institute of Classical Studies. 3rd ed. (1978) revised, enlarged by J. R. Green.

———. (1961) *Monuments Illustrating New Comedy*, London, Institute of Classical Studies, 3rd ed. (1995) rev. J. R. Green and A. Seeburg.

West, M. L. (1971) *Iambi et Elegi Graeci ante Alexandrum cantati*, vol. I (Oxford: Clarendon Press).

———. (1972) *Iambi et Elegi Graeci ante Alexandrum cantati*, vol. II (Oxford).

———. (1974) *Studies in Greek Elegy and Iambus* (Berlin; New York: de Gruyter).

———. (1985) Review, *Miasma: Pollution and Purification in Early Greek Religion*, *The Classical Review*, New Ser. vol. 35, No. 1, 92–4.

Williamson, M. (1995) *Sappho's Immortal Daughters* (Cambridge, Massachusetts: Harvard University Press).

Winkler, J. J. (1990) "The Laughter of the Oppressed: Demeter and the Gardens of Adonis," in *The Constraints of Desire: The Anthropology of Sex and Gender in Ancient Greece*, 188–209 (New York: Routledge).

Winkler, J. J., Halperin, D. M., and Zeitlin, F. I. (1990) *Before Sexuality: The Construction of Erotic Experience in the Ancient Greek World* (Princeton, New Jersey: Princeton University Press).

Winkler, J. J. and Zeitlin, F. I. (1990) *Nothing to Do with Dionysus?* ed. (Princeton, New Jersey: Princeton University Press).

Wysocki, L. (1988) "Aristophanes, Thucydides B. VIII and the Political Events of 413–11 B.C.," *Eos* 76, 237–48.

Zanetto, G. (2001) "Iambic Patterns in Aristophanic Comedy," in Cavarzere, Aloni, and Barchiesi, 65–76.

Zeitlin, F. (1981) "Travesties of Gender and Genre in Aristophanes' *Thesmophoriazusae*," in *Reflections of Women in Antiquity*, ed. H. P. Foley (New York: Gordon and Breach Science Publishers).

———. (1982) "Cultic Models of the Female: Rites of Dionysus and Demeter" *Arethusa* 15, 129–57.

———. (1985) "Playing the Other: Theater, Theatricality and the Feminine in Greek Drama," *Representations* 11, 63–94.

———. (1993) "Staging Dionysus between Thebes and Athens," in *Masks of Dionysus*, ed. T. H. Carpenter and C. A. Faraone, 147–82 (Ithaca, New York: Cornell University Press).

———. (1999) "Aristophanes: The Performance of Utopia in the *Ecclesiazousae*," in Goldhill, S., and Osborne, R., *Performance-culture and Athenian democracy*, 167–97 (Cambridge, UK; New York: Cambridge University Press).

Zimmermann, B. (1992) *Antiken Dramentheorien und ihre Rezeption* (Stuttgart: M & P Verlag für Wissenschaft und Forschung).

Zuntz, G. (1971) *Persephone. Three Essays on Religion and Thought in Magna Graecia* (Oxford: Clarendon Press).

Zweig, B. (1992) "The Mute Nude Female Characters in Aristophanes' Plays," in Richlin 73–89.

INDEX

Brumfield, A.C., 11
Bupalus, 70, 72, 193, 201, 205
Burkert, W., 20

Calamaia, 20
Calathos (offering basket), 28
Callias, 111, 112, 123, 127, 128, 213, 215
Callidice, 194
Calligeneia (Feast of Fair offspring), 24,
    118, 192
Callimachus, 87, 187, 205
Calliouloi (sheaf songs), 86
Callipais, 195
Callisto (Alcaeus), 116
Campbell, D.A., 92, 95
Cantharus, 114
caricature masks, comedic, 29
"carnival of women," 42, 50, 58
catabaulesis (winnowing song), 86,
    205
Cecrops, 223
Celeus, 39, 42, 51, 191, 194, 195. *See also*
    keleos
Centaur (Aristophanes), 204
Centaurs, 56
Cephisodorus, 128, 132
Cephisophon, 126–7, 214
Cephisus, 20
Cercylas, 125
Chalcidian Pursuit, 26, 187
chamber pot *(skaphion)*, 33, 199
Charaxus, 95
Charmides, 89
Charminus, 123
Charon (Underworld ferryman), 61
Charon the Carpenter, 110, 200
chastity, 24, 56, 82, 187, 196
Cheiron (Pherecrates), 116, 125
Cheirons (Cratinus), 111–2
Chios, 119
Choai, festival of, 185
choirion/choiros (piglet, vulva), 22, 173,
    223
Choiroboscus, 65, 199
choruses
    dithyrambic, 102, 104, 106
    old men, 186
    precomic, 103, 106
    women's, 83–4, 93, 109, 122, 123, 127–8,
        184

Chremylus, 174, 175–7, 223
Chrysis, 131
Cicero, 133
Cimon, 111, 112, 113, 211
Cinesias, 166
Cities (Eupolis), 119–20, 210, 212
Cities (Heniochus), 120
cities, personified as women, 119–20,
    212
citizenship legislation, 107, 111, 142, 211
City Dionysia, 12, 16, 149, 208, 218–9
    comic contests at, 104–6, 211
    exclusion of women from, 102
    women as spectators at, 136, 144
City of God (Augustine), 187
civic activity, impact of Demeter festivals
    on, 23
civic identity, 107–8, 183, 209
Cleisthenes, 105, 148
Clement of Alexandria (Church Father),
    17, 24, 52, 194, 195, 202
Cleoboea, 61, 197
Cleobulina (Alexis), 123
Cleobulinas (Cratinus), 123
Cleobulus of Lindus, 123
Cleomedes, 24, 187
Cleomenes, 165
Cleon, 140, 143, 168
Cleophon, 111, 123, 168, 220
Cleophon (Plato Comicus), 210
Clepsydra (Eubulus), 215
Clesithenes, 158
Clinton, K., 23, 27, 57
Clouds (Aristophanes), 122, 123, 126, 134,
    139, 169, 204, 206, 210
clowns, ritual, 221
Clytaemestra, 30
Cocalus (Aristophanes), 115
Colchis, 114
Colias, 162
collective identity, joking as, 4
collectivity, women as representation of,
    141–2, 146, 149–50
Cologne Epode, 70–1, 201
comedy, 98–144. *See also specific play*
    audience of, 135–8
    development of, 101–2, 127–8, 208–9,
        217–8
    and erotic mime, 213
    fantasy and utopia in, 117–8